DA

JAN 23 '90

D0856277

By

Apc 10/3/88

VANDERBILT UNIVERSITY LIBRARY

NASHVILLE, TENNESSEE

THE LISTENING EBONY

Gamu with his kudu horn, used as a percussion instrument by the Ebony diviners (see Chapter 5).

THE LISTENING EBONY

Moral Knowledge,
Religion, and Power
Among the Uduk of Sudan

WENDY JAMES

CLARENDON PRESS · OXFORD

1988

Oxford University Press, Walton Street, Oxford OX2 6DP

Oxford New York Toronto
Delhi Bombay Calcutta Madras Karachi
Petaling Jaya Singapore Hong Kong Tokyo
Nairobi Dar es Salaam Cape Town
Melbourne Auckland
and associated companies in
Berlin Ibadan

Oxford is a trade mark of Oxford University Press

Published in the United States
by Oxford University Press, New York

© Wendy James 1988

All rights reserved. No part of this publication may be reproduced,
stored in a retrieval system, or transmitted, in any form or by any means,
electronic, mechanical, photocopying, recording or otherwise, without
the prior permission of Oxford University Press

British Library Cataloguing in Publication Data
James, Wendy, 1940–
The listening ebony:,moral knowledge,
religion and power among the uduk of Sudan.
1. Uduk (African people)
I. Title
305.8'963 DT155.2U38
ISBN 0–19–823403–1

Library of Congress Cataloging in Publication Data
James, Wendy.
The listening ebony: moral knowledge, religion, and power among
the Uduk of Sudan/Wendy James.
p. cm.
Bibliography: p.
includes index.
1. Uduk (African people)—Religion. 2. Sudan—Religion.
I. Title.
BL2480.U38J35 1988 306'.6—dc 19 87–30976
ISBN 0–19–823403–1

Printed in Great Britain by
Butler & Tanner Ltd,
Frome and London

For the children of the
'kwanim pa

Preface

This book is distilled largely out of the same body of fieldnotes and texts as its predecessor, 'Kwanim Pa (1979). The original fieldwork was carried out between 1965 and 1969, from the University of Khartoum, and full acknowledgements are made in the Preface to that book. In the same place I promised a further account of religion, ritual, and healing among the Uduk. But as will be evident, it has not been easy to construct a coherent account of this field, characterized by the flux and flow of indigenous and imported practices, and the waxing and waning of Christianity and Islam. I have here attempted a historical approach to the analytical interpretation of the evidence; and if occasionally I have had to guess, well perhaps the best historians do this too, and I take heart from them.

I have been able to bring this account to fruition only through the help and backing of others, of institutions, friends, and family. Oxford University gave me a year's sabbatical leave in 1982–3, partly for the purpose of completing this book, and the Faculty Board of Anthropology and Geography gave me a grant to help with the expense of further travel in the Sudan. The first draft was completed that year, which was spent largely in Juba where my husband Douglas Johnson was employed on an archive project with the Southern Regional Government. In the context of travel partly connected with his work we were able to make a brief visit, via Malakal, to Boing in Meban country and across the Blue Nile Province boundary to Chali, in the heart of Uduk country. I am grateful for the appropriate research permission which was given by Dr Muhammad Ibrahim Ahmad, Secretary General of the National Records Office in Khartoum, on behalf of the Anthropology Board of the Ministry of the Interior. I was able to pick up old contacts in Chali and then spend a short time back in the hamlets of Waka'cesh which had been my base during fieldwork in the 1960s. This visit, with our two small children, though only a couple of weeks in all during May 1983, was a tremendous stimulus for the reworking of this book. I later offered a second draft for comments to a few patient colleagues and friends, and on the basis of their advice revised the text, as it was transferred on to disks at the

Institute of Social Anthropology. On these disks the third and final
draft was produced. For technical help with typing and word-
processing I am particularly indebted to Isabella Birkin, Isobel
Clark, Carol le Duc, and Sally Sutton; and for the index, to Stella
Seddon.

Those who have read this book in earlier drafts and encouraged
me with their attention and specific suggestions include my mother
Isabel Wilson; Gerd Baumann, Jeremy Coote, Ian Cunnison,
Christopher Ehret, Marie Isaacs, Godfrey Lienhardt, Elizabeth
Munday, Joachim Theis, and Alessandro Triulzi. Seminar papers
and lectures drawing on the material have been given in the Uni-
versities of Liverpool and Manchester, the Oriental Institute of
Naples, and the Free University of Berlin, as well as in Oxford,
and the comments and questions of students have often been sharp
and constructive. I have had the benefit of helpful general discussion
and correspondence with a number of people who have been
engaged in research in the Sudan and Ethiopia, particularly
Abdal Ghaffar Muhammad Ahmad (who assisted in the original
fieldwork), John Burton, Donald Donham, Peter Garretson, Jay
Spaulding, David Turton, and Bahru Zewde. The recent work of
others in the border region between the two countries has helped
me give a firmer historical and comparative base to my account,
and here I would like to mention in addition to those above Jon
Arensen, Lionel Bender, Christian Delmet, Gabriel Jal, Charles
Jedrej, Akira Okazaki, Taddesse Tamrat, Serge Tornay, and Patrik
Wallmark. For the candid insights of a friend in a completely different field, I am indebted to Jaynie Anderson.

During our time in the Sudan in 1982–3 I had the great pleasure
of seeing Stephen Missa Dhunya again, in Khartoum, and he
provided not only recent news but also assistance with new translations. In the intervening years I have had useful correspondence
and talks with Joshua Kheiralla Wallo, now employed in Saudi
Arabia. But it was very good to see old friends in Boing and Chali:
Moses Chidko and 'Tabke, Pastor Paul Angwo and his family and
the new church community. And it was for me a very special bonus
to have the chance of a reunion with William Danga, Tente, Ha'da,
Saba, Nyane, Bwaywanu, and other Waka'cesh friends from the
1960s, though circumstances in so many ways had changed. My
debt to them, and to all those mentioned in the text, has grown
with time, and I offer this book in acknowledgement.

Whatever merit might be found in this account, it must be shared with my husband Douglas, whose support as intellectual partner, travelling companion, and helpmeet has made its completion a reality. I would also like to thank Fiona and Roger, because the making of this book became a part of their lives too.

Institute of Social Anthropology
Oxford, February 1987

Contents

List of Illustrations

12. A sequence from Nyane's treatment, 1983 (see Chapter 6).

    a. The diviner Brushes Nyane's body with a chicken and presses it to her.

    b. He draws out 'foreign things' from her body, using hands and mouth.

    c. A colleague Straightens her limbs.

    d. Nyane can relax after she is anointed with oil.

Figures

Note on Texts

I have incorporated a substantial number of oral texts into this account, both as a primary ethnographic record and as evidence for my analysis of Uduk experience and knowledge. The majority of these texts were recorded between 1966 and 1969. In those few cases where a text was recorded more recently, this is made clear. In most cases, transcription was by Shadrach Peyko Dhunya, and translation was our joint work. I have presented many of the texts in this book in the form of conversation, to indicate the context in which they were elicited. The questions, printed in italics, are my own unless otherwise indicated.

Once written down, these oral accounts are of course a little diminished, losing the rhythm and stress of the spoken emphasis, the drama of the ideophones (which I try to shadow in transliteration) and the nuances of hesitation and silence. Where the written versions have seemed excessively slow, opaque, or repetitive, I have made a few deletions, but otherwise have allowed these voices of the Uduk to participate as freely as possible in 'my' account of 'their' beliefs and thoughts.

In the transcription of Uduk words and phrases, the orthography used is that of the Sudan Interior Mission, as employed in their mimeographed Dictionary of the Uduk language and in their published scriptures (for details see Chapter 4). Tone is not indicated. An apostrophe indicates implosion or explosion in the consonant it precedes; underlining indicates aspiration; and the oblique stroke represents a glottal stop. I have omitted the latter from the transcription of proper names for the sake of simplicity. A convention I should also note here is that the pronunciation of many Uduk nouns begins with a euphonic a-. Where the noun occurs on its own or at the beginning of a sentence, this is transcribed as a prefix (though this too has been omitted from proper names). Where it occurs in the middle of a phrase or sentence, it is transcribed as a suffix to the previous word. Euphonic suffixes of m, n, ŋ, or ny are commonly added to words ending in a vowel and spoken in a phrase or sentence, and where these occur in a text they are transcribed. Further information on the Uduk language may be found in Appendix 1 to my earlier book.

Note on Rites

Rituals for illness and healing, for hunting and the wild, and for marking stages in the life-cycle figure prominently in the Uduk villages. Descriptions are sometimes incorporated into the main narrative of this book, but in a number of cases the descriptions have been set apart from the main text by the use of italics and the present tense, to suggest both their dramatic unity and their common standing outside 'normal time'.

Note on Terminology

There are two dialects of the language usually referred to in the literature as Uduk (agreed by all commentators to be a member of the 'Koman' grouping and closely related to its other core members, Komo, Kwama, and Shyita). Northern Uduk speakers (about 7,000 in the Tombak and Ahmar valleys) refer to themselves and the speakers of southern Uduk (about 3,000 in the Yabus valley and the hills to the south) as 'kwanim pa. Occasionally included also in this category are some speakers of the Shyita language (which Uduk term Pur) in the Daga valley to the south. The southern Uduk call themselves K̲amus, and may include northern Uduk in this or distinguish them as Bun'cesh. Speakers of the northern Nilotic languages refer to the Uduk and neighbouring peoples as Cai, while Arabic speakers use the blanket term Burun.

My knowledge is primarily of the northern Uduk. When I refer to the southern Uduk this is made clear. Reference to 'the Uduk' without qualification or other context should be taken to mean the northern Uduk.

Introductory Essay

The world as the Uduk-speaking people knew it was almost destroyed in the closing years of the nineteenth century. Those who had not been enslaved, or enserfed by chiefdoms of the Sudan–Ethiopian border, had fled as refugees away to the north and west. The three valleys of the Ahmar, Tombak, and Yabus which they had made their homeland over the previous century or so were deserted. In my previous book, *'Kwanim Pa: The Making of the Uduk People: An Ethnographic Study of Survival in the Sudan–Ethiopian Borderlands* (henceforth abbreviated as *'KP*),[1] I have described these events and their continuing relevance for our understanding of the society the Uduk have recreated since the early twentieth-century pacification of this region by the Anglo-Egyptian government of the Sudan. They see themselves as having made a fresh start after so much loss and death. I described hard-working cultivators (a population of some ten thousand), drawing skilfully upon the resources of the forest, valuing these above those of the field and above the modest flocks and herds they kept; subsistence hoe-cultivators by necessity, but very shy of the commercial market, of individual gain or profit, and of the appearance of inequality among themselves. These communities, measuring the bonds of kinship in the substance and metaphor of connection through women, were able to absorb refugees and other strangers while refusing to allow the marriage of their young womenfolk by bridewealth to outsiders. The acceptance of bridewealth smacked to them of slave-dealing. For them either transaction would in principle create distance, even potential enmity, between the parties. The absorption of a stranger had to be on the basis of potential reciprocity, eventually transmutable into the idiom of kinship; and the motif of re-creating the society of the *'kwanim pa* in this way dominated not only their view of the 'historical' past but also areas of their myth and ritual.

This book is a sequel to *'Kwanim Pa*. It takes up religious and moral aspects of modern Uduk society, but in a wider context both

---

[1] *'Kwanim Pa: The Making of the Uduk People: An Ethnographic Study of Survival in the Sudan–Ethiopian Borderlands* (Oxford: Clarendon Press), 1979. References to further sources on the Uduk may be found in the bibliography of *'Kwanim Pa*.

of time and of regional political relations. The analysis seeks to look back beyond the events of the late nineteenth century, for which we have some definite evidence, to the 'pre-historic' past of the Uduk as a predominantly hunting and gathering people. For this earlier era we have little conventional historical evidence. But it seems to me essential to set this account in a temporal dimension, and in order to give some inner momentum to my analysis of the changing events of this century, I have made a number of assumptions, hypothetical though I believe justifiable, about the remoter past. From this source must surely come those elements of basic cultural knowledge which we can now see to have endured through many documented changes in social and religious practice over the last two generations, and which promise to survive further.

This study, by comparison with 'Kwanim Pa, is extended forward in two senses. A revisit to the field in 1983 made it possible for me to update some of my first-hand observations from the 1960s, the 'ethnographic present' of my earlier book. But in addition, the present study explores ways in which the Uduk themselves have looked, and are looking, to the future rather than remembering the past. As they do so, they draw not only upon the past as they consciously represent it, but also upon the long-accumulated cultural deposit of unremembered events.

(i) Moral knowledge and the cultural archive

The ritual practice, cosmological theories, and religious notions of the Uduk today display intimidating variety. There would seem to be such a jumble of different cults, rites, practitioners and 'beliefs' as to defy coherent description. At different times since the turn of the century, Uduk communities have appropriated Bertha oracles and festivals, Nuer, Shilluk, and Meban spirits and Jum Jum healing cults. They have also shown from time to time, in a qualified way, enthusiasm for both Islam and Christianity. They retain an assorted repertoire of rites which are undoubtedly 'authentic' to their own cultural past, but these do not provide in any obvious sense an explicit ideology or religion. Indeed it is only rarely that the 'older' and supposedly authentic rites are performed. The commonest practices, which lend themselves more readily to exegesis and the construction of 'ideological' positions, are largely drawn from neighbouring peoples. It is necessary that in part we look to these for 'integrating' themes, and for those articulating frameworks of systematized knowledge, that in French may be encompassed by the term *connaissance*.

But what might it be that the Uduk thus need to integrate or systematically to articulate? It is true that somehow they have had to accommodate the political and religious experiences which have confronted them since the middle of the last century. But into what vernacular context are these accommodations made? There has been at the same time a spontaneous, undirected quest to bring to light and redefine those received elements of fundamental knowledge of the world and the self which lie partly dormant in the 'archive' of their culture: what in French might be distinguished as *savoir*, knowledge not of the pre-structured or demonstrable kind, but of that spontaneous experiential kind almost inseparable from the knower. *Connaissance* is a noun, like knowledge, made from a verb-stem; but *savoir* is also a verb, a *knowing* as well as a form of wisdom. In making these distinctions I have taken my lead from the writings of Michel Foucault.[2]

It is quite impossible to give an account of the intellectual and moral world of the Uduk corresponding to the older anthropological image of a coherent tribal cosmos, an integrated system of discourse, an orthodoxy perhaps authored 'from above' and endorsed by secular power. It is necessary to make some primary analytical discriminations before the mass of evidence concerning Uduk symbol, rite, faith, and knowledge can be untangled for description, since the strands do not adhere in that 'seamless whole' so often taken as a working model of 'culture'. The history of competing sources of power in this political no man's land is the essential framework for analysis. Not only do the small language communities receive ideas from powerful neighbouring or encompassing civilizations, but the people themselves appropriate and modify, and they respond intellectually, emotionally, and politically to some extent within the terms of reference offered them. Competing outside powers, presenting themselves as often as not in the discourse of authoritarian religion, may come to supply major elements in their publicly presented ritual practice and stated creed.

---

[2] See particularly *The Archaeology of Knowledge* [1969], translated by A. M. Sheridan (London: Tavistock), 1972, and *Michel Foucault: Power/Knowledge: Selected interviews and other writings 1972–1977*, ed. Colin Gordon (Brighton: The Harvester Press), 1980.

But then we should surely seek a level below that of such publicly enacted rhetoric, a level at which implicit certainties about human experience perdure and from which response to imported religions must ultimately stem. Foucault's general concept of an *archive*, below the level of the explicit statements and formulated theory of the day, persisting through a period of history and underwriting a certain coherence through times of superficial change, lends itself to our project of analysing Uduk moral knowledge. Not describable as a whole, perceptible only in part, like the evidence of the archaeologist, the archival depository of cultural representation nevertheless offers crucial clues to any understanding of the way that articulated creed in its most recent forms has been received and reshaped among the Uduk.

A suggestive analogue of what we may seek to illuminate by the 'archaeological' method can be seen in language itself, and language use, among the Uduk. As a language community, 'the Uduk' are very permeable. Individuals frequently travel, and may be bi- or multilingual. Indeed a majority of people can probably speak something of at least one neighbouring tongue—Bertha, Kwama, Komo, Ganza, Meban, or Jum Jum; and most men, at least, have a smattering of Arabic, and a few of English. Uduk-speakers enjoy the sound of foreign tongues, often adapting elements from them as personal names for their own children. Vocabulary is freely incorporated into Uduk, most conspicuously from the Nilotic languages, and from Arabic. It is stylish and witty to use foreign terms in one's conversation or in naming things (for example, a couple of puppies might be called 'Yes' and 'No' in friendly acknowledgement of an English-speaking guest).[3]

But in spite of what appears a high rate of lexical borrowing and other linguistic exchange, all is not flux and flow. One of the remarkable features of the Uduk tongue is its extreme conservatism with respect to phonemes, especially consonants. Its spoken form has adhered over time to a complex pattern of consonants which gives it a unique place in the comparative study of African languages. This pattern discriminates, for example, between five different manners of articulation at each of three different positions of articulation in the mouth, and between four manners of articulation

[3] Further details of naming may be found in my article 'Ephemeral names: the Uduk case', in *Aspects of Language in the Sudan*, ed. R. Thelwall (Coleraine: The New University of Ulster), 1978.

at two other positions. The recent work of Christopher Ehret suggests that the Uduk language may be that descendant which preserves most nearly the consonantal pattern of proto-Nilo-Saharan, the language assumed ancestral to tongues now widely spread over the Sudanic belt of Africa.[4] This language was spoken over 7,000 years ago, and possibly as much as 10–15,000 years ago. The Uduk tongue therefore appears to be flexibly innovative on the surface, but this appearance cloaks an astonishing conservatism. A good many statements will include borrowed words, even explicitly and intentionally borrowed words; while collectively, and perhaps without deliberate motive, Uduk-speakers stick doggedly to complicated consonants which are difficult for others to hear, let alone copy. Perhaps this combination of conservatism in *la langue* and flexibility in *la parole* could help to illuminate, by analogy, the way in which implicit vernacular knowledge can persist through many changes of religious allegiance and profession of belief. I suggest that, at least in the Uduk case, we may usefully guess at the presence of an archive of substantive notions about the varieties and distinctions of primary human experience, not always clearly described, and indeed often obscured behind the changing modes of overt discourse.

These questions could be extended to the whole range of 'pre-Nilotic' peoples straddling the Sudan–Ethiopian border. In different ways, the evidence suggests that sets of vernacular cultural elements, whether or not embodied in a surviving language, can persist at a partly hidden level to a surprising degree, while the visible features of social practice and cultural discourse can accommodate themselves to a prevailing lingua franca, dominant religion, and the regional demands of political and economic life. Among the 'pre-Nilotic' peoples living in Ethiopia, we find various communities using Amharic, Oromo (Galla), or Anuak as a second language; we find some adhering to the Ethiopian Orthodox Church, some to Protestant churches, some to Islam, and some to the teachings of Nilotic prophets. On the Sudan side, some again subscribe to Islam and others to the Catholic Church or to Protestant Christianity, while yet others have accepted a dominantly Nilotic definition of the religious world. The Meban and Jum Jum,

---

[4] Professor Ehret has recently discussed his forthcoming work on this topic with me.

as well as some of the groups known as Hill Burun, present the intriguing combination of Nilotic language and religious cosmology with what we can now identify as 'vernacular' traditions of myth, of ritual practices, and of kinship and interpersonal relations, which they share with their 'pre-Nilotic' neighbours.[5] Indeed we might seek, at the archival level, connections not only through periods of time but across 'ethnic' classifications and language boundaries in this borderland region, itself a historical as well as a geographical niche. This comparative question is discussed in Appendix 1.

In the Uduk case, the strong commitment to a vernacular idiom goes far beyond the apparently careful conservation of the difficulties of their own language. The evidence I present in this study indicates that there are levels at which we may discern stubborn and substantive concepts, often to do with the way in which human beings experience the world and often cast in characteristic imagery drawn from a hunters' tradition. These notions do not necessarily form, in themselves, a system or an articulated theory, but, like an archive, may constitute a lasting base of past reference and future validation. They may at times rest dormant but on occasion be drawn upon for the formulation of new discourse. The elements of this cultural archive, revealed as much in the repertoire of habitual ritual action as in language, constitute the foundations of a moral world. They refer in the main to the emergence of fresh human life from its animal context; to the sound growth of the person and the maintenance of a proper inner balance of experiencing parts, both by positive training and by defensive measures against overwhelming spiritual invasion; and to the struggle to control illness, bodily decay, and death. At this level of felt knowing, perhaps of *savoir* as against *connaissance*, of things taken for granted about being human (and only partially revealed in exegesis), there is no standing 'Other', no divinity set against the human estate, to form a point of primary reference. For the Uduk, as far back as evidence and memory goes, the gods have been powers introduced by outsiders, and have been met by responses shaped through their own practical wisdom and their hunters'

---

[5] The term 'pre-Nilotic' was coined by V. L. Grottanelli, in his article 'I Pre-Niloti: Un'arcaica provincia culturale in Africa', *Annali Lateranensi*, 12 (1948), 281–326. Reference to recent work on the Koman peoples and other border groups may be found in Appendix 1.

experience of fleshly life and mortality. I have distinguished this cultural repository as *moral knowledge*, a fund of implicit guarantees upon which they have drawn both to meet, and to counter, the various claims of authoritative religious teaching which have confronted them.

It is more difficult to trace the shared elements of such fundamental knowing than it is the outline of a particular religious discourse, with (almost by definition) its formal pronouncements, explicit exegesis, public ceremony, and defined participation. There is no exclusive priesthood of moral wisdom among the Uduk, no single or specifiable source of moral guidance. What is known for certain is rarely put into dogmatic statements. This is partly why those verbally transmitted religious claims which seem for a time to have made headway with the Uduk are not actually disagreed with or openly rebuffed. There being no authoritative 'centre' of knowledge, whether in a cosmological or social sense, it is not possible to set up a confrontation between spokesmen for the newer religious systems and the older wisdom respectively. At the same time, new teachings cannot easily survive intact the quiet erosion of an everyday practice proceeding from different assumptions. Let me introduce some of these assumptions, for which evidence may be found in Part I of this book.

Within the human person there is a vital organ, which we may term the Liver (*adu*, used also in the simple anatomical sense of the liver). Here is concentrated the circulation of the blood, and that animating force or spirit, *arum*, which carries us through life as it does the other animals. From this source surge up our uncontrolled feelings, our anger, our affection, and our spiritual potency. It is also the nerve-centre of our spiritual vulnerability to external powers, to the stench of evil and sickness, and to the unknown gods. Invasion of the Liver by such powers may overwhelm a person. But the discipline and training undergone throughout life, especially through medicinal and dietary control, strengthens the conscious will and the directed self; for the Uduk, the exertion of reflective and deliberate will is an exercise for the Stomach, as against the Liver. Set also against the vulnerable passions of the Liver is the highest form of individual receptive consciousness, the capacity I term the personal Genius, *k̲ashira/*. The Genius must be ever-watchful against the dangerous invasiveness of spiritual powers, *arum*.

Arum has become differentiated within the world as a result of our separation from the rest of the animal realm, our organic individuality, and through the events of human history. In so far as *arum* exists without the body, it is never a separate god, divinity, or self-existent Spirit; it is rather in essence the spiritual residue of lives which have been lived before, of bodies, both human and animal, which have now decayed and gone. Disembodied *arum* is present in the world in two main forms today. First, since in some sense it outlives particular bodily vessels, it exists in the land of the dead. The *arum* of those who have died are reconstituted in communities underground, and occasionally these may be encountered above ground. Second, in the bush and forest there are wandering *arum* of those who have died out there and never been properly buried. There are also various loose *arum* of animals killed by hunters in the past. Moreover, in an important way there is a surviving presence of *arum* in its primeval form in the still living bodies of our kin in the bush, the wild animal species.

Ritual practice among the Uduk has two main foci. The first is upon the gradual building up, strengthening, maturing, and repairing of the person as he or she goes through life. A common theme of both developmental and healing rites is the careful feeding of persons with victuals and medicines that might otherwise prove harmful to them, in order to strengthen their resistance. Wholeness, soundness, freshness must be worked for and maintained, and measures taken to avoid weight-loss, slowing down, damage to the protective faculties, in particular the Stomach and personal Genius, in order to stave off the eventual decay of the body and detachment of the *arum*.

The second focus of ritual practice is the continuing defensive struggle of humankind against the wild, and especially the powerful wild animals. Many medicines are possessed which protect the community from the effects of killing a large animal (and from other dangers). These medicines themselves can however cause sickness to those in close touch with them; one of the commonest reasons for 'elephant sickness' today, for example, is inadvertent contamination by Elephant Medicine. Treatment is usually on what we would call the 'hair of the dog' principle; the patient (usually female) is treated with the very substance that made her sick, on the assumption that what is required is protective acclimatization. The modern principle of vaccination provides something of an analogy, as 'advance' protective acclimatization. There are direct parallels in Uduk medical lore for this too.

The theme of building up the person through the application of 'homoeopathic' techniques, by accustoming and thus strengthening the body through administering an element of the substance or danger which represents a threat, is not only a key to medical practice but it has shaped in part the responses Uduk have found to what they see as the dangers of foreign theism. In tracing the contours of moral knowledge among the Uduk, we discover that it has often enabled them to find a defensive response to the teachings of dogmatic theology, brought nearly always by teachers with the backing of wealth and power, represented explicitly as a threat in themselves. At different times, the Uduk have regarded Nuer and Meban teachings, and Islam, in this way; and it is possible to view their recent embrace of fundamentalist Christianity, since the departure of foreign missionaries, in the same light.

One rich corpus of rites and practices which the Uduk have appropriated in recent decades, and made their own with great enthusiasm, has presented a very different face. An Order of diviners, or perhaps practitioner-performers (*ŋari/*), stemming in the last years of the nineteenth century from the Bertha and spreading widely through the Kurmuk region, has not only penetrated Uduk society but has become the chief means whereby the Uduk have been able to revitalize their own cultural existence. Diviners and adherents of what we may call the Ebony Order, after their chief oracle, have drawn upon the archive to redefine the world. They specialize in celebrating with their music, dance, rite, and drama their new vision, a vision drawing on the older certainties which informed a hunting people's experience. The success of the Order in the Uduk villages has been remarkable. By the mid-1960s, about a third of all adult men in the central valley of the Tombak, together with a few women and children, were members (in my usage, 'Ebony Men'). Other practitioners had become informally linked with the Order, and large numbers of lay people, including many women, were drawn into active participation in the Ebony rites.

The key operation of the Ebony Order is the consultation of their distinctive oracle. A thin, peeled wand is obtained from the tree known in Sudan Arabic as *babanus*. This is strictly *dalbergia melanoxylon*, an ebony substitute, but is commonly referred to in

the Sudan as ebony, and I follow this usage. The diviner kindles
the wand in the fire, and holds it over a gourd of water. The
observers wait attentively. Patterns discerned in the manner of
combustion, and in the water below, gradually provide the diviner
with his diagnosis. It is the nature of ebony, people say, as it grows
wild in the forest or bush, to 'hear' signals about what is going on
in the human world, and it is these secrets which are revealed in
the consultation. The ebony knows the grumblings and sufferings
of the people; with its help, what is assumed to be a true picture
of the people's condition is reflected back to them in the watery
mirror. They offer the ebony their problems, attend its signals in
silence, and seek their salvation through it. The ebony can aid the
people because it has *listened* to their voices. In strident contrast,
spokesmen for the new religions loudly proclaim their prescriptions
for faith, counting as their victory the silencing of others. None
have noticed the quiet indications of the ebony, sensitive to the
inner *arum*, the health of the Stomach, and integrity of the personal
Genius.

At the same time missionaries of all sorts, Nilotic, Christian,
and Islamic, ignorant or careless of these inner conditions of well-
being, in their various ways have attempted to reify *arum* as an
external, and often demanding, divinity opposed in its essence to
humankind. The main aim of this book is to offer a descriptive
interpretation of these efforts, and of the way the Uduk have
responded by drawing upon the 'archival' roots of their tradition.
In this way, following the authority of the Ebony Order, they have
endeavoured to reconstitute their moral world, and to revalidate
their sense of personhood, in the face of the overwhelming powers
of the new Arum. The first part of this book is inevitably a
little disjointed. It presents the source materials of interpretative
knowledge; a catalogue of the archive, as it were. Part II deals with
today's various competing religious discourses within the Uduk-
speaking field. Those which have in recent times been backed by
explicit political claims and economic pressure include Nilotic
theistic teaching, fundamentalist Christianity, and Islam. Part III
analyses the success of the new diviners' movement, the flourishing
Ebony Order, as a covert counter-strategy (of shifting tactics):
that is, as a new partial articulation of elements of 'subjugated
knowledge'. Many individuals have been obliged to find their
own syntheses, and construct their own explicit statements: in the

Epilogue I include one such extended account from an Uduk pastor, and compare it with the formulations of others who though not Christian remain in an important way a part of the same moral community.

To make my analysis plainer, I have used the written form *arum* when my informants have seemed to intend the older, primary or archival sense of the word; that is, an initially embodied spiritual power which has been with us since our early history, which is still immanent in persons and which survives us in the timeless world of the dead. This *arum* is certainly a source of life as much as it is a reality which lies beyond life; but it is not distinct in its origin from human beings themselves, and not a 'Creator' in any cosmological sense. Where this *arum* has been refashioned in the encounter with theism, whether in the authoritative declamations of foreign advocates or in the Uduk endeavour to meet them half-way, I have used the written form Arum. Without this device, what is a real ambivalence in modern Uduk discourse would be plain confusion for the reader. Many new, disturbing, and dangerous trans-formations of *arum* have appeared to enter the Uduk world in living memory, and we can share the nostalgia of the older generation for an earlier age when there were fewer spiritual complications.

Let me quote from one of several conversations with the sceptical Bukko, who in 1968, mourned the simpler wisdom he recalled from his own youth. He has himself died since, though at a reasonably ripe old age.

You speak of *Arumgimis* [the Biblical 'God on high'], *aruma'cesh* ['spirits of the ground' or the Biblical Satan], *caah*. The earth was not like this long ago. Not at all like this in the past. These things are now spreading everywhere, though these 'Arum' practices came only recently.

Many people die now, when in former times people stayed alive. Only the old people were the ones who died occasionally. There would be several years without any deaths, and an old man would go on living, sitting under the eaves of his hut and eating well. As we are now getting old! He sits and eats, sits and moves around his hut with his hands on the ground. Children play at attacking him. He says, 'Oh, you children'—for he is already blind. 'Children, don't hurt me like that.' People come and chase the children away, and the children run off laughing.

Death used not to be died as it is now. People didn't die in the past as they do nowadays ... there was no 'Arum' practice then. Just one death would happen, and then nothing for a year. People cultivated crops. And then later people would make beer to treat the grave; the dance music was

silenced, so that people would not dance, for death happened rarely....
[But today's] kind of death is very bad. Death is attacking us repeatedly....
We are coughing things, coughing too, and dying, dying too. This 'Arum'
is different. This 'Arum' comes from many areas around us; that's why
we die like this. Do people understand the talk of 'Arum'? People planted
things in the past; now people say, 'Give it the proper ritual': but there
were no rituals [for crops] in the past. Things were planted and they just
grew up.

Our exploration of the cultural archive takes us back into the
world of a hunting people. This is a world now more of the
imagination than of everyday experience, but the primary assumptions about bodily life and death and a large part of the idiom of
moral and spiritual language are firmly rooted in it. The modern
Order of the Ebony diviners has brought together a large area of
new Uduk experience by drawing upon this archival repository.
The modern diviners, like Bukko, also find something to fear in
the new foreign powers; but the wild ebony offers some reassurance.
The people may freely cull it from the forest; the diviners may use
it, mirror-like, to help the people relocate themselves, to confirm
their sense of orientation and identity. Through the diagnostic
readings of the ebony the encroaching High Gods are kept at bay.

(ii) Chali and its hinterland: religion and the extension of power

The Uduk-speaking people established their present home in
what was the southern periphery of the Funj Kingdom of Sennar,
probably during its closing era in the late eighteenth to early
nineteenth century. The region from Roseires to the Yabus valley
is still known generally as the 'southern Funj' (former spelling,
'Fung'), and it still constitutes a partially administered marchland
from the viewpoint of the northern Sudan. It is also still a frontier
zone for Islamic religion and social custom, with which the state
has been associated in varying degrees since at least the sixteenth
century. The growth of chiefdoms in the hilly country of the upper
Blue Nile, in the region of Bela Shangul, was in part the result of
the extension of power from the Nile valley, and it was from these
chiefdoms that extreme pressures were exerted upon the Uduk in
the late nineteenth century. The expansion of the Ethiopian state
at that time was a factor in the political turmoil of the borderlands,
and the frontier settlement agreed in the early years of this century

included the better part of the Bela Shangul chiefdoms within Ethiopia.[6] The fate of the Uduk since then has been shaped primarily by their relationship to the establishment of Sudanese state control, the growth of economic and cultural activity in the southern Funj region stemming from state policy, and challenges to state authority in the region both from across the frontier and from recurring civil war. Of course there have also been changes in the political character of the Sudanese state itself, and its consequent attitudes not only to Islam and Christianity, but also to what has fashionably become known in Sudanese discourse as 'animism'. Such wider patterns of political history and official cultural policy constitute the primary framework within which we must interpret the responsive, shifting scene of religious and symbolic activity among the Uduk.

At the close of the last century many Uduk were living in close contact with Bertha in serf communities attached to the Bela Shangul chiefdoms. It was almost certainly at this time that they first appropriated for themselves the practices of the *ŋeri* diviner, whose standing amongst the Bertha was already that of rival to the Islamic holy man. On returning to their home areas after the 1904 pacification of the border region, the Uduk brought their own version of the *ŋeri* practices with them. With the developing policies of the Anglo-Egyptian Sudan government, and in particular the eventual establishment in 1938 of a mission at Chali in the heart of Udukland, the scope of what the Uduk term *ŋari/* widened. From being the antithetical pole in relation to Islam, this figure came to represent the chief rival to Christian evangelism. The events of recent Sudanese history, in particular the 1964 expulsion of foreign missionaries and the renaissance of state-endorsed Islam in the late 1970s and 1980s, have thrust the diviners back towards their older role. In quietly co-ordinating the responses of the people to these external pressures, those we can term the Ebony Men now find common cause with a new, post-missionary wave of indigenous Christianity. Whatever their changing hostilities and alliances, the diviners' movement has, however, remained acephalous. There is no open leadership, no particular centre. They are not concentrated in Chali, still today the one 'modern' market-village and admin-

[6] A detailed account of this border region may be found in Alessandro Triulzi, *Salt, Gold, and Legitimacy: Prelude to the History of a No-man's Land, Belā Shangul, Wallaggā, Ethiopia (ca. 1800–1898)* (Naples: Istituto Universitario Orientale), 1981.

istrative centre of any size, which at different times has been a disseminating point for the two main 'religions'. On the contrary, the diviners flourish in the outlying zone of tiny dispersed hamlets, away from the roads and from the eyes of most travellers. Along with the bulk of the Uduk population, of whom most live in this peripheral relationship to Chali, they have always viewed the arbitrary powers, the officialdom, and the pious demands of that place with deep suspicion.

Since its establishment in the early years of the century, the village of Chali has increased in local importance for a number of reasons. In addition to the expected functions of market centre and minor administrative outpost, it has been a small but significant political pawn on the frontier between the 'North' and 'South' of the Sudan, having been transferred from one to the other more than once and having been of strategic importance during periods of civil and international war. It has harboured, and subsequently lost, a flourishing fundamentalist Christian mission. Today the surviving church community faces a new mosque, an Islamic Institute, an army garrison, and many times the Muslim population of the 1950s–60s (quite apart from a few feelers put out by the Roman Catholic Church). The changing political, economic, and cultural character of Chali has constituted, for the Uduk, the nature of the state in which they live, and their social history during the present century has been a story of their relationship to the changing fortunes of this small centre. Chali has maintained at different times a series of threatening postures towards its own periphery, to the network of tiny hamlets scattered through the bushland which shelters most of the Uduk. For them it has represented the power and danger of the commercial market; the power of police and the law; the power and discipline of the mission; and in recent years, once again, the old dominance of Islamic society and the arbitrary power of an armed garrison. Chali by national standards is a puny place; but locally, it represents the outside world, or at least the gate to the outside world, for the surrounding population. In a modest way they have responded defensively from their base in this periphery, though at the same time individuals have been drawn into the changing opportunities of the centre.

This spatial model of a political pressure point and its environs, of an enduring asymmetry of power between Chali *as a central place* and its hinterland, helps us to interpret the proliferating religious and cult activity of the past two or three generations. When power and effective authority change hands in Chali, quiet reactions may be expected in the outlying settlements. For this reason I have repeatedly discriminated in my analysis between events in Chali itself, and events in its periphery. To generalize about 'the Uduk' is not always helpful; for example in the context of Christianity, it is possible to ask why activity among 'the Uduk' increased enormously after the departure of the missionaries in 1964. But the answer must discriminate between 'the Uduk' in Chali and the rest, for the periphery appropriated Christianity to itself only after the collapse of exclusive mission authority at Chali and the rise of a new Islamic presence there. Only a few years earlier, in 1953, at the height of mission power (and the arrival of Sudanese nationalism, which seemed to challenge it), large numbers of Uduk men from outlying settlements had 'become Muslims' temporarily. These matters are analysed in detail below, and contrasted with the steady persistence of the activities of the Ebony Order, whose practitioners have always based themselves permanently in the periphery, and never moved into positions either of clientship or of patronage in Chali. They have consistently maintained a defensive, if covert, resistance to the successive orthodoxies and shifting social and political demands of that centre. They have been identified as prime opponents in turn by Christian and by Islamic advocates in Chali: but have shifted their suspicions and antipathies accordingly. We can trace a similar counterpoint in their relation to the world of Nilotic religion.

There is good reason for the perceived arbitrary and threatening patronage of Chali. It has had precious little opportunity to settle down as a centre of peaceful commerce and benevolent civil administration, let alone 'legitimate' government. There have been only three periods of relative peace this century in the Uduk homeland. Each has been overtaken by insecurity and disturbance, and violent fighting has come close to the Uduk on each occasion. The issues have rarely involved them directly. But the very arbitrariness of the political quarrels they have witnessed adds to that tangible insecurity which must form the background to any analysis of their thought and experience. The spectacle of embattled armies has sometimes seemed to represent a dangerously capricious side of the gods they often champion.

The first period of remembered peace followed the pacification in 1904 of the international frontier and the quelling by military patrol of Ethiopian border raids. Incidents, including the capture of persons into slavery, did continue in this region until the 1920s, but on the whole northern Uduk communities could develop undisturbed. By the late 1920s, the market village of Chali was firmly established as the commercial and administrative focus of Uduk country. It had two centres: Chali el Arab, named after a watering place of the nomadic Rufa'a el Hoi, and Chali el Fil, after the first government-appointed chief of the Uduk, nicknamed 'El Fil', the Elephant. During the 1930s, the village grew, and was drawn increasingly into the framework of administration. In 1938, the Uduk and 'Koma' areas (the latter, a term applied to groups we now distinguish as Kwama, Komo, and Shyita) were transferred from the old Fung Province to the Upper Nile Province, partly because of the affinity of their people to the African south rather than to what was seen as the predominantly Arabic-speaking and Islamic north of the country, and a station of the Sudan Interior Mission was established at Chali in the same year. However, this first period of peaceful development came to an end with the Second World War. The Italians invaded and bombed the nearby border town of Kurmuk, the Chali missionaries were evacuated, Swahili-speaking troops of the King's African Rifles were brought to reinforce Sudanese troops on the Ethiopian border; and although the period of disruption lasted for less than a year, it is remembered clearly by the Uduk as a time of disturbance, and referred to as 'the anger of the Italians'.

After the Italian defeat in 1941 peaceful development returned, with a fresh start for the mission's work and the gradual expansion of commerce and government control into Chali. The village grew steadily, especially after 1953 when the Uduk and 'Koma' areas were transferred back to the Blue Nile Province, successor to the old Fung Province, for greater ease of administration from Kurmuk. The mid-1950s were a time of growth and prosperity for Chali, both for its trading community of mainly Bertha origin and for the mission community up on the rising ground above the market area. Like other parts of the country, especially in the north, Chali was caught up in preparations for the 1956 independence of the Sudan. But the outbreak of army mutinies from mid-1955 in the south, leading to full-scale civil war by the early 1960s, meant that the bustling activity of Chali, focused mainly on the mission, was gradually stifled. The foreign missionaries at Chali were finally deported in 1964, leaving behind one Uduk pastor in charge of the mission. The trading community had also declined with the shrinkage of the mission and the spreading insecurity.

It was in this situation, of commercial quiet and a decaying mission station, that I first arrived in the field in late 1965. Chali did not change much during my fieldwork visits up to 1969. The market village had a forlorn look. The two shops had virtually bare shelves in the long rainy season, and not much more in the dry. The mission buildings up the road were physically crumbling and the school, twin orphanage, medical dressing station, and other buildings were empty. The church was operating from week to week, but with a declining congregation. There were few easy connections with other places. In the dry season occasional lorries passed through from Kurmuk to Boing in the Upper Nile Province, but there were none in the rains, when transport was on foot or occasionally by mule or donkey. The old mission station had formerly been served by the small planes of the Missionary Aviation Fellowship. Now the airstrip was thickly overgrown, and as often pointed out as a place where the people used to take shelter from Ethiopian raids as it was described as a landing strip.

From the somnolence of the small police station, manned by half a dozen, one would not have guessed that here was the threshold of the vast South, and the civil war; but tensions were not far below the surface, and just behind the old mission were remains of trenches where troops had dug in a couple of years previously. As far as I know this did not happen again, and Chali remained a backwater until the Addis Ababa Agreement of 1972, which was a plan for peace in the Sudan. A semi-autonomous Southern Regional Government was set up in Juba, the new southern capital.

Ironically, this securing of the national peace had a galvanizing effect on Chali. No longer a faded village in a forgotten marchland, it became a strategic staging post on an active frontier of commercial, religious, political, and military expansion from the north. Moreover, it was an area to which the South now laid a claim on historical grounds, but to which the now fiercely nationalistic North clung firmly.

In 1983, when I had the opportunity to revisit Udukland, the population of the Chali market area was several times the two hundred or so it had been in the mid-1960s. The village was quite transformed. Many small businesses had arrived, especially from Kurmuk, and there were two or three dozen shops (though mainly kiosks and stalls rather than solid brick structures). There was regular traffic to Kurmuk and Boing, including a daily bus service in each direction. The countryside too appeared more heavily used by the seasonal nomads, and they also contributed to the business and social life of Chali market. There was a large and flourishing (Arabic language) elementary school, and a very imposing *mahad* (Islamic Institute). The latter had been built in the late 1970s under the patronage of Omda Talib, son of the famous El Fil, and attracted students from many parts of the Blue Nile Province. A splendid new mosque had been constructed in the very middle of the village, and was officially opened in May 1983. There had been a general expansion of Islamic religious teaching and activity in the Sudan during the previous few years, financed partly by Sudan's more wealthy Arab neighbours. But President Nimeiry had also proclaimed general freedom of religious activity in the country, and this together with the generally peaceful conditions up to 1982 had attracted a Roman Catholic presence; the Catholic Church, with the experience of the Comboni Foundation to build on, had established contacts from Damazin to beyond Boing, and Chali was a link in this newly-extended chain.

Ironically again, in contrast to the relaxed policemen of the mid-1960s, glad of the odd bag of tomatoes I could give them from my little cultivations, the new Chali boasted an upgraded police station and a conspicuous army post. The village now had more of a 'frontier garrison' atmosphere than during the civil war of the 1960s. Power within Chali had shifted firmly away from the old mission station to the police, army, and Arabic-speaking market area and tension was high.

The most serious incident in the previous couple of years had followed a relatively mild set of written enquiries from some of those originally educated at Chali concerning the possibility of the transfer of the Chali and Koma Omodiyas back to the Upper Nile Province, within the Southern Region. Along with some other specific border areas, Chali had been mentioned in the Addis Ababa Agreement of 1972 as a place which, having been formerly part of the old Upper Nile Province (until 1953), would be entitled to a referendum to decide on its possible retransfer. Although the enquiries were made to various levels of officialdom, and were perfectly constitutional, members of the community and signatories of the letters were arrested by army authorities from Kurmuk and Chali, harrassed and in two cases tortured. This occurred while the pastor was absent abroad, and on his return, he was interrogated in Kurmuk. Only with the intervention of local merchants (several of whom had acted as protective patrons of various Chali Uduk in the past) was the matter dropped. Subsequently, however, the soldiers stationed in Chali kept up a certain aggressive vigilance, making their presence felt in the outlying areas through rounding up people for compulsory labour.

The political tensions in Chali have increased further since my last visit. The dismantling of the Southern Regional Government in July 1983 and the national imposition of Islamic law in September fuelled the civil unrest already smouldering. Within a few months parts of the southern Sudan were plunged into full-scale civil war again, and areas of the eastern Upper Nile were in the hands of the Sudan People's Liberation Army. The fighting continued even after the deposition of President Nimeiry in April 1985, and towards the end of that year the SPLA mounted an attack on Kurmuk town and other places in the southern Funj. Further incidents followed.

As I complete this introduction to the present book in early 1987, travel southwards from Roseires to Kurmuk is not possible. The Khartoum government's authority stops short, in practice, of Uduk-land. The third period of peaceful growth in Chali this century, 1972–1983, has thus been interrupted like its predecessors by national or international politics, and the present conflict is reopening old wounds. Developments in the modern Chali, a brand-new mosque now confronting a revived Christian community, have entrenched its frontier character. With the original establishment of the mission, Chali became a symbolic battlefield. Recent events appear to have turned symbol into substance. The Uduk have been perceived by many others in the past as a people on the front line: but this position, now a suffered reality, is not one of their own choosing.

I have described the dramatic changes which have taken place in the village of Chali as a foil to the primary subject of this study, which is the experience of those in its outlying settlements. It is not surprising that the population of the peripheral villages, the ordinary Uduk, have on the whole kept their distance from the eventful developments in Chali itself. As in former periods (either

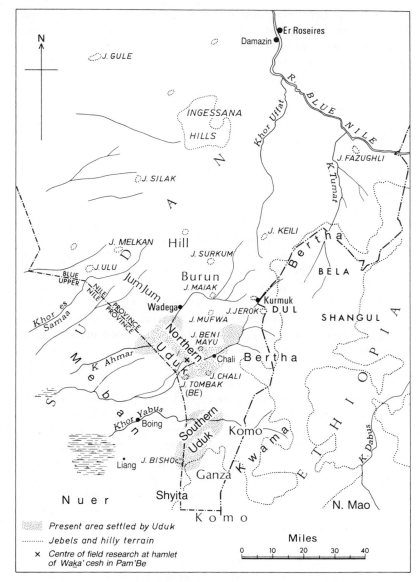

Figure 1. *The Uduk homeland and the southern Funj region.*

of bustling prosperity or of that ominous quiet caused by war in the medium distance) they have continued to exercise discretion and to guard as far as they can the relative security of their tiny but normally self-sufficient hamlets in the bush. On the surface, there were visible differences between the mid-1960s and 1983, especially in such matters as dress. There is a widespread, if intermittent, new interest in Christianity. Certainly money is more in use, and people seem to have more regular contact with Chali, at least in the settlements down the Tombak valley. In 1983 many of these seemed visually to have become extensions of, and dependent on, the new Chali. But in spite of the enlarged commercial market, the new pressures of Islam and the revived activity of Christian evangelism, I found during my brief revisit to Waka'cesh in May of that year that the older ritual practices were still flourishing. In particular, the consultations and rites of the Ebony Order were just as prominent as during my first stay in that village in 1966.

There were undoubtedly new aspects to life in the outlying settlements. The effects of the commercial growth of Chali were evident, and perhaps inevitable. It now constituted a permanent market where any villager could take a load of sorghum or maize, and acquire money for salt, onions, coffee, clothes, beads, shoes, and so forth; the goods themselves, all 'luxury extras', were available as they used not to be, and with the current high level of inflation, ordinary Uduk villagers (perhaps thinking of last year's prices) may have felt they were getting a good deal. Of course the market makes demands; a great deal of wood has been needed for building, and continues to be needed for firewood in the new Chali. Uduk women know that they can easily obtain money by collecting firewood, and both sexes can help in cutting and carrying building wood. This is a tempting and easy way of acquiring money. When I saw the fragile state of the woodland around the settlements to the west of Chali in 1983, I was taken aback. The very long dry season that year partly explained the thinness of the vegetation cover, but it soon became clear that this was real deforestation. The woods which used to screen each little hamlet are being sold off, and it seems doubtful whether they will recover.

The new money goes mainly if not entirely on consumables. Village women these days regularly wear clean wraparound cloth skirts; many wear pretty coloured dresses, and only very few wear the strings of beads and old ochred cloths common in the 1960s.

Virtually no men in the Pam'Be area now wear beads, as most used to do with their shorts; they now wear vests, T-shirts, or buttoned shirts with their shorts or trousers; some wear the short Sudanese *jibba* and *tagia* cap, though not always together, and not necessarily indicating conversion to Islam. These clothes of course look tattered very soon, as they are lent, patched up, and borrowed around. To a visitor's eye the people do sometimes appear poverty-stricken, in a way they used not to. However, on Sundays large numbers come out in their brightest and best, and the tiny hamlets in the bush look far more prosperous than they really are.

For the hamlets have not really joined the cash economy as deliberate producers. They sell what happens to be there, as it were, but they do not (at least as yet) sow crops or rear animals specifically for sale in the cash market. A good sesame harvest, as always, in addition to procuring goats by barter, will make it possible to bring in extra cash, but this still gets dissipated in the enjoyable extras of life. Cash received is not invested in further production. A small number of Uduk in the environs of Chali are setting up tiny shops, but these are often ephemeral. Money circulates more freely than it used to, but the old prohibition upon engaging in labour for another person for money is as strong as ever. Money is treated as one of those extra little luxuries; it is certainly an increasing temptation, and it has even become perfectly in order to brew beer for money. A man will get his wife to brew, using his grain, and he will give a share of the proceeds to her, or buy her clothes. Money circulates in ceremonies and rites to a much greater extent than it used to, coins for example being brought to 'greet' new twin babies. My old friends and their newly-grown-up offspring even brought coins, among other gifts, to greet my children.

But whereas it is very convenient to have money, and money has become a necessary or useful currency for some transactions, it is still regarded as a 'commodity' in itself, and has not become a means to subsistence. One still can, and should, live through reciprocal labour and shared access to land. Money has not at all become a means whereby one villager can impose dependence or indebtedness on another to any new degree; and as yet it has not become the means through which the communities peripheral to Chali have been reduced to obligatory dependence on that market. Whatever their wish to resist such reduction, which I sense is still strong, it could of course happen (especially through deforestation and deterioration of the land).

Perhaps the most fascinating visible change in the formerly pagan settlements of the Tombak valley, and I understand in the Ahmar valley too, is the network of tiny new churches, chapels, and other Christian meeting places. The upheavals caused by new religious activity from the late 1960s onwards are described below; and today's evidence could easily lead one to assume a most profound change of belief among a large part of the northern Uduk. A small church was even operating in Waka'cesh in 1983. Moreover, a dramatic change has occurred in the attitude to, and treatment of, twins. During the mission period, many had been saved from the early extinction that awaited them in the villages by being rescued and brought up at Chali. A real dilemma had been felt by village women over this problem in the mid-1960s, but a resolution had taken place in the 1970s. Twins were being saved through the network of Christian churches in the outlying settlements. Nor was this all. A ceremony for the 'saving' and 'socializing' of twins had also been adopted from the neighbouring Jum Jum, a ceremony that had nothing to do with Christianity, but had parallels with the Gurunya cult (also taken from the Jum Jum) for saving certain children from the death which had already claimed their elder siblings ('KP: Chapter 7). In resolving the problem of twins, the people drew on the new Christianity, but at the same time on a range of other social and cultural resources.

The newest branches of the Ebony Order had also spread to the Uduk from Jum Jum country, though originating like the earlier versions with the Bertha of the Ethiopian foothills. The Uduk have returned again and again to the wisdom of the diviners' oracular and healing techniques, in spite of the repeated assaults on their world by secular pressure and the official advocacy of 'Religion'. When I arrived in Waka'cesh in 1983, I found an enormous cleared space; it was being used by young men for dance-like gymnastics, to the rhythm of a staccato whistle. They were copying the exercises of the army garrison at Chali, for their own amusement. But only a couple of weeks previously, the dance-space had been prepared specially for a very large gathering to celebrate the graduation of two local Ebony diviners, Koro and Yuha, to senior status. I knew them well; their ceremony had been anticipated as far back as 1968, and my notes record disappointment at not seeing it in 1969. That year the harvest had not been good enough, and for various reasons it had been postponed again and again. I only just missed the eventual celebrations; but from all accounts, some hundreds had been present for the several days of energetic dancing and drinking (supposedly anathema to the new Christians, who nevertheless swelled the ranks on this occasion). The rite had taken place with all the old enthusiastic energy, and most of the people of the village still bore the signs when I arrived—red ochre on the principal Ebony Men, black oil on the bodies of the women and girls who made the beer, commemorative charms around their necks and claw marks on their thighs. Was this the ancient unbelief against which the mission had struggled so hard? Yes, in a way. But the Ebony Men were no longer so harshly condemned, and were themselves smiling upon the new Christianity. In dovetailing these different 'faiths', the communities of the periphery had found a new way of defining themselves in contradistinction to the dominance of Chali, in its new guise of military power and Islamic propaganda.

PART I

The Archive of a Hunting People

Discourse has not only a meaning or a truth, but a history.... The archive is first the law of what can be said, the system that governs the appearance of statements as unique events ... it is that which, at the very root of the statement-event ... defines at the outset the *system of its enunciability*.... Between tradition and oblivion, it reveals the rules of a practice that enables statements both to survive and to undergo regular modifications. It is *the general system of the formation and transformation of statements*.

Michel Foucault, *The Archaeology of Knowledge*,
translated by Alan Sheridan.

PART I

The Archive of a Historic People?

The Forest and the Animals

We were wild animals ourselves.

Buḵko

The Uduk often speak and behave as though they were surrounded by thick woodland, tempting them with rich rewards for the skilful hunter or gatherer. It is not so very long since this image had some basis in truth. The hilly country to the south of the Yabus, whence they have come according to their own account (and now inhabited by Komo and Shyita) is still relatively well forested and the larger game can still be found. A graphic picture of these hills as a 'hunter's paradise' is sketched in a government report for 1931, a picture recalling (apart from the threat of Abyssinian poachers) the primeval scenes of Uduk myth in which they perceive the first emergence of humanity. The description refers particularly to Jebel Dute and the Khor Matuk (see Fig. 1).

This forms the focal point of a hunter's paradise. The whole neighbourhood is covered with a network of Elephant tracks, and the Elephants came and drank within 100 yards of my camp at night. . . .

I also found a few tracks of buffalo, and heard several lions and leopards close by at night. In the country immediately to the South, Giraffe, Hartebeest, Tiang and Roan were met with in large numbers. Also various species of gazelle and one herd of Wild Pig.

It is obvious that what happens is that by the early rains of each year, the other watering places nearly all dry out and practically the whole of the game becomes concentrated on Dute. It is then that the poachers arrive from Abyssinia. . . .[1]

With their move north to the valley of the Yabus, and beyond to the Tombak and Ahmar, the Uduk found themselves in thinly wooded savannah country, which at best would have supported less game. But human agency has in recent times depleted the forest and animal resources of the whole region. There is a denser settled

[1] A. W. M. Disney, Report on expeditions to Warragarra (Daga), 1931. Southern Records Office, Juba [SRO] END 66. B. 1 Vol. 2.

population in the northern valleys than further south, and more serious has been the increasing use of the region by nomadic peoples, especially Fulani- and Hausa-speaking groups and Rufa'a el Hoi. Their seasonal invasion (December–May) with vast flocks and herds, and a network of camping sites, has impoverished the woodland. The increasing use of firearms has almost cleared the region north of the Yabus of major game.

Nevertheless, and in spite of the fact that the Uduk have long subsisted mainly upon the hoe-cultivation of sorghum, maize, beans, and sesame, and the raising of a few cattle, goats, pigs, and chickens, their imagination still conjures up the rich prizes of the wild. They still draw on the forest world to inform their representations of humanity and the moral life. Idioms of speech and symbol take their cue from the life of the forest, and a few illustrations will serve to introduce this chapter. Colour reference is one instance.

It has been shown convincingly how the cattle-keeping peoples of North-east Africa draw their colour terms and imagery from their cattle.[2] In the case of the Uduk, descriptions of 'colour' are largely constructed from elements perceived in the wild environment. There is no way of talking about colour in the abstract; one refers to *jamas piti*, 'its appearance', which includes what we would call pattern and texture, as well as hue. There is in the first place a double discrimination: the brightness contrast of dark and light (*'thi* and *kush*) and the hue contrast of red and green (*'per* and *dhi/*, or *gwo'd gwo'd*). This alone would give the impression that the colour discrimination of the Uduk language was very poor, on a 'universal' colour scale. These terms are less descriptive, however, in use, than symbolically assertive, especially the contrasting trio of dark, light, and red. Maturing crops, for example, can be referred to as 'black', if a rich, fruitful green, and 'red', if withering in a drought. But in the second place, at the level of 'descriptive' representation there is an abundance of terms drawn from the world of animals, birds, and butterflies; they are employed in all kinds of ways, from conventional cliché to brand-new metaphor.

---

[2] See particularly E. E. Evans-Pritchard, *The Nuer: A Description of the Modes of Livelihood and Political Institutions of a Nilotic People* (Oxford: Clarendon Press), 1940, 41–8; R. G. Lienhardt, *Divinity and Experience: The Religion of the Dinka* (Oxford: Clarendon Press), 1961, 11–16; and David Turton, 'There's no such beast: cattle and colour naming among the Mursi', *Man*, 15 (1980), 320–38.

Thus, for example, the term recently applied to a type of blue bead is *jaloŋ*, after a blue bird.

There are numerous images drawn from the wild to describe the markings and colourings of domestic animals: for example, *koro*, brown and rough, a 'colour' said to be like the bark of the *balanites aegyptiaca*, or the skin of a frog; *gawul* (fish eagle, said to be black with white stripes on sides); *waro/* (shrike, with patches: a general word for 'spotty'); *nyuruny* (hyena, that is, dark spots on light background), *lis* (kite, used for chickens, grey and white flecked), *pinyamath* (grey, as the ash of the *math* tree), *apumbule/* (butterfly, applied to whirly patterns). One finds goats, cows, pigs, and dogs with appropriate markings thus referred to as weasel, lizard, leopard, or caterpillar. Patterned cloth is often 'butterfly' or 'leopard'. There are other evocative words, including ideophones such as *diŋ diŋ* for a spotty pattern; but terms drawn from the wild predominate.

Animal images are seen everywhere, even in the stars; part of the constellation we call Orion, Uduk term *dir biṟ*, 'Leading Cattle', pointing to three cows being led by a man, and trailed by a hyena. The Milky Way is *por je*, 'The Elephants' Trail'. Animal images even occur on the human body—the middle finger, because of its length, is called the 'Giraffe Finger'. Aesthetic judgements are also frequently expressed in images from the wild; for example a beautiful young girl may be compared to a gazelle, or her skin to the softness of a certain root. There is an even wider range of metaphors for the ugly and repulsive.

A hilarious pastime is the verbal sparring of those who are entitled to hurl abusive 'jokes' at each other. These are persons classed either as *amugu* (double in-laws, especially a man and a woman married respectively to a sister and brother), or cross-cousins. Large numbers of persons are 'entitled' to joke with each other, though only a few excel at the art. Most of the fast-flung witty insults draw upon the animal world. Thus a pair will snap at each other 'Hyena's buttocks!' 'Red eyes like one who peeps from a hole!' 'Spiky-toothed like the one who lives in the river!' 'Shimmering eyes!' 'Your fingers are spiny like a lizard's!' 'Your head is mottled like the *lwanya* bird!' and so on, indefinitely. Experts can keep up these exchanges throughout an afternoon. Another kind of entertainment is swapping tales of hunting and travelling expeditions, on which all imaginable hazards are faced and represented with dramatic sound effects. I have a collection of these hunting and adventure tales, not only from the Uduk, but also from the Komo, and the Gumuz.

Wild bird imagery, like that of the Gurunya (glossy starling) cult ('KP: Chapter 7), is characteristic of Uduk speech and rite. Akira Deguchi (working on African myth in Shimane University, Japan) has suggested to me various structural and symbolic connections between the bird and human world; Iris Gillespie (now building on her earlier studies of West Africa) has also written to me about Uduk bird symbolism, pointing out that the starling, while having no song of its own, copies the songs of others—a most apt idea for this context. No doubt these topics could be taken further.

The psychological and moral language of the Uduk, stemming from the 'archive', is shot through with hunting idiom and metaphor. For example, the term *pal* is the stem of the verb meaning to try or to test, and can mean attempting any kind of task, but specifically and literally refers to pointing a weapon (spear or bow and arrow) without actually throwing or shooting. *To'k* is to straighten something, as an arrow shaft; but it can mean to correct a person, or *to'k ki gwo* can mean to correct a person's speech. *To'k* is also used of Straightening a person's body in the ritual context. (In this and other examples I am drawing both on my own understanding of the language, and on the Uduk Dictionary.) *This e* is a term meaning lost, in the material sense of a domestic or wild animal being lost and wandering out of sight; but it also means to forget, or to doubt something. To help a person is *woth*, and is commonly used both in a casual everyday sense, and in the special sense of a healer treating a patient. Compare however the Dictionary gloss 'to deliver, deliver from, drive off birds, locusts (save from), to save, to correct, to scare away, to help'. *Thuk ki e* is to follow with the eye, while *thuk gwo*, literally to 'follow the word', is in the Dictionary 'to trace a thought through; to speak to the point; to search out a matter; used in school for the outlining of events, etc.' The hunting reference *thuk sho'k*, literally 'follow the footprints' is 'to follow tracks as of animals; to track'.

The very word for the fox, *mak*, doubles as deceit or hypocrisy, and an untrustworthy person runs away with the eyes of a wolf. The important term *cesh*, which I came across first in the context of 'magic and witchcraft' practices, and which can be translated 'bewitch', in the hunter's context means to catch, to snare, to trap; *cesh e*, which is an intransitive form, means to cheat.

There are two very common words with a wide range of application, *bu'th* and *'kosh*, in their most general senses meaning to take hold of or seize, and to strike or kill, respectively. The use of *bu'th* can mean to dominate and control, in a political context; and *'kosh* can mean to attack and fight, a rather different concept of power. *'Kosh jwa*, to 'kill to death' is also an idiom for 'finishing off' something. Both *bu'th* and *'kosh* appear too in the context of healing practices and relations with *arum*, which can either seize and possess, or strike and kill. But the clearest and most literal application of these notions of power is in the hunting field, where you seize hold of or strike at an animal, or it can do the same to you. These images are strong metaphorical material.

The inventiveness and flourishing imagery of these and other common idioms of everyday speech have deep roots. Serious talk on almost any topic of human affairs is likely to lead back at least implicitly to the forest context whence we came, whether in recent history or in its timeless mythical analogue. An archetypal representation of early origins is the scene of the great dance, the dance in which all the animals joined, before our own emergence from their midst.

(i) The primeval dance

Common to the Uduk and the Komo, and I suspect to all the Koman peoples, is the vision of a primeval gathering of all the creatures, including early humankind, to enjoy the music and dancing of the *baraŋgu/*. This is a type of dance music produced by an ensemble of long gourd flutes, very rarely performed today and itself regarded as an antique form. The dancers, as in modern forms, move in pairs or groups of the same sex, or singly, in an anticlockwise wheel around the musicians. In the myth, there was no particular enmity between the various creatures at first, but teasing and trickery during the dance mounted to the point where real hostilities broke out for the first time. A major incident, whose consequences still dominate the world today, was that with the help of the Fox-Dog, human beings managed to foil a conspiracy by the other animals to attack them, and seized a pile of spears to take pre-emptive revenge upon the other animals. Human beings at that point became physically differentiated from the class of hoofed creatures, to which they had belonged, and a number of other species also differentiated themselves from their class and joined us as domestic animals.

The second major permanent change in the world whose source lay in the struggles at the great dance was the breaking of the primeval cycle of life, death, and rebirth. Various stories account for this, many light-hearted in the telling but all with the same dire message: that death, once died, is now final, and only in the most remarkable circumstances can be overcome. There are other separations: of earth from sky, and the earthly creatures from the moon, a motif which the Uduk and the Komo share.

Linking our present world with that of the early dance is the presence of that same life-generating force which is the ground of existence shared by moving creatures today: the force *arum*, which is less a 'spirit' added on to a material body than a life-principle inherent in it from the start. *Arum* today is present in all living, moving creatures, and in the same essential form animated the beings of primeval times. It did not then, and does not now, operate or manifest itself as an identifiable divinity, or creator, or entity of a discrete kind. It is true that if Uduk are cross-questioned, they can be manœuvred into a position where they will acknowledge that *arum* was there from the beginning, before the time of people, and itself created the world we see around us. But this theory does not appear spontaneously, and out of context gives a distorted account of normally implicit assumptions. The presence of *arum* at the start of things is not separate from the being of the animals; they are not 'creatures of' a creator spirit; they simply are *arum*, in themselves. The primeval cycle of life, death, and rebirth implied that the body and spirit of beings remained essentially conjoined; only with the breaking of the cycle, did they become separated, at least at the end of an individual human life. The primeval *arum* still inheres in the living wild animals, which constitute a kind of permanent reservoir. The villages of ordinary living people today are thus separated from *arum* in two senses: from the primeval undifferentiated *arum* in the wild bushland, and from the individual *arum* of those who have lived and now died, to reconstitute their own communities underground.

The main classes of animals, and even many species, were already distinct at the time of the great dance. But from the events and encounters which took place there, many species developed the particular characteristics they still have today, and the seeds of many lasting feuds were sown. Of these, the greatest is that between ourselves and our domestic allies on the one hand, who live in the village, and the generality of wild animals outside. This divide cuts right through the animal world. Nearly every major zoological class, as the Uduk see it, has given rise to a domestic member. The primary principle of classification is by the type of feet a species has, or its mode of movement.

There are thus the 'clawed animals', *toŋgwapi/*, which include for example the lion, the hare, and also the dog. There are the 'hoofed animals', *tonycuk*, including for example the antelope and the goat and cattle. We ourselves are derived from this class. (The monkeys were later derived from us by reverting to the bush.) There are then the 'feathered creatures', *tonyjeshe/*, including both the starling and the chicken; the 'earth creatures', *ton'cesh*, including snakes and lizards, and of which there is said to be a domestic member, the 'diviners' snake'. The class of water animals, *toyi'de/*, including fish, frogs, and crocodiles, does not seem to have a domestic member. But the pattern of correspondence between domestic and wild predominates even where class membership is not always agreed upon. For example, the giraffe and the camel are linked as a pair in this way even though it was pointed out as a problem that their feet are different from the other hoofed animals, and similar comments were made about the wart-hog and the domestic pig. There were particular problems about the python, associated ambivalently with the Rainbow; the python is an earth-creature in its movement and its normal habit, until in the guise of a Rainbow it leaps into the air, or sleeps like a swamp-snake in the watery pools. This classic ambivalence was pointed out to me quite spontaneously.[3] In the case of the elephant, another animal which has become the focus of elaborate rite and symbol, my friends were puzzled and at a loss to suggest where it could be fitted in the main classification. It is certainly conspicuous in having no domestic

---

[3] Compare Franz Steiner, *Taboo* (London: Cohen & West), 1956; E. R. Leach, 'Anthropological aspects of language: animal categories and verbal abuse', in *New Directions in the Study of Language*, ed. Eric H. Lenneberg (Cambridge, Mass.: MIT Press), 1964; and Mary Douglas, *Purity and Danger: An Analysis of Concepts of Pollution and Taboo* (London: Routledge & Kegan Paul), 1966.

partner, and thus stands magnificently apart as the greatest of the wild creatures, figuring as I explain below both as a chief and as a symbol of the wild in general.

It is impossible to obtain a single unified account of the primeval dance. There is rather a large repertoire of individual stories and story-motifs about the animals and their encounters, which can stand on their own as 'folk-tales', but are usually prefaced by the clue 'The animals were dancing, and . . .' This signal links the story with the primeval dance-context even though the plot may take us far from it. Elements of the stories are split and recombined in the telling, and may refer in different texts to different animals. There is a good deal of light-hearted story-telling for its own sake, in which the Hare or the Tortoise teases and tricks the Elephant. The fun of the stories lies partly in the way listeners take the side of the trickster animal. Other tales portray the Hyena as the clumsy big animal being tricked, and the Fox as the trickster (that is, Dog in his pre-domestic form). Animals are sometimes referred to casually, as members of their kind, but sometimes treated as individual heroes or villains. Some examples of these popular stories, which are told simply for entertainment, are included in Appendix 2. Other tales are told with seriousness and carry more obvious moral weight.

In one of these, the elephant is explicitly represented as leading the music with the main deep flute (known as the 'mother' of the _baraŋgu/_). It may even be represented as a chief, _tapa_, whose downfall is procured by the smaller and cleverer animals. The elephant is sometimes referred to by the name it likes to give itself, Ko Dwaya, or 'Mother of Dwaya', implying that it is female, as in the text below given me by Dhirmath.

In this tale the chief's position is usurped by the Warbler Bird, who takes over the heavy flute from her. However, this leads to the bird's death, as he falls from the sky. He is revived with a little Moon Oil. A point made later was that the Warbler had been singing about being cursed by his mother, a reference I take as referring to the Elephant mother chief. Although the Warbler was revived with Moon Oil which had spilled on the ground as the Moon fell and also died, the old cosmic pattern was broken, as well as the relation between chief and follower, mother and child, for the sky had fallen and the place had become dark. The story is more than simply light entertainment. In some ways, Uduk would regard the essentials of this tale as true.

People were dancing the *baraŋgu/* up there, and the Elephant was the one playing the leading *baraŋgu/* flute. The *baraŋgu/* went *bur-pupush, bur-pupush*. She was criticized by the Warbler Bird. The Warbler criticized her *baraŋgu/* playing strongly, and repeatedly like that. He criticized her and then said, 'Please bring that thing for me myself. Why are you playing it badly like that, you great big creature, blowing the *baraŋgu/* with your crooked mouth like that?' He snatched the great mother-instrument, took it away and blew it, *buug-buug-buug, gunyambe* [a bird]; *buug-buug-buug-buug-buug, gunyambe*. Then he went up into the sky. Went up into the sky there, and a great cloud of dust rose and settled behind him. Then the frog was squashed by the Elephant's foot, squashed like this, *'daw!* He spat, for there was blood in his mouth. He was crushed by the Elephant's foot in the dance; for everyone was dancing, the snake included. The frog was crushed by the Elephant's foot and spat out blood; it was Ko Dwaya, he said. Then that little Warbler came down at last, with the big leading flute in his hand, and landed on the ground, *'bwo'k*. People said, 'Oh, oh, our great chief is dead, oh, oh. Put the children to the breast, oh.' People had been absorbed in the great dance, not realizing what was happening. 'Put the children to the breast. You were all absorbed in the dance while our great chief is dead,' they said. People brought a little Moon-Oil to help him, by soaking him behind with a little Moon-Oil. He revived.

The Moon had died together with the Warbler, *waap*. And then people soaked the Warbler's anus with oil, Oil of the Moon. For the Moon had also died, and they took his Oil from the ground there, to use on the Warbler.

There is another story that at the time of the great dance, there was an exchange between the earth and the sky. The Moon would spit down for the people to catch his spittle, and thus to reappear after death as the Moon reappears after three days; but a certain lizard refused the spittle and broke the cycle ('KP: 74–5). This story of the spittle seems to be separate from that of the Moon Oil, which in the text above is released upon the fall of the Moon to earth. There are other accounts of the Oil being kept in a gourd, and used for anointing people to heal and revive them, but the gourd was dropped and broken when two lizards (a rough and a smooth respectively) struggled over it. Such developing hostilities were legion, as for example between the snake and the scorpion, who exchanged poisons. But the greatest hostility was that which divided humankind and their friends from the rest.

At the great dance in the sky, according to accounts given me by Bukko, people walked on all fours and had hoofs; we were kin with the other hoofed animals. The story goes that the others were planning to fight us with spears; but with the help of the Fox or Dog, who tricked the other animals and the old woman who was guarding the spears, we managed to get the upper hand; we stole the spears, and since then have hunted the other animals. At that time, we were transformed into upright creatures, and with the help of the Dog again, who gave us not only spears but also language and fire, we became civilized, creatures of the home ('kwanim pa). Some of the other hoofed animals also changed into a domestic form at the same time. The conversation between William Danga and Bukko, in which much of this appears, runs in part as follows (referred to also in 'KP: 83–4):

The dog is a thing of the Uduk. When he sits there, sits and lies down on the ground, he sits and hears what is said.

The people were once dancing, and were about to kill us. For we were hoofed creatures.

We were hoofed creatures?

Yes, we were like that, and became human beings at last because he [Dog] heard what was being said, and he took the spears that were being put ready to kill us. Then people domesticated him, for he is ours, he lives with us.

We were hoofed creatures ... we grew feet while we were still speaking gibberish. We spoke gibberish from long ago.

But people danced the *bargum* [an 'old word' for the *baraŋgu/*]. People danced the *bargum*, gathered together to dance the *bargum*, the tortoise too, everyone. The elephant too, everyone. And people danced. The Dog was lying there. They stuffed earth into his ears, they stuffed the Dog's ears with earth thoroughly, for they said he would tell people something. But all the time one ear was just lying against the ground. He stayed still and heard their talk, all of it. The tortoise was sitting being admired by the elephant. . . .

And we were the ones with the appearance of hoofed creatures; we were hoofed creatures they say. And then spears were brought and piled up near that old woman. . . . They brought spears and piled them up near that old woman, *kana'd, kana'd* [sound of spears] as we do to go hunting and kill things. *Çaaw!* The Dog [appeared to be] deaf.

Which people had the spears?

Those wild people that we now kill. Yes, we kill them. Those hoofed folk. They had the spears. And then ... what was the Dog waiting for? He ran off and shook his ears *poto poto*! He went along like a giraffe just like that, saying it was the giraffe coming, *thuku'b, thuku'b* [sound of giraffe's steps]. 'You old woman, please collect up those things and hand them over to me. People have had enough dancing. Please hand me those things all left with you. They were left with you, please hand them over.' He gathered up the things, came and divided them among us people completely.

Çaah! The others came and cried in wonder, *huugu, huugu, huugu.* 'We've treated the Dog like this, we can't survive [in peace] now!' One said, '*Çaaw!* I'm going to take revenge with my horns.' Another said, 'I'm going to take revenge with my horns.' And another said, 'I'm going to take revenge with my teeth.' The snake said that. The snake said that and the scorpion too. . . .

And what were people like at that time, when wild animals were about to kill them?

We were wild animals ourselves.

We grew feet like them?

Yes, it was these feet [pointing to his hand] which enabled us to go upright. These feet here. They made us go upright at last by growing like this. Our feet were just like those of hoofed animals.

At the time of the dance were we still going on all fours?

Yes, it was while we were still in the form of hoofed creatures. . . . We went upright when we spoke real language. . . . Our hands were all the same, like hoofed animals. Our hands split up later [into fingers]. They split up when we spoke proper language. We were still hoofed animals. For Dog, didn't he bring fire, when we at last spoke proper language, from Dog. Dog is the one who came and taught us how to speak.

A part of the large Lake birth-group is known widely as *golga/*, after the tiang, and this was taken up by Bukko who indicated that they were not the only group among the Uduk to be associated with specific hoofed species. The contrast was drawn with the *Pan'thamu* people of some nearby Bertha hills, notorious for their capacity to change into lions. Danga opened with the question:

Those Lakeŋ Golga, are they left from the time that people were still hoofed creatures?

They are the ones who stuck to the tiang while we were hartebeest. They are the Lakeŋ Golga you mentioned.

Are they real tiang?

Yes, that's why they are called Lakeŋ Golga. We were all hoofed creatures, all of us. Those people together with the 'Pesho'k people called Borfa, weren't they waterbuck? Yes, they were waterbuck, they were waterbuck. Don't you see how dirty they are? They are waterbuck. But we people of this area, we were hartebeest, all of us.

And the Pan'thamu, were they lions?

Some were mixed with the hoofed creatures. Those Pan'thamu, do they like the hoofed creatures? They are afraid of them. For if one is pierced by a hartebeest, taken on its horns, he will dry up completely. Those are the real Pan'thamu. They have always feared the hartebeest in the hunt, up to now. If you decide to go for the hartebeest [in a hunt today] they won't like that situation at all. They will all move together away from here, while the hartebeest are coming, they will run away, leaving the way open for the hartebeest to come, *buw*. . . .

The gazelle, in his case he became a goat among us. And the *yul* [a small cob] became a sheep. And the wart-hog became a pig, and was kept by us . . . and cattle were roan antelope. . . . The giraffe became camel, and the francolin, chicken. The Dog was formerly called Fox; it changed together with us. . . . We kept the *yul* while we were still wild. We were to have been killed together with that sheep, the *yul* . . . but we pushed the *yul* on one side, and we now kill them together with the hartebeest.

A great division thus opened up between those animals who took sides with us, who helped us in some way as the Dog did or who took on a domestic form, and those who remained wild, and whom we now hunt. Among the former were some unexpected friends; for example the little rat *dhothany'cena* who taught women how to give birth properly (see Appendix 2); among the latter were careless and even malicious animals, through whom, in part, death was introduced into the world. These various stories do not all fit into a neat sequence, and it would be difficult to put them together as one creation story. But a grand pattern does emerge, with repeating themes of life, death, and separation.

The second set of stories accounting for the beginning of death deal with human beings, and the way they used to visit the great dance, in this set of tales located at the top of the legendary Birapinya tree. Some versions include the explicit point that a girl went to the dance having risen from the grave. She stank, and people cursed her, and her own mother was angry at the people for criticizing her daughter; or in some cases she was angry with the daughter for not taking notice of her, and going straight on to the dance. Because of this, the primeval state of the world in which people lived again after death was spoiled. This is Puna Marinyje's version:

At the time when people appeared from the Birapinya that you spoke of, people however would have been revived after death. People would have revived after death in the past.

And a person died, a young girl, long ago. And others said, 'Ay! Who is stinking like that? Smelling like the grave [*wuruŋgu'b*].' So the mother acted: the daughter was hidden by her in a certain hut, she was hidden by her. And the body was stinking like that from that place. And another said, 'What is stinking like that?' For people reappeared [from the grave] long ago.

And it was that woman who spoiled everything. The mother became angry while the people were going to dance the *bargum*. The *bargum* was danced on high long ago, for the Birapinya existed, and went up to the sky. People danced the *bargum* there.

And that girl too, was about to go to the dance. People said, 'What a stinking person.' Then the mother became angry. Lots of people were gathering up there. She was smoking a water-pipe, *'doko, 'doko*. She threw a cinder from the pipe to the foot of the Birapinya there. And the Birapinya, the fire burned it, *'tha, 'tha, 'tha*, and snapped it, *dhu'th*!

All those people were cut off up there. Up in the sky. And those up there dropped down; they went dropping down for the Birapinya was destroyed by fire. That's why it's not there now. But its great hole is there now, it is said. That's what people say. Its hole has not disappeared. Its hole exists now.

Komo versions of the great dance are closely parallel. One Komo version may be found in Appendix 1, in which the mother of the risen, stinking girl, knocks her back in the grave. The Komo versions are, however, not set in the above, at the top of a tree; as I have already suggested (*'KP*: 68–84) the Birapinya tree motif of the Uduk is rather shared with the Meban.

In my earlier discussion of Uduk myths I have emphasized the social and political interpretations the Uduk make of these stories in the light of their recent historical experience. Here I wish to present the tales as fragmentary discourse about the way in which the presence of *arum* in the world today came to take the form it has. There are clear logical, if not theological, implications in the stories. There was no separate *arum* power which could be seen as creator. It seems evident that the primeval world of the animals in the forest was in itself a manifestation of *arum*: we have seen how the original male creature was in himself *arum* (*'KP*: Prologue), and how our forebears were transformed from being *arum* in the shape of animals at the great dance. The association between early times, wild bushland, and *arum* continues today, and is discussed in many other contexts below.

A further reason why, in Uduk eyes, the beings of early myth were *arum* is of course the very fact that they did not die; through the cycle of death and re-emergence, they were in themselves *arum*, in sound body, decayed body, or healed body. At no point was the body permanently separated from the life-giving *arum* within, as it is now. With the falling of the Birapinya; or the knocking back into the grave of the re-emerged girl; or the falling of the sky, loss of the healing Moon Oil and so forth, death did become final, and with it came the separation of the living person from the *arum* within. The whole person no longer arose, but the *arum* did, and still does. I have elsewhere pointed out that this primeval break, in some versions, causes the separation of one part of the people from another, rather than the separation of God and Man, as with the myths of so many other peoples ('KP: 72–4). But here we can consider also the significance of the separation of a *part* of the very person from that wholeness which was enjoyed in life: at death, a part is taken, or sent, away, and except in very special circumstances, it is never embodied within a complete person again.

The origins and development of *arum* within the world are understood, I believe, as consequent upon the developing history of humankind itself. The differentiation of *arum* in that other world follows the differentiation of the world of living human beings. It is true that *arum* is spoken of as a general source of 'creation', but there is no question of an active Divinity, nor of a pantheon of gods. In its general sense, *arum* is a diffuse life-force without an autonomous existence. In the context of myth, there is no tragic cutting off of God from Man. But these stories do all explain how human beings came to be separated from the animals of the wild; from other, cut-off communities like those in the sky after the fall of the Birapinya; and from their own personal life-spirit, when they finally die. However, the *arum* in its primeval form remains with the animals in the bush, and with the primeval human beings cut off in the sky; and after human life, the differentiated *arum* of persons leave the grave for permanent residence in the land of the dead.

In certain respects the ancient connection of humankind with the animal world is still with us in an inner bodily sense. Certain birth-groups, that is groups of kin with common matrilineal ancestry, understood as a line of bodily or racial continuity by the Uduk, have carried forward an inherited animal link. The most striking of these claims is that of certain lines of the Lake birth-group, described above, to kinship connection with the tiang cob. Another example concerns the 'monkey people'. There is a tale of monkeys having originated from a human brother and sister who were badly treated by a stepmother, and so ran off into the forest, became *çiŋkina/* (foundlings), and refused to leave the trees (*'KP*: 65–6). One birth-group today is regarded as having monkey descent. The The historical situation is likely to have involved the rescue and adoption of a matrilineal forebear of the birth-group in question, Yakon. They are now scattered in various parts of Uduk country, but the monkey connection is said to be important in the Yabus valley rather than in the north (where I was based). It is said that one has to be very careful in any dealings with the 'monkey people', for if they get angry, monkeys may come into your field, break and eat the growing grain. Young men in particular are very careful not to offend 'monkey girls' during the rainy season when the grain is maturing; and for this reason, a 'monkey girl' will find that nobody courts her at this time of year.

Those who have inner inheritance from the animal world can be seen as a potential source of danger to others, particularly when there is a threat that the power may begin to affect other birth-groups; real dilemmas may present themselves in this form. As I describe in the next chapter, during a large part of recent history, Uduk have acted to try to eliminate physically those known as *dhathu/*, those born to birth-lines thought to be in this state (most notoriously, twins). Except in this extreme case, however, embodiment of power from the wild has always been controllable, in principle, by human agency.

(ii) Mastering nature

In facing the bushland and forest, the Uduk today still think of themselves as 'man the hunter' and, perhaps, 'woman the gatherer'. In practice, the gathering of wild foods (leaves, roots, fruits, seeds, and certain barks for soaking to provide thickening for sauce, and woods to provide ash for flavour) is still a vital supplement to the staples of the field (sorghum, maize, sesame, beans, pumpkins) especially in poor years. But hunting has declined sharply in the last few generations, and although the men may occasionally come home with a smallish animal, big hunts are rarely organized and when they are, the catch is disappointing. Direct encounter with a dangerous animal, such as a leopard, buffalo, or elephant, is virtually a thing of the past north of the Yabus River. In so far as the Uduk eat animal food these days, it is of goat, chicken, pig, or occasionally beef, nearly always in the context of ceremonies which entail animal offerings. Virtually all a man's productive time is now spent in cultivating the fields. But in spite of the fact of practical dependence upon cultivation, the Uduk do not invest much imagination in this activity. Even when involved in weeding a field, they see themselves as combating the invasive forces of the wild, and employ a range of devices, practices, and rituals to keep away the wild birds, insects, and so forth, which threaten the crops. As Bukko said in the passage quoted in the introductory essay, 'Things were planted and they just grew up;' if protected from the wild, crops need no special attention in themselves. The human struggle is envisaged not so much as being *for* the crops, even though this is now the mainstay of physical life, as being still *against* the wild forces, an epic strife of rivals, and of kin.

Practices and cults which are oriented to the control and mastery of the wild are not inherited in bodily fashion down the matriline, as are innate conditions. They are often *taught* and always *ritually transferred* powers, dependent on aids such as special stones, or medicines, and a repertoire of special ritual techniques. These powers, in themselves a co-opting of *arum*, inhere in the relevant medicines and other equipment but more particularly they enhance the personal presence of the holder, or 'master', of the practice. His (or occasionally her) inner life-power or *arum* is itself strengthened by the acquisition of a ritual practice, and while this confers potency on the master it creates around him a charged aura which can harm others, more especially his close matrilineal kin. They seem to be peculiarly vulnerable to accidental, involuntary contamination, and he is the one to treat them for it. This pattern, whereby the one who causes a condition is also the person able to correct it, it is very common in Uduk thinking about disease. The same principle is seen in the cults for dealing with the wild, and indeed it is an 'archival' model for understanding the way the Uduk have reshaped some of the foreign religious cults to which they have been introduced, as I discuss in Part II.

Because the enhanced powers of a master who deals with the wild can be dangerous to his bodily kin, his practice is not passed to one of the matriline, but to someone *outside* it, such as a son, or a brother's son. If a practice is held by a woman, she passes it to a brother's son, for example, but not her own. The practices and cults are thus transmitted by patrilateral links down the generations, and bring together many small local matrilineal communities, conceptually and practically, in a common effort to overcome the depradations of the wild, and to wrest its fruits.

In this struggle there is an engagement of *arum* on both sides. In the wild bush *arum* is present in many forms. There is first of all the primeval elemental *arum* which has animated all life since the origin of things, and which is present within the living wild animals today. Sometimes the animals, especially antelope, are spoken of in this idiom; for example they may be said to have 'just come out of a hole', as though directly from the realm of *arum*. The presence of *arum* in animals is just a fact of nature, as the Uduk see it, and not a matter for special concern if the animals die naturally. But if one, or many, are killed by human beings, there may be a risk of danger from the *arum* of the creature, as I show in specific cases below.

There are also in the bushland and forest many *arum* which have one way or another been the product of the historical passage of human life and death. In normal circumstances, the *arum* of a person buried in the ordinary way will go to a special underground home, as I describe in the next section. But those not so buried will be hanging about in the forest, their *arum* left permanently in the wild. In the case of men, these personal *arum*, as well as the *arum* of those whose final burial rites have not yet been completed, may themselves assist living men in hunting the wild animals.

(a) Hunting and Fishing

A generation or two ago there were large, collectively organized hunts. Men from various territorial areas would join in—and those of each area, or territorial cluster of settlements, would co-operate with each other. Large areas would be surrounded at the time when the grass was fairly high in the early rains (though not so high as to make hunting dangerous). Or at the start of the dry season, an isolated grassy area would be fired, as part of the hunt strategy. These big hunts were organized by particular men, 'masters of the horn' (*com çe*, of whom Ngau was one). Responsibility for the hunt was passed on from a father to a son, or brother's son, and not down the matriline. Fathers and sons hunted side by side, as they fought together in battle.

It is said that at night, Ngau can see where the animals are grazing. He herds them by night sometimes, as other people herd the goats and cows by day. He can direct people to the place where the animals are. In June 1966, Ngau was preparing for a big hunt, I was told, watching to see where the animals were. When he would give the word, the news would be passed around by the blowing of a special horn in each hamlet, and people would join in this (Beni Mayu) hunt from as far away as Chali, and the Meban villages. Ngau would give instructions to everyone, the basic plan being a wide circle which closes in. If people were to see a really dangerous animal like a lion, they would let it through, but would spear any gazelles or other smaller animals which attempted to break the circle. The main weapon was normally the spear, though bows and arrows and throwing sticks might also be used. The big hunt did not happen that year, though two had taken place the previous year.

Danga said that when he used to share a hut with Ngau, he would hear him talking in his sleep about the animals and 'opening a door carefully to let them out', and 'telling them to stay in their holes'. Ngau's eyes were getting poor, and people said that was because he had not organized a hunt for a long time and as a result the antelopes (*bothoŋ*) had hurt his eyes. To treat him, an antelope's tail should be burnt on the fire, so that the smoke could cure his eyes.

One evening, Danga borrowed my torch to fetch Ngau because Tenge, a young woman who was his sister's daughter, was making strange animal noises. I went along and found her apparently unconscious, being held by several people and patted on the abdomen. She was twisting around and kicking her feet but not really violent. Her eyes were closed, her cheeks tear-stained, her mouth falling open, and her limbs flabby. She was making clicking noises with her teeth and in her throat, and a sort of lapping sound; and there was intermittent speech—I heard several references to *bip* (cattle). Ngau came. People seemed to expect him to blow a big horn, but he brought only the small (4-inch) horn I had sometimes seen him wearing round his neck. He smeared this with ash from the hearth, Touched and Breathed it to her nose (for her to inhale), smeared ash on her arms, Straightened her arms and fingers, drew the horn down each leg, and Straightened her toes (these ritual actions are described in Chapter 2 (iii)). He talked of *arum* and said he would do something with a chicken the next day. Ha'da, a man of the *arum* Leina cult, then came and rubbed some crushed Wild Mint (a special medicine of the cult) on her head, and breathed it to her nose, ears, and belly—spitting a little on it. He then did a full Straightening of the body.

Danga and others explained to me later that Tenge had had a dream as a girl, of being attacked by wild animals. Her legs were hurt, and 'her daughter had no teeth' (people believed that they were kicked out by the animals). What I had seen was quite common with her—she was 'herding the animals by night'; when she said 'cattle', she was referring to the antelopes. She was making the clicking noises that people normally make when they want to calm the cows for milking; but Tenge was wanting to drink milk from the antelopes. The lapping sound was the sound of drinking; but the animals were kicking her too, and the cries of 'Ish!' 'Ish!' were those that people make to drive away or fend off domestic animals in the hamlet. Tenge herself laughed the next day and said she was *'kosh ma bip*, struck by the cattle; but everyone agreed she was really *'kosh ma tombwasho*—struck by wild animals. She went to her own hamlet (of the Yakon birth-group) for the treatment with the chicken the next day; I did not go but Danga said some of her hair would be put with the chicken in hot water. This should have been done after her dream as a child, but had not been, and so now was urgent.

Ngau, Tenge, and Shara all belong to the same birth-group from Borfa which 'looks after' the animals; they herd (*ur*) the antelopes (*tonycuk*), take them to the water, the grazing, and so on. Various members of this birth-group have dreams about it at night. The dreams may be about releasing the animals from their enclosure, but sometimes they can stampede, kicking you in the process—and this is what was happening to Tenge. Tenge's little sister had a similar dream when small: she got sick, and her top teeth came out—they were 'kicked out by the animals'. People may dream these things; but Tenge, Danga told me, was not dreaming this time. She really was with the animals. The clawed animals, *toŋgwapi/*, are the 'dogs' of those people who 'have the horn' (*ta gi çe*).

To hold such powers can be dangerous. For example, if a master of the horn has pain in his eyes, this means he is 'hit in the eye by an animal's tail'. The Ebony diviners can treat him, by Extraction (*ye*), sucking out of the hairs of the animal's tail from his eye. They then cut a white chicken, and splash a little of its blood in water on his eyes; and they finally burn some hairs or fur of wild animals, for him to inhale the fumes under a blanket. Tente told me that Ngau was about to go blind because of an antelope tail which had hit him in the eye, and that the Ebony diviners couldn't do anything for him; it was only other masters of the horn, in his case, who could help. Not only the man himself, but his birth-group kin may suffer in the same way; for example, a young mother may find that her milk has run dry, because it has been 'drunk by the wild animals', and there is nothing left for the baby (this also happened to Tenge). Association with a master of the horn is a danger always to his matrikin, and this is often given as the reason why the specialism is passed on to a son, brother's son, or someone else *outside* the matrilineal birth-group. In this way it can be better controlled, and its spontaneous effects on close blood-kin minimized; though I believe a birth-group associated with the horn remains vulnerable even when the practice is passed on.

Here is Danga's account of the way that *arum çe*, *arum* of the horn or the hunt, operates, is acquired, and transmitted:

Ngau says: 'If a man has the horn and he goes to stalk, goes to stalk, he won't go seeking the animals' tracks. The animals know their master. The man goes into the forest there, and the animals come to him. They come out, and follow him to his village. He knows from a dream at night, from going to stalk there.'

If he wishes to blow the horn [to call people] then he can blow the horn. He blows the horn and leads the people to encircle the animals, without any tracks having been seen.

For example, one year, people went hunting in the area of Baŋa, and there were no animals. There weren't any animals, and people had not seen any tracks on the ground. Baŋa commanded people to surround a great empty bush area. People made a circle, and there were still no animals. And people then said, 'Where are the animals? Where are the animals?' While the animals were there, right in their midst. The animals then made sounds of movement from a great hole in the earth there, *buur*! Some were very thin and frail, because they had only just appeared from the hole. Then they were speared. *Arum* was very content indeed. The animals came out, and people killed them, killed them, a very large number.

But if a man calls a hunt, and his brother is speaking bad words, people will not find any animals to kill. They will be very elusive—they will run very close, as close as Dhupa here, a man will throw a spear and it will not stop. It will slip by. Very elusive.

How did Ngau's people, the Yakon people, get this special job?

From the dying of a man of theirs. One of their people died over there. And so they then took over that area.

He died hunting?

Yes, hunting. The hunting place belongs to another man first; and if your relative is struck by something [a weapon] there and dies, or if he is wounded by an antelope and dies, you will take over that place. For it is your place now.... If he is killed by a wild animal, like a lion, if he is killed by a hartebeest or a roan antelope and he dies; his blood is the blood of your place there, which you will hunt in. Heh! It is the same as the river. If the water kills people, it is the same. This business of hunting is the same as the river.

The relationship to the wild of the man who controls hunting is therefore predicated upon the prior loss of a person in the wild, in the context of the hunt. This person may or may not have been buried, but if buried would have had a special rite setting him apart from the ordinary community of the dead in the next world. His blood remains out there in the forest, and this gives future generations that special control of the wild, and connection with the *arum* of the wild animals, required in a leader of the hunt. It is the *arum* of the deceased which if content will lead the animals forward.

Danga went to discuss the analogous situation with respect to fishing; his father's people had acquired special control over the river through past drownings:

Many of my father's people have been drowned, long ago. And they are involved in the place where we now go fishing. They have great power over it. If they don't want people to find fish, they will turn the pot upside down, and people won't find any fish. Similarly, at the place in Dhopanyala/ here, a man called Baru is in charge. It is from their people—one of their people too in the past—[he drowned and] they took over that place. And there is another pool, called the pool of Nola, where it just the same. It is from your people who died, the water carried them and deposited them there, and it carved out a pool because of the blood of that man. The water carves out a big pool, and you [plural] will say your place is there. You will keep it and spread the news, and people will kill fish in it. If you are angry and unhappy, you will stop the fish from coming; the fish will disappear. People will not find fish.

And my father's people have a great deal of work with the fish which are dammed up in the river while the water is still flowing. While the river is flowing, they have a place to dam up the water and then people will find plenty of fish. If you are content to give people fish, people will find fish, and there will be so much fish that they won't be able to eat it all. There will be plenty of fish for several months, and even the pigs will eat fish [from the storage holes in the river bank]. The pigs will eat as much fish as they please, because there is more than people can manage. But if my father's people are angry, they will not let people have any fish; the fish will disappear. This is what it means to have *arum* of the water. For it is from their people who were drowned and carried to be kept in that place. My father's people, many of them were drowned and that is why they took this part of the river and made it their own. And the fish will hear their words, and will disappear if they tell them to go.

Clearly, even if a drowned person is retrieved for burial, which would take place in the forest, the blood—specifically mentioned here—and the breath would be left in the river, and this implies the continuing presence of the *arum* there too. In this case too, power over the wild comes about through the loss of a person, who does not go to the normal community of the *arum* in the villages of the underworld, but remains in the bush. There, the *arum* is in close contact with the wild animals, and if human survivors co-operate with it and do not offend it, they may benefit from the relationship.

At the final Beer for Settling the Grave of a deceased adult man (see below Chapter 2(iv)), I am told it is a custom to go hunting. This takes place on the day the beer is fermenting, before the day on which the grave is treated. The point is that the *arum* of the newly deceased is out there in the bush, with the animals, knowing what their movements are; maybe this *arum* too can lead the animals to its living relatives. After the settling of the grave, the *arum* retires to the land of the dead, in villages separated from the wild forest, as are the villages of the living. But in the intermediate stage between the village of the living and the village of the dead, the transitory *arum* can make a final gesture for the benefit of the living. This hunt is held particularly for a deceased master of the horn, or anyone close to him. For a master of the horn is made by *arum* to herd the wild animals, both in dreams and after death, and is himself a hoofed creature. The people go out to hunt as the beer is maturing, and all the meat killed should be brought home (that is, not left out in the bush). Women go with the hunting party to carry the meat back on their heads. If there is a great deal, some may be roasted and eaten in the bush and the rest brought back. When they return to the village, the wailing can start; and the next day, the wild meat is boiled into stew, together with goat killed in the village. The grave is fixed, the beer is drunk, and there can be dancing again. Once, in Borfa (I was told), people who had the horn were dancing for a deceased man of theirs, and a *cish* (a small gazelle) came right into the village, entered the cattle enclosure, and people killed it without any need for a chase.

Tente said, 'If (the) *arum* is happy with people, it will give plenty of wild animals to be killed.' The sense was less that of a responsive divinity graciously permitting the hunt to be a success than a reference to the specific attitude of the deceased towards his surviving relatives. If content, he would be willing to drive the animals in their direction. If the *arum* in this sense is unhappy, there would be no animals. Sometimes, however, people say a living master of the horn doesn't want to lead the hunt, but to drink the milk of the antelopes himself, and so no game will be found.

Hunting at a final Beer for the Grave does not, however, take place for a diviner of the Ebony Order. If people went hunting after the death of an Ebony Man, it would be very dangerous as they would find only the clawed animals, *toŋgwapi/*: the lion, the leopard, and so forth. The living Ebony Men are themselves sometimes spoken of as 'clawed creatures'. In Part III, I describe this Order of diviners in detail.

(b) Leopard Rites

Ordinary hunting, in which antelopes and lesser game are sought, is seen as part of a regular process of give and take between humankind and the wild. But occasionally, the opportunity comes to attack and kill one of the major large beasts. When people are able to manage this feat (with only spears, throwing-sticks, bows and arrows) it is celebrated as a glorious victory. Some of the larger animals, such as buffalo or elephant, can of course provide a great deal of meat, but this is not the main reason for the joy and excitement of the kill. It is a moral triumph over the largest and most dangerous animals the wild can produce; a symbolic vanquishing of the wild realm as represented in their being, and a time to recall that primeval conquest of the other animals with which we began our journey into human existence.

In the Gumuz villages of the Blue Nile valley in Ethiopia, I had the chance to witness the fervour and enthusiasm of the celebrations which followed a leopard kill. The killer became a new hero, and the dancing, music, and rites went on for more than two weeks. I have not see anything of this kind among the Uduk; nor has there been for many years the opportunity for killing large game in the northern Uduk valleys. But Mary Beam and Betty Cridland, formerly of the Chali Mission, have told me of seeing the leopard rites, describing them as the biggest of all Uduk ceremonies. Girls were set aside in the huts for the leopard killer, and it was 'very immoral'. I can believe the scale of the rites and celebrations, and have been told something of them. For the Uduk as well as the Gumuz, the killing of a leopard is in some ways equivalent to the killing of a man, and amongst both peoples elements of the same rite were formerly performed after homicide.

Before a leopard killer can be treated in such a way that he will not suffer from the awful consequences of his action, a Leopard master must be found to administer the appropriate protective antidote, *mushu*. (The same medicine is also used to treat a person who has committed homicide.) The Leopard master, *com mushu* (master of *mushu*) will hold a large gathering and the special hunting songs (*gwaya kaŋis*) will be performed, with dancing and stamping of feet.

Here is a popular example, the 'leopard song':

Leader: *Coma Walka ka mugu bu'th*   Father of Walka! His
     ma kwa 'kup   comrade's head, seized by
                                  the leopard!

Chorus: *Akwambil yan sonu*   'That fearful swamp leopard.'
Leader: *Ka mugu bu'th ma kwa 'kup* His comrade's head, seized by
                                  the leopard!

Chorus: *Akwambil yan sonu*   'That fearful swamp leopard.'

Leader: *Akwa ŋari/ mugu bu'th ma
        kwa 'kup̱*

Oh leopard-diviner! His
comrade's head, seized by
the leopard!

Chorus: *Akwambil ya sonu etc.*

'That fearful swamp leopard.'

The killer, and then the whole assembly, will be treated with the medicine and then Sit Black for a period following the rite (Sitting Black, without red ochre or beads, characteristically marks the middle, transitional stage of Uduk rites of passage; see *'KP*: Chapter 7). Those who dance together, and go through this rite together, are subsequently known as *kaŋis* to each other. When a leopard is killed, its blood affects people's Livers (*abasa kwa mi'd 'kwani adu*); the Liver 'goes up and down', and people get thin. It is the same as with the blood of a person who has been killed, which can make you angry and want to kill others. So in most cases your Liver must be calmed down; you must be *dil adu*. This is done by pressing the appropriate place with the medicine horn, and applying *mushu* to little cuts made on the abdomen. Later, after the period of Sitting Black, beer is made, and there is a rite for Hair-Styling, *thes 'kup̱*. Beads are put on again, and people are anointed with red ochre. There is a general exchange of beads and bangles, and people 'make friends', *mii amugu*. Subsequently, each pair of friends uses the reciprocal name *mojunyu/*, and avoids (*ga/*) each other's real name.[4] Tente and Medke still call each other by this name, and Tente still shows the marks of the *dil adu*, the calming of his Liver with *mushu*.

Although leopards are very rarely encountered or killed by Uduk today, the *mushu* rites probably still take place following homicide, though this would now be arranged very circumspectly.

(c) Elephant Medicine

By contrast with the Leopard rites, the rites surrounding the practice of Elephant Medicine (*cwany je*) are very conspicuous, even today. The killing of an elephant has consequences which last over the generations, and the administration of the Medicine is an occasion for the richly symbolic re-enactment of the original mythical conquest of the animals, and the fresh start which was thus made possible for humankind. As with *mushu*, the primary use of the

[4] Compare the reciprocal friendship names commonly used between pairs of friends, described in my article 'Ephemeral names: the Uduk case', in Thelwall, *Aspects of Language in the Sudan*.

Medicine is to calm and protect the elephant killer. In due course he can administer the Medicine to others, and then pass his special responsibility to a son, or a brother's son. Occasionally a woman will take on the administration of the Medicine, usually from her father.

There are many 'medicines' known to the Uduk. Most are roots, barks, or leaves from the forest. The Elephant Medicine is an acrid-tasting root. I was once travelling with Tente and a few others in the Yabus when he went off on his own to dig up a supply. The plant, for which I am afraid I cannot give a botanical name, is common in the Yabus but not in the northern valleys, and he wanted to restock his collection of medicines back home. Tente is a senior graduate of the Ebony Order; but he has been an Elephant master for even longer, and easily combines it with his wider work as an Ebony diviner.

I have already indicated the place of the Elephant in the stories of primeval times. She was at one point leader of the whole dance but was usurped by the Warbler; and at other times tricked by many small animals, by Tortoise snipping away inside the great body or Hare paring off the soles of her great feet (see the tales in Appendix 2).

The wider context of elephant hunting in this region should be mentioned. There were formerly large herds along the Sudan–Ethiopian border, and the ivory trade, intermittently significant for many centuries past, reached a peak with the greatly enlarged demand from Ethiopia following the late nineteenth-century expansion of that state under Menilek II.[5] Even the remotest communities were drawn into the proliferating network of ivory supply and trading, and even at the furthest points there was an inflated reward to be found in elephant hunting. Though not operating on a major scale, the Uduk were among those indirectly caught up in the supply of ivory through many middlemen to Ethiopia. Although the herds had dwindled in this region by the 1920s, the significance of the elephant today is derived not only from the older mythical representations but also from its having been a hazard-ridden source of windfall wealth within living memory. Such wealth is itself perceived as a danger to the fragile social balance among the Uduk,

[5] See Donald Donham and Wendy James, eds., *The Southern Marches of Imperial Ethiopia: Essays in Social Anthropology and History* (Cambridge: Cambridge University Press), 1986, esp. ch. 1, 2, 6, and 9.

and the symbolism of the cult of Elephant Medicine as it is practised today reflects this in some degree.

The way in which the Uduk might summarize the business of Elephant Medicine is as follows: a man kills an elephant, or rather initiates the killing, for it requires many people to assist. He, and the community as a whole, obtain much meat, and also perhaps much wealth, from the killing. But there is a danger, from the *arum* of the elephant, which will strike him and also others if they are not given protective rites and treated with Elephant Medicine. This root from the bush is thought so powerful that it can itself make people ill. The main symptom is a skin disease, in its earlier stages indicated by rough itchy patches and flaking like an elephant's hide. The condition as defined by the Uduk may include what we call leprosy. Treatment is by an Elephant master, who acquired his practice either from having killed an elephant himself, or from the hand of a father, or a father's brother, or other patrilineal relative through similar links back to one who did kill an elephant in the past. One of the commonest sources of contagion is by carelessly eating things of an Elephant master who is a (matrilineal) birth-group relative, such as mother's brother. However, it is also possible for the Medicine to 'catch' you as you wander about in the bush, where it grows, or as a result of your 'eating things in many people's houses'. Whatever the cause, as soon as you see that you have a rough and itchy skin, you know, without going to an Ebony diviner for formal diagnosis, that you have been caught (*bu'th*) or struck (*'kosh*) by Elephant Medicine, and so you approach an Elephant master. Masters frequently act together, and thus constitute a quasi-professional association for the protection of the community from this particular danger. The details of the rites explicitly evoke the mythical struggle to overcome the wild and act out the conquest of the Elephant.

To recollect an elephant killing is a heady memory for the Uduk. In the imagination swarms of people foregather, the beast resists the repeated attacks with spears and arrows, the struggle is prolonged after the creature's death by everyone cutting it up and scrabbling over the meat. It is perceived as a dangerous occasion in many ways (not least from the chances of injury, and from the mound of flesh, no doubt still quivering as it releases its life, and starts to putrify in the hot sun). The custom is for the person who throws the first spear to retire from the fray, leaving others to follow it up; the first is also the most vulnerable to the *arum* of the elephant, and following the first spear, the antagonism between them is translated on to a 'spiritual' plane. The hunter has to sit cool and quiet and not even drink water, in order that the elephant be quite vanquished. The Elephant master arrives on the scene to play his part. Tente explained:

It is from the *arum* practice of long ago, from the people of old who killed elephants. People killed an elephant; but maybe this man who attacks the elephant is not very brave. He will throw his spear at the elephant and run and sit in the shade. And it is the other people all around who chase the elephant and kill it, while he stays in the shade. And he doesn't drink water. He doesn't drink any water. He stays like that, for if he drinks water, the elephant will not be killed. The elephant will not be killed to death. The elephant will go on living.

And after he has gone to sit in the shade, the elephant is killed while the sun is here [indicating low in the sky], and then dies. . . . And a man who knows the Elephant Medicine well, when the elephant is struck, he goes and stands where the spears are piercing the body of the elephant there, *dug, dug, dug, dug*. The man chews the Medicine in his mouth and goes to the place where the elephant is. The elephant moves away, leaving people their spears. He shakes his body, *puur!*—flinging people their spears in the ground. The elephant goes away, and people pick up their spears. And later people go and kill it, *ta'b, ta'b, ta'b, ta'b*. . . . It dies at last, and people cut it up. It is cut up for all the villages from the whole of 'Penawayu to the whole of the other bank there [all of Pam'Be]. This one elephant supplies all these people with meat by itself . . . but the effects of it are not good at all. If it is eaten when the sun is here in the morning, people will not be satisfied. They eat like that, on and on until sunset, still eating. People are seized with hunger here very soon like that, immediately; it provides no satisfaction. It is eaten like that until people are tired.

Tente went on to describe the continuing need for the Medicine. In some way, the power of the elephant's *arum* enhances the 'contagious' power of the killer himself, and that of later masters of this Medicine. We were discussing the particular case of Mondi̱t, a girl who developed skin disease from eating the meat of animals derived from ivory proceeds that had benefited her birth-group in the past:

And for those whose fathers have killed an elephant: its *arum* is still there. For example . . . my sisters' children are here today, living here. If they touch something which I have made with my hands, and they eat, they will get skin-disease [*go̱p*]. Their bodies will itch very much. . . . And if food is brought to them to eat, they will eat it while it is very hot, and then leave it. And in the morning they won't eat sesame paste ... [which] is the thing to carry skin disease from the Medicine.

There is a Medicine [*dawa*, Arabic] for this condition which helps people.... Now the Bunyan [Arab or European] doctors, don't they give medicine to people? Are there not various medicines to help people's bodies? To help people with itching bodies, and rough places. You will itch, your whole body will swell in lumps, *gotolagotol*. You will go to a person who washes you with medicine, to make you better. You will recover.

And later, people will brew beer because you are better ... and finally put you right [*nyon*]. You will be completely cured. It will not affect you again. But if you cheat [that is, on the food prohibitions], ah! you won't recover. You will get worse. You will be diseased for ever and build a house alone, as a man with leprosy does.... From cheating a man will become very diseased and people will not eat together with him. He will live alone.

W. Dhupa: *Why was Mondit struck by Elephant Medicine?*

She found something to eat from her mother's brother. For her mother's brother killed an elephant ... long ago, before I can remember. And he bought [*yol*] things with the elephant tusks. The things remained. They ate those things; goats or cattle ... the old ones of the mother's brother are still living.

The contamination of animals acquired as the proceeds of ivory sales can thus be a continuing problem for the matriline.

I was also told that if you kill an elephant, you and the people in your own village do not eat the meat. It is for the people 'outside' to eat it. Your people must not eat anything at all until beer is prepared, and you are all treated with Elephant Medicine. If anyone eats before this treatment, they will be ill—*uni mina cwany je bu'th mo* (they will be caught by Elephant Medicine). Ridan, an old lady, was an Elephant master, and this had come about through her eating food after her father had killed an elephant, before the beer was prepared for treatment. She was caught, or seized, by the Medicine, and then treated by her father. Ever since then she has been able to treat others. Her son Laga often helped her in this, but the practice was to be passed on by her to a brother's son, and not to her own son.

I have not seen the primary treatment given to a person suffering from Elephant Medicine. But I have seen, three times in all, the Head-Shaving ceremony to mark recovery; this is the rite which follows a period of convalescence, during which the patient is allowed to eat only the plainest of food, and there are restrictions on his or her movement. Beer is made, and the patient has to hand over a number of items to the master in payment; if the debt is not met, the master can cause further sickness by putting the Medicine on the fire.

The Head-Shaving rite quite explicitly enacts a new beginning for the recovered patient. Foods of every type, both domestic and wild, are collected together, and ritually Blown to the patient's nose by the master. He also Offers these foods to the patient, who tastes them carefully, rejecting them once before swallowing, as a part of the 'reintroduction'. If the patient is a woman, her hand will be carefully led by the Elephant master over the grinding stone, and in other actions which are the daily work of women; she is thus 'reintroduced' to the tasks which are her part of making the community home. Even more striking is the reintroduction of fire. For the cooking and brewing fires on this day, 'new fire' is made. The master goes out to the bush for a soft stick to bore into with his fire-drill, in the ancient manner, making a fresh spark to light the domestic hearth. Normally, for healing rites as for everyday purposes, fire is begged and borrowed from house to house. But for the day on which the Elephant is conquered, new fire is required.

Throughout the day the theme of killing the elephant recurs; the goat to be offered does not have its throat cut in the usual way, but is dispatched like a wild creature with a spear thrown from the side. People crowd into the beer-hut exclaiming 'Let's go and kill the elephant!' [that is, have a taste of that beer] 'Let's throw a spear at the elephant,' 'I'm going to throw too!' [*mar je amee*, a hunting term to throw a second or follow-up spear at the elephant].

I will give a few details of one case. Lajia's baby developed lumpy sores on its lower legs and buttocks, and was treated together with Lajia by Tente in the rainy season of 1967. It was assumed that they were caught by Elephant Medicine from 'eating something in another village somewhere'; by implication, something either derived from the proceeds of ivory sales, or from the food prepared in the house of an Elephant master. Lajia ate something bad of this sort, and through her milk, the baby got the sores. Tente cut the sores, and applied a little of the Medicine. Following treatment, the mother and baby ate only within their own household, not in other villages or even in other huts of the same village. Their foods were also of the plainest. Fortunately, they recovered, and the beer-party for Head-Shaving was held the following April. Food for the feast was collected from all the surrounding villages, and included as wide a range of types as could be found, wild herbs and roots from the forest as well as cultivated crops from the fields. The beer was prepared by Lajia's own people, and she returned to their village for the ceremony from her married home elsewhere. During the day of the ceremony, many guests brought token contributions for the specialists, such as bangles and spears.

Elephants are one of the main threats from the wild that the Uduk have known in historical times, and have assumed in addition some of the aura of danger associated with trade and wealth. Knowledge of a Medicine which can counteract the threat of the Elephant, even though it may occasionally contaminate its possessors, is valuable. No wonder that its successful use is celebrated with rites which recall the mythical establishment of the very first human community, when wild nature was first vanquished and fire and cooking first introduced. No wonder also that in considering the Uduk reception of a variety of religions and cults that have been introduced into their world in recent decades, we are reminded again and again of their response to the *arum* of the Elephant.

(d) Further examples and discussion

A cult which I have not come across in my own work has been described by earlier observers as 'Lion Eyes'. I have heard rather vague statements about 'some people' being able to change into lions, mainly some of the southern Bertha, but have not traced a ritually transmitted lion practice among the Uduk. However, it is very likely that along with many of the older concerns of Uduk ritual, such a practice could have been overtaken, and partly absorbed, into the activities of the new Order of Ebony diviners. The account in the MS notes on the Uduk from Chali Mission, however, dating from the mid-1940s, is of interest in several respects:

Mabans say that the lions are in reality "*Kwanim pa*' who have changed themselves into lions. This has some foundation in fact, in that the Uduks on the Yabus have the custom of initiating some babies into the cult 'Lion Eyes'. A parent who has that distinction himself will 'give' such eyes to his children, girls or boys. In such cases a newly born child (one day old!) is taken from the mother, and a hole dug under the woven wall of the house. The child is passed under the wall from the outside in, and then taken outside and thrown onto the roof of the house, so as to land on its stomach. As it comes sliding down backward, it invariably snatches at the thatch with both hands, 'like the claws of a lion'. When that child grows up, he is then said to have another 'self', that when hungry goes out hunting in the form of a lion and gets meat for himself. They say that such lions kill only wild meat, not goats, etc., although the Mabans do not agree. A 'lion man' can tell when he has been out at night be [sic] waking up with a full stomach, and often the next day, they say, may go out and lead the people to carry home the meat from kill [sic] made the night before.

The advantage to the people of such power is in the fact that such people will 'never be hungry'.

The Bertas have the same custom, we are told.[6]

Like other powers connected with hunting, this power is transmitted from father to child (the 'parent' referred to takes the masculine pronoun), which suggests that this is not an inborn power but an acquired practice. As we shall see later, in Part III, the modern Ebony Men are represented as 'clawed' in several contexts, and in some rites are similarly thrown up on the roof of a hut to cling on with their hands. It is very striking that in the rite described above, such new-born children are passed through a special hole in the hut wall from the *outside* in; this presumably precedes their emergence into the social world through the front door. I have already described a rite, for the new-born Gurunya child, which requires that the baby is passed from inside the hut to the outside, through a side-opening of this kind ('KP: 213–14). The Gurunya child is defined from then on as incompletely human, and as outside society; the baby in the lion-eyes rite is being defined as having entered human society, through the front door, but only after originating from the outside.

This rite is also interesting in that the powers transmitted are used by the holder for purely private benefit (though the expectations may be that the meat hunted at night should be shared out). This theme, a sensitive matter for the Uduk who are very cautious not to appear selfish or exploitative of others, also runs through the practice of using rainstones.

---

[6] 'Customs', typescript notes, Sudan Interior Mission, Chali, n.d., p. 2.

I have described the use of rainstones in some detail elsewhere.[7] Briefly, a considerable number of birth-groups possess rainstones, which are normally administered by one of their number. They are kept in the ground and brought out in the early rains, when they may be washed, anointed with oil, and, if the need is great, sprinkled with the blood of a chicken. It is expected that rain will fall; the dark stones bring steady rain, but the red and white are liable to bring thunder and lightning storms. One property of the storms thus caused is to wreak damage on recalcitrant debtors, who typically have owed debts of animals to the rainstone holders for many years. Grumbling by the creditors may activate their stones. Storm damage, when it occurs, is appropriately diagnosed by an Ebony diviner, and arrangements are made for the repayment of the debt (often plus 'interest'). Rainstones may be administered for a while by a son of the owning birth-group, and he may recoup old debts of his own with them, but like animals the stones are the property and responsibility of birth-groups and must return to them. There is a stronger personal, or rather birth-group, interest in rainstones than in other ritual techniques for controlling the environment, because of the potential economic benefit. Problems over the use of rainstones, of course, can lead to a good deal of the grumbling which encourages storm damage.

There is one further major stimulating wild presence: the rainbow, sometimes exercising as fearful an effect on the imagination as any ordinary animal—indeed more so. It seems likely to me, though difficult of proof, that the relative importance attached to the rainbow in recent decades has probably increased, perhaps even as the encounters with wild animals have become less and less frequent. There is no remembered ancient ritual specialism which dealt specifically with the rainbow, even though it can embody *arum*. Accounts of dealing with the rainbow are rather like hunting stories, of escaping from hair-raising situations by using one's wits, as one might from a wild animal.

The Order of Ebony diviners, however, which has become established among the Uduk only this century, confronts the rainbow head on. Rainbow Medicine is one of the Order's special emblems; and one of the diviners' main tasks, in Uduk rhetoric, is to 'fight

---

[7] See 'The Politics of rain-control among the Uduk', in I. Cunnison and W. James, eds., *Essays in Sudan Ethnography: presented to Sir Edward Evans-Pritchard* (London: Hurst), 1972.

the Rainbow' or 'ride the Rainbow'. This topic will be explored further in Part III.

There are ordinary rainbows, and special ones, which we may term Rainbows. Both are *pe'do/* in Uduk, though the latter is also spoken of as a python (*sum*). Morning rainbows in the west seem to be harmless; but the afternoon ones in the east may be the dangerous ones. You should never point at a Rainbow. If it chases you, and you cannot get home, people say you should take shelter under a thorn tree. The Rainbow will come and curl itself round and round the tree, to swallow you up with its mouth. Just as it is about to get you, you dash off home, leaving the Rainbow caught up in the thorns and unable to unwind. A Rainbow is sometimes said to have a camel's ears, and other strange attributes. It lives in water-holes in the ground. It is indubitably *arum*, at least in the contexts in which it becomes active.

I find it quite impossible to state what 'the Uduk really believe' about rainbows; there is no easy line between their own notion of the physical or even zoological reality of the rainbow/python and its active role as *arum*. It is of course only rarely seen in either of its 'natural' states; and the powerful imagery of the aggressive Rainbow creature seems to displace observation or memory. People enjoy tales of encounters with the Rainbow, and each community has a good repertoire, often told along with their hunting stories. The circumstantial detail is perhaps the most difficult part of these stories to assess. Tente told me about one exciting encounter.

People used to take women along the path in the red soil area there, to dig for the [edible] *cu/* root. The weather had clouded over. We carried the root in our pouches, and we also collected some honey. I was carrying the honey in my shoulder-pouch. We were with Buta, and Mare, and my brother-in-law Mongo, and my friend Dwaj. We were going along, and other people were making a fire in the distance. The rain-clouds were moving overhead. Perhaps we had reached a place where the Rainbow is to be found. We passed on. My friend Dwaj went to relieve himself in the bush back there. We left him behind. Then I looked back, as he was crouching down. 'My friend Dwaj! What is that? There is a great Rainbow behind you!' He said, 'Oh, oh, my friend, stop!' We ran towards each other. As the Rainbow appeared, the rain came down.

The Rainbow came and surrounded all of us. My brother-in-law Mongo dashed forward, to the mouth of the Rainbow. Buta stayed in the middle, and didn't go to the mouth of the Rainbow; he was afraid of the

Rainbow. He stayed in the middle, and said, 'Oh no! You go to the mouth of the thing!' Mare ran to its mouth. Dwaj and I went to the other end. There were two of them, Mongo and Mare, together. We shot at it, at the distance of about that tree there. It came toward us, and we ran away, I was running, but I kept looking back at the Rainbow all the time. I was carrying the bag of honey. Then I fell over and squashed the honey on the ground. I got up and ran off, shouting all the time, 'Wayaa! Wayaa!' I called out, 'My friend! My friend!' My friend Dwaj was saying 'Get up!' I got up again. I took my throwing stick. I threw it at the Rainbow, and then it moved away. I ran after it. I took the bag of honey and hung it on a tree. Then we shot, and shot, and shot again, *jira, jira* [sound of arrows hitting prey]. We don't know whether the arrows stuck in the body of the Rainbow or not. We went to the place where the arrows fell, but we couldn't find them on the ground. Maybe those arrows were in the body of the Rainbow.

We shot and shot again, until it was as far away as Thayo's place from here [i.e. about one hundred and fifty yards]. The Rainbow went into a tangle of briars, and didn't move away from there. We shot at it in the middle of the briars. But we were extremely tired, so we left it there. As we came away, I put the bag of honey on my back.

Then the Rainbow came again. The ground was slippery, and I fell down again, and squashed the honey once more. I took the bag and hung it on a tree. We started shooting again, until it went back to its hole in the middle of the briars. We came away and I put the bag on my back again. We moved far away, but it stayed in the middle of the briars.

We came and found people building a very big fire. They were also shooting at the Rainbow, but over *there* [pointing to a different place]. We had been shooting at the real thing, but they were shooting at nothing. We were the people shooting at the very body of the Rainbow. We found them making a big fire. We found them right here. As we put our bows down, the Rainbow appeared one more time. Everyone said, 'You people! The Rainbow's here again!' Everyone was scrambling for his bow. Everyone began to shoot again, and then the Rainbow retreated. And it stayed away for good.

The Rainbow as a motif is also found among neighbouring peoples; I once asked a Bertha visitor if the Bertha feared the Rainbow as the Uduk did, and he replied very firmly, 'No, no, not at all.' Then after quite a few minutes' reflection, he added, 'It's only bad Muslims who fear the Rainbow!'

Given such an explicit antithesis, which must have been established earlier among the Bertha (who have been partially Islamized for a century or more), it is tempting to regard the Rainbow as already a major 'symbol-in-waiting', an element from the archival stock, before the Ebony Order appropriated it as a major emblem.

Nature and history blend into each other in the bushland of the Uduk imagination. The Rainbows I have just described may be the vehicle of *arum* of the dead, anonymous or otherwise; and at the same time, there are named *arum* of a shadowy kind which are sometimes referred to as lurking in the bush. For example, one hears occasionally of *arum ma Miṭi*, which in the singular or plural is said to 'race horses in the late afternoon', gun in hand. There is also *arum ma Badhiya*, which is said to be a one-legged man and associated with a certain tree by the Uduk, while the word *badiya* itself in the Komo language means rainbow. No one has seen these *arum* for a long time. It may be that they are historical residues, fading political memories; of the military *bashi bazouks* of the Turco-Egyptian period in the first case, for example, or of former Komo contacts in the second. Numbers of unknown *arum* from the past cluster around particular features in the bush, for example large trees (like the great baobab near the Chali mission which fell when the missionaries finally left), certain stretches of river, certain hills and rocky places. A brief sickness of mine was attributed to the *arum* of Beni Mayu hill, which I had just climbed; it was not, as I had at first thought, the 'spirit of the mountain' but rather the shades of the past which gathered there.

(e) Birdrites

The old practice of *ḳoŋgoro/* rites for environmental control, especially of birds, and the observance of its rules for disciplining noise, exuberance, and sexuality, are no longer kept up very well. But Puna Marinyje claimed that *ḳoŋgoro/* was an ancient and authentic '*arum* practice' of the Uduk learned from nowhere else. It consists of a series of rites administered by a male specialist I shall term a Birdmaster, who would take over the responsibility from a father or father's brother. The rites are designed to ensure the survival of the crops. One might assume these rites to be aimed at the fertility and maturation of the crops in themselves, as are the rites of so many agricultural peoples, but in fact they are intended solely to deter the enemies of the crops—the wild birds and insects which might invade and consume them. The rites in fact are more appropriate to a hunter-gatherer tradition, with the emphasis perhaps particularly in this case upon the 'gatherer' elements. The main theme running through the rites is the careful damping down of excitement and stimulation, the reduction of noise and sexual activity in the community, the collection and 'tying' or bottling up of errant insects, and the use of the 'cool' black colour. The cooling and calming of the community, and the avoidance of provocation, is intended to have a corresponding effect on the wild. This theme recurs in other contexts where the Uduk are dealing with the threats and dangers of the wild—and indeed those stemming from social and political causes—and it is therefore of some interest to record the *koŋgoro/* rites in a little detail (though I have not witnessed them).

The Birdmaster has special equipment, including a gourd of oil for collecting insects, and black stones (which like black rainstones bring only safe drizzle, not storms). In the early part of the season as the crops are coming up, he will go to the fields (in the morning when it is cool) and pick up the insects *manduruny* which destroy the maize, bite them with his teeth and put them in his gourd with a creeper to 'tie' them. He also collects the worms which destroy sorghum, and the grain eaten by birds, and puts everything in the gourd. He keeps an eye on the crops right through the rainy season, and during this time his wife refrains from the normal practice of throwing their household ash outside. She stores it in a pile at the back of the hut. If the Birdmaster is angry, say with someone who has taken pumpkin or sweet corn from his fields, he can take a little ash, throw it outside, and mosquitoes will torment that person.

At the most vulnerable part of the year, when the crops are almost fully ripe, the Birdmaster will collect sesame from everyone, make oil to anoint the sorghum, and declare a special *koŋgoro/* period. He will take a chicken for the fields. It will be dispatched by having the head twisted off and the body held firm, so that it does not flap around, causing disturbance. During this time there should be silence especially in the fields, and no whistling or blowing of instruments. There should be no joking or abuse between *amugu* (double in-laws or cross-cousins). If a man and a woman have sexual relations at night, they should not go to the fields the next day; nor should a pregnant or menstruating woman go to the fields. If a pregnant woman insists on going, her feet should first be brushed with a lighted grass bundle. If anyone 'cuts the rope' of these rules (that is, breaks a prohibition), *arum* may cause sickness (this signifies the *arum* of the Birdmaster himself) and the birds may eat the grain. The birds might even 'follow the path' of a man who had slept with his wife; presumably this is a 'hot' trail, and like the hot ash, would provoke bird attack in this cool time. I heard of a case where a girl was taken by force in the fields during the ḳoŋoro/ time, and the ḳoŋoro/ people claimed a fine.

When the crops are fully ready, the Birdmaster gives the signal for the harvest, and a big beer feast is prepared. Beans are brought by every woman to the Birdmaster's wife, and she cooks them and mixes them with sesame; also animals are killed and the meat boiled, but like the bean mixture, this meat is allowed to cool until the next day before being eaten. At this feast, the whole year's ash is scooped up and taken out through a special hole cut near the ground in the hut wall, and thrown away.

It is worth noting that the ḳoŋoro/ rites deal mainly with sorghum and sesame. In the case of maize, a historically more recent crop, the first fruits should be taken to an Ebony diviner for his blessing. 'Ta'bko gave an account of the ḳoŋoro/ rites; he was himself a Birdmaster.

I practise this because of birds. It is done by us because of these things, and also when the sorghum is eaten away [by beetles etc.]. We go and do something. We take some oil, dip a hand in and drop a little into the sheath at the top of the plant, and the sorghum becomes healthy. It recovers, improves, and afterwards I rest at home again. Later I put oil in my hand and pull the leaves with my hand like this.... Later again, I bring ash when the grain has flowered, and take the leaves in my hand, I cut some creeper, chew the leaves in my mouth, and spit on to the seeds. I treat them with oil, and drop a little ash on top. Then I go along the path with ash; people will see the ash on the path there. I find little beetles, and I go off the path and seize them, and put them in my gourd and shut it up with the creeper, 'te'b! Then I go back home, find a chicken, make the children chase the chicken, and I seize it and cut [i.e. kill] it.... People store up my ash in the hut. It is not to be taken anywhere else. My ash remains in my hut.

If my wife strains it, to make sauce [a common method using salty wood-ash], it is put back in the storage pot afterwards with the rest.

Later on, when people have finished threshing, they will tie little bundles of sorghum ... and a few of sesame, and bring them to my hut. They are kept to be soaked for making beer ... when it is ready, lots of people gather, with chickens in their hands at my hut there. We pierce a hole in the hut, under the eaves near the ground and carry the ash out through it. And people cut goats, chickens, and pigs. Now we boil [the meat] in pots. People boil it, but they don't eat it. It remains there, until the next day. People [on the first day] eat grain food and drink beer, but the next day we all rush to these things and eat, while they are very cool. We eat meat at last, while the meat is very cool. We eat it all in the morning, and then we go our ways. That's how it is.

Are there koŋgoro/ *stones?*

There are stones: they are black. The stones are deep black. I have stones now—there are two ... they are in the oil now. They are in the oil, waiting to seize birds. They are seizing birds, because they sit eating little husks on the ground. I go and pick up the husks, and throw them in among the stones, throw them on top of the stones. Then I cut creeper, to seal the mouth [of the gourd with the leaves of this creeper]: and the [birds] will not eat anything more. They will stop eating the sorghum.

How did you learn koŋgoro/?

I am doing it from my father ... in the village over there. Long, long ago, it came from the old people. Because it is not newly invented. *Koŋgoro/* is a thing of long ago, while we people here don't know [its origins]. Even the man who gave it to me, doesn't know.... He took it from his father. His father also got it from his father first. That it how it's passed on.

Did your father treat you before you could do the koŋgoro/?

Yes. He treated me. He cut a chicken and put the blood on my hand here, mixed with the stomach-contents of a goat.

Have you told people not to make a noise in the fields?

Yes, I told people not to chatter a lot because the animals will eat things. And then it was finished. I let them do as they wished, because the grain had dried out. That man, I spoke to him about eating beans; I said, 'Why are you going to eat beans early? Because of the talk of Jesus? You should go about quietly still, and wait for the word from me.'

Danga explained that if the bird nuisance persists, people may decide to do something active about it.

People will challenge the birds; they will all shout very loud in the middle of the sorghum field. There are not birds [this year] and that is why people are silent. Otherwise people would not sit and chat at home. All the children too would gather in the middle of the sorghum, and each take a different place and stay there; people would tell them, 'You stay here. You stay here to shout at the birds. You must keep the birds on the move up there until the sun goes down. At midday, you can stay in the shade, for the birds too hide in the shade. In the late afternoon, you must go and shout at the birds very loudly, to stop them.' This makes it difficult for the birds. Those of Chali, they eat the grain every year ... it is very bad in Chali because the water is very near.

This alternative, so aggressive by comparison with the peaceful, wary strategy of the Birdmaster, can never be very successful. Compare, however, the rather beautiful story of the man who could calmly attract the birds to his spear-point, which Danga also told me:

Long ago, we planted those fields here. There was a man called Banga. He said to us, 'Where is my food?' He came from a place of beer that day, while we were coming from the water. That man, he was a mother's brother of Martin Lipa. At that time the birds were eating a lot in this place where the grain was sown. They were about to finish the sorghum, and so people went and called that man. They called that man for he had the *koŋgoro/*. He came, came and placed his spear like this. He placed his spear like this, and the birds came down and perched on it. He took the birds in his hands. Yes, with the *arum* of *koŋgoro/* which is very strong. He placed his spear like this, and the birds landed here on the spear; he seized the birds and took them home. He put them inside the gourd. Then, the birds stopped eating for good; not one would be heard calling '*koleg*! No, there was no calling of birds.

The forest and bushland is the depository of the Uduk archive. Not only are many of the demonstrably 'older' or 'authentic' Uduk rites drawn from that rich store, but newer notions and practices too must be sustained from the same source to survive. Healers and prophetic teachers of every age must locate themselves in this ancient landscape of remembered, half-remembered, and even unconscious knowledge.

When Tente was young he was 'seized by the *arum* of wild animals' (*bu'th ma rum tombwasho*). It was thought that this was the hunting *arum* of his father's people, who were masters of the horn. It appeared to have become active because he used to hunt a great deal, and kill many animals. He used to dream of antelopes (*bothoŋ*). One day he dreamt that his leg was injured by them. It swelled up and became painful, on the side of his left shin. He went for treatment to Leina, the already-famous healer who lived in Meban country beyond Boing, and who was to exert a powerful influence upon the Uduk, as I describe in Part II. Tente was led to Leina's home by his father Naka (who became involved in the healing practices of the Meban cult) and Lyife (the name is pronounced as two syllables, *lee-fay*), a key acolyte of Leina's among the Uduk. Lyife, who spoke Meban, interpreted for Tente. Leina told him to kill a chicken and make stew, and to put this on his leg. He did this, his leg got better, and he has not been bothered by the wild animals since. The authority of a really great healer, even from outside Uduk country, will always encompass the realm of the wild.

Persons

The human being, as the locus of knowledge of self and others, is the experiential centre to which we must return again and again in exploring the regions of 'symbolism', 'belief', 'religion', and 'cosmology' among the Uduk: domains which the ethnographic tradition has too often separated from embodied experience. In this chapter an inevitably lengthy account is given of the experiential foundations of personal knowledge among the Uduk, an account which acts as ballast to the discussion of innovative theistic cosmologies in Part II. The Uduk themselves return to the touchstone of personal knowledge in their encounter with religious discourse and in doing so they draw again upon the archival base of their culture.

(i) Human beings: body, experience, and understanding

The representation of the person, as a framework for the interpretation of experience and perhaps for the very shaping of that experience in the first instance, must constitute a part of every 'culture', though it is not always fully described in ethnographies. Questions of translation are here particularly delicate, and bring into fine focus some of the paradoxes of inter-cultural transposition. But if there are no broad lines of agreement possible about terms of reference for the discussion of experience and personality, such as contrasting dimensions of body and spirit, emotion and reason, waking consciousness and dreaming, outer and inner, senses and responses, how can any such translation take place? For the practising ethnographer, translation must be assumed to work, if roughly. The assumption made here is that we are able to use our most general tools of linguistic discrimination to explore the *experience of personhood* in another culture.

(a) Substance, vital circulation, and senses

The body, *buŋgwar* or *is*, the tangible and visible part of the person, is kept healthy and alive through the circulation of the blood, in the Uduk view (which in this respect tallies quite well with modern medical opinion). Blood is the essential carrier of life for the person, as for the matriline or 'birth-group' from which the human body of flesh and bone is derived. Food, exercise, and work keep the blood circulating and the person fit. Old or ill people get up and struggle to the fields to work, because too much resting at home would slow down the blood circulation and weaken them. Loss of blood may be fatal, and this is given as the reason for death following a variety of illnesses or even mishaps. For example, if you are knocked hard on the head, this will 'send the blood down' to the heart, and you will die. If the limbs are wounded, life could be endangered by a heavy loss of blood. If the heart or liver are pierced, even by a small instrument like a safety pin (often used for such small operations as removing splinters), the loss will be fatal as these are vital centres of the blood system. If the throat is cut, the primary vital circulation link between the head and the heart is broken, and so much blood is lost that death results.

The blood is sent round the body by the heart (*kwasinycama/*). It goes up to the brain, and this is why it is said 'the heart holds the brain up there'. Blood is also sent to the various limbs, whence it returns to the heart. The function of the heart is to keep the blood moving. The liver, by contrast, retains the blood, acting as a kind of reservoir. In all these respects, the bodies of animals function just as ours do.

The heart in itself is not the seat of any part of the human 'psyche', and is not associated in Uduk physiology or metaphor with any intellectual or emotional function. Nor is the head (*'kup*) with the physical brain (*tula/*) important as a part of the mental or psychological make-up of the person. 'The head of a man is just like the head of a pig; there's nothing there at all!' Another amused comment on my queries was 'The head is just there to hold up the eyes, ears, and nose.' Uduk informants were astonished at my explanation of European notions of the thinking brain and the feeling heart.

The sense organs, the eyes, nose, and ears, in particular, are regarded (as among ourselves) as externals, or appendages to the person, the functions of which we share in common with the other animals. For the Uduk, these organs register the impact of stimuli, but do not themselves experience or process the information received. From the eyes or nose the information 'goes down' to the experiencing centres of the Liver or the Stomach for processing, and from these founts of the person's being, a response may emerge (as I describe below).

(b) Liver (adu): Being and Feeling

Although Uduk do not distinguish head and heart as we do, they do make an analogous distinction between the controlled, conscious will on the one hand and the spontaneous, passionate inner nature of the personality on the other. The physical placing of this opposition however is between stomach on the one hand and liver on the other, which as aspects of the experiencing person I distinguish as Stomach and Liver. The Liver (*adu*) certainly has a bodily function, not only as the main concentration of blood in the system, but also in relation to digestion—it 'catches the food on its path and sends it down'. But beyond being a key physical organ of the body, it is the vital centre of a person's sensations and felt response. The Liver receives impressions and produces emotional reactions. Moreover, as the primary focus of *arum* or animating power within the body it is an essential life-centre.

There is a proliferation of expressions referring to the Liver. A person of peaceful temperament is said to have a cool Liver, a hot-tempered person a hot one. These expressions are physically 'embodied' in a stronger sense than (for example) the Shakespearean 'lily-livered' or 'hot-livered'. If a person's bad temper leads to evil doings, he or she is said to have a bad Liver or to have 'gone bad in the Liver' (*a'di shi'da du*), a very serious condition. By contrast, to be strong of Liver, *'bi'th ma du*, is to be brave (according to the Uduk Dictionary).

It is the Liver that fears, hates, and loves; it 'beats' with these emotions. Uduk may say simply that 'My liver will beat' (*adum pem midi mii*) meaning that it will beat in fear. The Liver leads us into sleep (*adu sus ana ish e*), and wakes us up in the morning. These functions are beyond our control, we follow the lead of the Liver in many respects and are controlled by it. It registers information at what western psychologists might term a 'subliminal' or 'unconscious' level. For example, when you are asleep, your ears may hear the cock crow, or the cry of the hyena; these sounds 'go down to your Liver', and then you wake up. In general, you see things with your eyes, or hear them with your ears, and they go down to your Liver. If they are bad things, your Liver will respond, and you will involuntarily become angry. This feeling starts from the Liver, comes up to the heart (by implication perhaps, along with the blood circulation), and then to the eyes, mouth, and outwards; you speak angry words and may fight. When I asked what part of a person remembers and forgets, the revealing answer was the Liver; in our everyday psychology too, this capacity is analogously by definition far beyond the conscious will, however much we may try to discipline it.

The Liver also experiences pain, which is a very serious matter. People may say his or her Liver is painful, *adum piti shwa'da nyor*, literally 'burns with anger', or he or she is struck with pain in the Liver, *a'di 'kosh ma du ka nyor*. When a person has become insane, a condition which we associate with loss of rationality in the brain, the Uduk say 'the Liver is running about' (*a'di gusu'd adu*). The sense is that the human being is no longer a 'self'; there is no self-control, no himself or herself, no reasonable interaction with others. Almost always implying an affliction by *arum* from outside, the condition carries one beyond 'self-possession'. A man who was known to have had recent experience of contact with a new manifestation of *arum* once explained to me why he had not spoken to me very much previously. A man speaks from his Liver; if he is discontented (*shina bwa*, literally bad in the stomach) from his Liver, his tongue will be held tight from inside and nothing will come out. If his Liver is beyond his control (in this case because of invasive *arum*), his tongue goes down, and he is held from speaking.

Air, winds, and the scents they carry are a part of the environment to which the Liver can react. Through breath, the essence of a thing can make direct contact with the Liver inside the body. Air, and scents, may be the proper element for the transmission of *arum* itself, channelling this power straight to the Liver. A person with a strong Liver will be able to breathe well. To be out of breath is to be failing in the Liver, *wuwa du*, a phrase which can also indicate possession by an external *arum*. Good scents will calm and cool the Liver, while bad smells will upset it to the point of causing one to vomit spontaneously. There are parallels with our modern notion of 'allergy'. Thus people may find that the taste or smell of a given food upsets them. Goat meat, especially when roasted, and a certain mushroom (*disha wulul*) which smells in the cooking rather like goat meat, are found disagreeable by many individuals, who therefore avoid them (*ga/*, to avoid in a ritual sense). Muinyke, a young mother, explained this:

I don't eat those things [mostly meats]. I just sit there. Even fish, I don't eat it. But I do eat chicken, and also pig. I can eat pig because people give me medicine, and then I can eat it. I used to refuse pig, because when it is roasted, *caah*! Its smell comes rushing into you, to the Liver there, and your Liver goes *guug*! And you vomit, *woog*. So you refuse it there, and you just keep to yourself. And from that time, they will treat you so, and so, that's why it's done. And I don't eat clawed animals, or rats. All those things, I stay without them. It is from the Liver, from the Liver here. It gives me a lot of trouble....

Did you get this from your mother?

No, my mother didn't do this.... [My mother's people] ate everything. But there are many things I do without. Peanuts too, I don't eat them.

So, did this come from your father?

No. Not from my father. It was just brought to me when I was too small to know. ... It just comes from the Liver, I myself in my Liver ... but the actual meat of goats, I can eat the stew of that.... If you are like this, and don't eat everything, then you will stay quietly, your Liver will lie down quietly and not bother you. But if you go and find something at another place, you will vomit from finding the smell of something bad in your nose. From rushing into your nose, it goes to your Liver there, and you vomit. Your body weakens from vomiting like that....

Yes, the medicine of the Ebony Men is very strong. This strong medicine will be given to you, and all those things you avoided can be eaten. You are able to survive. The Liver will be affected by the medicine; your Liver will lie down and be quiet.

Very new, young things, especially anything to do with new-born babies, can also upset some people, and such people 'avoid new-things', *ga/a nyolos*. Thaduse told me how her grown son would even run to vomit at the sound of a new-born baby's cry, and she herself, when she had given birth, couldn't eat anything until the remains of the cord had dried up and fallen off, and even then she might vomit on taking food. Only when her child was taken ceremonially out of the hut, could she keep food down. She also has a reaction to the meat of sick goats. In her case, her sensitivities were taken over from her mother, and she has given them to her sons.

Bad smells as from dead things (*wuruŋgu'b*, the smell of death), very raw things such as fish or eggs (which are *tu/atu*, that is very freshly from a living body), and also body smells can upset people. Meat which is 'cold', that is found dead rather than being killed, can upset a weak Liver. *Arum* encountered in human form can be recognized by a bad smell, or a bad breath, and 'witchcraft' is often carried through bad smells. These smells go straight to the Liver, and when serious, have to be dealt with by specialists in matters of *arum*. In healing treatments, substances are often 'breathed in', including the fumes of medicine, while the emblematic medicines of the Ebony Men and the *arum* practitioners are scented—Spice and Wild Mint respectively. When these specialists are restoring a person's lost Genius (*kashira/*: see below), an element of the individual psyche for which the visible shadow is an analogue, they touch it to the nostrils first, so that the patient can breathe it in.

Scents, sounds, sights, all channel received experience directly to the Liver, and scents especially convey the impact of psychical and spiritual encounter to this centre of the person's being. Spontaneous response comes from here too, response which may overrule the prudence of conscious control. For the person is also able to reflect, to consider, to exercise control and judgement: but these functions do not stem from the Liver. Nor are they initially present in the baby or child, as yet without experience and knowledge. The Uduk Dictionary gives an interesting sentence under the entry for *uci*, children: *uci 'kon ma du ki 'kos*. This could be translated 'children have Livers which are still free', meaning 'children are still ruled by spontaneous feeling'. As context, the Dictionary gives 'eyeing cloth and wanting it. "Covet." ' In later life, the adult in wisdom comes to exercise restraint over such feelings. In the case of the animal world, my evidence suggests that the liver of a creature, at least of the larger creatures, responds impulsively in the same way as it does in human beings, but like young children, the animals lack judgement and self-restraint.

(c) *Stomach* (bwa): *Reflecting and Willing*

Contrasted with the Liver is the Stomach, *bwa*. The term can also be used of the abdomen in general, sometimes specifically in the context of pregnancy and giving birth. A first-born child is *bwan-yara*, from a girl's belly, with the sense almost of 'first fruits'. As a verb stem, *bwa* can be translated 'to conceive' or 'to swell with pregnancy'. In its most general sense, the word suggests the inside of something, its capacity, as in *bwaŋ gu'b*, 'inside the hut'.

The notion of *inside* is however intimately connected with the idea of the stomach, as the capacity which must needs be filled regularly through eating. Images of the good life and happiness are those of plentiful food and a contented stomach ('*KP*: 98–9; 119–21). Several common expressions refer metaphorically to the stomach, such as *bwaŋ'kush*, a 'white stomach', meaning generous, and '*kunya bwa*, 'sweet in the stomach', meaning glad or pleased. But there are stronger senses in which the stomach is indicated quite literally and directly as an organ of the experiencing self, and not simply as a metaphor for an inner nature other than itself. When the term *bwa* is used in this strong sense, I write Stomach. In the Uduk idiom, one cannot get closer to specifying the essence of a person's own, individual, and self-conscious being. By comparison, the English 'I could not stomach (or digest) the news' is relatively weak metaphor. The Stomach is in an important way the organ of a person's autonomous thought, and will. What has been learned from experience is stored in the Stomach, and the sense of 'I' as an inner consciousness which can act upon the world is asserted from it.

There are common expressions such as *aha/ ona bwa*, 'my Stomach tells me' or I want; *aha/ 'tena bwa*, I don't want; *aha/ 'bora bwa*, 'I am good in the Stomach' or I am content, happy; *aha/ shina bwa*, 'I am bad in the Stomach', I am sad, sorry, disappointed, resentful. There is another very common idiom *mmokulum i bwa*, 'to turn things over in the Stomach' or to think, to consider, and reflect; and more specifically, *kulum gwo bwa*, 'turn words over in the Stomach', to consider what has been said. To 'keep in mind' something (or as the Uduk Dictionary puts it, to 'memorize'—which has rarely happened outside mission school) is *kar i bwa* or *dhu em bwa*, keep or put in the Stomach. I have also heard *a'di 'tu'd ma nyor i bwa*, 'his Stomach is filled with anger', or *anyor caaca i bwa piti*, 'there is a lot of anger in his Stomach'. This is a distinct notion of 'righteous' or reasonable indignation, not the spontaneous fury of the Liver. Here too in the Stomach is the seat of considered covetousness and envy, *'thoth bwa*, according to the Dictionary, which also includes an interesting term new to me, *apulp̱ucu/*, glossed 'rumor, stomach'. A common idiom is *ki bwam̱ piti, ki bwam pem*, 'as he wishes', 'as I please'. The Dictionary also has *miiyi ki bwa*, to do something continually, 'with a will', and also a phrase *bwa ma Arumgimis* for 'the Will of God' (literally the stomach of *arum* in the sky). Problems of this kind in the translation of religious language are discussed in detail in Part II.

It may be thought that linguistic expressions of the kind Uduk use in connection with the Stomach are no more than metaphors or analogues for the way personality really works. But the Uduk 'theory of the person' is not merely an intellectual 'representation', detachable from the embodied way they register their most intimate and self-validating personal experience. The physical cycle of hunger and satisfaction, experienced by all communities living at subsistence level, is perhaps particularly pervasive in the accumulated cultural idiom of those with a hunting and gathering past. In the Uduk case the presence of that past is almost palpable in their 'psychological' language of the Stomach. The workings of the Stomach are moreover uniquely human, and opposed in their capacity of conscious direction to the spontaneities of the biological liver. When I asked Nyethko which part of you is being used when you read or write, he replied firmly that it was the eyes *and the Stomach*. Nyethko, whose knowledge of the uses of script in school, church, or courtroom did not extend to the thrills of fiction, nor to the possibility of revelation through scriptural text, saw no question of the Liver being touched by the written word.

The pervasive and elaborate reference to the Stomach made by Uduk-speakers contrasts with their almost complete neglect of the head which, as I remarked earlier, is not the seat of any psychic or moral function; nor does it, in itself, experience anything. Through eyes and ears and nose the head does receive signals from the world, but this information does not register any impression there. It 'goes down', either to the Stomach (as with reading) or to the Liver (as with the cock-crow at night, or in encounters with dangerous animals and so forth). Tente told me that in this sense the head and the Liver work together: 'You see things with your head, and they go to the Liver; if they are bad things, your Liver gets angry and the anger shows in your face.' I have heard expressions which might belie this view of the head as not in itself important—for example of people who do not know how to make angarebs (the Sudanese wooden bed)—they *dar gi bwam 'kup*, they 'have nothing in their heads'; and *aha/ thisa 'kup e*, 'I have lost my head', I have forgotten something. But these expressions (as Jon Arensen has pointed out to me from his knowledge of the Murle) refer to practical skills, the sort of thing you can acquire by watching and listening and copying rather than by employing reflective wisdom. When asked whether, after all, there is something in the head, Nyethko replied 'If you are blind, can you know anything in your head?—or in your Stomach?' The implication was that the head *sees*, because the eyes are there, and shares what it sees with the Stomach; but what does not go down to the Stomach cannot be registered as experience.

In dreams, in addition to the wakefulness of the personal Genius, it is only the eyes, and perhaps ears (there was room for argument on this between informants) that are being used—they see and hear things, but these things do not always make sense when (later, on waking) they are thought about. Not only must you be able to see and hear things, but also to reflect on what they mean, and it is here that the Stomach is involved. The physical brain, *tula/*, plays a part in stimulating the exchange of blood between the head and the heart. Tente told me *tula/ kar ana ki e*, 'the brain keeps us alive', and that if the *tula/* is removed, a creature dies. But the *tula/* has no particular work. Tente like others was amazed that I should consider that thinking ('turning things over in the Stomach') should go on in the head. He made it as clear as an informant could that thought came from the Stomach in a substantive sense. The idiom was not merely 'a manner of speaking'.

It would be inappropriate to treat as quite separate the way in which Uduk understand the functioning of the senses, like 'seeing' with the eyes, and the processes of registering impressions through reflection, understanding, and emotional response. The receiving of signals, and the moral registering of experience, are linked in the way the Uduk represent the working *together* of the eyes-and-Stomach, or eyes-and-Liver. In the first case, the integrated function

of recording-and-processing information is expressed in the Uduk
language by the verb *mish*. This can be translated 'see' and also
'know' or 'understand'. It can be used in a fairly casual way;
'There's beer today, you know'; or it can be used in a much more
substantial sense, such as 'We do not understand the world very
well.' It is used also of 'knowing' a person, both in an easy colloquial
sense and in a serious sense, and it can be used of understanding
specific things which have been learnt. The Uduk Dictionary gives
the further range of 'to be able' and 'to love', though I have not
heard the latter usage. *Mish* is the word used also of seeing and
knowing things from dreams. A common phrase, *mala e*, includes
direct reference to the eye, *e*. It means to be absorbed in something
you are doing so that you don't know what is happening around
you; you don't see or notice it. The phrase can mean 'asleep', but
the usual indication is of wandering attention, of failing to keep
fully alert. It is tempting to regard the way in which Uduk associate
intelligence and understanding with the capacity of eyesight, not
only in their lexicon but in their view of the inner functioning of
the human system, as a cultural inheritance from their hunting
past.

(d) *Genius* (kashira/): *Dreaming and Knowing*

There are further aspects of knowing and experiencing, which,
while stemming from organic human existence, do not involve
particular bodily parts, but rather, special operations of the alert
human intelligence. The outstanding case is that of the attribute
commonly spoken of as *kashira/*. This term refers in a *mundane*
sense to a shadow, the shadow of anything. By day, this shadow
is the visible analogue of a principle active by night. It grows and
matures with age and general experience. A small boy skipped by
in the late sun, and a woman exclaimed with satisfaction, 'Just
look at his *kashira/*!' There on the ground was his dark, dancing
shadow, pretty, we might say, in a Puck-like way, and I think
captivating, almost entrancing to my companion.

In the context of the personality *kashira/* connotes a special
capacity of psychic intelligence. Before this is understood, it might
invite the translation 'soul', or even 'mind' or 'consciousness', that
is, in some way the spiritual or intellectual counterpart of the body.
Although the missionary translators at Chali have used *kashira/*

for the 'soul' of Judaeo-Christian discourse, one problem I discuss further in Chapter 4, I believe we should be very careful here. The *kashira/* is not an entity in itself, nor a counterpart of the whole person, as the Biblical soul is often envisaged. Nor is it an 'intellectual' function needed for managing everyday life, like seeing-and-understanding. It is rather an extra-ordinary aid to knowledge in the Uduk view, a sensitive capacity, a gift for registering out-of-the-ordinary experience. It is close to what in ordinary English we mean by a 'sixth sense' or 'psychic powers', with the specific function for the Uduk of having, or rather 'doing', dreams. A dream is *jaan*, to experience a dream is *shu'b jaan*, and to be affected by what happened in a dream is *miin ma jaan*. Some suggest that a person sleeping, maybe dreaming, should not be wakened suddenly, for their *kashira/* may be far away (compare our English idiom, 'He was miles away').

A literal translation of *kashira/* is not possible. However there is a word of Latin origin with a complex and evocative history, conjuring the double sense of an ethereal guiding spirit, and also of an innate disposition, a human and subjective capacity for apperceptive insight. My use of *Genius* as a gloss for the Uduk *kashira/* deliberately draws on both classical and modern nuances of the word. The *kashira/* does at times appear to behave autonomously as a 'spirit' or tutelary image of a person (and is undoubtedly vulnerable to invasive spirit powers); but it remains essentially, in my view, a human faculty serving the knowledge of one's own identity and that of others. More than a higher consciousness 'belonging' to a person, the *kashira/* in some ways *is* that person, in his or her singularity as it is perceivable by others. It is not that individuality of the inner will or of self-control which is the Stomach; rather, the personal Genius is the marker of a general category of psychic individuality.

Kashira/ is something possessed only by human beings. Everyone in discussion of this topic was agreed that cows, goats, or wild animals did not possess it. There was, however, argument over dogs. Those who thought that perhaps dogs did have this capacity pointed out that they do *dream*, as anybody can see from their grunting and twitching during sleep. This was diagnostic because the crucial role of the *kashira/* is to be alert and receptive even when the person is asleep and the everyday senses are inert. It has been suggested to me that the Genius can leave the body lying there on the bed, and wander round the village. Dreams, remembered in the morning, are evidence of this activity, a special witness to events. The Genius cannot be perceived by others, even in their dreams; it is not in essence a *manifestation*, or a *representation*, but part of the integral person, operating more as we might imagine a psychic searchlight or radar monitor. It registers evidence mainly about the activity of *arum* and persons of spiritual power, especially of harmful intent. In particular, dreams can indicate the hostile dispositions and acts of *dhathu/*, those supposed to have powers we may gloss as 'witchcraft'. To be aware of such actual or potential danger is obviously a defence in itself, and this is what the Genius can provide.

The information revealed in dreams is useful primarily as a forewarning of evil presences. There are many graphic descriptions of such dangers. This is a typical dream-story about *dhathu/* ('witches') stealing grain, given me by William Danga:

People who are *dhathu/* come for the grain, they lead people with baskets on their heads. They wrap up little bundles [of grain]. The grain is not carried by itself. . . .

And you will know this in a dream at night; you will follow them and chase them on foot . . . run, run—you strike them, strike them, strike them. They run—some of them are very agile and they will throw everything down on the ground, and run, to escape. Then these *dhathu/* people will fly away, like bats. Leaving you on the ground there, they fly up like bats, fly up and escape. And they . . . give you death while they have flown away, and people can't kill them.

They flee away and the grain yields very heavily at their place. It all bears very heavily and there will be nowhere left to store everything. There is a heavy crop. And then [your people] will start to die . . . and people come to understand . . . saying, 'People took things; all these things which yielded so well. That is why those people died.' For some people have seen this in dreams. Some people know through dreams.

In this passage, the Uduk word *mish* has been translated both as to see and as to know or understand, according to context; it is used as though to see, especially in a dream, is in itself to understand or know.

But there are many other dreams which can reveal general facts about the world of *arum*, and bring wider horizons of knowledge of all kinds. When the old lady Emed asked me why I spent so much time reading and writing, I explained that in a book you could see words that other people had once spoken. These people might have lived long ago and were now dead, or they might live far away and you would never see them. But by looking at the marks in the book, you could find out what they knew, and what they wanted to tell you. 'Yes,' she said, carefully; 'I suppose it's like dreaming.'

I should elaborate briefly on dreaming. To dream of something is to have direct knowledge of that matter; and it is the Genius which goes out in a dream and acquires the knowledge. What you see in dreams are actions of beings you do not see by day, and although these may be harmful to you or ones near to you, they may also be good. Through dreams ordinary people without ritual powers have access to a hidden world, although the Ebony Men and *arum* practitioners can see even more clearly into this hidden world, with and without the help of dreams.

Dreaming can moreover be a source of creative and joyful discovery. William Danga described how dreams are the source of new songs. They are not 'composed' by the conscious effort of the singer; they are a spontaneous revelation, or discovery, made by the nocturnally active Genius. Without expecting this answer, I had asked where songs came from:

It is from sleeping. You will go to sleep, as I slept, I slept, and then: a man, a man will come up to you. He comes and he has a lyre with him. And while you are asleep, he will play his lyre for you, to teach you a song, for you to play. You take the lyre; he puts the lyre into your hands. The song which he has taught you, you take it from him and play it. You practise, practise, practise it, until you get hold of it and know it.

You keep it, and if you want to get up soon after you have learned the song, you practise on your lyre in the night. Then you try again in the morning, and by then you will know the melody from the man who came to you in the night while you were asleep.

The occurrence of dreams, if not always their content, is very conspicuous among the Uduk. When they have had a dream, they often smear a little ash on the temples or forehead before coming out in the morning. For some time, I assumed this was only for bad dreams, as a kind of protection. One morning I asked discreetly about Saba, who had emerged with a heavily powdered forehead, singing loudly; I discovered there had been no ominous sign, but that she had dreamt a catchy new song for the *athele/* dance flutes.

Joshua Kheiralla, with a good deal of travel experience and

education, used to sing for the lyre in a style which blended something of the old with a 'modern' Sudanese romantic idiom. Here, slightly condensed, is an interesting song of his which again intertwines the notions we distinguish as knowing, dreaming, reading and writing, a blend which I have tried to capture in translation:

Aa 'kon ma cim daka	A few days later,
Aa 'kon ma cim daka	A few days later,
Aa mina jaan 'te	I had a dream
Ak ka yim kayaa e	Saying that she remembers me.
Ka warka/ yan kali gwony jaan 'te	This letter brought me just dream words,
Ak ka yim kayaa e	Saying that she remembers me;
Ka mina jaan 'te	For it was just a dream,
Ak ka yim kayaa e	Saying that she remembers me.
Ka warka/ yan kali gwony jaan 'te	For the letter brought just dream words,
Ak ka yim kayaa e	Saying she remembers me.
'Bira 'kup ki cwa mo 'taa	Did I stumble against some tree?
'Bira 'kup ki cwa mo	I stumbled against a tree,
Ka mina jaan	For I dreamed
Ka yim kayaa e	That she remembers me.
Ka warka/ yan toraa gwony jaan 'te	But the letter brought just dream words,
Ak ka yim kayaa e	Saying that she remembers me;
Ka mina jaan 'te	For I was dreaming
Ak ka yim toraa gwon gana/	That she was telling me the truth.

The normal functioning of the Genius is essential to human well-being, over a period of time. The most common preliminary diagnosis by the Ebony diviners in a situation of everyday illness is 'loss of Genius', and people who are not feeling too well may frequently call in the Ebony Men to check what has happened to their Genius. It can be separated from the person, particularly if entrapped by 'witchcraft', and get literally stuck in the mud, at a graveside, or in the river, or an old village site. Treatment must include the physical recovery of the mud in which the Genius has become stuck; sometimes the Ebony Men do this by rooting around in river banks, dead trees, and so on, and sometimes they make as if to catch it on the wing. Suddenly, one may lunge forward, grasp at the air, glance this way and that as if following an insect, grab again and sigh with relief, wiping his fingers with a leaf on the end of his spear. The Genius has been caught. It will later be 'breathed in' by the patient, as the diviner holds the mud or leafy bundle to his or her nostrils. If you are without your Genius, you may miss, in your dreams and perhaps directly, vital information about who or what may be harming you, and in addition you may slowly deteriorate from the very absence of the Genius itself.

I have heard several times, though in passing, of the foolishness of sleeping during the day, or allowing one's attention to wander—we would call it 'day-dreaming', but for the Uduk, dreaming belongs to night-time sleep when the Genius is normally alert. Dozing off in the daytime is quite dangerous, because the Genius is not usually alert, and you are therefore vulnerable. In a text quoted below, a young woman imagines herself pregnant and sleeping at midday, and the other women warn her against this: 'Don't sleep at midday, you will not see in a dream what is being done to you, for the thing which is brought to you from far away;' that is, in this case, she may find herself bearing twins (see (iii) (c) below). It is the function of the normal senses to inform you by day, if you stay alert. The Genius is your watchful guard by night.

When I asked where the Genius of a new-born baby comes from, Nyethko, who was a senior Ebony diviner, said that *arum* puts it there when it creates people. I then asked whether it came from the father's or the mother's side, and he replied quite firmly that it came from the mother's side. 'You mean it comes with the blood?' 'Yes.' He added that the Genius was finished when a person dies (which is not surprising if we accept that it is an integral capacity, like the senses, and not a 'soul' counterpart).

In certain contexts, the Genius is spoken of in the idiom of its physical image, the shadow. When an Ebony Man sponsors a boy apprentice, it is sometimes said that the Ebony Man's Genius, shadow-like perhaps, is 'on top of him'. The effects of one or another power of *arum* may be spoken of in this way too. For example a certain *arum* may be said to have 'covered up' a person's Genius, as though it were obscuring a perceptive sense like sight, hearing, or smell.

My understanding of the *kashira/*, to summarize, is that it is an aspect of individual psychic being and consciousness that provides access to the world beyond the capacity of the waking senses, and informs the person's intelligent and creative activity. Like our notions of intuition, giftedness, or 'sixth sense', the *kashira/* does not exist autonomously as a thing in itself, it does not stand as a counterpart of the whole person, and, except for appropriating information in dreams, it does not do things of its own accord. Moreover, it does not survive death, any more than a hypothesized 'sixth sense' would. With death, the individual Genius has gone, for it belongs to this world that we know, and not the 'other world' of *arum*.

Shortly after the old lady Umpa had died, she appeared to a daughter in a dream. As yet not understanding the word, I asked if this appearance was her Genius. 'No, of course not,' came the impatient answer. 'It was her *arum*.' The next evening people played the dance flutes near her old hut, to please her.

(e) *The animating spirit:* arum

The Genius is encompassed by the mortal person. But behind the whole person, and sometimes standing for that whole person, is the *arum*. *Arum* is present in every human being but is not located in any particular organ, except for being primarily associated with the Liver as the centre of vitality, and blood as the sustainer of life. Moreover, blood and breath are vehicles for the transmission of *arum*. *Arum* however does not 'function' in any particular way within the system. It is simply there, and is the grounds for life itself. *Arum* is not exclusive to persons. All animals, including wild animals, have *arum*; the living body with breath, blood, and movement entails the presence of *arum*, as a condition of that very existence. *Arum* is neither good nor bad in essence. There are no particular signs of its normal presence within a living person, and in many ways it is just taken for granted. But it is that part of a person which survives death.

It is helpful to consider the body and consciousness of a person, with its various attributes already discussed, as the outside form; and its *arum* as the inner driving force. Contact with this inner nature is possible through the breath, as air and smells are inhaled; through food, which is absorbed into the body and can disagree with it; through sexual relations; and through the blood. Chickens are treated as though they were particularly vulnerable to *arum*, and when they are cut (that is, have their throats cut) at the start of a rite, they will show by the way they react, and especially by the way they die, whether the rite is to be successful. If *arum* is not content, the fowl will die quickly on its front; if content, the fowl may flap around a good deal and die on its back. The life and movement so evident in a chicken, even in its death throes, is a vigorous sign of the presence of *arum*.

Thus for example, the very simple rite of Brushing a chicken against a person should establish contact with the *arum* in that person. In this action, the healer of a patient or the host to a guest from afar holds the bird's legs and moves the creature steadily up and down against the body, as it flaps its wings. The *arum* within the patient or guest will be calmed and settled down. If you were a guest, for example, your *arum* would then know the village, and you would sleep well. And then if blood, even from a tiny cut on the toe of a chicken, is touched to your nostril, for you to Breathe in (*pi shush*), that will please and comfort the *arum* in your body. Tente explained these things clearly, leading on to a (slightly leg-pulling) account of how there is *arum* in every part of one, and how even my *arum* was strong and content, since it led me about so much; but that I (through not knowing about Brushing) didn't know how to look after it properly. The Uduk custom of Brushing, Tente said, was there from very long ago. As the beating chicken is passed across the body, it is pressed to each shoulder, to the sides, and to the Liver. I quote from Tente's account:

A person who comes as a guest, as you came before—a chicken should have been taken for you, to Brush your body. That makes you a guest. And we would Brush you, and then cut the chicken. And to welcome you, people gather together here, to pay their respects to you. To sit and chat; we sit and chat happily, enjoying conversation around you. And then to greet you, lots of people hear the news, our friend has arrived. Our friend has arrived. Where is she?

There she is, they Brushed her with a chicken in the afternoon there. In the afternoon, people will Brush you with a chicken, as a guest. You will be able to sit well and then sleep.

Lay people may thus Brush a guest. When I asked why the Ebony Men use the same action, for a patient, Tente gave a fuller explanation which made quite explicit the presence of *arum* within the body, both of the Ebony Man and the patient:

It is *arum*. The *arum* of the Ebony Man. The *arum* of the Ebony Man is here in the shoulders too; it is Brushed and treated too in the shoulders here. His *arum* is in the shoulders here, he will take that chicken, to treat your body. To treat that man, his body too. And cut the chicken, to put a little blood on his forehead. *Arum* will then be content with him. It will say, that is my man.

I asked him to elaborate on *arum* being in the shoulders, and he replied:

Arum lives in the shoulders. Yours is there too now, that's why you go about like this. Yes, you know this. Your *arum* is there now. Yes! Very content. That is why it is leading you about so much!

His is there too [indicating a companion]. Yes, that man has *arum* in his shoulders. When sleeping at night, doesn't he go *ook, ook*, doesn't he cry out at dreams in the night? He cries out at dreams in the night. Heh! What is it but the *arum* in his shoulders—that's why he cries like that.

Don't you know how Ngau always shouts out *wooh, wooh, wooh*? The *arum* is there in Ngau's shoulders. Yes. And yours is certainly there, you sleep and dream at the same time too. You are not without *arum* in your body. Your *arum* is there, very strong too. And you—you don't know what to do about it, saying, 'Oh! What am I going to do, my *arum* is behaving like this, where am I going to get a chicken from to Brush my body in order to sleep well?' For you have never had this thing in your country. Our custom has always been like this, from long ago.

Tente then mentioned how the Ebony Man touches blood to the body, to the nose, the forehead, the sides, the shoulders, and finally the region of the Liver. I asked naïvely whether *arum* was in the Liver. This was such a silly question he began to make fun of it:

In the liver, *arum* is there; in all of this body that we have there is just *arum*, all of it. Our bodies are full of it. All of the body! The eyes too! Your eyes have *arum*, your nose has *arum*, your mouth has *arum*. Your ears have *arum*, your hair has *arum*! Your fingernails have *arum*, your teeth have *arum*. If the teeth of your *arum* go bad, all your teeth will decay, all of them. If the teeth of your *arum* decay and drop out, you will be toothless!

Of course there is *arum* in people, the textbook answer might go. It is there in the blood, and therefore concentrated particularly in the Liver. It keeps us alive, but rather than being a particular part of the workings of the whole person, it is the pulse of life itself, even outliving the mortal flesh and its psychic intelligence. The *arum* within us is a guarantee of our organic and individual vitality. This is at all times under threat from various external powers, which may invade and take us over.

(f) Special powers

Right at the core of the human community today there is present a special power which is inborn, which has come down through matrilineal continuity from the early mythical days to the present and which is found in some birth-groups of the numerically preponderant Lake. This innate and special power was described for me and some companions from Waka'cesh mainly by Puna Marinyje of the southern Yabus valley, whose father, a Lake, had embodied it. In the northern villages some ambivalence was expressed about such people. There were dark hints of a special and dangerous quality to the Lakeŋ Golga (Tiang Lake). Puna however spoke proudly of an inborn power which might lie dormant, but to certain persons who were true Lake might reveal all the secrets of healing. These people would become 'diviners' (ŋari/ in a generic sense) in and of themselves, without having to be taught, or sponsored. They simply 'had *arum*'. I have included some of Puna's account in my earlier book ('*KP*: 114) but it is worth returning to here. He was telling us of the children of the first female person, conceived from her *arum* alone, who were followed by the birth of a tiang cob. 'A real hoofed creature was born from that same woman. They were called Lake, Lake, because they were wild people, together with the hoofed creatures. *Arum* from the bush.' This *arum*, in antelope form, apparently strikes people in the eyes with its tail (or their tails) and then the Lake (Puna's father's people) are able to treat the person. Here is Puna's description:

Arum ma golga/. The one of the *golga/* from Marinyje is very old.... Look: it acts like this, as we are sitting here, it will come for no reason, come and beat us in our eyes with its tail, *dhu'th*! *dhu'th*! and our eyes will water, and we will sit, waiting, and then heh! [the skin of a tiang will be found] and we look at its hide, people will cut it, *'the'b*, and put it on the fire for you here and surround you with the smoke, in your eyes here.... Then he will take his horn [the man treating you] like this to Touch (*wuḳ*) you like this, like this, like this, and you will bend sideways, sideways ... then it is rubbed on you, all over here; and you will recover.

Algo gave an account also, on another occasion:

Marinyje practised the *arum* of Leina [a Meban-derived cult], very powerfully. And there is also their own real thing, something which they did not get from anywhere else, this thing was different ...

In what way?

Look: his own thing which he practised here, see how it strikes us like this, without us knowing how it strikes us at all. It comes to strike us here, *arum ma golga/*. It strikes people, from his *arum*, their *arum* which is held by them alone; they are *ŋari/* [diviners], just in themselves. They have the *arum* of the diviners just like that [without being instructed]. It is their *arum* just automatically.

There is an ambivalence about the *arum* of the tiang, which is spoken of with quiet pride by some, who are perhaps connected with it, and awe or even fear by those who are not. It is possible to ask, though not at present to answer, the question as to whether the special character of the *arum* of the tiang might stem from an earlier encounter with the expanding power of the Nuer people. In the first half of the last century, the Gaajak Nuer were moving north-eastwards in the regions north of the Sobat. Their north-ernmost section is named Thiang; this section has both attacked and offered protection to the Meban in the early decades of the present century, and might well have had a similarly ambivalent relationship to other groups of what they call Cai at an earlier period. *Thiang* is a word common to Nuer and Dinka for a particular antelope species, *damaliscus lunatus,* and the Nilotic term has entered English (the species is also known, in East Africa, as topi or 'bastard hartebeest'). The acquisition of *arum* through the appropriation of an external representation of power is a common motif in Uduk history, as the second Part of this book shows, and it is at least possible to suggest that such an appro-priation might lie, though forgotten, behind the now mythical origin of the Lakeŋ Golga.

The special status of the Lake birth-groups associated with the tiang is taken much more seriously than the theories of Bukko, quoted in the previous chapter, about certain categories of people being waterbuck, hartebeest, and so forth. The diffuse image of the *'kwanim pa* in general as antelopes, and sometimes specifically as hartebeest, is very commonly encountered; but it is usually intended as *metaphor* (though of a strong kind). The difference with the Lakeŋ Golga is that they are thought to stem organically from a line that has a direct connection with the ancient animal world. The former and still potential 'priestly' role which some attribute to them contrasts with the dread which lies just below the surface among other sections of the population, who may fear that the negative side of this power can seize them, and transfer itself to them. I have heard, though in indirect and guarded terms, of at least one homicide against a member of this group for supposedly evil influence; and I have heard it suggested that all members of the *golga/* groups are *dhathu/*—a word only whispered—or 'witches' because of their birth to this line.

Serious suspicion, however, and action based upon it, has led to quite a number of homicides throughout Uduk society in recent generations. Before giving some account of the way Uduk represent such evil, as requiring such action, it is helpful to consider the pattern of the good, straight, and true life: which springs, essentially, from a good birth, and a good birth-line.

(ii) Individuals and selves

Uduk frequently evoke in their everyday language the special quality of the *singular*. They are noticeably concerned with the singularity of times, places, events, and beings. Persons especially embody the notion of the singular, each a uniquely interactive combination of elements and circumstances. The attention paid in healing rituals to the proper functioning of the *kashira/*, which I gloss as the personal Genius, marks dramatically the moral singularity of the person. It is not, however, an isolated or isolable aspect of personhood, but rests upon other, complex layers in the linguistic and cultural representation of individuality, and in particular of human individuality.

Terms and expressions referring to human beings in the Uduk language are exceptional in that they normally take both a plural and a singular grammatical form. For example, words such as those for 'child' or 'woman' take either the singular or the plural form (*a'ci, uci* and *a'bom, up* respectively). This sets them apart from most nouns in the language, which like the English word 'sheep' do not admit distinction of number. We take for granted with most words in English that the 'ordinary' form of a word is its singular, and the plural is the specially modified form. But do we not think of 'sheep' initially in the collective rather than the singular? I believe that in the Uduk tongue, the vast majority of nouns for which number is not marked can be as well understood in their 'ordinary' form as collective, rather than singular referents. They do not call to mind the singularity of a thing, without further indication, any more than the English word 'sheep' does.

In this context, the distinction of number made in those terms which refer to *people* appears to mark a special case of individuality, acknowledging the particularity of persons thought of in the singular. Indeed even groups of people are often spoken of by modifying a single person's name; to refer to Tente and those with him, for example, one would use the pluralizing prefix I-, to form I-Tente. Personal names themselves are in principle uniquely coined, fashioned from seemingly arbitrary elements of spoken language echoing passing events; they are not consciously repeated, and not inherited or otherwise transmitted. The name disappears with the death of each person.[1] The one exception to this pattern, which in itself confirms the general principle of individuality in personal names, is the name given in the first instance to certain infants born to mothers who have already lost children: the name 'Gurunya' and the special rites through which the child passes, mark its prolonged and safeguarded journey towards personhood. As a 'Gurunya', it is not yet an acknowledged person (*'KP*: Chapter 7).

Discussions of 'ethnicity' and 'identity' often take for granted a person's belonging to a collectivity, whether explicitly through the use of a collective ethnic term, or implicitly, in the way the problem is posed. A stereotype of externally defined 'personal' identity and selfhood has perhaps been too easily accepted in the comparative ethnographic debate, and contrasted too glibly with 'Western' religious and moral notions of autonomous, and interior, selfhood. Mauss's classic essay on this topic pays scant attention to ethnographic representations of the inner person or the voice of individual experience in non-Western cultures, but with better ethnographic evidence we are now in a position to take the discussion much further.[2]

In the Uduk case, it is fruitful to consider how far the expression *wathim pa* is more than merely a technical singular of *'kwanim pa*,

---

[1] I have described the personal naming system in 'Ephemeral names: the Uduk case', in Thelwall, *Aspects of Language in the Sudan*.

[2] Marcel Mauss, 'A category of the human mind: the notion of person, the notion of self' [1938], in *The Category of the Person: Anthropology, Philosophy, History*, ed. M. Carrithers, S. Collins, and S. Lukes (Cambridge: Cambridge University Press), 1985. This new translation by W. D. Halls is accompanied by a set of essays on the topic. See my review article 'Mauss and the Tortoise's Predicament', in *Journal of the Anthropological Society of Oxford*, 18 (2), 1987.

the collective self-name of the Uduk. The term *wathi/* alone can refer casually to 'him', 'her', 'it', 'the fellow', 'this one', 'someone', and so forth, in referring to any person or, in a narrative context, an animal or deceased person's *arum*. Qualified as *wathiŋ gwath* or *wathim 'bomi* it means man and woman, or even male and female creatures, in a story. But *wathim pa*, the 'one of the home' (*pa*), distils a special sense of moral personhood beyond that of the mere individual referent. As with its plural, *'kwanim pa*, it may be used to discriminate between human beings and animals, and between human beings and spirits from the land of the dead. Even though such an animal or spirit might appear and even speak in an adventure story or a legend or myth, it would never be termed *wathim pa*, person. In the ethno-historical sense, the *'kwanim pa* are those who have become over time a civilized human community, carving out and maintaining in the face of environmental danger and death a home (*pa*) for themselves in the midst of the forest. The individual *wathim pa* has been moulded by participation in the struggle, and continues to participate. It is true that at the level of collective ethnic terms, *wathim pa* means 'an Uduk' as against a Nuer, or an Arab, or one of the English. But through close social association with an Uduk community, such an outsider can be (at least rhetorically) claimed as a *wathim pa*, even a 'real' one, *wathim paŋ gana/*.

To qualify an object, such as a stream or a plant as *gana/*, is to underscore its identity and validity; it really is such-and-such a stream, or plant. To add *gana/* to a claim that a throwing-stick is yours or mine, is to insist on its true ownership. To qualify the spoken word thus, as *gwoŋ gana/*, is to assert its truth, and to speak thus of a 'true story', *gwololop gana/*, gives it a seriousness beyond that of ordinary tales. If one wishes to speak of a given person as a true friend, a 'genuine' person of good character, an admirable and upright example, one might well use the expression *wathim paŋ gana/*. The Uduk Dictionary gives 'faithful, trust worthy' for *wathiŋ gana/*. Such a person is a good neighbour, relative, or friend to claim as 'ours', or 'of our home'.

These expressions are concerned with the whole person; and wholeness, or completeness, is crucial in the representation of personhood. At a pragmatic level, we might note that the Uduk number system is based upon the body. They use a counting system of sets of five, often pointing to fingers and toes as they do so, and four such sets complete the largest unit of the system, that is twenty or is *'de/*, literally 'one body'. A hundred would be 'five bodies'. At a more abstract level, the theme of the proper completeness of the body-and-person runs through rite and symbolic action; to anticipate accounts below, I will just mention here again that one of the commonest corrective treatments is the Restoral of the lost Genius (*kashira/*) to the person. Again to anticipate a little, the whole person is composed of many elements; and the notion of the *wathim pa* encompasses these, in their proper working inter-relation. Beyond indicating an individual member of the *'kwanim pa*, it entails an elaborate image of the internal man, woman, or child, built upon that physical framework of the structure and capacities of personhood which gives form and substance to moral and psychic potential. These representations of the inner per-son are not only a point of reference for the Uduk themselves in talking about their experiences of life, learning, death, and revela-tion; but they are at least sometimes also the very bodily grounds of those experiences. An account of them must precede any in-terpretation of the way Uduk have responded to religious, theocen-tric discourse. But first, a few notes on the pragmatic setting of 'selfhood'.

Among the Uduk I have had no doubt of their strong sense of the moral autonomy of the individual person, a sense of 'I' and 'thou' as self-directed and responsive beings. The human being is the creature of no ruling god, no inner passion, nor are persons mere puppets of an external social order. Uduk view the arrival of a new-born baby as a unique event with unknowable potential. When a young woman has her first child, she and her husband as well as the child are firmly described as 'new people'. There is a clear notion of bodily continuity through the matriline, but upon that foundation, social relations are fresh-made by individual persons as they establish their lives with others. I have described the way in which affinity, metaphorical kinship, friendship, alliances, and other historical connections are thus 'man-made' in my earlier book. Here I want to suggest that in important ways, for an outsider observing the Uduk, their view of the integrity of the individual is associated with a sense of responsibility and freedom more 'modern' than is often attributed to non-literate cultures.

A man has a wide degree of choice in practice as to where to live, with which group of his relatives to settle and work, and whom to marry; and in all these respects, a woman has almost as much liberty. There is a strong sense of the right of persons to live their own lives in the way they prefer, without interference from others. Outside the matrilineal birth-group, even within marriage, no person can demand the labour of another. Such labour should be given without coercion or strict accounting. Wage-labour is abhorred, and is likened to slavery. Selling one's labour for cash, like being sold into slavery, cuts one's kin ties and reduces one to the status of *çiŋkina/*, like the lost foundlings of history, a helpless thing rather than a person. Bridewealth payments, also abhorred by the Uduk, smack of the selling of people into slavery. A woman should always be able to return to her people and leave her husband, should she wish, especially if he beats her.

The marked sense of personal integrity which Uduk display often leads them into petty squabbles and conflicts. Criticism and insults are jealously detected all the time. People don't turn up for work in the fields, they suddenly leave beer-parties, they move house, or they publicly quarrel and threaten to fight. They have anger (*nyor*) in their Stomachs, because they have been insulted. People easily aroused are said to be 'hot'. There is a common phrase, *a'di pishi'd*, 'he/she went off-in-a-huff'; when someone does this, others shrug their shoulders and wait until the person has cooled down. If a real fight blows up, bystanders will be expected to force the combatants apart, to prevent injury. People expect that others will get upset and annoyed about things from time to time; there is a feeling that each person should be entitled to a little space around themselves, and if they are angry they are given a wide berth for a time. Certain people are known to get excited easily; Tente was one, and people just knew that they had to be careful not to offend him, especially at a beer-party. For an Ebony diviner to have an excitable temperament is not necessarily a bad thing. With dogs too; I once brought a dog with me, and people asked if she were dangerous (*shwa'danyor*, literally 'burning with anger'). I assured them that she was very good and quiet. This was disappointing news; but she suddenly bit Tente, and people were delighted! That dog had something about her after all. Uduk feel that if a person has a grudge, it is better for it to come out. People who habitually sit quiet may be building up resentments. They may eventually be suspected of being *dhathu/*, 'witches', and practised at concealing hostile feelings. The honest, straightforward, and forgivable thing to do is to express one's feelings openly.

Whatever might be privately concealed, honesty in public statements—perhaps rather 'verifiability'—is expected among the Uduk. They have the reputation among administrators and former missionaries of telling the truth as they see it without guile or equivocation. Even when accused of a serious offence, they tend to describe and justify what they did (of course their reasons may well include the hidden, malign disposition of others).

There is a marked feeling that a person is responsible for his or her own actions, in so far as anyone can consider and reconsider what they do by 'turning things over' in the Stomach (*kulum gwo bwa*) or 'thinking'. But if something external affects the Liver, the impulsive, responding centre of being, then a person is no longer able to help what he or she does. An extreme condition is madness—when the Liver is out of control. Then help from a specialist in matters of *arum* is necessary. But apart from extreme conditions of this kind, each person is judged and judges as an autonomous agent. A person is admired particularly for those virtues, however, which orient him or her to the interests of others. Generosity, a concern for fairness in the community as a whole, for the keeping of promises, the fulfilling of obligations and repaying of debts, dominate the way in which judgements are made of behaviour, and severe criticism follows those who appear in the slightest way selfish or who break understandings with others. Moral approbation and censure are perhaps the more marked in Uduk communities for the lack of such formal legal institutions as village courts. When the Uduk come up against 'the law' and are arrested, imprisoned, and tried in Kurmuk or Rosieres, they tend to see their experience as one more eye-opening encounter with the unpredictable and arbitrary powers of a government, and a governing people, best kept at arm's length. When things go wrong in their own communities, they make their own judgements and sometimes take their own action, and only rarely refer the matter to the constituted authorities. The most extreme deliberate action taken in the villages is the killing of a person suspected of being (and in their eyes proved to be) a dangerous 'witch'. Such persons, because of the contamination of their being from birth, are not responsible for their harmful effects on others; the evilness arising from their inner being cannot be controlled by their own 'rational' capacities.

By comparison with many of the African societies familiar to us
from the ethnography, the Uduk have very few automatic sanctions
upon individual behaviour emanating, apparently, from symbolic
representations of the social order. The kind of pollution or trig-
gered sickness produced by the transgression of rules 'protecting
the social structure', discussed for example in Mary Douglas's
work, is uncommon.[3] It is true that one can become sick through
pollution from senior in-laws (a condition termed *gu'th*), and
that one's father's people have special mystical power over one
(one may be *'kosha 'twa/*, struck by their words). The recently
dead may also harm their living kin. There is also a complaint,
piyan, from which a man may suffer if he and his brother have
sexual relations with the same woman. Uncontrollable bleeding
from a wound is a sign of *piyan*, as is the swelling of a dead man's
body.

But otherwise, there are few mystical dangers which could be
interpreted as sanctions. There is no mystical consequence even to
'incest'. Sexual relations within the birth-group are likely to lead
to fighting, and thus to the possible anger of the spirits of the dead.
A response I have heard more than once to the idea of incest is the
puzzled comment: 'But if there were a child, it would have no
father's people.' This pragmatic and prudent view is characteristic,
and illustrates the kind of reasonable common sense they assume
to guide most people. For Uduk, the immediate social world is not
perceived as a structure closing them in, either with the prescribed
authority of others or with a hedge of 'symbolic' rules and threats.
They are free, in most respects, to make their own social relationships as they go along. Occasionally individual persons are dangerous to their fellows. And at a distance, there are threats: from the
forest, from powerful foreign peoples, and from the market-place
and the government. But in relation to such potent dangers, as
with those closer to home, one can take a defensive position,
acknowledging their reality by self-protection.

(iii) Growth and completion of the person

We have examined some of the 'working components' of the
person; but the whole encompasses more than the sum of these
parts. That whole, the moral person, is moreover specifiable only

[3] Compare Mary Douglas's *Purity and Danger*, esp. ch. 7 and 8.

within time, and within experience, the reflexive experience of others and of self. From each new starting-point begins a specific personal history, a history of the building up of a particular self, through encounters with events, other people, the active efforts of the will, and response to ritual action. It is useful to consider 'developmental' rites as part of the 'making' of a person, and 'healing rites' as dedicated to the 'repair', 'correction', or 'protective maintenance' of a person in the face of damage or threat. The common ritual practice of the Uduk forms a repertoire of bodily treatments which specifically concern the condition and inner balance of the person in relation to other persons (rather than the state of relationships with the divine, or the cosmos). Taken together, they do not constitute a formal discourse; being only partially explicit or 'meaningful', however, they do not oppose the construction of formal discourse, theory, or ideology at another level. Many elements of the ritual repertoire recur, significantly, among a variety of neighbouring peoples, who speak different languages and may hold explicit religious or other theories which differ from those of the Uduk. The implication of a 'moral community' wider than a linguistic grouping and underlying apparent differences in overt discourse is further discussed in Appendix 1. Here, I introduce first the individuality of the person as marked in time, and then the ways in which a person is properly fashioned through bodily treatments during the course of a given life, and beyond.

(a) New beginnings

By a 'beginning' I mean what the Uduk call *mompinu*: that is, the 'place/time of appearing out', as a plant might appear from the soil, an animal from a hole, the new moon from its periodic rest, or the sun, either from behind a cloud, or more particularly from the horizon at dawn. The time-shape of a day starts with the appearance of the dawn sun and continues with its rising, passing overhead, and falling into a 'hole', from which it will appear again. Reappearance is a theme with many variations among the Uduk. In *'Kwanim Pa* I suggested how the Uduk view themselves as having made a new start in their own history; in the discussion of Elephant Medicine above I have pointed out the making of a fresh beginning after sickness, echoing the fresh beginning of mythical times; and

I have touched above on the way each new human birth is seen as a new emergence.

Even in respect of what we might call environmental, or cosmic time (as against historical, social, or biological time), the Uduk like to pin-point 'new beginnings'. A 'new moon', described as such in the Uduk idiom, does mark a new phase of time. Activities in the field, especially harvests, are postponed until 'the new moon comes'. If *athele/* flute dancing starts in a hamlet, it will continue on alternate nights as long as people have the energy; but even if they dance for only a few days, no other hamlet should start dancing until 'the moon has changed'. The new moon may 'bring the rain', or heavy rain may 'extinguish' the old moon. The moon, together with the seasons, marks the periodicity of 'time' in general, or *yil*. This term can mean a year, qualified as this year or that year, or last year or next year; or less specifically this time or that time, a long time ago, or in the future (*yilaŋkamu*, another time, next time, or next year). Uduk say *apee aḵ yil e*, 'the moon changes the time', in the sense that it marks a shift from one time period to another. Important rituals are geared to the new phases of time provided by the moon, and people plan their personal lives by it, for example postponing journeys until the new moon. Commonly heard is the phrase *yil piti*, 'its time', or proper season, which may or may not have arrived. It does not seem good to start a project while the moon is waning.

The developing phases of the moon are not, I believe, seen as cyclical in the sense of mechanically repeating each other in an endless round (as we see the cycles of the clock hands, for example). Nor are they seen as linear, in the sense of succeeding in a long neutral continuum. Each month marks a new start, with its own peculiar pattern of events. No month is like the one before it, for all sorts of climatic and social reasons, and so there is little feeling of mere repetition. Nor is there a notion of a fixed cycle of months co-ordinated mathematically or symbolically with the yearly or seasonal periods. The months do not even have names in Uduk (though I have heard individuals using Arabic or English names).

The longer time-shape of a year, itself termed *yil*, is also marked by the freshness of its start, that is the time of new growth, when the early rains begin in April and May. This is when projects for planting extra grain for specific purposes, usually big rituals, are begun; and it is the time when last year's stores are running low—

even running out—giving the feeling that the previous year is now approaching its end. Some grain has been set aside for planting, of course, and this is now brought out. Joachim Theis has told me that the Komo pull up and throw away any chance seedlings that appear in the new fields, that is self-sown seedlings. The new crop must be entirely from what they themselves have deliberately planted. This may very well be done by the Uduk too, and certainly echoes the general understanding I have of their purpose in cultivation, that is to protect what has been planted from the haphazard intrusions of the wild species.

As the year progresses, there is a lively sense of developing momentum through the named seasons towards the main harvest time in December and January ('KP: Chapter 3). When a new harvest is reached, in addition to the satisfaction of having 'completed' an anticipated 'natural' cycle, there is a sense of being further on than at the time of last year's harvest, of being older, a sense reinforced when there have been many deaths during the year. At the same time, a fresh start is anticipated with the next early rains, an anticipation reinforced when there have been births, and especially if more are due. The historical and social aspect of development in time, from circumstantial and particular new starting-points, is quite explicit, and seems to help define the shape of cosmic or environmental time.

In the context of humanity, there is an assumption that each life has a proper course ahead of it, a progress in growth towards maturity and fulfilment. To this end, since this progress is not made automatically, there are specific developmental rites through which everyone normally goes. In addition, because there are many hazards and diversions from what is explicitly represented as a 'straight' course, there are corrective rites. The commonest interference is illness; and in practice, this is the most frequent reason for rites dedicated to re-straightening a person's course. As virtually everyone experiences illness, healing rites can be regarded almost as 'rites of passage' in themselves. Like the regular stages of life defined by developmental rites, they mark less regular, but no less normally expected, crises through which a person must steer a course. The chief elements of ritual practice are found in both these categories of rites, and all deal primarily with the proper development, correction, repair, and reorientation of the person. The main aim of these rites is to nurture and preserve the fresh,

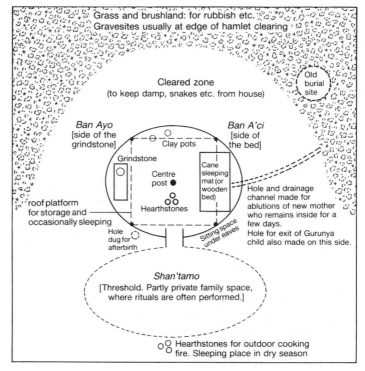

Figure 2. *Diagram of the Uduk homestead.*

sound body and its functioning parts, including its immaterial aspects; to fight against decay and putrefaction; and to ward off those diseases that can invade or interfere with the functioning body and bring premature degeneration.

(b) Rites of development

The first marriage of a young woman and the birth of her first child is the key starting-point in the ideal cycle of family and personal life. This is the epitome of a new beginning, a fresh start, for the Uduk, and many other new beginnings are modelled after it. Choice of marriage partner is very free, and marriages are often initiated by elopement ('KP: 124–40). A first marriage is not, as in so many other societies, the product of a pre-arranged liaison to carry forward the social investments of the respective families, but a fresh bond struck between the individual parties. It is potentially the setting for the birth of a series of 'new' persons. It could be the start of a new matriline or 'birth-group'.

After a period of discreet and even secret courtship, a young couple will disappear from their homes to live in a shelter in the bush or in a distant friend's house. The girl's family will eventually trace her, and bring her home. The two young people are covered with blackened oil (*jiso*) and will have to remain apart for a while. They are known by a special term, *nyaŋa'b*, which we could translate either 'betrothed' or 'newly-wed'. They should not travel far, should not cross rivers, and should remain apart.

The young man builds a hut, usually in his own birth-group hamlet with his mother's brothers, and when this is ready the bride will join him. She will prepare food alone for a while, for herself and her husband. Then for the first time she will start to prepare beer for a work-party in the hamlet. This beer is known as *Asum Mash*, Marriage Beer, or *Asum Ur Me'd*, Beer for Guiding the Hand. In the old days this 'wedding feast' was usually held at the husband's father's hamlet, but it is now more often held at his own. People say that 'in the old days' these feasts were more elaborate than now, when so many people have casual affairs, and marriage (they say) is not taken so seriously. Proper wedding feasts are certainly rare, and the *de facto* setting up of married households common.

In theory, at any rate, there were certain essentials to the wedding feast, which marked the way the new bride was ritually brought into the husband's community and recognized as a fully adult woman. In the course of a typical ceremony as described to me, the bride's right hand is held by her mother-in-law and others of the husband's people as she pours water into the beer mixture, as she kneels to smooth the rough dough with the grindstone, and as she stirs the cooking-pot. She is symbolically Offered food by her in-laws (in this action, a person being newly acclimatized takes a little food into the mouth, rejects it, and then swallows the second offering). The young couple each have their heads shaved, and are anointed with oily red ochre by his mother. The bride's long fighting stave, *kura/* (with which she may have to defend her marriage; see *'KP*: 129–31) is also touched with red ochre. The couple are adorned with new beads, and the bride is given feathers and a long tail (*ras*) of cowrie shells by her mother-in-law. At this stage the couple can be referred to as *gowal*, a species of showy red bird. There will probably be dancing, to the *athele/* flutes and beaten logs, which are dusted with ash from the domestic hearth and Brushed with a chicken before use. If the feast is being held before the young man has built a hut, the womenfolk will escort the girl back to her village, brandishing their long sticks. If they meet women of her village on the way, they will stage a mock fight. The girl is installed temporarily with her own people, and her husband brings her back when the hut is ready. The marriage rites are then concluded with a beer-party for Hair-Styling (*thes 'kup*), when the couple have their new growth smartly or decoratively trimmed.

It is hoped, and expected, that a newly-wed young woman will soon give birth. If she does not become pregnant after a year or two she will seek advice from a diviner. It is thought that the most fertile time for conception is just around the time of menstruation, and although intercourse is avoided during the actual flow, the proximity of the blood is thought to make conception likely. Sexual relations are avoided in the weeks immediately following a birth, because it is thought that the remaining blood of the birth-process may result in a second (and premature) conception. It is better to wait until regular menstruation has been re-established.

There is *arum* within a new-born baby. It is generated from the time of conception, and is particularly associated with the role of the father in creating and moulding an embryo from the mother's blood and later shaping its appearance and character ('*KP*: 117–19). This is in contrast to the rest of the child's substance, including its Liver, Stomach, and personal Genius, which are derived, with the blood, from the mother's side. But in spite of the undoubted generative link with the life-giving powers of the father's side, the child's own vital being, its *arum*, is not an 'inheritance' from the father, nor is it in any way a reborn 'spirit' from his ancestors. In so far as there is spiritual continuity with the past, it would in fact appear to be on the mother's side, through the blood and the Liver (for example, see the discussion of special inborn powers above, section (i) (*f*), and the abnormalities, to be discussed in the next section below). The personal Genius, the *kashira/*, however, while it appears to be derived from the same matrilineal bodily source, is as yet undeveloped in the child. It grows to distinctive maturity in adulthood. The new-born child appears to

the Uduk as a fresh creature, a new sprouting of *arum*, already
with the potential for adult personhood.

A woman usually goes back to her own hamlet for the birth of
her first baby, though subsequent children (who are said to 'follow
behind') are normally born in the husband's home. Women may
give birth inside the hut, or outside, in the bush behind. The mother
then remains secluded for a few days. She washes herself and the
child in hot water, 'to make them both strong'. Giving birth is
normally a very good, auspicious, and 'cool' event. Mother, child,
and father too are 'very cool' in their bodies, and need warming.
The father may also bathe in hot water on the day of the birth. He
may avoid hard work or rough actions, which could 'harm' the
baby, though this is not a strictly observed prohibition.

The water used by the mother for washing in the hut drains
away, through a hole cut in the side of the hut behind the bed, and
along a special channel dug by the women in the direction of the
bush. The child's navel cord may be cut by the women, or in more
recent times by the men of Arum. The afterbirth used to be flung
up into a thorn tree, I understand, but is now normally buried.
When I saw this done, it was buried in a narrow hole about a foot
and a half deep just outside the door of the hut, on what counts as
the right side (see Figure 2). The afterbirth itself was put at the
bottom of the hole, and the cord carefully stretched up towards
the surface. The women explained to me that this was 'the way in
which the baby had been born', implying an analogy between
the earth and the mother's body. The child's afterbirth, they emphasized to me, was called *mom piti*, which can mean 'his (or
her) place/time' (though I may have missed a tonal difference);
I had previously only known the more ordinary anatomical term
tor.

Birth produces a state of extreme 'newness' (especially of a first-
born), a newness which can in itself upset some people. Mothers
may be not just cool but cold because of this state. It is termed
nyolos, a word indicating the quality of rawness or freshness. Some
people find such freshness upsets the Liver. They avoid (*ga/*) such
things as very young maize and 'very raw' things (like raw fish or
eggs) with a particular aura described as *tu/atu/*. These are things
whose potency seems to stem from the presence of raw life still
within them, which seems to cause queasiness in those especially
sensitive. These people keep away particularly from new-born

children. The aura fades in the case of foods with age or cooking, and in the case of children, with age and appropriate 'ritual processing'. The new baby, and the *arum* within it, are soon greeted by the enactment of its first rites.

There are two variants of the sequence of rites through which a normal new-born baby passes. In the case of a child born in the mother's own hamlet, and more particularly in the case of a first-born, there will be two separate rites. The first, after a few days, is Bringing out the Baby (*ḳal a'ci ka pije/*), and is fairly modest and simple (see Plate 1a). This is followed some weeks later by a bigger rite, Bringing the Baby Home (*ḳal a'ci pa*), that is to its father's hamlet. In the case of a child born in its father's home, the rite for Bringing out the Baby will be more elaborate, in a sense condensing the two rites into one.

At its very simplest, probably in the mother's hamlet, the initial rite will be carried out by the immediate relatives. The women will cut the navel cord (with a sharp grass or corn splinter), and lay people will themselves Brush the child with a chicken. If however the cord is cut by the men of Arum or the diviners, which is likely for a first-born or for a child born in its father's home, then the rite will be more elaborate, there will be beer and the child will be anointed with red ochre.

For the first-born (son) of Losa and Barpen, married for the first time, two Arum men and two Ebony diviners supervise the rite of Bringing out the Baby at the father's home. Barpen goes to the river early to collect water, for the first time since the birth. The child is brought out and she sits with him on her lap at the doorway (shan'tamo) of the hut, the place where all personal and domestic rites are performed. Mother and child are Brushed with a chicken, which is then cut, and a goat is also cut. Heads of mother, child, and also father are shaved clean, leaving only a patch on the baby's soft spot. Girls and women are busily preparing a meal to follow the rite. A strip of skin from the goat is tied around the right wrist of the mother, and then the baby, where it will remain. Food is brought to the parents and Offered to them. 'They are all new people,' it is explained to me. The diviners dip a little porridge in the stew, Blow it gently to the mother's nostrils and ears, then put a little in her mouth; she spits out a little to the left, then to the right, and then eats it. The same is done for Losa, the father. Then the Arum men take a little red ochre on the end of a sprig of Wild Mint, their special emblematic herb, and Blow it to Barpen's nose and ears. Then they Touch the ochre to her body, on forehead, chest, abdomen and sides, and back. The ochre is smeared all over. Father and baby are done in the same way. The new family go in the hut, and then the general meal is served out.

Some weeks after a baby born in its mother's hamlet has been 'brought out', beer is again made, both in this hamlet and in that of the baby's father. This is the rite of Bringing the Baby Home. Since in recent years the wedding feast itself has become atrophied, this rite of bringing the baby home to its father has become the main occasion for the formal meeting of the respective relatives of wife and husband. The day's ceremony establishes a balance between the two sides, each, for example, Offering food to the other. The day has a threefold structure: the focus is at first on the wife's hamlet, then upon the formal procession through the bush (during which the young wife is made 'a real woman') and finally upon the husband's hamlet.

The son of Baden and Lishka already has two names (these are given informally and do not require ceremony). He was born in the home of his maternal grandmother and about a month ago had his initial rite, Arum men Shaving his head, Brushing him with a chicken and cutting it, and anointing him with red ochre. The parents were also shaved and anointed. The baby now wears the feathers of the chicken on his wrist. Baden is summoned by Lishka's brother and arrives in the early morning at his mother-in-law's hut, escorted by Cinge, married to a brother of his. He sits with his back to the women, not speaking, while they grind red ochre. Food is being prepared outside, and Lishka's brother comes in to Offer a little food to Baden and share it with him. This is the first food Baden has taken from the village. His brother-in-law cuts a chicken for the stew. Baden has his hair trimmed, in the rite known as Hair-Styling (thes'kup). He is decorated by the women of the village (wives of his brothers-in-law, and thus amugu to him), with the beads of a woman including head band, neck ring, and anklets. Then he is smeared with oily red ochre by his mother-in-law. The main serving of food is now brought in, and two of the older men of the village (Baden's mar, senior in-laws), his mother-in-law, and various of her sisters, Offer food to him in turn. Each person dips the porridge food in stew, and feeds it to him with the right hand. He then pushes it away with his right hand and makes the other person finish it. He is then led outside by his wife, in solemn mien and his 'female' finery.

The procession then forms up, led by two of Lishka's brothers and a sister of Baden who carries the baby on her back, Baden himself in red ochre and Lishka still black, followed by the rest of the hamlet's women, and then the men. The remaining food is also carried with them, and the red ochre.

About half-way to our destination, Lishka is escorted off the path by Ciŋge (married to Baden's brother and thus jil to her). A brief but essential rite then takes place. This is the Bush Rite (mii bwasho) or True Women's Rite (mii up gana/). It is, they say, 'to make Lishka a real woman'. Ciŋge hacks off a long piece of soft bark from the tukh tree with a stone, rolls it, and gives it to Lishka together with a new waistcord (mantom) of homespun cotton and a tail (ras) of cowrie shells. Lishka disappears to put these things on, 'to be a real woman'. (Strips of bark from the tukh tree are normally used for hygiene at times of menstruation and childbirth.) The gift of the new cotton waistcord recalls the other main occasion when a girl is 'incorporated' into a new home, that is for the adoption of a foundling from the bush, a ciŋkina/ ('KP: 62–6). Lishka is then given a bead apron and other outer clothes to wear by Ciŋge. We then rejoin the path and the procession which has been waiting for us.

The procession is met outside Baden's hamlet by one of his uncles holding a small chick. Lishka's brother takes it and leads the procession right round Baden's hut (anticlockwise), before escorting the baby and its parents inside. The chick will be reared as the child's own. Lishka washes the child, and then she has her hair Styled and is lavishly adorned with beads by the women here. Her mother-in-law smears her all over with oily red ochre, and the baby (already wearing some from earlier) is brought forward for more. He is given beads to wear by his father's sisters (black beads are especially suitable for small children).

Lishka is Offered food by her in-laws just as her husband was; she eats a little, pushes it away, and the person Offering it eats the rest. They also feed her a little goat meat, and she is then conducted to her husband's hut. The general meal begins. This includes food brought from Lishka's own hamlet. There should be beer but on this occasion grain stocks are too low. After the meal Baden's mother covers Lishka's mother with red ochre, and then various others of her people are anointed by a younger woman of the village. Those who are amugu *to either wife or husband (i.e. those married to Baden's sisters or Lishka's brothers) appear to share their status as* nyaŋa'b, *'newly-weds', and should remain indoors until sunset. Baden and Lishka should each have an* amugu *to lead them out of doors if they wish to go.*

Baden takes off his female attire informally in the evening. The next day his wife's people bring water from their home to wash him, and his people wash Lishka and the baby. From this point on, the couple may eat food in each other's hamlets, drink beer, and speak freely with people there. This makes life easier in particular for Lishka, now able to participate fully in the life of the hamlet she has married into.

The rite of Bringing the Baby Home sets the seal on the marriage of a young couple. The focus throughout is on the parents as much as their first-born, particularly upon the mother, who through this rite achieves maturity as a 'real woman'. At the birth of subsequent children, which is likely to be in her married home, she will be aided informally by the other women there. When the baby is Brought Out there will probably be beer, and red ochre for both parents. The father may again be adorned in women's beads.

In the special case of a Gurunya child, who is required to Sit Black for a prolonged period after birth, in order to avert the death which has already claimed one or more elder siblings, there are variations on the rites just described (*'KP*: 212–21). The child is brought out not through the front door, but through a hole in the side of the hut; it is later taken on a procession around the neighbouring hamlets, to supplicate for gifts; and only then do all the neighbours gather to drink beer and anoint the child and parents with red ochre. The father on this occasion too is decorated with women's beads; it is a kind of Bringing the Baby Home.

From its fresh beginning, each life has the potential to develop along a straight course towards maturity and completion. For a girl, the main achievement is marriage and motherhood in her turn. For boys, fatherhood is also an integral part of personal fulfilment. But in addition, it seems that achievements in hunting have also played a part in the celebration of adulthood for men. He who killed a wild animal was formerly accorded great prestige; his own inner vitality was thereby strengthened, both by the overcoming of the beast and by the assimilation of appropriate protective medicines (see Chapter 1 (ii) above). However his achievements did not take precedence in any simple sense over those of the woman. From one point of view, the successful hunter was modelled upon the new parent, where the representation of femaleness dominates the symbolism: he was adorned in women's beads, just like a brand-new father welcoming his new child. Today there are few opportunities for hunting achievement. But it seems likely that the rites of the diviners' society, the Ebony Order, have to some extent taken the place of hunting rites as an option open to young men advancing to adulthood. This theme will be taken up again in Part III. Here we might just note that newly-initiated diviners, too, are dressed and treated as women—or rather brides (see Chapter 5 (v) below). The same strong metaphor underlies the recurrent role-reversal of all these rites of achievement for young men.

The road to maturity and completion is not a natural or inevitable course. Progress takes place through experience and training, and has to be monitored. Where things are going wrong, there has to be intervention; the commonest obstacles on the road are illness as the result of affliction by the invasive powers of *arum*, from the wild or from the dead, or the attacks of *dhathu/* ('witches'). These are described below. Episodes of illness are unfortunately very common, and although their management is not normally classed in ethnography together with 'rites of passage', they are for the Uduk part of what may be expected in the course of a child's development. We may even bracket the treatment of illness together with the 'rites of passage' already described as bundles of analogous techniques in the 'making and maintaining' of a person. Certainly, when we look in detail at the repertoire of ritual action, both in passage rites and in healing rites, we find a good deal of correspondence and overlap (see (d) below). This can be best understood if we view the growth and development of a person as a continuing process, both of internal maturation and of increasing accommodation with, and mastery of, the external world. Classic rites of passage, like those of marriage and birth already described, are in the Uduk case especially concerned with adjusting the person to the normal processes of the external social world; healing rites in the strict sense are concerned primarily with the internal state of the person when, in abnormal encounters with others, it has been upset.

What is aimed at in the course of developmental rites, of whatever kind, is the controlled maturation of the person. The personal Genius grows in strength with age and experience; the Stomach is vulnerable when the person is young but can be trained, especially through dietary regulations during illness; the *arum* within can be protected by avoidance of those sources of danger which have already made themselves known, and the person's movements can be carefully regulated during vulnerable periods of ritual transition or illness. Strengthening of the Stomach, watchfulness over the state of the Genius, and care in keeping the *arum* within calm and cool can all help to protect the person from those invasive powers which may upset the Liver.

All the elements of the adult are present in the child. But their interrelationship is not yet that of an adult. The Liver of tiny children is 'free', they are still close in body and being to their mothers, and mother's milk is thought to be the main route whereby sickness can affect the baby. Nursing mothers have to be very careful about what they eat, for it may upset the baby. Many illnesses of babyhood are attributed to the mother having eaten something affecting the milk, which is then too strong for the baby's stomach. The baby is described as *'kosh ma ko*, hurt by milk. A young child's stomach is as yet delicate and untried, and has to be treated with care. The foods a mother will find safe include grain porridge moistened with plain water, the stew of certain fish and mushrooms, pig meat, and various antelopes; and those which are forbidden include chicken, eggs, sweet sorghum, the strong-smelling mushroom reminiscent of goat meat (*disha wulul*), most wild animals (except antelopes), honey, and sugar. Meat of cattle and goats may be tolerated by some but not all—each woman will test it out herself.

Even when a child is weaned, and up to adolescence, it is likely to be treated for any sickness together with its mother, and they may even undergo the same restrictions during convalescence. One of the commonest of these restrictions is that on diet: another is that on physical movement. It is as if the digestive system has to be carefully disciplined in order to bring a person through a period of convalescence, while the free movement of the person is held in rein for a while, to combat the unfortunate effects of the invasion of sickness—something which primarily affects the Liver.

In a young child, the training of the digestion, and the controlling of physical freedom, has only just begun. This training will eventually come to impose its own discipline upon the Liver, which, while 'free' in the youngster, is held in check, to some extent, in the adult. Dietary discipline, quite literally, seems to be one of the ways in which the adult Stomach, the source of deliberation and will-power, is consciously developed. By eating things all over the place, in ignorance, and thus perhaps encountering and ingesting various dangerous *arum*, you may get ill: but by being careful, knowing what you are eating, and avoiding things of certain kinds, and in certain places, where they may infect you, you may protect yourself to some degree.

Moving into strange territory and out in the wild bush can be dangerous; you may be entrapped by the way, especially in the river. A tiny child has a *kashira/*, a personal Genius, but like the Stomach it is not yet developed, and does not give a child the psychic autonomy of an adult. It develops with growth, and with experience. It can easily be dislodged from a youngster (less easily from an aware adult). If this should happen, the Ebony diviners are there to restore the *kashira/*, and supervise the diet, of a child who becomes ill. If the disturbance has seriously affected the Liver, an Arum man will be brought in. Ideally, the Stomach and personal Genius will mature sufficiently for the Liver to be given some protection. In the adult there should be a reasonable balance between the working of these parts.

(c) *The balance upset*

Persons can be diverted from the straight and sound course of proper development. What are often seen as external sources of spiritual power can invade the Liver; dislodge the Genius; upset the Stomach; and, in extreme cases, interfere with the birth of whole and healthy children to a matriline. Those born to such a 'spoiled' line may adversely affect others around them. In this section I focus on this major crux of Uduk understanding and attempt to place it in sociological context.

Certain events may signal that the normal development of a matrilineal birth-group has been blighted. The main sign is the birth of abnormal children, including twins. The moral significance of such departures, and the practical action taken in relation to them, have varied at different times in remembered history. But for a good part of the present century, at least, Uduk have taken an extremely negative view of abnormal births. They have been notorious for their practice, continued until recent times, of killing one or both of a pair of twins. Such births are signs, which in the middle decades of the present century at least were interpreted as meaning that the blood of a given birth-group, or matriline, had undergone a damaging change—a sort of mutation, for which there was no known means of correction. Sources external to the birth-group are usually held to blame for causing the abnormality, termed *dhathu/*, a word spoken in lowered whispers, and applied to those affected. The condition is transmitted down the matriline; when the birth of twins, for example, has established it, not only will the mother and the twins themselves be regarded as *dhathu/*, but all subsequent children born to the mother, and those born to a female twin or younger sister of twins. The condition seems to become more entrenched with time, so that not only are afflicted individuals more dangerous as they grow older, but children born at a later stage down the female line—for example, children born after twins—are more dangerous than those born before.

There is a strong element of animality in the idioms used in speaking of *dhathu/*. The word used of plural birth, *wol*, is different from the normal word for giving birth (*dho'th*); *wol* is otherwise used only of animals like cattle and goats. The effect might be echoed in English by saying that a woman had littered. Sometimes one hears of a pregnant woman having 'a snake in the belly'; sometimes that she has a 'forked belly', recalling the divided after-birth; and in these expressions there is suggestion of reversion to the the animal state. A woman dreads the possibility of having twins; from her point of view, she herself is not inadvertently contaminated. Someone else must have brought the blight on her, or it must have come from the realm of *arum* in the ground. I saw a young woman terrified after a dream; she was pregnant, and I learned later that her dream had been about a neighbour (already suspected of *dhathu/* activity) digging up the corpse of a recently buried child, and bringing it to her.

Dhathu/ are thought to cause sickness and death around them, especially to their own matrilineal kin (case studies may be found in Part III). Their powers are at least partly involuntary, and their actions take place partly at night. This is why they can be seen in dreams. But in waking life they can be active too, and the expression 'evil eye' (*en thus*) is sometimes, though not frequently, used of them. It suggests that the evil within, especially in the Liver, comes up spontaneously, without restraint, and shows through the eyes. Another term which is heard occasionally for this condition is '*bo/a'bo/*, as an adjective, or its grammatical variants. The baneful attacks of *dhathu/* usually begin with the entrapping of one's own psychic sensor, one's personal Genius.

In the old days, in principle, the evil was removed by the quasi-judicial killing of both the mother and her children. I do not know how generally this occurred, but it is certainly true in recent generations that many mothers who bore twins have escaped to neighbouring, non-Uduk communities, and found refuge there. In some cases certainly, where twins were born, both might have been killed (with a firmly suffocating pressure on the chest, I understand). But very often, I would judge (and informants agree), only one would be disposed of, and the other allowed to live. From the individual mother's point of view, she is not at fault; she does not wish to lose her children; only one may be the bad one anyway; and who is to know if one is allowed to survive, and nothing is said? This principle of course leads to a situation where almost anybody could be suspected of being born to a contaminated line. It is certainly this motif to which Uduk always have recourse in justifying the killing of adult men and women who have been repeatedly revealed, through dreams and specialist advice, as harmful *dhathu/*. Such killings have been by no means infrequent, and only with the closer administration of the Uduk area from the early 1950s has this declined. People say that they are 'afraid of the Government', and diviners of the Ebony Order, who used at the least to channel the popular verdict, no longer name names. But, at least in the 1960s, the publicly avowed dread had not really diminished. The rescue of twins from the villages was a priority for the missionaries at Chali. I have heard how no sooner was an expected twin birth reported there, than the missionaries would jump in their Land Rover and fetch the mother, and her babies if they were delivered, for safe keeping at the mission for a while. There was a twin orphanage, perhaps the most famous institution of the Chali Mission, where a large number of children were brought up. Shwamge, a wife of Tente, had twins in Waka'cesh during the first few weeks of my fieldwork. Everyone was clearly aghast. The Bertha midwife had already been escorted by Tente from Chali, and she was in a state, warning the gathered people in a trembling voice that if anything happened to these babies, 'By God, I will tell the Government and you will be punished.' The poor mother, normally a bustling and cheerful lady, was blank and exhausted. 'We can't send them to Rasha's now, can we?' Rasha, that is Pastor Paul, had been left in charge at Chali on the deportation of the missionaries some two years previously, and the orphanage no longer functioned. Most of the children were fending for themselves back in their own villages, without having come to any harm, and a few still lived around the Christian community. But no new babies were being fostered. In the event, as I had a vehicle that year, Tente asked me to take the midwife, mother, and babies to Chali where they could stay at the Dispensary for a while. I did this. Unfortunately, one child died spontaneously that evening; the other child survived only a few years, and poor Shwamge herself died not long after that.

On the basis of my work in the 1960s, I could foresee no way in which the situation over twins might change. There were obviously many more cases in which twins had been disposed of than those I knew of. Apart from the twin birth I have just mentioned, there were no twins in the genealogies I collected. But by the time of my revisit in 1983, there certainly had been a change, at least among the northern Uduk. Women who were rearing twins brought them to visit me. I shall return to consider this dramatic change in Part II.

Evidence from informants' own accounts of the 1960s conveys something of the fearful nature of contamination by *dhathu/* as it was then understood. The following is from a young man, already interested in the new Christianity, and therefore willing to talk more openly than most:

Where do dhathu/ *come from?*

Dhathu/, of course people say that they come from those who give birth to two.

Why?

Çaah! I don't know.

Is it bad to give birth to two?

Yes! It is cursed by Uduk. Uduk say it is very bad.

Why?

People are said to have bad eyes, because of the afterbirth which is forked. And this business, *ҫaah*. It is just *arum* which brings a person and reveals him to you, reveals a person in a dream, as though you see these things done by a person in a dream. You will then accuse the person [behind his back to others] of being *dhathu/*, from just seeing the person in a dream. But he hasn't done anything to you in the dream, to harm you, nothing.

But why do women kill little children?

They kill them dead. Yes! They kill them dead if two are born.

Both?

No, just one. They kill one and keep one.

And they kill one?

Yes! It is not killed in the open, just secretly, so that not many people will know. It is taken secretly to be killed.

Do they kill the child so that other people won't know this thing?

Yes, they will not hear the tale. They will not know that the person bore two. And one little child, she will keep it and people won't know. Until the word will come out gradually. From the telling of the story, that the woman gave birth to two, gradually [from one person to another]. The word goes around very slowly, and then comes out at least.

A more graphic account comes from a young married woman in a state of some excitement, willing to talk in front of the tape recorder only because we knew each other quite well. Her account hints at the dread that women felt about this matter in the abstract, while at the same time reflecting the bewilderment of a woman who suddenly finds herself in this position. The account is not consistent over whether it is another *dhathu/* person who may bring the bad thing to you, or whether it is brought by some *arum* presence directly from the earth. I have left the inconsistency as I found it:

And we don't know this *arum*; it comes to give birth to two like that. We don't know why. Yes, *arum* is the one who creates it, in the belly while we are unaware. And you don't know that you are going to have two. We just discover this [from seeing the babies] on the ground.

Everyone says: 'Why is that woman going around with such a big belly? Is she going to have two? Yes indeed, she's surely going to have two.'

And people will name you [call you, accuse you], 'Ay! you are a witch [/E 'bo/on], you have done something to me. You are a witch, you have done something to me.'

It is from *arum* which created something in your belly here, and you don't understand it. Lots of people have-twins [*wolon*] like that nowadays, all over the place.

Does this come from the arum *of someone?*

Yes, it is from the one which we can see at night. As you are sleeping at night, it [*a'di*, which can be he, she, or it] will come. You will be unawares, at night, and it will come. It knows that pregnant woman. She is unawares, and later it brings a child, and goes and puts this other one in when the first has grown quite strong. That woman is fast asleep and she doesn't know about it, as the child is placed in her belly.

She says [to herself], 'Ay! Why am I so stiff; do you think I am going to go wrong?' She doesn't know. She says, 'I am stiff for no particular reason. There can't be two children.' And at midday you will sleep, and the others say to you, 'Don't sleep at midday, you will not see in a dream what is being done to you, for the thing which is brought to you from far away.' It is brought and forced into your belly. You will go wrong, have-twins, have-twins, when you never had-twins before. You had always given birth to children one at a time. But something came and cut this off [i.e. cut the line of good births and diverted you], and contaminated [*bul*, to rot, to spoil] your belly, and you will have-twins.

The arum *which comes, is it* aruma *'cesh, or is it the* arum *of a particular person?*

Çaah! No. It is not *aruma 'cesh*. It is not the *arum* of a person which comes to do this to women, no.

Arum comes of its own accord from the place where it is in the ground there [*mo gi dina a'di 'ceshi mun*]. Nobody knows the one who brings the thing. You don't know, you are sleeping, you found this unexpectedly, and say, 'Why is my belly hurting with pain like this for no reason?'

For something is there, two of them in the belly. Yes, you will say, 'Ay! I can't do any work. I am stiff and I can't sleep.' It is because of the children which are there, your belly grows right up to here. Your belly divides here, while one child is here, and another there [indicating]. If it wants to move about, two of them, they move about, *uluc!* When one child moves about, the belly will divide and the other one will be separate. Yes, it is from another child being brought, while the child which you conceived properly is all right. But the one which is very bad, was brought to you from some other place which you don't know, and that person brought you the child.

Is it not from the father?

No, not from fathers. From just the woman. It is just from women ... yes, it is from her own belly.... No, not from your own belly, from outside, it comes and deals with you, and people call you a witch [*dhathu/*]. 'You are *dhathu/*.' 'What do you mean by *dhathu/*? I was not borne by my mother as-a-twin. So was I visited and bewitched [*ceshku*]? To have two children while I didn't know anything about it.'

I have already noted how, in the case of the Laken Golga, and the people with 'lion eyes', there is a moral ambivalence: they are people whose powers can be represented as being for good or for bad ends. This ambivalence of spiritual power as conceived by the Uduk (and not only they) is important for our understanding the question of *dhathu/*. The evidence suggests that the Lake, or at least that core of the Lake birth-group whose continuing matrilineal descent from early times down to the present gives some unity to their conception of themselves as a people, are associated with an inborn power of *arum*. That power itself connects them with the proto-world of antelope ancestors, and in (possibly idealized) former times, before the disruptions of recent history, that power was a source for good among the people. Those Lake who practised in its name could heal others, including those hurt by it. It seems evident that among the effects of this power on others was the dislodging of the Genius.

With the wholesale disturbances affecting the Uduk in the last century, birth-groups became dispersed and many fragmented groups, including outsiders, became absorbed into the new amalgam of the modern Uduk. Many such are said to have been protected by the Lake. It seems that the potentially dangerous powers of the old Lake line have become infectious in recent times; they can now seize and damage others, whom they affect morbidly, causing a kind of 'mutation' to the line. The endeavours of modern diviners are largely devoted to the detection and elimination of the consequences of this situation. Were the ebony oracle's revelations first directed at the baneful influence of the Lake and their relatively powerful position as patrons of many others? There is scarcely a distinction today between the Lake and the rest of the Uduk; all are in the same boat, however, with respect to outside powers. To these powers is sometimes attributed the welling up of abnormality within the birth-lines of the Uduk, itself a major cause of sickness in the communities of those affected.

It is very interesting that although *dhathu/* were being represented to me in the 1960s as almost wholly evil, my elderly informant Buṯko did inform me, in conversation with William Danga, that in the very old days, *dhathu/* were not so feared. Their powers could be beneficial to the village, for they would go out in the night and kill meat, or at least locate the animals; and in the morning they would be able to guide the people to the meat.

Oh no. People used not to bewitch; there were no witches in the past. *The people who had twins in the past, did they bewitch others?* Oh no. This witchcraft is a new thing.

Witchcraft was recently introduced by people, since all of you have grown up. Was witchcraft spoken of in the past? People didn't know witchcraft in the past.... It was the recent generations, I told you, who introduced this witchcraft talk. There were witches when I was young; but few and isolated. Were there many? No! It's only just now that witches are appearing all over the place.... It comes from the birth; from the afterbirth which divides. The afterbirth divides, and that is what is called *dhathu/*. But they used not to be active.

No. They cultivated as men do, cultivated together with the men, among the people there, and ... they never took things. They cultivated with ordinary hoes. You invented this story, saying: 'Something has been taken to that village. Something has been taken to that village.' You invent these stories and kill fellows for no reason. Nowadays you call people witches, but who called them witches in the past?

This business of having twins, it has been happening a lot lately. Were people always having twins in the past like that? Oh no. Now they long for it! They pray for it! People are just longing for twins nowadays. And I say [to myself]: long for it then, but behave properly and don't do evil things. Live as they did in the past ... when there were just a few women who had twins, and they lived quietly without being pointed out: 'That's a witch!' The children they bore, were not pointed out as witches.

Now they say: 'That person is giving birth with a snake-belly.' You have invented this, calling it a snake-belly, to kill you as you have killed the others. Did people know these things [in the past]? *Dhathu/* became numerous only since you were born, after the time of the old type of *dhathu/*.

The real *dhathu/*, which looked after people in the past, looked after people. [And if people were ill] they were *lat̲* [the Genius was Restored] and it was finished. They looked after people well. They led people to the bush harmlessly. If a person was *dhathu/*, he would say: 'Go and stalk over there. Stalk ... there is something over there, I saw it on the ground. Please go.' You hear this, and you go and pick up that animal in your hand by its legs.... Did they kill people? Certainly not; they would kill a gazelle for you, *te'b*. Then they would tell people: 'Go, please, go to the fields, go and look around at the far end of the fields, go as far as the top end of the fields.' You would stop there and pick up an animal.

Bukko continued in this vein and introduced the idea that it was only since the arrival of the missionaries that women had begun to have so many twins.

Yes, it was begun recently, when Miss Beam had just arrived. This was not started from long ago. When Miss Beam arrived, was anything like this being said? The state of affairs comes from Miss Beam.... People only recently started having-twins. Did people have-twins before? *Caaw!* They used to have-twins just here and there, here and there. But it is praised by those people now. This having-twins is praised by them now. But are people goats?

Bukko explained how these days, it was not merely a question of a few birth-groups bearing twins, but that *dhathu/* were now passing this condition on to many others who had been free of it.

Now people [he means *dhathu/*] are seizing others, and giving it to them. People seize each other among the Uduk. People seize others, and give you witchcraft [*dhathu/*] in your body for no special reason, so that they will all be called *dhathu/* together. *Caah!* People who have-twins [*wol*], they deal with others, give others evilness [*thus*] gratuitously....

How long ago did Miss Beam go? When people were having-twins all over the place.... People pass on this type of birth to others and call names, saying this and that. By saying: I am capable of bewitching [*Aha/ 'bo/a*]....

[In the past] people gave birth according to their practice of giving twins from long ago. They follow, follow, the line of the afterbirth [*tor*: used as a common image for the matriline].... And now you do this thing indiscriminately, while it should follow on ... yes, from their grandmothers who bore twins long ago.

Bukko's evidence indicates that there was a time when the Uduk took a much more easygoing attitude towards *dhathu/*. Persons in this category certainly had special powers but they were not turned against the human community. On the basis of this testimony, admittedly only one voice, we could suppose that a totalitarian attitude to *dhathu/* as an evil within the community, to be rooted out by physical elimination, developed only in the course of the present century, when the Uduk became particularly conscious of their internal vulnerability.

Therefore we need not try to construct a moral apologia for the practices I have described of the killing of adults and infants classed as *dhathu/* as they operated in the middle decades of this century, any more than we need defend, on grounds of a need for liberal tolerance, the racial or other atrocities which have characterized any particular period of the history of another nation or society. Bukko's testimony of an earlier era can now be matched by recent accounts of how twins and other *dhathu/* are no longer feared as they used to be (see Chapter 4). It is no longer necessary to think of twin-killing as a permanent aspect of Uduk 'custom'. There always have been different ways of looking at the event of a twin birth, as I have suggested; and what it so be done about it is a complex matter with a political as well as a moral dimension. The notion of *dhathu/* in an older sense, people of a special capacity by virtue of an innate link with the world of animal *arum* from which we all came, constitutes a potentially strong metaphor for the concentration of power within people. During the specific period of the middle decades of this century, it became a metaphor for the source of evil emotion so strong as to become a reality for which blood was shed. But the nexus of connection between such a reality and its metaphorical image is not fixed for all time. The notion of *dhathu/* as incurable evil which cannot be accommodated has shifted over the years. Perhaps this may be linked with shifts in power relations both between central and peripheral Uduk birth-groups, and between the Uduk and the outside world as represented by their Meban neighbours, or by the mission in Chali.

(d) Models for healing: the elements of lay ritual practice

Two main terms are used for healing rites. One is *thoson*, glossed in the Dictionary as 'to prepare, to arrange, to fix, to mend'. In the mission it was also used of making restitution after a wrong. If couples ran off, a church wedding could later be held to *thoson* them, just as the wedding beer in the villages was held to *thoson* an eloped couple. Many healing rites also entail the repairing, or rearranging, of something that has become disordered or damaged. A second term sometimes used of healing rites, but never, as far as I am aware, of passage rites, is *nyoŋ* (which does not appear in the Dictionary). This means to correct something that has been broken, bent, or otherwise gone quite wrong. In the context of healing rites, the term is used of rites to correct a serious affliction, usually involving *arum* and affecting the Liver. These would normally require blood offerings.

Both passage rites and those for healing deal with the whole person, and attempt to restore the proper balance of internal elements. Very few, therefore, deal exclusively with a single organ or symptom in isolation. Most include a variety of acts, each however dealing primarily with one organ or function of the person. It is part of my argument in this book that these acts, and the way they are understood by ordinary people, constitute an enduring body of practical knowledge of the human condition, not easily dislodged by new religious or moral teaching. In the course of observing these rites today, it is not easy to disentangle what may be innovation in the practice of a healing cult like that of the Arum of Leina, for example (see Chapter 3), or in the practice of the Ebony diviners (see Chapter 6 (ii) where a number of healing rites are described). The bulk of the ritual techniques employed by these practitioners can be found also outside these cults: either in rites of passage, or in the undeniably 'older' rites for hunting and the mastery of nature which I have described in Chapter 1 (ii) above, or in the wide miscellany of domestic treatments which still persist and do not necessarily require the attention of specialists. I therefore speak of the repertoire of 'lay ritual practice', and set out here a rough inventory of basic techniques through which we may seek the 'archival' roots of what the Uduk know of themselves. By drawing upon this inventory, and employing the same or similar ritual acts, the latter-day Arum men and Ebony diviners have been able to construct their own acceptably familiar systems of treatment.

A healthy body is cool (*'thupa'thup*), one feels light in weight (*po'dapo'd*), or rather 'nimble and lively'. Health is also dependent on having plenty to eat and being what the Uduk call 'fat'. Losing weight is experienced (often with good reason) as sickening, and people often may be heard saying 'My body is too thin; I shall go to the dispensary to drink some medicine.' Illness brings a hot body, indeed the general terms for sickness is the same as that for heat. A sick body, is *'batha'd*, means at the same time a hot body. The main reason for becoming ill is that you have encountered something which damages or spoils you, and causes the onset of decay. The trigger may be a substance you touch or eat, or a power of *arum* carried directly to you through the air or the water, or in the person of someone with a concentrated, and uncontrolled, force of *arum* within them. The *arum* power, if major, has to be calmed and led away, or somehow eliminated. If minor, or if you have encountered a substance which has harmed you, treatment can aim at accommodating you to the encounter, even reinforcing your own inner strength by appropriating something of the power of the minor *arum* or substance you have met. The principle of fighting a disease on its own terms commonly underlies these practices.

A minor complaint illustrates some of these ways of looking at illness. There are a few individuals around whose urine, even in small traces, can produce a sensitive reaction in others. In one case, a person's urine may be supposed to cause headaches, or in another to cause swellings on the knee. If you have such a complaint, you can approach the known source of the trouble, and he or she will give you treatment, which includes the use of a little urine. The whole complex of the complaint and its treatment is just known as 'urine', *dhara'c*, sometimes qualified by reference to the part of the body affected. With the simple rite of treatment, the matter is completed, and no debt is incurred.

With more serious and prolonged illnesses or complaints, treatment rites follow a clearly structured pattern, very similar in outline to the structure of passage rites. Once people are defined as suffering from an illness, that is by approaching a healer, having a diagnosis (usually by kindling the ebony), and accepting treatment, they Sit Black for a while. This may mean simply taking off their normal beads, or it may mean that they are anointed with the black oil *jiso*. During this time they are vulnerable, and likely to be observing restrictions on their physical movement by not straying far from home. They will be eating carefully, avoiding rich or strong-tasting foods (which may disturb Stomach or Liver). They are likely to allow their hair to grow. After the course of treatment, if they recover, beer will probably be made for the rite of Head-Shaving to mark their restoration to health. Their hair will be shaved, and they will be anointed with oily red ochre and resume their beads. They will move freely in the bush, crossing rivers and visiting neighbouring villages as before. They will be able to eat normally. Their debt (*amure*, cognate with *amur*, hair) to the healer will be paid off.

It is in the pattern of rites for prolonged illness that we can see most clearly the analogy with passage rites, both in the general structure and in the detail of ritual action. A descriptive glossary of the commonest elements of ritual practice follows, elements we can describe as 'lay' ritual because they exist independently of those healing cults known to be fairly recently adopted by the Uduk (in particular the Arum of Leina and the Ebony Order), and can be administered by non-specialists.

With respect to the Stomach

Fasting: During periods of treatment for illness, during convalescence, and also during the middle period of some passage rites, there are restrictions on a person's diet. It is safer, the theory goes, to abstain; and when recovery is established, foods can be gradually reintroduced. Restrictions on movement outside the home can be relaxed.

Offering: When a new food is introduced to a patient, he or she takes a tiny bite, and spits it out; then takes another bite, chews, and swallows it. This rite is termed *çi 'twa/* in Uduk, literally to 'give to the mouth'. It often occurs in other rites, for example when the new mother's people are received in the hamlet of her husband; when senior in-laws are receiving younger people; even when a stranger is received in the village. Hands are not washed before Offering food, as they are before a normal meal.

Medicines: Most medicines are ingested and directly affect the stomach. A few medicines are designed to 'combat' a condition; but in my experience, most follow the model of homoeopathic vaccination or prophylaxis. They are sympathetic in action rather than allopathic, substances which in the right quantities and conditions reinforce your defences against their own powerful nature. Many medicines, like the Elephant Medicine for example, are so powerful that they themselves cause illness around them. Having been affected in this way, however, you will then be treated by the same medicine.

Medicines may be Breathed in, or swallowed, or both—the implication being that they are going both to the Liver and the Stomach. Medicine may also be Sprayed on, from the mouth of the practitioner.

With respect to the Liver and arum

Brushing: The action of Brushing the body with a chicken (see (i) (e) above) or *wup is*, a reflexive form referring to a person's body or self, helps to make contact with the inner *arum*. (The same word *wup* is used transitively of a hen sitting on eggs, or clouds covering the sun.) This action may simply calm the *arum* and settle it, help it to be acquainted with the new state or surroundings of the person, or it may be a means of discovering the nature and disposition of the *arum* within, especially if there has been invasion by an external power. When the chicken is killed, the manner of its death will suggest whether or not the treatment will be appropriate and successful. To 'die well' on the back is a good augury, while death on the front, with head down, is an inauspicious sign.

Making Blood: I am following closely in this term the Uduk *mmomii abas*, to make blood by cutting an animal with a knife or spear, usually in the throat. It could also be glossed as 'a blood rite'. (There are other methods of killing which do not release the blood and breath, such as knocking on the head or suffocating; these are used mainly at funerals.) The term 'sacrifice' does not always seem appropriate, as it carries theological overtones which may complicate our understanding of these acts (Patricia Holden has recently worked on this question[4]). The Uduk 'make blood' in order to render *arum* passive or content; and perhaps to lead a dangerous *arum* power away from a person, sometimes literally along a trail of blood that is made, and sometimes as it seeps or is washed into the ground. Patients may be washed in water from a gourd, into which some blood has been spilt. Blood may be used to Touch (*wuḵ*) people in quite everyday contexts, such as visitors from one's father's village, or other guests. An animal may be cut, to make blood, in the clearing of a new field; this will calm or settle *arum* in a general way.

With respect to blood

Some pains, especially a headache, may be attributed to bad blood, or 'black blood', and this is a reason for blood-letting, done with the help of a small horn. (The sucking out of foreign objects from the body by the Ebony diviners, *ye* or Extraction, is limited, I believe, to the diviners' practice, but blood-letting provides a lay model.)

With respect to the personal Genius

After vivid dreaming, a person will smear a little ash on the temples; this is protection for the *ḵashira/*, which can be dislodged. The rite of *laṯ*, or Restoring the *ḵashira/*, has become a hallmark of the activities of the Ebony diviners, but there is evidence that it predates

[4] Patricia Holden, 'Aspects of Sacrifice in the African Ethnographic Literature', M.Litt. thesis, University of Oxford, 1984.

them (see Buḵko's account above of non-malignant *dhathu/* who could dislodge the *ḵashira/*). The demand for the rite for Restoral of the Genius has grown dramatically in recent decades (see Part III). It consists essentially of retrieving the Genius from where it has been entrapped, usually by scooping up some soil or mud with a few leaves, and Blowing this gently to the nostrils so it may be breathed in. The mixture may also be rubbed into the body, sometimes together with a little medicine or a little blood from the chicken which has been used to Brush the patient; the leaf bundle is pressed to the shoulders, body, and forehead. These actions are known as *the*, which has the overtone in this ritual context of making connection, of offering, of joining; the everyday greeting by snapping of the fingers is known as *the me'd*, literally the joining of hands.

With respect to the outer body

Straightening: The general alignment and tension of the body may be corrected, by pulling straight the arms and legs of the patient, pulling the toe and finger joints, bending back each shoulder in turn, and turning the head from side to side. This is known in Uduk as *ṯodosh is* or *toḵ is*.

Anointing: The act of covering either the head, or the whole body, with an oil (*'kosh is ka yin*). Plain sesame oil may be used (*ayin 'thi*, or 'dark oil'), or it may be mixed with powdered charcoal to make *jiso*, black oil, or powdered red ochre, to make *yin 'per*, red oil. This is likely to take place at the end of a passage or healing rite, after a thorough washing of the body, and whether plain, black or red oil is used will depend on the place of that rite in the whole scheme. A sick person, treated but not yet recovered, may have plain oil; someone going into the middle of a passage rite, or withdrawing after a hunting encounter, may have black oil; but at the conclusion of a passage rite or recovery after convalescence, a person will have the red oil.

(iv) Death and death rites

A tangible feeling of the physical presence of death, of the loss and the nearness of the dead, is evident in Uduk villages. There is of course a high child mortality rate, and adults too are struck down, sometimes in their prime. The sites of graves, close to the edge of

a hamlet, are remembered and pointed out even in overgrown
former settlement sites. Death provokes anger and resentment; this
is publicly displayed especially at funerals where people may shout
general accusations and threats, bring their weapons and feign
attacks on death in general, and their known enemies and suspected
causes of death in particular. Sometimes real fights break out.
Death is the subject of many songs, which are in themselves a
memorial to those who have died, and at the same time a veiled
reminder to the world, and enemies in particular, that these deaths
will not be forgotten, nor the ill will of those who may have wished
them. Many of these songs are sung individually to the lyre, by
men, and pass from one singer to the repertoire of many others. I
recorded this song from Tente in the 1960s. By recalling the death
of a mother's brother a generation before, at the same time it
quotes back, ironically and warningly, the scornful remarks of a
neighbouring village who have observed how Tente's people are
always dying:

Kapki ko jwa ka yeyempa/	'Let them wail for their dead and wail again;'
Kona wuna 'bwah pem mo	I wailed for the death of my sister.
Ta denum jwa ga 'ceshe?	Why do you tremble over the dead of the earth?
Ta dotum jwa?	Why do you question the dead?
Ta dotum jwa ga 'ceshe?	Why do you question the dead who belong to the ground?
Ta denum jwa?	Why do you tremble at death?
Kapki ko	'Let them wail;'
Jethdhu aa dotu po/ 'taa?	Jethdhu, they ask me where are our people?
Kapki ko jwa ka yeyempa/	'Let them wail and wail again;'
Koni 'dapa wuthee	They wail and they suffer from cruel talk.
Kapki ko jwa ka yeyempa/	'Let them wail and wail again;'
Aa kona wuna 'bwah pem mo	I wailed for the death of my sister.
Ta denum jwa ga 'ceshe?	Why do you tremble over the dead of the earth?
Ta denum jwa?	Why do you tremble at death?
Ta denum jwa ga 'ceshe?	Why do you tremble over the dead of the earth?
Ta dotum jwa?	Why do you question the dead?
Kapki ko jwa ka yeyempa/	'Let them wail and wail again;'

Koni 'dapa wuthee	They wail and they suffer from cruel talk.

William Danga sang another lament, for the death of a sister's child; here are pictured his sister's children playing in the graves, as *arum*; Ha'da is called to dig until his hands are blistered. 'Tirko' is another of Tente's names. The brief refrains, *Eeyee*, evoke the falling notes of the funeral chant.

Gona 'bwah pem mo kanoo	My sister's crying like that,
Ta ti gona 'bwah pem mo kanoo?	Why's my sister crying like that?
Goki'di nana	She's chanting to comfort
Gona 'bwah pem mo kan	My sister's crying like that,
Goki'di nana 'ci	Chanting to comfort the child.
Tirko goki'di wan ka ta?	What can redeem Tirko's grief?
Tirko goki'di wan ka ta?	What can redeem Tirko's grief?
Ta ti gona 'bwah pem mo?	Why's my sister crying?
Nam pem pena lo'bi jisa rumee	My sister's children are playing in the caves of the underworld,
Inam pem pena lo'bi jisa rumee	They are playing in the caves of the underworld.
Tirko goki'di wan ka ta?	What can redeem Tirko's grief?
Tirko goki'di wan ka ta?	What can redeem Tirko's grief?
Ta ti ona 'bwah pem ya golu kan?	Why does my sister cry wherever she goes?
Ta ti ona 'bwah pem ya golu kan?	Why does my sister cry wherever she goes?
Eeyee	Ah,
Jwa ti 'bakaa eyee	I am exhausted by death, ah.
Jwa ti 'bakaa e	I am exhausted by death,
Eeyee	Ah.
I'bwah pem goki'di nana 'ci	My sisters chant to comfort the child,
I'bwah pem goki'di nana	My sisters chant to comfort.
Ta ti gona 'bwah pem mo kanee?	Why's my sister crying so?
Ta ti gona 'bwah pem mo kanee?	Why's my sister crying so?
Ee	Ah,
Ki bur	Blistered.
Ha'da, kunyi uni wa	Ha'da, dig for them,
Bur me'd ki bur	Dig till our hands are blistered.
Inam pem pena lo'bee	My sister's children are playing,
Inam pem pena lo'bi jisa rumee	My sister's children are playing in the caves of the underworld.

Finally, I quote Nyane's song; she is another sister of the same birth-group as Danga and Tente, and her song also refers to the death of Jethdhu. It is primarily about the death of the girl Corke: and Nyane calls on her brother Ḵasar to begin the chanting, but also on the men in general to fight. She demands to know why people are accepting death 'coldly', that is without fighting those who have caused it; she herself threatens to go to the Bunyan, that is, to make accusations to the authorities; but 'we are afraid of the word of the Government,' and so do not immediately seek vengeance. Fighting leads to police, courts, and imprisonment, and the courts do not accept witchcraft as a justification for retaliation, even sometimes punishing those who point out witches.

Ḵasar ṭela ko ntwa/a	Ḵasar, begin the chanting first
Kanyke biri gwath n'kosha 'kosh	Kanyke is urging the men to fight
Gopa Corke ka pije/	Dig up Corke [from the grave]!
'Kosh ma kapen ta?	Struck with fear of what?
Jwa ma Jethdhu mane?	Where is the body of Jethdhu?
Ki jwa 'bakaa e	I am exhausted by death.
Ona gus Bunyan mo 'te/ ba	They say they will go to the Government
Nyane 'kosha' kosh mo 'te	Let Nyane fight,
Ata mina ana ça'bi wu jwan 'thupu'd ka yempa/ kan?	Why do we sit and accept death coolly?
Kona ḵona dhalku/ ki 'kosha'kosh	Let us weep, weep and not fight;
Gwath mane kun mina ana biri 'kosha'kosh?	Where are the men we can urge to fight?
/E ti go ko jwa ga 'cesh moye	You are weeping for the dead of the earth,
Haga mina wu mo	While I am going to die too.
Gwom Bunyan koka aman	We are afraid of the word of the Government.

Between my fieldwork in the 1960s when I collected these songs in Waḵa'cesh, and my revisit in 1983, not only older individuals but also a number of my contemporaries had died, including one woman in childbirth, and an unknown number of small children. Tente had lost during this interval not only his mother, but a sister, his brother Ḵasar, and a child. He had become too tired of all this death and had in fact left Waḵa'cesh to live in another hamlet on the far side of the river. Over the course of his life and a succession of marriages, he had lost something in the order of ten children. I mention these things because they are the painful context in which we have to evaluate 'the ethnography'. Death is not hidden away by the Uduk or other Koman peoples, as apparently it is among some of the Nilotic peoples.[5] News of a death is advertised immediately by taking up the dramatic musical chant which accompanies the whole period of the funeral rites and remains vivid in the memory over the years. When death is very close, relatives may gather before it actually occurs; and there is some evidence that relatives may even help out the last breath. Mary Beam and Betty Cridland (former missionaries at Chali) have told me of going to visit an old man who had been sick for a long time. They had been called in at the end to give him an injection. They refused, as they could see that he was dying. Mary Beam looked at her companion and shook her head; whereupon the sister of the dying man pushed on his chest with her hands, releasing his last breath. This account seems to make explicit what underlies the whole range of funeral ritual, not only among the Uduk but among their Koman neighbours where burial may be long delayed (see Appendix 1). The main point seems to be to separate out the life which inheres in the flesh, blood, abdominal organs, and breath, so that the disembodied *arum* may go quite safely to the underworld. If the *arum* inhering in live bodies is allowed to linger on in decaying organs, blood, and flesh, *that* may indeed be dangerous. The re-emergence of a body decayed but still animated by *arum* is a vision to instil dread and awe.

I have already referred to the idea of *arum* motivating the body, leading it about, and so on, and to Tente's (only partly joking) suggestion that if the *arum* of a part, such as a tooth, decays, then that part will itself decay and fall away. It is as if advancing senility, assisted by disease, is itself seen as a general decay setting in, and death is the eventual outcome of that decay. The decay leads to death, rather than being the result of it. The contrast between sound young flesh on the one hand, and ageing, almost decaying flesh on the other, and the processes of slowing down, injury, and putrefaction, are powerful images for a people with a hunting past.

Before describing the modern burial rites of the northern Uduk, I should introduce something of their wider context. There is good evidence, going back to the last century, to suppose that among the Koman peoples classic 'double death rites' have been practised:

---

[5] Compare Lienhardt, *Divinity and Experience*, p. 289.

that is, the body (at least of important persons) was disembowelled, dried, and later buried in the earth after a long period of time, perhaps years. These practices, or their analogues, are still found among the southern neighbours of the Uduk, and within living memory have been known among the southern Uduk themselves. Mary Beam and Betty Cridland told me that in the 1940s, in the Yabus valley, they smelt a body in the roof of a hut. It had been disembowelled and the innards buried, and would itself be buried after six months or a year. They claimed the Chali people used to do the same. Further evidence of the regional context of delayed burial practices may be found in Appendix 1.

By their elaborate and protracted burial rites, the Uduk and the other Koman peoples are not so much trying to keep the deceased with them, as to make sure the 'spirit' (Uduk *arum*) is able to make a complete and clean break with the body. If a person is prematurely or improperly buried, the separation may not so easily take place, and the spirit may hang around too long in the rotting flesh. This is surely the reason for the women at a funeral described by Malcolm Forsberg shrieking at the body of an old woman not to come back, and closing her eyes with cherry-stones;[6] and this is the reason why, among the northern Uduk today, long-buried bones are sometimes dug up, checked on, and touched with a spot of red oil.

There is a close affinity between these practices and the rites analysed for the Dayak of Borneo by Robert Hertz in his classic essay on the representation of death.[7] For the Uduk too there is a dramatic enactment of the translation of the deceased spirit from this world to the next, as the body decays, and the living mourners readjust themselves. But for the Uduk, the effort is primarily towards the active disengagement of the spirit from themselves, and to keeping the living 'outside', well away from that slide towards decay and death which draws on everyone. The double death rite is here not an automatic 'rite of passage' to restore a state of normality, but an active struggle to maintain a safe distance between the world of the living and that of the dead. But let us return to the funeral scene.

[6] Malcolm Forsberg, *Land Beyond the Nile* (New York: Harper), 1958, pp. 200–1.
[7] R. Hertz, 'A contribution to the study of the collective representation of death' [1907], in *Death and the Right Hand*, trans. R. and C. Needham (London: Cohen & West), 1960.

News of a death spreads quickly. The death chant (*ko jwa*, to cry for death) is a vigorous combination of falling notes, in three or four parts taken up by voice after voice descending in echoing cadence. There are some cries and interjections, such as '*Ҫiŋkina/*! We are all *ҫiŋkina/*!' ('We are lost! Bereaved!') rising over the wailed or hummed notes. From inside the hut of mourning, the chant soon carries over the air, to a distance of some miles on a calm day, and youngsters are dispatched with the message to the homes of remote relatives. Even for a child, there will be a large gathering, and for an adult, it may comprise hundreds. New arrivals will hurl themselves in the hut to cry and join the chanting, and if closely related, to embrace and weep over the deceased. Periodically, those inside the hut, sweating and crying, will leave for a break, while yet others press in.

There are many tasks at a funeral, but there is no sense of hurry. People say that in the past, a burial would not be completed for two or three days (more in the Yabus). Today, because of former mission and government urging, burial is completed more quickly. If the death occurs in the night or the early morning, it should be over by the evening, but if an adult dies during the day the business will not be finished until the next morning. The body is first washed and shaved. Animals are provided normally by the father and mother's brothers of the deceased. For an adult, it is likely that a goat or a sheep will be placed alongside the body, facing it; its mouth will be held closed and it will be suffocated as people sit on it. This is known as *dil abor*, press to the chest. One or more goats may be killed outside by being knocked hard with heavy sticks. It is said quite explicitly that these deaths, without the loss of blood or breath, are intended to keep the *arum* within the body, so that the whole animal, body and life, may survive in another place. If a very senior person has died, and an ox is to be killed at the funeral, this may also take a form of *dil abor*, pressing to the chest. But in this case, the beast will be tethered with a rope around its neck, and the rope passed through the hut door to the right hand of the corpse. The people will then spear the animal. I have even heard of a funeral where a herd of cattle was let loose at the funeral, and spears were sent flying at them from all directions (which evokes the scene of the hunt). I have been told of a particular funeral where live ewes were placed in the grave before it was filled in, so that the deceased might drink milk in the next world. This was the 1949 funeral of Jibirdhalla, a leading 'man of Arum' in Chali. At the funeral goats and cattle may also have their throats cut in the normal way, to 'make blood' for *arum*, rather than to send an animal with the deceased. A skin will be prepared for the corpse to lie on in the grave, and a number of women will be threading cotton waistbands and beads, or grinding sesame and red ochre for the anointing of the body. A number of men will be digging the grave, a site having been chosen near the edge of the hamlet.

The old-style Uduk grave is a rounded chamber, big enough in the case of an adult for two women to enter and arrange the corpse. The chamber is round 'like a hut' so that the deceased can be enclosed, and not 'out in the open'. The grave is constructed by first excavating a fairly wide saucer-shaped depression in the earth, and then digging a narrow, deep hole in the middle of it, which will be the entrance to the main chamber below. A great deal of work is involved in constructing this type of grave, and it is now fairly common to make a 'Bunyan' (in this context, Sudanese Arab) grave instead. This is shallow, rectangular, with a narrow trench at the bottom for the corpse. The trench is sealed with logs before the grave is filled in. This style of burial still seems exposed, 'out in the open', to an Uduk eye. In the old-style burial, the corpse is richly covered with beads and red ochre, and with new waist-cords and cowrie shell tails for women; but increasingly, especially with the rectangular grave, the body is simply wrapped in a sewn shroud of new cloth, and sometimes also in the woven cane mat the deceased used to sleep on.

For the actual burial, the corpse is normally laid on the left side with the head towards the hill from which the father's people came. This is the territorial community to which the deceased remains linked. There are gourds of oil and various personal possessions close at hand, lying on the prepared skin and perhaps covered by another. When the grave is filled in, all can wash; and then perhaps, if there is a little coffee available, or some other refreshment, it may be taken. But the funeral meat is normally divided among the groups of guests, to be taken away and eaten in the forest on the way home. It is dangerous meat, especially in the case of those animals killed without the letting of blood. Funeral meat is not eaten by those with a vulnerable Liver, or by children. The next morning, a chicken is likely to be used to Brush the grave, and is then beaten to death on it.

The deceased is said to sleep for three days in the grave, and then to come out. It is during the period that follows that it may disturb people, making noises and movement in the old hut, and people may see it in their dreams. This is the time when it can suddenly become very dangerous, and strike people: in this state it is the *aruma 'cesh*, the *arum* of the earth or the ground, which can knock people down in a sudden wind, send them into fits, or even kill them. This can happen at random, but is likely to be directed at the surviving members of a birth-group who have been quarrelling, for the unleashed force of the deceased's being can apparently take this retaliatory form. We might first assume that this *aruma 'cesh*, the 'ground' *arum*, is perhaps a separate type of spirit. The fact that it is feared, even dreaded, and only rarely spoken of openly, suggests that it belongs in a separate category within the range of 'spirits'. This has been the view taken by the missionary translators at Chali, who have treated *aruma 'cesh* in the Biblical context not only as an evil spirit, but as the very epitome of evil, assimilated to Satan (see the detailed discussion in Chapter 4).

The fundamental idea, however, is not that of a distinct type of spirit, but rather the life-power of a deceased person in the initial stages of escape from the decaying flesh, in its freshness carrying with it the very stench of death. It is scarcely surprising that those who buried it, and gathered for the funeral, may find their Livers upset. It is common for one to feel aches, pains, and nausea after a burial (for which there are good reasons we would also recognize). More than once my own odd bouts of fever or exhaustion were attributed to recent funerals. But the dangerous aura of the burial, attributed to the release of the *aruma 'cesh*, is not permanent, nor is it morally evil in a 'satanic' sense. The danger will pass with time, and eventually the *arum* will be quite freed from the residue of the body and go permanently to the underworld where it will not pose a threat in the same way at all. To make this clearer, it might be possible to render *aruma 'cesh* as '*arum* of the grave', rather than of the earth or the ground. The earth referred to is the earth packed around the corpse in the grave, rather than the earth as opposed to the sky.

For youngsters who die, it has long been common practice to hold a small rite a few days after the burial, cut an animal, and then treat the whole thing as over. For infants, not even this need

be done. There is an increasing tendency, I discovered on my
last visit, to hold a minimal concluding rite of this kind even for
adults, modelled on Islamic practice and known as *mii apurash*.
However, in the past, there was an intermediate period lasting
weeks, months, or even years after an adult's death, concluded by
a very important rite. Close relatives during the long mourning
period Sat Black and many others would refrain from wearing
beads, dancing, and so forth. The full concluding rite is known
as *asuŋ 'kupaje/*, the Beer of the Grave, and still takes place for
senior persons.

A large amount of beer is brewed, and the night before it is
ready, fresh chanting takes place. On the following morning, the
grave is Brushed, and the men start work on what is said to be the
main purpose of the rite, 'fixing' or 'settling' the grave (see Plate
1b). Today it is common simply to dig up a good deal of material
from the top of the grave, and then to pack it down again more
firmly. However, there is more to this act than is immediately
apparent. The general practice in quite recent times, even among
the northern Uduk, was to dig out one or more of the bones, and
anoint them with red ochre, before returning them to the grave. At
one rite for Settling the Grave I asked the men digging if they were
going to get up a bone, expecting a strong denial. They explained
quite casually that on this occasion they were not, because another
burial had just taken place in more or less the same spot, and they
didn't want to disturb it. Otherwise, they would have taken a bone
and put red ochre on it. Red ochre was on this occasion, as always,
freely used to cover various belongings of the deceased. Among
these, for a man, are his weapons and musical instruments, which
will be returned to his father's people (see Plate 2a). Red ochre is
also used to anoint the close relatives who have been in mourning.
Then there will be *athele/* dancing (Plate 2b), and great rejoicing.
The *arum* of the deceased is now quite separate, and has moved
finally to the land of the dead.

I would like to quote from a conversation with Rusko, which
took place in 1983. By this time he was an enthusiastic Christian,
but happy to elaborate on some of the views he had come to reject.
I had suggested that perhaps the *aruma 'cesh*, rather than being the
Evil Spirit of the Bible, was simply the human spirit left behind by
one who had just died, and that after the beer for fixing the grave,
it would go. He seemed to agree.

Yes, that's what is said among the Uduk here! If a man is buried today, then he stays for three days; he stays for three days, and then he appears out, and gets busy bothering people in their homes there, creates a lot of disturbance in his village there, in many huts, *gur, gur, gur, gur*. People say, 'What's that over there? It's *arum*; there isn't anyone to treat him.' After a while, people hold a small rite for him, and treat him with beer. They dig up his grave a bit, then fix it properly, and then it's finished, we are happy, and he goes. He doesn't bother people again. Just occasionally.

The place where the spirits go is known as *pam arum*, or *bampa ma rum*, villages of the *arum*, or in a more general sense 'land of the dead'. This land is underground, and the particular settlements of the dead are supposed to be under the various hills. Each hill is associated with a territorial cluster of birth-groups, and the allegiance of a person to a territory is normally through the father's birth-group; this is why people are usually buried with the head towards that hill from which their father comes. All a man's children will join the community of the *arum* under that hill. Graves are not publicly marked, though their sites are privately remembered by close kin.

There is a special category of deaths which I should note here, and to which I shall return. This is the category of those who do not die in the village and have a village burial, but die out in the bush. Most commonly, this happens as a result of hunting accidents, or from fighting. If a person dies in this violent way, the special hunting songs (*gwaya kaŋis*) are sung, with dancing and rhythmic feet-stamping, which I have described above in connection with the Leopard rites (Chapter 1 (ii) (*b*)) and which have now been assimilated to the rituals of the Ebony Men (see Chapter 5).

The deceased is buried in a shallow grave with white ash, no animals are offered, no mourning takes place, and no Beer for the Grave to conclude mourning. The body is covered with leaves. On rare occasions a person is lost, or drowned, and not buried at all. Like those given the burial in the bush, these *arum* never make their way to the underground settlements of the dead. The wild bushland remains their abode.

For the Uduk death rites should be done thoroughly. Embodied life should be thoroughly disposed of (which is not always possible today). They are afraid in some way of the embodied life lingering and returning. They do not mind seeing ethereal apparitions from the underworld, but they are in awe and to some extent dread of 'resurrection'. The main bodily resurrection of which one hears in the Uduk villages (or did in the 1960s) was that of the former prophet-healer, Leina; and when he emerged his body was eaten by white ants (see Chapter 3). The case of Leina, as a potent risen healer, is often compared with that of Jesus Christ. But here I am anticipating Chapter 4.

(v) The land of the dead

Uduk are of the opinion that life in the land of the dead, that is the realm of those thoroughly and properly buried, is very realistic and much like that they already know. Villages are inhabited by all—old and young, women, men, and babies; there are even cows, goats, and chickens. Normal activities such as watering animals, or dancing in the evenings, are carried on in the same way as among the living. There are many, many 'people' in the land of *arum*—all those in fact who have lived and died before us. Sometimes the Uduk say 'Only a few of us are left outside now;' meaning '... outside the grave.' Those who have died are buried in the earth, inside holes in the ground. As with the living body, the *inside* is the place of the essence, the *arum*, whereas the outside is the temporary place of stay. People go on existing in the land of the dead—they do not seem to die there, nor are new babies born. In ordinary villages 'outside', however, life is very insecure, and death is known to be very close. Life is punctuated by regular deaths, of people of all ages; and the landscape is littered with the graves of people one has known. *Arum* can take anyone away at any time; *arum* is more often spoken of as the bringer of death than the giver of life—you may be struck by *arum* (*'kosh ma rum*), or *arum* may 'cut your throat' (*'cith e'kus*) and finish you off at short notice. It is quite true that *arum* is commonly represented as a form of 'life force'. But the imagination of the Uduk seldom focuses on that force as an originator. It dwells more on that force as it is *now* concentrated (because we have had so many deaths) in the land of the dead. There is, moreover, a feeling that we are all on our journey towards it.

How do we know what *pam arum* is like? There are perhaps three levels of seriousness at which the Uduk tell stories of the land of the dead and its inmates. To take the most light-hearted: at a beer drink, people may exchange anecdotes and stories which include encounters with *arum* by night, and which Uduk usually find hilarious. Sometimes these *arum* are said to have long hair and pale skins. Also they may smell bad, with the smell of death (*wuruŋgu'b*). Characteristically, a young man is returning home from a beer-party or a dance at another village, when he hears chattering or the beating music of the *athele/*. He goes to join the dance, or asks the dim figures the way in the dark. But the dancers suddenly disappear, or his companions chase him, and in the morning he realizes what he has seen. Maybe a woman going for water at sunset finds a man at the river, who suddenly seems not to be a human being at all. A traveller may take shelter in an empty hut and find '*arum*' companions there; or a young adventurer may follow some flirtatious girls at sunset. They are elusive, and turn out to be *arum* girls. In the early evening—when light is fading, and sleeping animals are beginning to stir: a good time for experiences by the river—people frequently report the lowing of *arum* cattle from below the water of deep pools, and even 'goat droppings' rising to the surface. (Methane gas is a possible explanation for this effect.) These stories are told in a jokey vein and rarely seem to have a serious outcome. They circulate widely and are popular with children, and, though throwing light on 'the other world', are not regarded as major experiences of contact with it.

1. *Ha'da*

People ['*kwani*] were dancing the *athele/* at Pandhudhu aYoma. [Yoma is the name of the big baobab at the Chali mission.] I went along and I was young, as small as this [indicating]. The *arum* called me by name, 'Ha'da!' I said, 'Yes!' 'Where are you going?' 'I am going to dance, going to dance *athele/*.' They came and surrounded me ... I went along in the midst of the *arum* like that. The *arum* were close around me, as we are sitting now. Some were leading me on the path, others were bunching behind me, and yet others came in the middle, on both sides of me, with a *haw, haw, haw*. We came along thus; I went on and on, and arrived at the dance. But the *arum* left me at the dance-ground there. I said to myself, are all those people of mine gone over there, who were gathered round me? Where are my people who came with me? Goodness! They had completely disappeared. I considered this. I thought a little and said, 'Ay! What did they all surround me so strangely for?' I didn't know they were *arum*. I thought they were human beings ['*kwanim pa*], as we came along together....

It was my father's people they say. They came to call my name. My father's people, with Sirko and others, are said to have died there.

2. Dhirmath

A man was sleeping alone in the last remaining hut of an abandoned
village. Gwarayo was his name: he was my father's brother. The villagers
had all moved to a new site, but he refused to go with his brothers, and
stayed behind in the old site. It was raining, and he was sleeping up in the
roof.

Now, some *arum* outside thought that the hut was empty, although in
fact there was a human being sleeping up in the roof. They were running
along, chanting, *atajintaj, U-uh, atajintaj, U-uh* . . . [unintelligible rhythmic
noises] and they entered the hut, where a small fire was smouldering. They
warmed themselves, and said to each other, 'Ah, now we're getting warm
at last.' All the time the man was up there in the roof. He took a wooden
stool, and smashed it on the head of an *arum*! They scrambled outside
and slithered about in the mud, like that.

3. Saba

Bade came back from drinking beer, and went to sleep. But he wanted to
urinate. He got up and put his penis through a gap in the [woven wattle]
wall of the hut. He put it through the wall. He put his penis through the
wall and urinated outside. An *arum* seized him by the penis, *jip*. He cried,
'*Waah, waah, waah*! Ko Kanthi [his wife], help me, *waah*! Ko Kanthi,
help me, *waah*! . . . Manyci, Manyci, help me, *waah*! Manyci, help me,
wa-ah!' The *arum* had seized his penis; that's why he cried so loudly. He
cried out a great deal. The *arum* then let him go, and he went to bed. He
climbed up into the roof, leaving his wife down below. He was trembling
severely. He slept up there. It was weak of him to cry like that.

At a rather more serious level, stories are told of experiences or
encounters with *arum* which had, or might have had, sombre
consequences. For example, there are certain holes in the ground,
in the bush, which lead down to *pam arum*, and it is very dangerous
to fall down them. I heard of a man in Bellila who was called out
at night to chase a hyena from the village. He ran out after the
animal, and fell down a hole. He came out in *pam arum*, and it
was midday. He slept one night there and then came back. An
experience of this kind might make a person very ill.

I have heard several versions of a story of a woman going to fetch
water from the river at a place called Gumyi'de, notorious for
arum. She was foolish enough to go in the late afternoon, was
frightened by an *arum* man, and later died. In the wet season,
particularly in times past, Gumyi'de is a place where a deep and
wide pool forms, and you may expect to hear lowing, bleating,
barking, and crowing, all from beneath the water. Here is one

version of the story, by Shara. She described it as a true story, *gwololop̱ gana/*.

A woman went to the river in the late afternoon. And the water *arum* of Gumyi'de was sitting there carving a throwing-stick. And he was called by the woman, 'You fellow there, carving that throwing-stick, come and lift this water for me.' The man replied, 'You won't run away from me?' She said, 'Why should I run away from you? Who are you, that I should run away?' He repeated, 'You're not going to run away from me?' She said, 'Who are you anyway? Please come and lift this thing for me. I'm going home as the sun is setting.' And so then the man got up and came, came slowly, slowly. He had been covered with red oil by his wife, and was sitting under the tree carving his throwing-stick; but he got up and came, came, came, and lifted the water for the woman.

But the woman fled at the sight of his great red armpits. They were red, bright scarlet, when the man raised his arms. He raised his arms up in a great sweep like this; raised them right up. The woman cried, '*Waaah*!' and dropped the great water-pot, *dush*. She fled; and at the time she was pregnant. She ran, and the man also ran. And after a while the man spoke, and said 'Go: and call the child Gumyi'de, Gumyi'de, Gumyi'de; Wanos, Wanos, Wanos [this means 'Break the pot'].' And later it became dark, and people went to sleep. But that woman died, with the child in her belly.

In another version of this story, the *arum* man came after the woman, beat her until she was dead, and then he married her.

At the place of Gumyi'de, there are many *arum* living at the bottom of the water. Danga told me that a man was caught by *arum* once, and taken down into the water, to the *arum* village at the bottom. It was a dry place, with no mud, and the *arum* made fire and cooked things as we do. The man lived there for some time; but he did not eat anything, and came back. It is a crucial matter not to share the food, drink, or tobacco of the *arum* people; nor to have sexual connection with them, for these actions seal your fate. You will not return alive, but will be incorporated into the *arum* community. The *arum* do often seem to take the initiative and behave provocatively; I have heard that if the *arum* at Gumyi'de do not like you, they can make the water muddy (and not good for drinking or washing). If you comment on the dirty water you will get sick. At the end of the rainy season, the water becomes stagnant; but if you go to drink there, you should not scoop off the scum, for the dung of cows, goats, and so forth, will come to the surface. At the mission I once heard that the water is *dhathu/*, but I did not hear this in the villages. One young man (named Washan) from Borfa was said to have met an *arum* in the forest, and being *bu'th ma rum* (seized by *arum*) he became confused and ran very fast towards Gumyi'de (to join the *arum* people there). Fortunately the people of Gindi managed to catch him just in time.

Not only Gumyi'de, but all rivers and especially pools are potentially hazardous as places of *arum*. The *'kwanim pa*, people say, are afraid of the water (*ko yi'de/*). 'Why?'—'Because there is *arum* in it.' The frogs (abhorred by people, and said to have taught them the death-chant) live there, and birds, and if you imitate the sounds of these creatures you will get sick. One part of the Tombak river is called 'Gurmin', that is *gure/mi* (goat dung, of *arum* goats).

Danga told me various tales of people being lost to the *arum* of the water. Others were nearly lost, but just survived to tell the tale.

Some Mufu people came [from Jebel Mufwa] ... and wanted to drink the water at Gumyi'de ... they cleared the surface of the water like this, and there was just goat dung coming up.... And the Mufu went on trying to clear a place by splashing with their hands, saying 'Let's drink some which is clean.' One of them was dealing with the water, and the other began insulting [the *arum*], *Ruth gure/ ka 'dol!* [an insult in the Mufu language], 'Why do you treat us badly like this, mixing up the water?'

Then these *arum* chased them ... they fled, and the water itself chased them. A mass of water chased them, and they fled. *Thu'b, thu'b, thu'b.* They punched great holes with their feet, they punched holes, *bup, bup,* but found they couldn't run fast. They went down into a hole. They went into a hole, *gurug!*—a hole over there.

And another time, girl *arum* came to play outside. They came from under the water. And human boys came to chase them, thinking they were girls, ordinary human girls. They chased them because they were wearing lots of beads, and were covered with red oil; they were very beautiful like human girls.... They wore bangles here on their ankles, and bells here. They went towards the bush there ... and some boys found them and said, 'Ay there are lots of girls over there, lots of girls.' They chased them, chased them, wanting to take hold of them and have sex.... But they could run very fast. The girls could run so fast that they kept ahead of the boys, and threw themselves into the water, *goow!* The boys cried *'Waawoo!* We have been chasing a crowd of *arum* girls!'

The dogs of *arum* bark, they say *haw! haw!*—like that. And Harpa [blind, but a very entertaining storyteller] said that he once trod on a little *arum* baby with his foot. It was a little child mislaid by *arum*, put on the ground, laid down to rest on the ground!

On the point of death, a person may expect to glimpse *pam arum*. Few recover to report their experience, but occasionally this does happen. Danga gave me a very circumstantial account of Yuha's experience of the land of the dead. Yuha was a 'cousin' within the same birth-group.

Yuha has seen the land of *arum* ... when he was sick and about to die. ... He said there were very many cattle in the land of *arum* ... and he saw his brother who is in the grave there, called Mura, and also 'Ba'bko, our brother, who was born after Tente and who died and is in the grave there. He saw them in their graves. And a big tobacco gourd ... which was red ... was given to Yuha, with a lot of tobacco [snuff] inside; they were saying, take some snuff. And Yuha took the gourd, in order to tip out some snuff. But the brother of 'Ba'bko was angry with Yuha, saying, 'Eh! Yuha, what are you doing this for?' He knocked the tobacco from Yuha's hand.

He prevented him?

Yes, prevented him. If he had snuffed it, he would then have died. If you eat the food of the *arum*, you will die. You will not remain alive. You will die. You must not eat the food of the *arum*, for you live among people. It is your Genius which goes to the land of *arum*. And Yuha saw his Genius come back from the land of *arum*. ...

Yuha said it is very nice there.

Why did the man prevent Yuha from staying?

So that he would stay outside longer. 'Don't die,' he said.

Danga went on to tell me of the experience of Madhe, who fell in a pool while fishing, near a Bunyan village, and later, in a dream, visited a village of Bunyan *arum*.

And then, Madhe. Yes, he went ... right to the Bunyan village [near Borfa, or Gindi]. He went to fish ... at a place called Kokota. ... They beat the fish with throwing sticks; there was a great pool of fish, very big, and deep as that tall tree over there. And he chased a great fat fish like this ... with fire, until he went and fell in the middle of the pool. The fish were making a noise, *'do 'do 'do 'do.* ... Then he came out, and made a dash, and started to shiver ... and became sick immediately ... in one day after doing this. ... People led him home and he slept, and he went [in a dream] and saw the village of the *arum* Bunyan.

All the Bunyan came to speak to him. He was covered over with a cloth; Mahde was in the hut of the *arum* there ... he was sick and lay on the ground in the hut of the *arum*. ... And all the *arum* wore long *jellabiyyas* [Arab dress]. Great turbans were coiled on their heads, and they carried big sticks in their hands. They were trailing their sticks along the ground, saying, '*Salaam alekum*' [an Arab greeting]. They came in the hut to see their guest and chat with him. And some spoke thus: 'Ay! This man is a guest and his place is very far away. It is not near to our village. Don't do anything bad for him. Let him go back to their home.' Some spoke like this. The *arum* Bunyan said, 'Don't let this man do anything. For he is a man from afar. Leave him alone and he will go home.'

And eventually Madhe got better. He came home. He didn't want to stay in Borfa there, but fled home to Pam'Be for good. He stays in Pam'Be, and says he will not go back there. He doesn't want to for he knows the land of *arum* in the hole there. Madhe wanted to tell you this story himself properly but there were too many people ... because he knows the land of *arum*. The village of the *arum* Bunyan in the hole there. He used to say, 'I'm telling you seriously. Maybe you think I'm deceiving you. Ay! I almost died. I really have seen the Bunyan village: the great Bunyan village in the hole of *arum* there.'

Again, the mother of Bagi saw *pam arum* when she was very ill. The people there had chickens, goats, and cows (explained to me on this occasion as coming from funeral killings). The *arum* people cook food, while you are sitting there as a guest. Some of them will say 'Eat', while others may dissuade you. If you begin to eat, some *arum* may knock your hand away from the food, saying 'Don't eat!' If you eat you will die, but if you don't eat you will get well. The mother of Bagi saw her father there, and he said, 'Where have you come from? No, I don't want you to come here. Are you giving her food to eat? Don't give her anything, let her return, I don't want her to come here.' She did not eat, and she recovered from her illness. Then she told the people this story.

William Danga told me of eating together with *arum* in a dream; he became ill, but fortunately recovered. He then sang this song, with the lyre (I quote only the basic lines, on which there are many recombinations and variations in the performance):

Pos 'kakika	I have eaten grain.
'Kana posa rum	I ate *arum* grain,
Aha/ 'kana posa rum	I ate *arum* grain,
Pos 'kakika ki jan	I have eaten it in a dream.
'Thina dhan'thi	I got dysentery,
Çika ta'da mme'd	Passed it on to mother.
Rapka ba/ cuyi mis	Rapka, up you get please!
Suska ta'da Pany Jale/	Lead mother to Chali.

Rapka was Danga's sister; at Chali there was a small medical dispensary. Danga also told me that in his dream he had shared a gourd of boiled sorghum grains with some *arum* people. The grain was dressed with oil, which made it particularly dangerous.

The incidents I have described above indicate a certain 'give and take' between the world of living people and that of *arum*. With prudence, you can avoid risky contact with *arum*; you can be sensible and avoid sleeping in deserted hamlets, going to stagnant pools at sunset, falling down a hole at night, and so forth. It is difficult to avoid dreaming of *arum* however. If you are ill, perhaps on the point of death, it seems that your Genius may be tempted by food or tobacco, which would take you fully into the land of *arum*. In cases of this kind, the *arum* themselves cannot be said to be malicious, or fatally powerful, and they are not spoken of with terror or awe. Almost everyone knows somebody who has survived such an encounter.

However, at the most serious level of encounter with *arum*, terror and awe do predominate. It is only in a subdued tone that a reference is made to *aruma 'cesh*, *arum* of the earth, ground, or grave, for this is *arum* in a form that can take an aggressive initiative, and attack people, even striking them dead. As I have explained previously, this danger comes from the recently buried, and others not properly settled in the permanent villages of the dead.

When speaking of the actions of *arum* upon living people, there are two distinct expressions used by the Uduk. One is *'kosh*, to strike, to kill; and the other is *bu'th*, to take hold of, to seize. *Arum* in a variety of modes can either 'strike' or 'seize', but the *aruma 'cesh* only strikes. It is as if it were a blind force, and not a 'person', even metaphorically, in itself. *Aruma 'cesh* do not hold dances, herd goats, and so forth; they do not make appearances in human form. However, the force of *aruma 'cesh* is very real. It can knock people down or roll them over into the fire, and when it strikes, it is a matter for the attention of immediate kin within the birth-group.

A period of bad gossip or quarrelling within the birth-group is the context in which *arum*, especially in the form of the *aruma 'cesh*, is thought likely to strike. A mild affliction may be diagnosed as the action of *arum* long dead, people of the birth-group in a collective sense—this is spoken of as *arum pa pana*, the *arum* of our village. But the most dramatic incidents when people collapse and faint, or have fits, are likely to be attributed, even without a formal diagnosis, to the action of the *arum* of a recently buried member of the birth-group, that is, *aruma 'cesh*. Among the many healing rites I have seen in connection with *arum* matters, only a few were held because of the action of *aruma 'cesh*. But they were certainly the most urgent and people were fearful, even shaken, in a way I had rarely seen. Relatives of the birth-group are immediately summoned to spray water from their mouths on the person struck, and there must be an immediate blood offering ('*KP*: 190).

With the completion of the death rites, the *arum* has left the brief fulfilment of its fleshly existence 'outside', and joins the timeless world beyond the grave. In the realm of *arum* there are no fresh beginnings; there is a direct and unbroken continuity with the first great beginnings described in myth. There is even a tradition that some beings seen out in the wild may come directly from the primeval Birapinya tree. They look human but are really *arum* in the wild sense.

Losko, one of my best historical informants, was once giving us accounts of specific events in the past, when he paused and then volunteered a story which he clearly regarded as being true in the same way as the events of conflict and flight he had previously been describing. He had been a boy in the region of Jebel Bisho, and in that place people used to see a curious thing, he said. He had seen it himself, although it is no longer seen today. Beings known as *lem* or *yinya* would come, in single file, like people, walking along in the distance and carrying great earthenware pots (of the type normally called *lem*, after which they were named) on their heads. They would always disappear in the river, at a place called Bwata. They came from Pur (the Daga valley home of the Shyita, a people encompassed by the Uduk self-name '*kwanim pa*). They were very black. They spoke among themselves, but nobody ever ventured near enough to hear what they said, nor even to hear what language they spoke. Losko paused for a while and then added, 'They came from the Birapinya. They were maybe *tombwasho* [wild creatures], *arum*, *arum thus* [bad *arum*].' Medke, a woman of middle years who was listening soberly to this account, commented in a matter-of-fact way that these beings were probably human beings ('*kwanim pa*) who had died long ago, and who had come to life again with the *yina pe*, the Moon Oil.

Several threads were thus drawn together. Beings actually seen at first hand, or claimed to have been seen, were *arum* not only in the sense that they were *'kwanim pa* who had formerly died, and reappeared. They were also *arum* in the sense that they were the timeless things of myth. In general, before people became fully civilized human beings, they were *arum*, and in the account above, Losko and Medke referred spontaneously to the myths of the Birapinya tree, and the Moon Oil, which enabled people to revive three days after dying (*'KP*: 59–86). Only when the great tree was burned, and the gourd of Moon Oil broken, did death become final, and thus was created the gulf between the realm of *arum* and that of the *'kwanim pa*. The *lem* creatures were assumed to have survived from that early time, and of course they survived in the bush: they were 'maybe creatures of the wild'.

Death recurs endlessly in the villages. But the wild bushland and forest holds the key, and the promise, to the possibility of resisting it, and even of survival; this is the message perceived, and read in various ways from the signs, the memories, and the myths of the plants and the creatures out there. In Part III of this book I return to this theme.

On Moral Knowledge

> ... the central concept of morality is 'the individual' thought
> of as knowable by love.
>
> Iris Murdoch, *The Sovereignty of Good*

Tangible persons, such as, dear reader, you or I when we are off
guard and relaxing over a drink, are seldom encountered in a
journey through the academic texts. In Western philosophical and
sociological discourse (too often about 'ourselves') we find of course
a dominating 'I', but this is a distilled and rarefied ego spoken of
virtually in the third person, an 'I' with 'its' motivations,
conscience, will, soul, or rationality. Hypotheses constructed upon
this 'I' have sometimes been used to interpret society, religion, and
history.

But we are moving with less confident historical times and doubts
are creeping in: consider for a moment Derek Parfit's claims. 'We
are not separately existing entities, apart from our brains and
bodies, and various interrelated physical and mental events. Our
existence just involves the existence of our brains and bodies, and
the doing of our deeds, and the thinking of our thoughts ...'[1] As I
understand Parfit's work, it should be possible for us to disengage
ourselves from that notion of the soul-based individuality which
Marcel Mauss, among others, ascribed to the unique legal and
religious development of Western society,[2] and yet remain persons
within a wider moral community. Parfit regards *Reasons and
Persons* as pioneering the study of 'Non-Religious Ethics'.[3]

Doubts are spreading, too, over the treatment of 'other societies',
so often still assumed beyond some moral pale, as though their
self-consciousness were entirely encompassed by the wholes of
custom, structure, grammar, and tradition. Not only without our
domestic species of the potent ego, they have also seemed too often
without moral personhood in the pragmatic sense. David Pocock

[1] Derek Parfit, *Reasons and Persons* (Oxford: Clarendon Press), 1984, p. 216.
[2] Marcel Mauss, 'A category of the human mind: the notion of person, the notion
of self', in *The Category of the Person*, ed. Carrithers, Collins, and Lukes.
[3] Parfit, *Reasons and Persons*, pp. 453–4.

writes, 'The conception of "social structure" ... and of function that required the reduction to that structure of all that was not by definition given in it, ruled out of serious consideration most of the significance and all of the joy of human existence.... The loss of the individual was not the only defect of functionalism. It contributed also to the spread of moral relativism by appearing to suggest that the cultures studied by anthropologists were islands ...'[4] The dilemma itself is becoming clearer, as we see, for example, from the collection of essays edited by Carrithers, Collins, and Lukes, *The Category of the Person*, an extended debate over the implications of Mauss' view. Steven Collins' own monograph on the texts of Theravāda Buddhism, *Selfless Persons*, takes the question much further forward.[5] It is now possible, I take it, to give an intelligible account of persons, even of 'myself' and 'yourself', freed a little from that imperial ego which has so constrained our perception of others.

This study pivots upon the notion of the *whole person* among the Uduk, that pragmatic whole person who is both subject and object of what I have termed 'moral knowledge'. In making sense of 'the ethnography' we have thought too much of systems. Even that concept of 'morality' which can be multiplied as 'moralities', itself too little examined in ethnographic work, refers often to the systematic form of codes and conventions, rather than to the experiencing person. The locus of the 'moral', when it has been identified in anthropological writing, has too often been the morphology of convention itself, inevitably congruent with the forms of explicitly encoded religion, law, kinship, or whatever. Even in recent discussions of personhood and 'the self' in anthropological perspective, it is the person or the self as a *conventional category* that has been in the main under scrutiny. The person or self as the experiencing subject, and as touchstone therefore for understanding the world of others, has not often been in focus. But without a tangible knowing subject, it is difficult to specify (in a non-literate culture particularly) what may constitute knowledge, and especially so in the field of knowing human beings and 'society'. Exploring this field, which we may term that of 'moral knowledge', we must

---

[4] David Pocock, 'The Ethnography of Morals', *International Journal of Moral and Social Studies*, 1 (1986), 1–20, at p. 8.

[5] Steven Collins, *Selfless Persons: Imagery and Thought in Theravāda Buddhism* (Cambridge: Cambridge University Press), 1982.

use as our guide the self-understanding of real persons in 'another culture', and not allow them to be submerged in the formal systematization of conventional representation.

Of course there are systems and structures in society. But their existence should not be assumed as a fact of nature. Their existence is embedded in history and is inseparable from the exercise of power; knowledge in ordered and authorized format may itself become a vehicle for the further exercise of power, as the analyses of Michel Foucault have so devastatingly revealed.[6] Many notions of 'morality' have themselves been entwined, as again Foucault has shown, with the ramifications of power; but however far these may extend, the substantive person and his or her consciousness is still there (short of annihilation), to reflect upon and (even if inwardly) respond critically to their impact. What resources does this person have to call upon?

We do not need to invoke a metaphysical soul, a Cartesian 'I', or even the 'choosing individual' of Western sociology to recall the range of resources available to any competent human being. They would include a particular view of 'myself' in relation to others, and the capacity of my body and my psyche to respond to the world. They would include the whole range of (probably conflicting) ideas, words, advice, and encounters which have formed my previous experience. Where I have travelled, learned foreign languages, worshipped in different churches and temples, or otherwise had a varied and even discontinuous range of experience, so the resources will be wider. In so far as I have reflected upon the meanings of words and content of ritual actions, so will the resources run deeper. The repertoire of my mother tongue and cultural tradition will have accumulated usable resources on which I can draw; not a systematic or clear guide, necessarily, but a working fund. There is heterogeneity in this archive, as there is heterogeneity in the life-experience of all those persons who have contributed to it, or tried to draw systems from it.

My use of the expression 'moral knowledge' should not therefore be taken to indicate a rigid and enduring system of encoded prescriptions for behaviour. It indicates rather the store of reference points from which a people, as individuals or as a collectivity,

---

[6] An outstanding example here is Michel Foucault's *The Birth of the Clinic: An Archaeology of Medical Perception* [1963], trans. A. M. Sheridan (London: Tavistock), 1973.

judge their own predicament, their own condition, themselves as persons.

Of course the Uduk have constructed what we could, in a conventional sense, identify as a 'morality', that is a set of publicly sanctioned principles governing personal and general social behaviour. It is actually a very restrictive morality and based on rigid rules. Much of it is described in *'Kwanim Pa*, and in summary it seems narrow and intolerant in many ways, though oddly modern-looking in others. Strict reciprocity governs working together in the fields and in the village; animals and some other forms of property are the joint responsibility of members of a birth-group (a local matrilineage), who must shoulder each other's debts as their own; the products of the field must be shared and consumed, not 'invested' for the future except under the strictest conditions. Individual enterprise is frowned on, as it can only succeed at the expense of others. Transactions for cash or profit are severely limited, and a person's labour cannot be bought within the community. This would evoke notions of enslavement, as does the payment of bridewealth, which the Uduk observe all around them but refuse to practise themselves. Strong leadership and power are viewed with deep suspicion, and men who have become influential have been killed, even in recent times. Uduk communities for a good part of this century considered that they should rid themselves not only of 'witches' by chasing them out and killing them (which they often did), but should also eliminate children, like twins, who were regarded as signs, and carriers, of the stigma. It would not be difficult to 'moralize' about this set of rules, and to set up a debate on the relationship between 'morals' and 'culture', as though these were available as entities for comparison. By assembling a 'system' of enjoined practices in such a debate, one is almost inevitably left in the position of having to explain them *as rules*, and justify them as customary, that is timeless, law and morality, which of course results in accusations of relativism.

There is, on the other hand, sufficient evidence from various sources, as well as from my own fieldwork which has now spanned eighteen years, that the 'conventional' morality I have just sketched is not a timeless structure. As a system, it occupied, and still in part occupies, a specific place in the rapidly changing historical circumstances of the region, and the repeatedly disturbed re-formation of Uduk social relations within their present homeland over the last century or more. Rigidities over possessions, property, reciprocity, and a 'final solution' to evil within the community were not necessarily always part of 'custom', and, significantly, many aspects of overt morality are not shared by the other Koman-speaking peoples. No other group worries so much about witches, or kills twins, for example; and as I certainly disapprove of this practice, I am very glad to report that the Uduk themselves now seem to be abandoning it.

We can argue that there is sufficient evidence for historical change in the public codes of morality, understood as behavioural prescription, for us to reject the idea of comparing or judging it in absolute terms. (In the Uduk case there is I think a shadowy analogy with the familiar problem in European history of how far to include in the moral evaluation of a culture or a nation the very worst periods of its past.) But if morality as *system* is so fickle is there no sounder base on which serious comparative enquiry can be conducted? I believe there is a level at which one can more broadly consider the nature of constancy and of variation in moral thought. While, for example, the Uduk may one day prohibit, and another day allow, the selling of beer among themselves, one year dispose of twins, another year send them to be cared for at the mission, and a third year rear them at home, their basic notions of human nature and the character of human interaction are not so change-able. Modalities of the relationship between Stomach and Liver, for example, or as we would say between Head and Heart, or Reason and Feeling, are not immediately disrupted by the events of political and economic change, or those of encounter with other languages and societies; nor even, necessarily, with the arrival of new religious teaching. At this level, I suggest, translation and mutual understanding *is* feasible, and the problem of 'relativism', dubbed by Bernard Williams 'the anthropologist's heresy',[7] recedes. If you can conduct an adequate conversation across the cultural

---

[7] Bernard Williams writes, 'Let us ... look round a special view or assemblage of views which has been built on the site of moral disagreements between societies. This is *relativism*, the anthropologist's heresy, possibly the most absurd view to have been advanced even in moral philosophy.... A view with a long history, it was popular with some liberal colonialists, notably British administrators in places (such as west Africa) where white men held no land. In that historical role, it may have had, like some other muddled doctrines, a beneficent influence, though modern African nationalism may well deplore its tribalist and conservative implications.' *Morality: An Introduction to Ethics* (Cambridge: Cambridge University Press), 1972, p. 34.

divide about feeling and reason in human affairs, in one guise or another, then it should be possible to find a basis upon which the (inevitably mortal) rules and sanctions of a given political–social order could be critically reviewed.

A distinction of level of this kind between sanctioned rules, and the morally intelligible behaviour of persons, is very rarely found in the ethnography. I will return to a few instances from which we may draw some encouragement. But first it is illuminating to review some of the appeals made in our direction by contemporary philosophers, which I would read as pleas from the armchair for improved ethnography. It is certainly true that the varied species (if not the genus) of 'relativism' have flourished on poor quality ethnography. Sir Isaiah Berlin's lucid call must lead the field:

History is not an ancillary activity; it seeks to provide as complete an account as it can of what men do and suffer; to call them men is to ascribe to them values that we must be able to recognize as such, otherwise they are not men for us.... Acceptance of common values (at any rate some irreducible minimum of them) enters our conception of a normal human being. This serves to distinguish such notions as the foundations of human morality on the one hand from such other notions as custom, or tradition, or law, or manners, or fashion, or etiquette ...[8]

Berlin writes of the need to distinguish between subjective and objective moral judgements in the writing of history, and characterizes the latter by the degree to which the central values conveyed are those which are common to human beings as such. In spite of the variation of human judgement, this criterion is not 'wholly relative or subjective, otherwise the concept of man would become too indeterminate, and men or societies, divided by unbridgeable normative differences, would be wholly unable to communicate ...'[9]

Moral categories—and categories of values in general—are nothing like as firm and ineradicable as those of, say, the perception of the material world, but neither are they as relative or as fluid as some writers have too easily, in their reaction against the dogmatism of the classical objectivists, tended to assume. A minimum of common moral ground—interrelated concepts and categories—is intrinsic to human communication. What they are, how flexible, how far liable to change under the impact of what

[8] Isaiah Berlin, 'Introduction' to *Four Essays on Liberty* (Oxford: Oxford University Press), 1969, pp. xxx–xxxi.
[9] Ibid., p. xxxii.

'forces'—these are empirical questions, in a region claimed by moral psychology and historical and social anthropology, fascinating, important, and insufficiently explored.[10]

That 'minimum of common moral ground', note, is not a matter of behavioural codes or the arithmetical ethics of situational choice, but 'interrelated concepts and categories', to be discovered by empirical enquiry into cultural tradition.

Some people might expect to find in an ethnography about 'morality' a clear account of a people's ideas of 'the Good', or 'Right' and 'Freedom', and an academic exegesis of local orthodox conventions in their light. Some general notions might indeed emerge sufficiently from indigenous discourse for a comparative discussion to be possible, but it would distort the enquiry to make these abstractions banner headings for the conduct of research or the writing of an ethnography. We may take heart from Iris Murdoch's exhortation, in moral enquiry, to dispense with the primary general words and concentrate on the moral work done by secondary, specialized words. She believes that 'A moral philosophy should be inhabited;' and has explained 'My view might be put by saying: moral terms must be treated as concrete universals.'[11] Whereas the supposedly 'free' and 'empty' will of the existentialist–behaviourist moral agent was obliged to get along with 'only the most empty and general moral terms such as "good" and "right" ', we could alternatively picture the agent as 'compelled by obedience to the reality he can see, he will not be saying "This is right," i.e. "I choose to do this," he will be saying "This is A B C D" (normative descriptive words), and action will follow naturally.'[12] She explains further, after criticizing the limitations of an enquiry restricted to the bounds of ordinary language for its own sake:

We might, however, set out from an ordinary language situation by reflecting upon the virtues. The concepts of the virtues, and the familiar words which name them, are important since they help to make certain potentially nebulous areas of experience more open to inspection [. . .] For instance, if we reflect upon courage and ask why we think it is to be a virtue, what kind of courage is the highest, what distinguishes courage from rashness, ferocity, self-assertion, and so on, we are bound, in our

[10] Ibid.

[11] Iris Murdoch, *The Sovereignty of Good* (London: Routledge and Kegan Paul), 1970, pp. 47, 29.

[12] Ibid., pp. 41–2.

explanation, to use the names of other virtues. The best kind of courage [...] is steadfast, calm, temperate, intelligent, loving.... This may not in fact be exactly the right description, but it is the right sort of description [...] All I suggest here is that reflection rightly tends to unify the moral world, and that increasing moral sophistication reveals increasing unity.[13]

Iris Murdoch recommends, several times, that we remember the often forgotten (by philosophers; but perhaps others may feel the cap fits) figure of the 'virtuous peasant'. Among things 'theorized away' is 'the fact that an unexamined life can be virtuous and the fact that love is a central concept in morals. Contemporary philosophers frequently connect consciousness with virtue, and although they constantly talk of freedom they rarely talk of love. But there must be some relation between these latter concepts, and it must be possible to do justice to both Socrates and the virtuous peasant.'[14] This peasant is not without resources: 'The virtuous peasant knows, and I believe will go on knowing, in spite of the removal or the modification of the theological apparatus, although what he knows he may be at a loss to say. ...'[15]

However, although the work of ethnography may confirm the inarticulatenesses of the peasant (or the herder or the hunter), it can reveal, too, something of the range of his or her moral resources. It can also record the multifold cultural expressions of humble knowledge, which may only rarely be articulated in concise language, but more often approached through the relative opacities of art, music, movement, and metaphor. Perhaps, as is evidenced in the work of Pierre Bourdieu, the ethnographer's key entry to a culture is not through explicit discourse, but through a grasping of its practical metaphorical expression.[16] Here again, Iris Murdoch's vision is true: 'The development of consciousness in human beings is inseparably connected with the use of metaphor. Metaphors are not merely peripheral decorations or even useful models, they are fundamental forms of our awareness of our condition: metaphors of space, metaphors of movement, metaphors of vision.'[17]

Mary Midgley has written more recently on the need to distinguish the broader, from the narrower, sense of the word

[13] Iris Murdoch, *The Sovereignty of Good*, p. 57.
[14] Ibid., pp. 1–2.
[15] Ibid., p. 74.
[16] Pierre Bourdieu, *Outline of a Theory of Practice* [1972], trans. R. Nice (Cambridge: Cambridge University Press), 1977, esp. ch. 3.
[17] Iris Murdoch, *The Sovereignty of Good*, p. 77.

'moral'.[18] The narrower modern sense, of the hypothetical construction of principles of choice and duty by an abstract detached 'I', has dominated academic philosophy (and corresponds uncannily to a puritan moralizing streak in our everyday language). The broader and older sense, never quite displaced, does not easily form an abstract noun on its own, but defines its 'content' more naturally in conjunction with other nouns, in phrases such as moral enquiry, moral outlook, moral argument. The broader sense firmly includes substance along with evaluation, and, we could add, feeling along with reason. The narrow and the broad senses of 'moral', she suggests, have the relation of part to whole; and she persuasively recommends a return to the 'wholeness' of the older sense.

Official British philosophy ... has stuck to the narrow external behaviouristic sense of *moral*. But alongside this narrow sense, the old, useful general one has persisted. It is very common in such quiet, unemphatic phrases as; moral courage, moral feebleness, moral commitment, moral obtuseness, moral support. It is much like *spiritual*, but without the ontology. The main antithesis—moral versus material—has been enriched by several others—moral versus legal, intellectual, supernatural, conventional—and in these cases *moral* appears on the inward, the more central and personal side of the dividing line.... It means more, however, than just *inner*, because it conveys that these qualities—the moral courage, obtuseness, or what not—belong to the whole person.... The nearest synonyms are phrases like 'strength or weakness *of character*'. (*Moral* in this sense has in fact much closer connections with *mores* = character, than with *mos* = custom—which is the favourite sense of British academic discussions.) In this way it actually comes to mean 'comprehensive, affecting the whole person'....[19]

Mary Midgley has criticized the former preoccupation of anthropologists with 'very small and remote cultures'. They 'had often forgotten their own history' and made neat, self-contained subjects for study. They did not seem to have had that experience of the 'fertilizing mix' of ideas elsewhere so common, and apparently had not faced the 'problem of digesting and assimilating things which, at the start, they do not understand'. This she sees as a universal predicament, which the (undeniable) anthropological tendency to draw pictures of societies in moral isolation has obscured. She does

---

[18] Mary Midgley, *Heart and Mind: The Varieties of Moral Experience* (London: Methuen), 1981, ch. 7.

[19] Ibid., p. 117.

concede that anthropological judgements of tribesmen, as well as theirs of the anthropologist, have been refined with time; but whatever may be our judgement of the relevance of her criticisms to this or that particular account, we have to admit that a false (if 'tolerant') relativism pervades a good deal of what is offered, perhaps particularly at the popular level, as anthropological knowledge. A few more virtuous peasants striding through our pages, or across our television screens, might improve our accounts; for we have to agree with Mary Midgley that 'Morally as well as physically, there is only one world, and we all have to live in it.'[20]

Renford Bamborough's *Moral Scepticism and Moral Knowledge* is a lucid defence of the claim that there exist common grounds in moral discourse, whether between partisan disputants within one cultural framework or between apparently quite different views on 'moral' matters as between cultures; common grounds of a kind which hold out the promise of agreeing, finally, on matters of judgement. On this basis he justifies, as at least a theoretically attainable goal, *moral knowledge*, through an enquiry which engages feeling and reason together. He insists that we should disentangle a good deal of contextual circumstance before touching the inner nerve, as it were, of moral judgement. Ethnography enters his discussion too; even in extreme cases, such as Greek infanticide, he suggests that a large swathe of non-moral phenomena can be put aside to reveal the essential moral question on which some agreement might be found. A hypothetical sceptic might point to differences of moral practice and belief between one time or place and another. But, argues Bamborough, in collecting these instances the sceptic makes a contribution to the 'objective description of the objectivity of moral thought'.

When he reminds us that the ancient Greeks exposed unwanted children and left them to die, whereas we place them in orphanages or have them adopted, he does not, as he thinks, point to a clear case of conflict of moral belief. The effect of his citing such an instance is to open an investigation into the facts and circumstances of ancient Greek life, and how they compare and contrast with modern life, and a debate about whether the differences are such as to justify a difference of practice. If they are, then it will have turned out that in spite of superficial differences there is no moral conflict between the ancients and ourselves. If there turns

[20] Mary Midgley, *Heart and Mind*, pp. 74–5.

out to be a residual conflict, large or small, it may be that part of the difference is accounted for by differences in non-moral belief. If a man believes that a finite and temporal torment is the only way of saving a heretic from infinite and eternal torment, he may be prompted by motives of charity to reinforce his reasoning with the rack.... Our disagreement with the Inquisitor, which is represented by the moral sceptic as an irresoluble dispute about moral principles, is then seen to be a dispute which, whether resoluble or not, is not about fundamental moral principles, but about the truth or falsehood of some non-moral propositions—historical, psychological and theological.[21]

Without the presumption of a level at which a conversation on some such 'fundamental moral principles' can at least be sought, I do not see how the tasks of ethnography, and of analytical social anthropology, can be properly carried out.

Bamborough touches on a crucial distinction between the 'moral' and the 'religious' sphere in the passage above. Within anthropology, we have too seldom made this distinction. The possibility of setting the moral sphere aside from that of religion has indeed rarely been discussed outside a Western cultural context. The conjunction of Morality and Religion, whether the one or the other is accorded logical priority, has normally been taken for granted; it has been partially questioned only for our own society. No wonder the conjunction has been firmly assumed for all those other less sophisticated times and places. This attitude stems from a long tradition of evolutionary thinking about the emergence of 'modern' society, and it is still orthodox for anthropologists to take a view of 'primitive' worlds in which not only are morality and religion confounded, but are themselves jointly circumscribed by the fixed orthodoxies of public society, itself defined by customary law and constitutional hierarchies.

This confining picture, allowing breathing-space neither for history nor for the person as agent or subject of experience, can be found in archetypal form for example in some of Durkheim's writings. I quote (in translation) from *L'Éducation Morale*, a work written with the problems of inter-war France in mind it is true, but which significantly attempts to define the nature of modern morality by contrasting its form in undeveloped societies:

---

[21] Renford Bamborough, *Moral Scepticism and Moral Knowledge* (London: Routledge and Kegan Paul), 1979, p. 34.

It has sometimes been said that primitive peoples had no morality. That was an historical error. There is no society without morality. However, the morality of undeveloped societies is distinct from ours. What characterises them is precisely that they are essentially religious. By that, I mean that the most numerous and important duties are not the duties of man toward other men, but of man toward his gods. The principal obligations are not to respect one's neighbour, to help him, to assist him; but to accomplish meticulously the prescribed rites, to give to the gods what is their due, and even, if need be, to sacrifice oneself to their glory. As for human morality, it is limited to a small number of principles, whose violation is repressed less severely. These peoples are only on the threshold of morality.[22]

The category 'religion' has since Durkheim's time been overworked in anthropological writings, extended too far, and made to serve too many purposes. Is every recognition of an immaterial phenomenon, or a principle of cosmology or psychology, to be ascribed to 'religion'? There is plenty of room for intangible manifestations in our forms of psychology and psychoanalysis, and even for spiritual mystery in various forms of modern humanism; we distinguish all these easily from religion, but would probably agree they could properly be accommodated into an account of moral representations. Perhaps we have taken liberal understanding too far in allowing the dignity of 'religion' to each and every analogous motif in the thought of remote societies, to counter the stigma of the labels 'pagan' and 'heathen'. And yet, until recently, to account for those worlds in terms of *morality* or moral experience would have been problematic; for whereas 'religion' can be assumed to command a general acceptance of orthodoxy and obedience to its dictates, the idea of 'morality' *per se* evokes the notion of personal consciousness and the autonomous agent: a figure too often assumed to belong only to our own age and to be quite incompatible with 'earlier' and other supposedly undeveloped forms of society.

But there are signs of a new sensitivity to the older Aristotelian weightings in the discussion of moral phenomena, and their foundation in character, knowledge of character, and aspects of virtue. Consider Elizabeth Colson's study of heroism, martyrdom, and

---

[22] Anthony Giddens, ed. and trans., *Emile Durkheim: Selected Writings* (Cambridge: Cambridge University Press), 1972, p. 240.

courage among the Tonga of Zambia.[23] They may reject 'courageous' behaviour in what we see as its superior heroic cast, but this apparent failing they fully make up for in their evaluation of its other forms, of tenacity, endurance, and steadfastness in the face of pain and loss. Plenty of vernacular imagery, social context, and local experience are given; but in the final analysis, we are able to see moral sense in what the Tonga do and say, and indeed could transpose in our imagination their 'morality' in this field to people and societies we know elsewhere. The sillier questions of 'relativism' simply do not arise. A socially exclusive morality scarcely deserves the name. We cannot accept without further question that moral thinking can be adequately represented anywhere as a set of notions bounded by kin, language, race, or nation.

Grace Harris, whose account of 'casting out anger' among the Taita of Kenya[24] is one of the more detailed studies (since Evans-Pritchard's of Zande witchcraft[25]) we have of an ethical–medical theory about persons in society, has recently turned her investigations to ordinary American patients. She has demonstrated that modern American patterns of thinking about 'stress' as the ultimate cause of illness, a condition rooted in social relationships, follow remarkably closely Taita notions about 'anger'.[26] Close comparisons could be developed with the range of notions including 'anger' which were so beautifully described by Michelle Rosaldo for the Ilongot head-hunters of the Philippines.[27] Such explications of inner experience should surely be a point of reference for the comparative sociology of religion and morality. The collection of studies brought together by Paul Heelas and Andrew Lock on *Indigenous Psychologies* has surely a wider relevance than the strictly psychological; the questions raised here of how the inner constitution of the human being is represented in a given culture,

[23] Elizabeth Colson, 'Heroism, Martyrdom and Courage: An Essay on Tonga Ethics', in *The Translation of Culture: Essays to E. E. Evans-Pritchard*, ed. T. O. Beidelman (London: Tavistock), 1971.

[24] Grace G. Harris, *Casting Out Anger: Religion among the Taita of Kenya* (Cambridge: Cambridge University Press), 1978.

[25] E. E. Evans-Pritchard, *Witchcraft, Oracles, and Magic among the Azande* (Oxford: Clarendon Press), 1937.

[26] Grace G. Harris, 'Medical Cause and Moral Meaning: Studying Patients' Views in an American City', paper presented to the annual conference of the Association of Social Anthropologists of the Commonwealth at Keele University, 1985.

[27] Michelle Z. Rosaldo, Knowledge and Passion: Ilongot Conceptions of Self and Social Life (New York: Cambridge University Press), 1980.

point towards a way of grasping how human events are related to each other in the world, and therefore to sociological understanding.[28]

Self-knowledge is intimately linked with the possibility of understanding others, within one's own society and also way beyond it, within the world of those who inform the ethnographer about another. If we can give some account of those notions which elsewhere correspond to what *we* mean by head and heart, in varying contexts of vulnerability and power (and here I acknowledge how remarkably interesting I have found the recent work of Richard Fardon[29]), of how the world changed me yesterday, and how I shall change it tomorrow, we shall have done quite well.

[28] Paul Heelas and Andrew Lock, eds, *Indigenous Psychologies: The Anthropology of the Self* (London: Academic Press), 1981.

[29] Richard Fardon, 'Sociability and Secrecy: Two Problems of Chamba Knowledge', in R. Fardon, ed. *Power and Knowledge: Anthropological and Sociological Approaches* (Edinburgh: Scottish Academic Press), 1985; and other papers.

PART II

The Claims of High Theology

Instead of approaching religion with questions about the meaning of doctrines and practices, or even about the psychological effects of symbols and rituals, let us begin by asking what are the historical conditions (movements, classes, institutions, ideologies) necessary for the existence of particular religious practices and discourses. In other words, let us ask: how does power create religion?

Talal Asad, 'Anthropological Conceptions of Religion: Reflections on Geertz', *Man*, 18 (1983), 252.

3

The Nilotic Prophets and 'Arum i Mis':
Remembering Leina

Notions of a distinct divine presence have reached the Uduk as 'foreign' beliefs. It is likely that long before they encountered Islam (and, much later, Christianity), indeed when they were still settled in the Daga region, they had plenty of opportunity to observe the religious rites and practices of various Nilotic-speaking neighbours. Among these were the Nuer, whose eastward movement from the 1820s on was partly responsible for the pressures which led the Uduk and some of the other Koman communities to move north-wards, or further towards the Ethiopian foothills. In the well-documented religious representations of the Nuer and the Dinka, there is a central focus upon a Divinity whose realm is, geo-graphically and symbolically, the sky.[1] The claims of Nilotic religion are wide, even universal within the horizons of Nilotic experience. It is likely that in the past, the Uduk and other Koman peoples were drawn into the sphere of Nilotic priests and prophets. Indeed there is specific evidence that 'Burun' (a widely used term in Sudanese Arabic to include a range of Ethiopian border peoples and in this context probably Komo or Shyita), came to pay their homage to the great Nuer prophet Ngundeng at the Mound he had built near modern Waat, very far from the hills of the border country.[2]

Recent Uduk contact with the Nuer, Dinka, Anuak, and Shilluk has been limited. But the Uduk live on close terms with their immediate western neighbours today, the Meban. The Meban speak a tongue which is related to Shilluk. However, in their culture

---

[1] See especially Evans-Pritchard's *Nuer Religion*, ch. 1, and Lienhardt's *Divinity and Experience*, Part I.

[2] Personal communication, D. H. Johnson. The wide and still spreading influence of the Nuer prophet Ngundeng and the current impact of his prophecies is described in D. H. Johnson, 'Foretelling Peace and War: Modern Interpretations of Ngundeng's Prophecies in the Southern Sudan', in *Modernization in the Sudan: Essays in Honor of Richard Hill*, ed. M. W. Daly (New York: Lilian Barber Press), 1985.

and social organization, they have obvious affinities with the 'pre-Nilotic' peoples to their east, as well as with the Nilotes as we know them from the ethnographic literature. They may well have come to accommodate within their own world many of the ambi-valences that the rest of this chapter traces for the Uduk. They are classified as 'Burun' by Arabic-speakers together with the 'pre-Nilotic' Uduk and others; and as Cai, again with the Uduk and others, by the Nuer and Dinka themselves. Some recently dis-covered mission notes at Doro record that they place importance upon the matrilateral link, even having matrilineal descent groups, and this is confirmed by Douglas Johnson's enquiries.[3] This feature of their society, together with elements of myth and ritual, closely echoes what we know of the Uduk. There is, moreover, much coming and going, intermarriage, and blood-friendship between specific kin groups on either side.

Nevertheless, not only is the Meban language closely related to Shilluk, but the character of Meban beliefs seems outwardly Nilotic. Christian Delmet has claimed the 'Nilotic' affiliation of the Meban on the basis of their religion and its central act of sacrifice. This is characterized by the central dominance of the sky Divinity *juong* in their world, analogous to the place of the Shilluk *jwok*. Meban also employ the term *jok*, which occurs in a wide range of Nilotic languages, referring to a range of spirit powers.[4] Moreover, the Meban have lived with Nuer neighbours for a long period, and within the last two or three generations various Meban communities have been both exploited and protected by the Nuer. A pattern of leadership and prophetic inspiration, modelled on that of the Nuer, has developed among the Meban. In particular, a cult which sprang from the activities of a Meban prophet, Leina Muali, in the 1920s and 1930s, has taken root among the Uduk, where it still flourishes today. For some Uduk, the notion of an encompassing divinity has been transmitted by the teachings of Leina, himself drawing upon Nuer exemplars. For others, the message has been turned around; this is one more source of danger for the people, a

---

[3] 'Meban Information', typescript notes, Doro, n.d. [probably by G. A. Morrow], lent by Revd and Mrs Harold Walker. D. H. Johnson's fieldnotes (1983) confirm that the term *kem* or *ken* (presumably cognate with the Nuer *cieng*) appears to mean a matrilineage. Compare however the findings of Christian Delmet, who records important matrilateral links but only patrilineal descent groups, 'De curieux Nilotiques: les Maban du Haut-Nil', *Production Pastorale et Société*, 15 (1984), 41–58, at pp. 46–9.

[4] Delmet, 'De curieux Nilotiques', pp. 52–6.

Nilotic spirit-power which can cause sickness and death. It is perhaps never easy for teachings about peace spread by a powerful people to be taken in good faith by those they have exploited in other ways, at other times. The ambivalence is inevitable. But the Meban have never been terrifying enemies for the Uduk, as the Nuer have, and perhaps they have made more effective 'missionaries' than the Nuer were ever likely to.

In Uduk communities today, *arum* is indeed sometimes spoken of as a general power, with a degree of autonomy as a source both of danger and of healing. It then becomes appropriate to transcribe the term as Arum rather than *arum*. It is usually Arum as revealed through the cult of Leina that people have in mind when they speak of it in this abstract way. Practitioners of the Leina cult might wish to be known as *'kwani ma Arum*, people of Arum, in the generalized form; but the phrase is ambivalent, and carries at the same time the specific, and especially perhaps in the talk of sceptics, narrower sense of the personal powers of the deceased prophet, where we would transcribe *'kwani ma rum ma Leina* or 'people of the *arum* of Leina'. This reflects the ambivalence between the public adoption by the Uduk of the practices and discourse of the Leina cult and their uneasy response both to the universal claims of its theology and to the practical demands of its leadership, still in Meban hands.

Before giving a detailed account of the cult of Leina among the Uduk, I will sketch the way Uduk view one or two other, more direct, manifestations of Nilotic religion. I use 'Nilotic' here in the sense of the inclusive northern Uduk term Dhamkin (for the Nuer, Dinka, and Shilluk; though these are distinguished in the southern Uduk dialect as Zhwaŋge, Diŋun, and Culun—the latter two names matching Meban usage).

'Arum Dhamkin', the religious practice and spiritual power of the Nuer, Dinka, and Shilluk, has entered Uduk country (as they see it) several times. In most forms, it is known through rumour and repute rather than by direct experience, and is feared above other foreign Arum. The Yabus valley is the main part of Uduk country in which the Arum Dhamkin is to be found. Specialists of the Arum Dhamkin are known to have posts outside their houses, posts of Arum, and ordinary people are afraid to go near them. The Arum of the Yabus valley is reputed to be very strong in general, and people who have been treated by the Arum men there are avoided to some extent. For example, Ha'da, already an Arum

man in Waka'cesh, was given some treatment when he visited the
Yabus valley, and on his return, people said they would no longer
take grass from his roof (normally done casually, to light a pipe,
for example). When Yuha, an apprentice Ebony diviner, visited his
father who was a powerful Arum man in Yabus, he would not
sleep on the bed but only on a goatskin. A woman struck by the
Arum Dhamkin passed through Waka'cesh, and people were afraid
of keeping the cane mat she had used—some wanted to throw it
away in the bush, in case anyone else should be struck by the same
thing.

In the Yabus valley in the south, Arum Zhwaŋge (Nuer), Arum
Culun (Shilluk), and Arum Pur (Pur is the Uduk term for the Shyita
of the Daga valley) are known; though Arum Diŋun (Dinka) is said
to be found only far away in Meban country. These Nilotic Arum
are thought in general to be dangerous because they 'squeeze
people's innards' causing dysentery with blood (this can be fatal of
course, especially in children). I shall return to the Arum Zhwaŋge,
and its practice by the religious leader Jang, later in this chapter.

Ilo was a leading man of the Arum Pur in Yabus in the 1960s.
Even in the northern valleys Ebony Men were sending patients to
him, and he was collecting quite substantial payments for treatment
(in the form of goats, arrows, and sesame). One boy in Pam'Be had
been sent for treatment and Ilo later came to Pam'Be to 'set him
right' (nyoŋ) with the Arum. This Arum supposedly comes to a
person in a dream. He or she runs about, into the bush, and back,
and then to the home of a man of the Arum Culun, without even
knowing it. A person thus seized, bu'th ma rum Culun, must have
an ox sacrificed. This had taken place recently for the Pam'Be boy.
During the rite, he climbed, like a cat, up a bamboo post set up
outside the house. Later, around the beer pot, people saw him lay
his beer straw across the pot and climb up to sit on it, trembling
and shivering all over. This is something that Ilo himself does; it
used to happen in the vicinity of the Arum of Leina, but is no
longer seen.

(i) Activities of the prophet Leina

Leina Muali started as a relatively minor religious figure in Meban
country in the 1920s. (Uduk pronunciation of his first name seems
to me best rendered 'Leina' although official reports use 'Liena';

this may be a better transcription of the Meban pronunciation, which sounded to me 'Lyeina'. The Meban were known to the government as Gurra or Gwara, after Uduk usage.) Leina's importance was overestimated by the government of the day. A. W. M. Disney, who served for several periods in the Blue Nile in the 1930s and 1940s, has told me that Leina was thought to be attempting to emulate the Nuer prophets in building a 'pyramid', and a consequence of their persecution seems to have been a greatly enhanced reputation and influence for Leina locally. There was a movement among the Uduk to become followers of Leina during the 1930s, after his release from a quite unjustifiable imprisonment in 1929–30. They know little of the events connected with him before this time, but imprisonment made him famous.

The Sudan Government was extremely sensitive to the activity of religious figures during the early decades of this century, and in Nuerland this suspicion lasted longer than elsewhere. Throughout the 1920s brutal measures were taken against the western, central, and eastern Nuer.[5] Those men we know now as prophets, then labelled variously as *kujur* (Sudanese colloquial Arabic, usually translated 'witch-doctor'), rain-maker, wizard, and so forth, were suspected of inciting the population against the government and were hunted down. In the Upper Nile Province and bordering regions, therefore, a very careful eye was kept open at this time for ritual activities of any description. Leina Muali and some other minor *kujur* in the Meban area were noticed in late 1929. His name occurs first in the November Diary for Fung Province in that year. This reference was followed up the next month, with a brief report of Leina's arrest on 1 December. His activities, with the aid of his assistant Bilal Tonga, had allegedly been holding up road work. During the arrest, two of his followers were killed, and four wounded, by the police. The Civil Secretary requested a report on the incident, and this was submitted by the Governor of Fung Province, with apologies for the delay, at the end of January 1930. 'The facts' were described as follows:

[5] D. H. Johnson, 'Colonial Policy and Prophets: The "Nuer Settlement", 1929–30', *J. of the Anthropological Society of Oxford*, 10 (1979), 1–20. Government attitudes of the day to native religious activity are analysed in Johnson's article 'C. A. Willis and the "Cult of Deng": A Falsification of the Ethnographic Record', *History in Africa*, 12 (1985), 131–50.

A Kujur named Liena amongst the Gurra of Beni Chawa region South of the Yabus declared himself to be God towards the end of the rains; with powers of raising from the dead etc. No reports of anti-Government preaching by him were received, but as the Gurra from North and South of the Yabus were flocking to him; road work in the district being completely held up, as he was said to be flogging people who refused to come to him, and as he was said by some to be not a Gurra but a Nuer, it was judged prudent to bring him in for interrogation, especially as some trouble had been caused by another Kujur in the same area early in the year.

A party of Police with the Muawin, Sheikh Mohammed Zubeir arrested him in his village. His family called on the very large number of Gurra present to rescue him and their demeanour became so threatening that the police fired in self-defence, killing 2 and wounding four. The Gurra then dispersed and Liena and a disciple were brought to the Merkaz [Government office].

Assistant District Commissioner Kurmuk held a full enquiry and is satisfied that the Police were justified in firing.

The Gurra are reported to be settling down quietly again, convinced that Liena is not God after all. Road work was resumed without any trouble.

It is proposed to keep Liena in detention as a precautionary measure until the poll tax has been collected and then release him. He proves to be a Gurra.

Very shortly after the above another Kujur named El Egba (an ex slave) appeared in the Gurra district of Dar el Sagiy'a (about 10.15:30.30) [Map reference] with three disciples preaching resistance to Government taxation. They were arrested, in possession of four unlicenced rifles, without incident and are being dealt with.

The Assistant District Commissioner Kurmuk reports that he cannot discover that these apparitions are in any way caused by an underlying discontent among the Gurra.[6]

The Governor of Fung Province was reprimanded within a few days by the Governor-General himself: 'The incidents of December 1st, involving the use of firearms by the civil power were important in themselves and are just of the kind which lead to developments. They should have been reported at once.'[7] In the *Sudan Monthly Record* later in 1930 it is noted that 'The arrest of the Kujur Liena

[6] Governor Fung Province, at Singa, to Civil Secretary, Khartoum, 'Yabus Omodia'. 27 Jan. 1930. National Records Office, Khartoum [NRO] Civsec 36/4/13.
[7] Civil Secretary quoting the Governor-General, to Governor Fung Province. 5 Feb. 1930. NRO Civsec 36/4/13.

Muali has dispelled the faith of the tribesmen in his pretensions and the tribe have settled down quietly to normal conditions. It is proposed to keep Liena in detention as a precautionary measure. ....'[8] In some notes on the Meban in 1935, Wedderburn-Maxwell comments that 'Such Kujurs who came into prominence were discouraged from exercising any influence over the people: though no crime was proved against him, the rainmaker *LIENA* was imprisoned for a year for no other ascertainable reason than that he was a kujur: the hut of kujur Sidu was burnt. During the arrest of Liena, Province Police shot four of his followers dead [*sic*], alleging that they were attacked by overwhelming numbers: this story seems to have been accepted as true, as no one was punished: but it is surprising that none of the police were decorated for their heroism.'[9]

It seems that after his return to the Meban country on the lower Yabus, Leina's influence and fame spread. He was given hospitality in Chali on his return from imprisonment in Kurmuk in 1930.[10] He was then visited at his home for consultations by Uduk patients. I believe it was at this time that Tente himself as a very young man was taken by Lyife to see Leina. It was apparently in response to this kind of interest from the Uduk villages that Leina later made a formal visitation to Uduk country, a 'progress' in the course of which, through the Meban language or its interpreters, treatment was given to many sufferers and a select few were initiated as local practitioners of his new healing cult.

Ha'da, himself now a man of Arum in our hamlet of Waka'cesh, told me about Leina's visit to the Uduk country, sweeping his arm from the Meban horizon to the west, round through Pam'Be to Chali. In each village through which he passed, chickens were killed for the people to eat, and to put the village in a good condition. People danced for Leina in each place, to welcome and feast him. Then he went to Chali and slept in the house of Jibirdhalla (also known as Babu) whom he appointed a man of Arum. Ha'da pointed out that Jibirdhalla was not sick at this time, and was not drawn into Leina's orbit by the need for treatment. Leina then crossed the river, and came round to Beni Mayu, where he made three people men of Arum: Chenda, Munko (father of ŋule, still an important

[8] *Sudan Monthly Record* [SMR] N.S. No. 13, 1930. Para. 199.
[9] H. G. Wedderburn-Maxwell, 'The Maban', Nov. 1935, NRO Dakhlia I 112/16/105.
[10] 'Customs', Chali, p. 8.

man of Arum), and 'Kaya. None were appointed in Pam'Be, but
Leina returned to Meban through Pam Bigin, where Lyife was
appointed. These men, especially Jibirdhalla and Lyife, became
very influential and sponsored many others in the new cult of
Arum. Ha'da himself, after sickness, was initiated by Jibirdhalla.
After the latter's death in 1949, Lyife became by far the most
important Arum man among the Uduk, working from his base in
Pam Bigin and northern Pam'Be.

The cult of Leina spread rapidly and is still doing so. Today
there are representatives, almost exclusively male, in every hamlet
cluster, and at most rites in which they play a part there are two
or three such men of Arum. On special occasions there may be up
to a dozen. The men of Arum deal on the whole with serious illness,
where the *arum* within a person has been disturbed or where the
Liver in particular has been affected, even invaded, by *arum* from
elsewhere. Although the men of Arum represent a general power
of healing, claiming an almost 'priestly' role, it is not uncommon
to hear it suggested that the very strong *arum* of Leina within them
is in itself sufficient to cause disturbance and sickness in others.
But the beneficent authority of these men is largely accepted, and
they are frequently invited to take a leading role in rites of passage
and other activities which have in themselves a 'secular' character.
Most serious cases, in my experience, are eventually passed on to
the men of Arum even though other specialists, in particular the
Ebony Men, may have attempted cures. The cult, although derived
from outside, has taken root among the Uduk, and its practitioners
have gained some degree of acceptance in their priestly role.

The methods of the men of Arum are straightforward, centring
on animal offerings (*mii abas*: literally 'making blood'). Their
plain style contrasts with the complex paraphernalia and technical
wizardry of the Ebony Men. Moreover, the Arum men wear only
the white cloth Arab tunic, the *jibba*, or the full-length *jellabiyya*,
for ceremonial duties. Apparently both El Egba and Leina declared
that they received instructions from 'little men in clothes' who
appeared to them.[11] Even in the 1960s, the Uduk practitioners of

[11] 'In the rains of 1929 a kujur named Liena, claiming to be God and to have the
power of raising the dead, declared himself. He was arrested and detained for a few
months at Roseires. About the same time another kujur named el Egba, an ex-slave,
appeared in the Dar es Sigi'a, teaching the people not to pay taxes. He and three
"disciples" were arrested. Both he and Liena between whom there seemed to be no

the cult of Leina wore Sudanese Arab clothing on appropriate occasions, looking rather like Meban men, who adopt this style as a matter of course. The Ebony Men on professional duty, by contrast, add to the formerly common beads and bangles their own strings of charms, horns, roots, and cowries, whole animal-skin bags stuffed with medicines and magic objects, goatskins around the hips, feather head-dresses, and so forth. Like the Ebony Men, however, the men of Arum are only part-time specialists—all are cultivators, and take up their professional garb and demeanour only on appropriate occasion.

The distinct styles of these two main groups of practitioners in the Uduk villages seem to me to be external markers not of an ideological split but of partly competing, partly complementary discourses about *arum* to which all have common access. It is true that there is almost no overlap of membership between the two groups (I came across only a couple of individuals who were practitioners of both kinds). A certain division of labour is recognized between them, and even a feeling that if a person is absorbed into one cult, there is no need of, and no advantage in being drawn into, the other. In Uduk idiom, those caught by the Arum of Leina are not likely to be caught by the Spice medicine of the diviners, and vice versa. It would be mistaken to think that practitioners of the Arum of Leina are convinced of its claims to truth as against those of the Ebony Order; nor are the Ebony Men exclusively committed to a rival world-view. But the presence of these alternative 'faiths', in their practice partly complementary, partly competing, reflects a deep ambivalence in the world of the village Uduk, and to some extent this has become a dilemma within each man or woman's personal experience.

The authority of the men of Arum today is derived partly from the image of the figure of Leina himself, and the traditions of his miraculous life and deeds. Leina is remembered as a healer and a miracle-worker among both the Meban and the Uduk. Some mission notes from Doro, probably written in the early 1940s, state that 'The king of the rain-makers at present is Lyenna, who lives at Ban Lyan, south west of Doro, about 12 miles. There are other rain-makers of less importance in each district. Then Lyenna has a number of lesser representatives who are subordinate to him.

connection declared that they received instructions from "little men in clothes" who appeared to them.' L. F. Nalder, 'Gura' [Meban], NRO Dakhlia I 112/16/105.

Jirko of Doro is one such.... The rain-makers receive abundance of gifts for their efforts.'[12] Douglas Johnson was told something of Leina's life during historical research among the Meban south of Boing in 1983. Many went to Leina because of sickness; and Leina was able to bring the rain. He appears to have made prophecies about the coming of Nuer, Dinka, and foreigners to Boing, and forthcoming trouble. When he asked how Leina came to have these powers, Johnson's Meban informants claimed that Juong had made him like that; that it had seized him. Leina's first action was to speak to the birds, the small birds that eat the grain, and they fell and died; he spoke to them again, and they came to life. After that, Leina began to kill people. He would kill a person and put him to lie in the sun, and then would bring him back to life. When the government heard that he was killing people, they took him to Kurmuk and Roseires, to test him. They put him in a prison without any doors or windows or holes, but he escaped twice. This was a test, to see if he were an ordinary living man or a spirit. They did not take any action, but let him go, and gave him goats and cloth. He returned to his house.[13]

Douglas Johnson has drawn my attention to the 'Nuer' character of this image of a prophet. The ability to kill beings and then bring them back to life is commonly attributed in later tradition to the early acts of Nuer prophets; and of course 'seizure' by Divinity is the crucial event which makes a person a prophet (*guk kuoth*, or 'vessel' of Divinity) in the first place.

In the Uduk, as against Meban, versions of Leina's life, this divine 'seizure' as a prime essential of the 'Nilotic' representation of a prophet is missing, as far as I can discover. The miraculous achievements are, however, recited with relish and wonder. I have heard, for example, that after being imprisoned for taking too many animals from the people, Leina walked out through a door which opened by itself. He was put in again, but this time came out through the top of the building. Then they dug a deep hole. The police caught him and threw him in, but Leina jumped out, caught the policeman, and threw him in instead. All the police were then afraid of him and let him go home. The chiefs also tied him and threw him into the Nile for the hippos to eat, but he reached the other side safely, with the ropes loosened. Tente, himself a

---

[12] 'Meban Information', Doro.   [13] D. H. Johnson, fieldnotes, 1983.

senior Ebony diviner, gave me this account of Leina's imprisonment and eventual release, which like Meban accounts includes Leina's ability to bring dead creatures to life:

From the beginning of his activities, the Bunyan seized him and took him to Kurmuk, saying, 'He is a liar ... What sort of *arum* does this man have? He's behaving in a silly and dangerous way [*ta pus*]. There is no *arum* in him.' They seized him and fastened him with handcuffs, *'ce'b*, *'ce'b*. They fastened his wrists, and tied his body up like this and put him in a building. They struck a match, and set fire to the building, *sham*. They set fire to the house, while he still had iron cuffs on his ankles and wrists too, and his body was tied up in a bent position like this. The great flames burned up, *dugu, dugu, dugu*.

He burst the iron cuffs completely from his body and appeared and sat outside there. The great fire burnt up and destroyed that house for nothing. And the people said, 'Ay! Is the man really *arum* then?'

They loaded guns to kill him. But the guns didn't sound out *'boum!'* to strike him dead. The guns were extinguished right there, *taw*. The guns fired for nothing, they didn't strike his body. And when the bullets [literally 'seeds of the fire'] were all used up, the police said to him, 'Let us go,' ... They led him to look for antelopes to kill, and he commanded the police, saying, 'Ay! Kill that antelope!' The policeman shot it, *'duw*. The antelope died on the ground. They came up, they came up, and he commanded the police again, 'Ay! Beat that antelope with a whip.' The policeman whipped the antelope, but the antelope didn't get up. The antelope refused to get up. And then he said to the police, 'Give it me to try.' The police gave him the whip, and he whipped just once, *ciiw*.

The antelope got up and ran ... so there was nothing to eat!

Then the police put him inside the motor-truck, saying 'Çaah. We're going home.' They took him back, and told the chief officer, a very important officer in Kurmuk there. The Inspector said, 'Ay! The man is very strong indeed; perhaps he really is.' The Inspector said, 'All right. As he is so strong, let us take him to the north there.' To Renk there, the place of the hippopotamus.... Aren't there lots of hippos at Renk?

And they took him in a truck.

Now the hippos have very red mouths. The people tied him up, *'ce'th*, *'ce'th*, fastened his ankles with iron cuffs.... They threw him among the great mouths of the hippos there *gurug*.

All these iron cuffs were keeping him fast, but suddenly he was out from among all the hippos.... They cocked their guns again to kill him over there, but he was not hit. The guns just sounded in the hands of their owners there; they had gone out completely. And later, *çaah!* People said: 'Ay! This is a great man, a man made great by *arum* truly....' They put him in the truck and took him home. They [the Turuk] all collected a great deal of money and gave it to him. They collected a lot of money for him.

I assume the money may have been some sort of rehabilitation allowance, but in the eyes of the Uduk today it represents protection money paid by the Turuk (that is, the Government) to Leina, because they were afraid of his power. The events of Leina's arrest and detention, far from 'dispelling the faith of the tribesmen in his pretensions', are now recited not only to prove Leina's powers but to suggest that the government itself finally acknowledged them. In fact he was later seen as a mild figure. A 1940 report reads 'The Kujur Liene, who was imprisoned for some offence unknown in 1929 after the police fired on the people, was visited. . . . It seems that he still enjoys high repute and his devotees come from all over the Burun tribes as far as the Jum Jum bringing pigs and grain. He is in failing health, suffering from asthma and stomach trouble, but appeared to be a pleasant and sensible man. He seems to live quietly and innocently enough, and there was no trace of the "odd atmosphere" reported by District Commissioners in 1930 as pervading the village of Liang.'[14]

These tales are of Leina as a historical figure who died in the 1940s; but Leina as a vital presence is by no means gone from the scene. After sketching briefly the Leina cult as it exists now among the Meban, I give a fuller picture of its place among the Uduk.

(ii) The Leina cult among the Meban today

The focal point for sacrificial and healing activity among the Meban is the sky divinity Juong. It was in the name of Juong that Leina originally made his claim to spiritual power, and his successors base their appeal on a continuing relationship with Juong. Leina himself seems to have become to some degree an intermediary between the ordinary people, ministered to by the present-day cult leaders, and the sky divinity. The leading figure of the cult in the 1960s was Yakka, the son of Leina, while other members of his family held influential positions. Dali, his sister's son, and Fatma, who was described to me as Leina's sister (though she was far too young to be an actual sister) were leading figures in the 1960s.

On my return visit to the Uduk in 1983, we approached from

---

[14] Monthly Diary, Northern District, Renk, April/May 1940. SRO UNP 66.E.2.

Malakal and passed through Meban country. We soon learned that Fatma had become the leading religious figure in Meban; she had set up a special healing centre on the road a couple of days' walk north-west of Boing. Here, surrounded by her disciples, she held court. She was now settled far from Uduk country, but in previous times she had travelled a good deal. In May 1967 I had the chance to meet her, when she was still a relatively junior figure. I was in the Yabus valley, at Sheikh Puna Marinyje's village, and with my companions had travelled a few miles to a nearby Meban village, because we heard that Fatma, also then known by her Meban name Pangay, was coming to supervise the pre-planting rites. It became clear that the world of the Meban, in contrast to that of the Uduk, was oriented to notions of a sky divinity responsive to supplication and sacrifice, which could bring rain and blessing upon the work of the people in the fields. It seemed there was a more fitting place for a priestly figure among the Meban than the Uduk; or at least, an expectation of authority and hierarchy in matters of ritual.

Even in 1967 Fatma had an authoritative presence which I had not seen in any Uduk practitioner. When we got to the Meban village we found she had already performed and had moved on with her retinue to another settlement across the river. But there was a great deal going on, and so we spent the whole day there, awaiting Fatma's promised return. Hoes, digging sticks, and every type of seed contributed by the various homesteads of the village were collected and displayed outside the hut of beer, and a goat and a chicken had been sacrificed over them. Right through the day, the women of the village—quite a crowd as it was a big settlement—sang and danced in a growing chorus. More women kept arriving and others joined in as they completed the food and beer preparation. The women held leaves in their hands—either or both hands. They sang vigorous songs about God (Juong), rain, and crops. Some of the phrases were translated to me as 'Let God be pleased and bring rain / Let the crops be plentiful' and I caught the expression *juonga nyalo*, 'Juong in the sky', several times. As the women sang, the leader trilling from a high note to a falling melody, the chorus would reply with a roar of voices and a rhythmic stamping of feet, moving forward in a line, looking to the heavens, opening their palms wide to the sky and calling upon Juong. At the end of a song, they would sometimes fling their hands up together, calling for the rain, and shouting in unison, *WAH!*—'like

the thunder', my companion said. He added that their stamping
feet were like the pounding of grain. (Meban women use the heavy
wooden mortar and pestle set in the ground, like the Dinka, and
do not normally kneel to grind with stone on stone as the Uduk
women do.)

There was an obvious affinity between the sacrifice over the seeds
and implements, and the entreaties to God in the sky to send rain
so that the women could pound grain for food. This rite clearly
had a key place in the agricultural year of the Meban. The fact
that the women *en masse* joined with such gusto in the rain songs
showed that this was a well-known and thoroughly familiar part
of Meban ritual. I had seen nothing like this in the Uduk hamlets.
Women scarcely took part in the corresponding rites I had seen
there, that year and the previous year. The only occasions on which
I had seen enthusiastic mass participation by women were those of
the Ebony Order, and even more the Gurunya rites, when dozens
and dozens of women would sing and dance around the settlement.
But those occasions were nothing to do with agricultural ritual. In
other ways, the Meban rites I saw seemed 'foreign'; the extending
melodies of the music and song, for example, had a recognizably
'Nilotic' fluency strange to an ear grown accustomed to the beats,
turns, and twists of Uduk musical style. But the most foreign aspect
of the day's ceremony was the extraordinary formality and respect accorded to Fatma and her attendants when eventually they
returned.

During the afternoon there had been a collection of money,
and shortly before dusk Fatma appeared. A hush came upon the
assembly. A special angareb (Sudanese bed) was brought out,
placed in the open centre of the village, and covered with layers of
mats and skins. Fatma was led to it in procession, by an important
Meban 'Arum man', and she was followed by her own female
assistant and by Ilo, an Uduk Arum man and devotee of the Meban
cult. Fatma regally seated herself. I was escorted by Sheikh Puna
Marinyje, himself an important Arum man, and my companions
and I went in humble fashion to greet her. Fatma and her assistant
were a striking pair: they had shaved heads, and wore bright
flowered dresses, rubber pumps, and massed bangles and bead
anklets. They carried long decorated tobacco pipes (reminiscent
perhaps of Shilluk decorated pipes). An adulating group gathered
around the seat of honour and gazed. Fatma was exceedingly fat

by any standards. She remained seated to receive most greetings, but rose for the Omda's *ghaffir*, a rifle-bearing representative of the State. She then left in procession for a nearby hut, where small parties went to talk with her in turn. We went over to take our leave, as she was drinking the tea and coffee we had presented earlier. Through Ilo as interpreter, Puna invited her to perform a *mii arum* (Arum rite) at his hamlet the next day. We agreed to collect her in my Land-Rover.

(iii) The extension of Meban and Nuer influence: authority and religious synthesis in the Yabus valley

The rite at Puna's was minimal, and had a stagey air (see Plate 3a). Puna got out a few seeds, hoes, and so forth. Several Arum men had gathered, and first they and then Fatma took a chicken to Brush the seeds and hoes. Two chickens were cut, and died well on their backs. Water was poured over them. Fatma, her assistant, and the Arum men then took another chicken to Brush the place where the rainstones were kept, but they were not brought out. A goat was cut over the seeds and hoes, but with little ceremony. The men and women of the hamlet lined up, and Fatma herself and her assistant took a little grain in their mouths and then Sprayed it out on the hands and feet of the people. They were Brushed by one of the Arum men, who then dipped the cockerel in water and threw it up onto the roof of the hut. A party of Arum men then called at the other three huts of the settlement, and at each they were given a chicken to dip in water, Brush in the air, and then cut. When it was dead, they dipped their fingers in its blood, and then breathed on their fingers as they flicked them in the air. Some seeds were cast on the chicken's body.

After a few closeted consultations, during which I think some sort of collection was made, Fatma was ready to go; she took a late breakfast in my quarters before we drove her back, but I could not discuss much with her because of the formality of the situation and the fact that we had only rudimentary Arabic between us. It was quite clear that she had done us a special favour by coming to this small Uduk hamlet, largely because of the standing of Puna. However, there was no popular participation as there had been in the Meban village, noticeably by the women. Details of the ritual, moreover, such as the throwing up of water, of chickens, and the pouring of water on the roof of the hut, all consistent with the dominant notion of a sky divinity who may be entreated to bring rain directly, must have touched few chords among the Uduk spectators. For them, there is no particular divinity in the sky; there is no special connection between *arum* and the rain (rain is controlled primarily through rainstones, which in this case were not even brought out); and the whole notion of blessing the crops of the fields is, I believe, a foreign idea. As I have suggested in the first Part of this book, the Uduk are still oriented to hunting and gathering. As far as 'agricultural' ritual is concerned, it is a matter of protection of the fields from the ravages of wild animals, birds, and insects, rather than seeking blessings on the fertility of the crops themselves, or the people who grow them.

Nevertheless, the interaction and co-operation between Meban and Uduk so evident on this occasion had something of a history here in the Yabus valley, and had recently developed further. The key figure in the spread of Meban rites among southern Uduk communities during the period of my fieldwork in the 1960s was Jang (see Plate 3b). Jang, as an Arum man of long experience, saw no necessary conflict between the older practices of the Uduk, and the newer teachings of the cult of Leina; nor did he even see contradiction between spiritual claims from these sources and those of a Nuer visitor he had accommodated for a time, and who passed on directly something of Nuer belief and rite. For Jang, all was relevant to the welfare of the people, and all was the work of God.

Jang was by far the most *priestly* person I met among the Uduk, with a quiet conviction in his manner and a sureness of touch in his discussion which I had rarely come across. Jang was originally made a man of Arum by Aḵki, who had himself been a disciple of Leina's. Aḵki was a most influential figure among the Uduk, who knew him as 'the left-handed Meban'. He was an Ebony diviner even before he became a man of Arum of Leina. Moreover, his mother was a Meban, and his father Uduk (of the Ḵwamas birth-group). In Uduk eyes, Jang had received the Arum Gwara, or Meban Arum, from Aḵki 'long ago'. Perhaps approaching sixty years when I met him, he was by far the most important man of Arum in the southern Uduk settlements, ministering also to Komo and Ganza communities. He had acquired disciples throughout the region, and spoke of all the people from Yabus Bridge, north to Chali, and south to Jebel Dogobeli, as 'my people'.

Jang was widely respected, partly because he knew something of the 'ways of the government', having once been employed as a government guard. He spoke on spiritual matters with an authority which he attributed to direct instruction from Leina. In his youth he had spent some time as a novice at Leina's home, to 'learn the things of Arum', for which he paid ten goats. It was even today 'Leina who told him what to do' if the crops were poor: for example, the ceremony which was taking place in the hamlets that year (1967). This was, however, something of a figure of speech; it was actually Akki who had conveyed the instructions to the Yabus valley, through Jang, about the new pre-planting rite that year.

Arum, Jang insisted to us, was in the sky. We asked about the *arum* of those who die, and he agreed that of course these were in the ground. But, he insisted, it is Arum Above (*Arum i Mis*) which strikes people. We asked whether *arum* of the dead were not also dangerous, but he brushed this aside—'How can they be dangerous?' At one of the ceremonies he was supervising, Jang told us that there had been quarrelling at a similar ceremony recently. 'If people are angry and fight on a day such as this, when beer is made for Arum, Arum will be angry and there will be no rain. If people fight and shed blood, it will mix with the chickens' blood and Arum will be angry.' Nor should people come to a ceremony like this just to eat and drink. This will also make Arum angry. 'If the blood of men is shed, Arum will be angry and the crops will dry up.' He also explained that whereas you could fight with complete outsiders, you should never fight with your brothers; and that Uduk should not fight with each other. Nor should any of 'his people' fight with each other; this reference extended to many Komo and Ganza. Those who drink beer together, should not fight. 'If people fight, I will seize them and ask them, "Don't you know God Above (*Arum i Mis*)?" If blood is shed, he will say—this is the blood of a human being. But if he sees the blood of a cow, or a sheep, he will say, this is a thing which is eaten. And Arum will be pleased, and the children will not die of hunger.' By 'children', Jang here meant the people as a whole—a usage which is not commonly heard in the Uduk hamlets, but is here transposed from the Meban and wider Nilotic context of reference to people as the 'children', 'creatures', or 'ants' of God (extremely common for example in Nuer prayers, hymns, and the sayings of the prophet

Ngundeng).[15] Jang, and others in the Yabus valley, also frequently used 'Allah' in their discussion, which I had not heard in the northern communities. This was quite explicitly equated with *Arum i Mis*. One man said, 'Our country is spoiled. Our crops fail. What can we do? We don't know. There is just Arum there [and he pointed upwards]. The Bunyans say, "God is gracious" [*Allah karim*, Arabic]. That is all we can do.' Another layman responded immediately when I asked whether Arum was in the earth or in the sky, 'Arum comes from above.'

Jang told us (somewhat rhetorically) that before the Uduk had men of Arum, they just had *koŋoro/*—the Birdrites for protecting fields from damage by birds and insects (see Chapter 1 (ii) (e)). On other occasions I heard that nobody listens to the Birdmasters in the Yabus valley now, and that Birdrites have not been properly carried out there for years. Some suggested that this might be why the crops were so bad. It was also generally agreed that there were more men of Arum in the southern Uduk communities than there were Ebony Men—a clear contrast with the northern valleys.

Jang had already told me that he did not divine by the 'kindling of ebony', the key mode of diagnosis practised by the Ebony Order. Nor did he practise the Restoral of a patient's Genius, or other standard techniques of the Ebony Men. He informed us that the diviners (*ŋari/*) of the very old days in Jebel Bisho, when he was a boy, had done the same things as those of the present-day—including divination by kindling the ebony. But he also explained to us the limitations of the diviners' power: for example, he said, at one time the people were very hungry, and the Ebony diviners themselves said that Arum Above was not content, and that people should bring animals for sacrifice. They did so; and Arum Above was content, and the crops improved. The 'missionary zeal' of Jang had clearly ensured a hearing for the message of a dominant heavenly divinity among these southern Uduk communities.

But far from displacing other ritual practice, the Yabus Arum men were attempting to encompass it. In supervising the new (Meban) pre-planting rites in the southern Uduk hamlets, Jang had attempted to draw in some older Uduk rites under the general schema of a sacrifice for the coming season's crops. I saw the southern version of the ceremony three times in full (apart from

---

[15] Compare Evans-Pritchard, *Nuer Religion*, pp. 12, 26, 45–6; John W. Burton, *God's Ants: A Study of Atuot Religion* (St. Augustin: Anthropos Institute), 1981.

the occasion when Fatma visited Puna's hamlet, described above).
Jang was in charge on two occasions. Although he was absent on
the third, his instructions were clearly being followed. Rainstones,
elements of the Birdrites, and even of the Ebony Order, were all
found a place. Jang was the visionary and architect of a new
synthesis. He was to offer the newly-recognized Arum Above a
bouquet of rites and symbols to mark the start of the planting
season. I will describe in outline one of the rites I witnessed, with
a few notes on the other variants I saw, to illustrate the integration
of older ritual, and its reorientation towards a divine presence in
the Above.

We arrive at Bwaginzi early on a May morning for the Arum
Beer to Repair the Earth (asu arum mmothosona 'cesh). Things
have already been collected together at the hut of Shweyis, himself
a man of Arum. There are all types of seeds; hoes; digging-sticks,
pointing to the upslope sorghum fields, two gourds of Arum oil,
one closed (this is the Birdrite gourd). An Arum spear is leaning
against the hut. Two chickens have been cut already, and there is
blood on the hoes.

The place of the rainstones is Brushed and the rainstones are
brought out and added to the assembled objects. Some twenty men
of the hamlet are lined up, and Jang Brushes their bodies and feet
with a chicken. He points his Arum spear to various directions,
holding it high in the air (roughly to south, east, north, north-east
and north-west: the directions of the various cultivation sites of the
hamlet). In between each lifting of the spear, Jang Touches it to
the body of the chicken. Then he cuts the chicken; he seems to
make a point of never doing this very thoroughly but allowing an
animal to wander and die in the manner it wishes, 'to be guided
by Arum'. The chicken's blood scatters over the grain, the hoes
and sticks, rainstones and gourds. There is consultation in the hut.
Jang then rearranges the objects in front of the hut, pointing the
digging-sticks this time to the river meadows. A goat is brought
out of the hut, sprinkled with water by Jang, and laid on its back.
Other Arum men sprinkle the rainstones with water, and sharpen
the spear. The spear is Touched to the goat—it is brought gently
against the goat's body in three places, and then the goat is cut,
though minimally, in the throat. Water is poured over its body,
and blood spurts over the rainstones and seeds. The goat is dragged
(anticlockwise) around the hut and its head banged on the

threshold. It is then taken and left on the edge of the hamlet, to be skinned and cut up later. Then men of the hamlet all gather and paddle both hands in the earth where the blood was shed; more water is poured on, which washes the blood well into the ground.

All now rinse their hands in fresh water, and divide into two parties, one for the sorghum fields and one for the river meadows. They take black chickens with them: this is for the Birdrite. They should be black 'because of small black insects which destroy the maize—manduruny; then there are ants in the sorghum fields.' The Birdrite gourd is taken, and these insects are sought in the fields, bitten, and put in the gourd. The chickens would have their heads pulled off while their bodies were held—an old Birdrite practice, to keep the body still. The party for the sorghum fields also takes some of the 'blessed' seeds for planting—sorghum, groundnuts, sesame, and gourd seeds as well as two hoes from in front of the hut. The river meadow party takes seeds appropriate for those fields, and another two (white) chickens. (On another occasion a pig was also taken to the meadows for sacrifice there.) A part of the chicken intestines is to be buried in each river meadow, and the rest of the intestines burned in the fields (with some of the pig meat if this is available). After the business in the fields, all return to the village to drink beer. There is a collection of money, which is given to Jang, for eventual transfer to the Meban leaders of the cult of Leina.

Informants explained that some of the sacrificial meat was *burned* so that the smoke would rise up into the sky. This was a good thing, for the smoke 'goes up and greets Allah'. This was explained to me in the southern dialect of Uduk, the word 'Allah' being used without any sense of incongruity. 'These things come from Arum, from the Meban country, long ago,' I was told. The anthropologist does not often see a 'tradition' so clearly in the making, and only rarely knows what is indicated by 'long ago'. In this case, it was probably no more than two or three generations since the Arum men of the southern Uduk had begun to draw together some of their older ritual practices under the rubric of a theistic system. This certainly appeared likely from the detail of the ceremony just described, together with the other versions observed in the southern Yabus valley.[16] Women played only a

---

[16] There were some interesting variations on the other occasions when I saw this

background role in these new rites, busy with the food and beer but not coming forward for the blessing of hands and feet (in contrast to the conspicuous role of Meban women).

Jang's inspiration drew on the teachings of Leina, but at the same time on other sources. He had, for example, assimilated something of the world of 'Nuer religion'. Three years before we met him, and at a time of escalation in the civil war disturbances in the southern Sudan, Jang had had a visitor, who came to the Yabus from further south to buy tobacco. His name was Ngur Thiang, and he wore shorts and a leopard skin over his shoulder. He carried the skin of a wild cat (kura/), a sheet, a blanket, and a mosquito-net. From the vocabulary Jang remembered of his language, the man was clearly Nuer. Moreover, Jang remembered that he had the Nuer marks (six parallel lines) on his forehead.[17]

This visitor, about the same age as Jang, taught him about 'Arum Zhwaŋge', or Nuer Divinity. Jang translated this to us comfortably as 'Allah'. Specific names also associated with this Divinity were Makwei (an ox-colour) and Melut. The latter can also be an ox-name, though it refers to a place on the White Nile and occurs as a somewhat ambiguous talking spirit, kuoth (or kwoth) among the Nuer.[18] Jang insisted that Arum Melut did not strike people

---

ceremony in the Yabus; for example, at another hamlet Jang placed the rainstones in a gourd underneath the eaves of the hut, and poured water on the eaves so that it dripped off the thatch and into the gourd. This was rain 'coming from above'. At the time of sacrifice, Jang or the other Arum men would raise their open palms, as if in supplication to the heavens. This resembled the pleas of the Meban women I had seen dancing and singing for rain at one ceremony to the sky divinity Juong. At one ceremony, elements of the Birdrites were included. At another ceremony, the Arum men invited two Ebony Men present to cut an extra chicken; this was 'to greet the Ebony Men with a chicken'. At the conclusion of each day's rites, the Arum men touched oil on the bodies or foreheads of all those who had taken part. There were many other ways in which a range of ritual practices was being drawn into a new schema, with reference to an overarching sky divinity.

[17] The visitor might of course have been a 'leopard skin priest' but the fact that he was in possession of a leopard skin does not necessarily mean that he had this status.

[18] Maluth (Melut) has been recorded several times in the Nuer ethnography. For example J. P. Crazzolara mentions in his book Zür Gesellschaft und Religion der Nueer (Vienna: Anthropos Institute), 1953, that maluuth is a category of 'kuudh pieny', and that Maluuth (luth—lung-fish) lives in the water and takes the shape of a water-snake. It is said to be a Dinka spirit, like Deng; that it is not one of those spirits which are conjured up with rattles; that it is rather one of those which speak through the mouths of those they possess (pp. 136, 153, 157). Evans-Pritchard in Nuer Religion notes that Maluth is a fetish (kulang); 'Nuer have tried to assimilate them to an earlier model of Spirit, and this is indicated metaphorically by calling both types of spirits ... children of daughter(s) of deng, a Nuer way of saying both that they are Dinka and that they

harmfully. Ngur Thiang taught him how to deal with crops and people so that there would be peace and plenty. If the instructions were not obeyed, he said, Arum would be angry, the rain would fail and the people would die. Jang was taught how to deal with crops, with sick people, and with fighting. For the crops, animals must be sacrificed: chickens, pigs, goats, sheep, and cattle. He should really kill a 'cow' (presumably an ox); otherwise a goat would do. Sacrifices should be made at a special shrine; and Jang had indeed built a shrine outside his house, something very new in the settlements of the Uduk. It consisted of an upright forked post (of *balanites aegyptiaca*, commonly known in Sudan Arabic as *heglig*, a wood used also in this special context by the Nuer) surrounded by four small posts in the ground 'for Arum to sit on, as we sit on a wooden bed'. Some chicken feathers were tied to one tip of the shrine, and a special Arum spear leaned against it. The whole was described by Jang as *jath kuoth* (Nuer: 'the post of Divinity'). A beast should be sacrificed after being tied to the forked post with a rope, and speared once in the side (either side) with the right hand. A goat or other small animal should be held between the thighs and have its throat cut. Sick persons should sit in front of the shrine and have a chicken killed in front of them.

Jang was told to speak to Arum before spearing a beast or killing a chicken. This is the Nuer *lam*, or invocation, described by Evans-Pritchard.[19] Such ritual language is foreign to older Uduk practice, where there is no equivalent of verbal 'prayer'. Jang was told to speak in the Uduk tongue so that the people should understand

are spirits of a very inferior order' (p. 100). P. P. Howell notes in his article 'Some observations on "earthly spirits" among the Nuer' in *Man*, 53 (1953), 85–8, that Maluth, a type of kolang, cannot be purchased. It is acquired by a man who sees *wea*—a black and white snake associated with maluth. Like other kolang it operates in three ways: it may be possessed by, or possess, an individual who uses it to diagnose and cure illness; it may act as a free agent in attacking people and causing illness, but without ill will on the part of the owner; or it may be directed by its owner against his enemies (pp. 86, 88). Compare B. H. Macdermot, *Cult of the Sacred Spear* (London: Robert Hale), 1972, p. 80. Douglas Johnson comments that 'Maluth appears to be one of that type of "talking" *kuoth pieny* which has an indeterminate status. It does now seem to be bought and sold like any *wal*, but it must be treated more like a *kuoth nhial* than as an ordinary—and somewhat amoral—*wal*. Many Nuer associated with prominent owners of *kulang* or *wal* will claim that the *wal* was used to protect and cure people, just as with the *kuuth* of the prophets; they claim a different moral place for these *kuuth* than is generally accepted.'

[19] The word *lam* may be translated in a number of ways, for example 'to invoke', 'to sacrifice', 'to curse', 'to bless', according to context (see the detailed discussion in Evans-Pritchard's *Nuer Religion*, pp. 209–11).

him, on the following lines: 'Let the children [that is, all the people] be well. Let the earth be in a good condition. Let the children's bodies be cool and not heated.' Jang explained 'children' as *uçi Arum*, 'children of Arum', quite a new notion for many of his own flock. He repeated the prayer: 'Let the people be well, let the earth be well, let the children remain cool and peaceful. Let there be no anger among them.' For if sacrifices are to be made to Arum, there should be no quarrelling. This would make Arum angry. If human blood is shed, Arum will be angry and there will be no rain. If there is fighting, Jang should gather the people and ask what is the cause. He should take animals from the people and sacrifice them. If a man has no animals, Jang may give him to the Turuk (i.e. the Government). But if the people give him animals, he need not pass the case on to the Government. The work of the Government (*hakuma*, Arabic) and the work of Arum, he explained, 'is the same' (I understand from Douglas Johnson that many Nuer now say this). If there were no Turuk, then it would not be possible to do the work of God (Arum), for there would be no peace—people would be running about killing each other all the time (one is reminded here that Jang had direct experience of the power of Government, when he was in its employ).

These were the main things that Jang had been taught along with some unspecified Nuer medicines, which he knew by the name common to Nuer and Komo, *wal*. His visitor stayed some weeks, and Jang paid him £2 (Sudanese), two goats, and ten loaves of pressed tobacco. But by 1967, he had not yet settled a dispute on the recommended lines, nor sacrificed an ox at his new shrine, though he had sacrificed chickens and goats. He continued the while with his general 'work of Arum'; he saw no contradiction between his earlier Meban-taught practice and that brought to him later by his Nuer teacher.

Unfortunately, however, little more than a year after our interview, Jang became ill and died. I was back in the northern hamlets when I heard of his death. There it was assumed straight away that the new Arum Dhamkin had been too powerful for him to cope with, and it had killed him. 'His place', as the Uduk say, has now been taken by Dhajas.

Algo was the one person I knew well who practised as an Ebony diviner as well as holding Arum powers. He told us how Marinyje, Sheikh Puna's late father, had warned him off the Arum of Jang.

Jang had, according to him, unwisely taken on too many Arum. He was not the only one to die as a result.

Marinyje himself said to me, 'Ha! Don't take hold of the Arum of Jang. Hang on to the one Arum from Leina....' For Marinyje and Jang were taken [as disciples of Akki] together ... but Jang took his own way and left Marinyje, to go and collect from Pur [in the Daga valley] according to his own will [*ki bwam piti*, with his own Stomach].

He died. Jang died. And Marinyje told me earlier, 'You listen, Jang has many Arum. He took the one of Pur, and took the one of Nuer, and he already had the one of Meban. He gave up the Meban one, took the Nuer one, took the Pur one. He kept all these Arum. It was not good at all...'.

A certain man from my father's people called Thilyan ... went to Pam 'Beshok [Yabus] ... and said that he would take up that Arum of Jang, for which bits of wood are knocked in the ground [i.e. the Arum posts]; that would make him strong, he said, and he would be stronger than me in the work. Ay! Arum struck him and he died also.

(iv) Resistance to Nilotic influence: northern Uduk transformations of Leina and Arum i Mis

From the Meban point of view, the cult of Leina is controlled by a hierarchy of persons, authority resting in the hands of the immediate family of Leina. This authority is, on the one hand, spiritual, in the sense that instructions on the sacrificial and ritual requirements for particular occasions are issued from time to time. On the other hand, the Meban leaders' authority makes itself felt through periodic demands upon their constituency, for gifts, tribute, and payments of various kinds, backed by threats of withholding the rain or otherwise causing hardship. The lay Meban population may well respond to these demands, but Uduk communities, especially in the northern valleys, are at best reluctant and half-hearted. Demands may come not only from the main leadership but also from ancillary men of Arum. For example Akki, who lived in Meban country in spite of his Uduk connections on the paternal side, had toured the southern Uduk settlements in the early 1960s requesting grain supplies, 'because he was hungry'. The pattern goes back at least to the time of Leina himself, as I found from the Chali manuscript notes on 'Customs', which I would date to the early 1940s. Here it is stated that because of Leina's word, sorghum was planted 'this year and not planted last. Each year a delegation goes to him with offerings of goats, brass bracelets and money.' This annual delegation was led at the time by Jibirdhalla, who had first welcomed Leina into Chali and become the leading Arum man of the Uduk. After the death of Jibirdhalla (in 1949) the informal leadership of the cult passed to Lyife, then living in northern Pam'Be, where there were several other important Arum men. However, there was by then a growing resistance, led by Uduk of the Tombak valley, to the dominance of the Meban through the Leina cult. There was also a reformulation of the spiritual teachings of the cult, and of the image of Leina.

Even in the 1940s there were tales current among the Uduk which went well beyond the miraculous acts of Leina's earlier life. He was already thought to be not merely a human being, but to have risen from the dead, and to be therefore, not a person (*wathim pa*) in himself, but an *arum* from beyond the grave (see Chapter 2 (v)). The Chali notes state: 'Leena's [*sic*] influence in this tribe is comparatively new although it has been gaining power in the last two years immensely. Many tales are told of him. Among them; that he died and after several days came to life again, therefore is a spirit. He controls the rain, the locusts and sickness. He can live under water as well as above, and when taken a prisoner to Kurmuk by the English some years ago, escaped by continually breaking the heavy chains they bound him with so that they despaired of keeping him, and let him go home. . . . Each year a delegation goes to him with offerings of goats, brass bracelets, and money. Jibirdhalla became his deputy because he took him in on his way back from Kurmuk, fed him, and finally drank beer that Leena had spat in [*a characteristically Nilotic motif*], thus partaking of his powers. Hence Jibirdhalla is the chief rain-maker hereabouts and the most feared. He is the one too, who spreads the word of all that Leena can do—even he says, he is able to give life to one who has been dead—especially after one of his yearly treks down to see him.'[20]

Douglas Johnson attempted to discover during his 1983 interviews with Meban whether they too held a view of Leina as risen from the dead. His informants did not respond to this idea, and an Uduk family living in Boing assured me that Meban do not have this view of Leina.

Among the Uduk today, however, tales about Leina go even

[20] 'Customs', Chali, p. 8.

further than claiming that he was himself a risen *arum*. They claim that before the man Leina died, he was not a Meban at all but an Uduk, a *wathim pa* in every way. It was only with his resurrection, which happened for no particular reason to be in Meban country, that he lived as a Meban. But he was still essentially an Uduk, one of the *'kwanim pa* in the ethnic sense, though ontologically transformed. Thus, on the occasion Leina visited the Uduk country during his 'progress' in the early 1930s and was received by Jibirdhalla and others, he is now represented as 'revisiting' his own people, and his own country. Some versions of the tale have the original Leina 'dying' somewhere out in the bush, and then coming home and becoming alive again.

The strongest version of the Leina story holds that he actually lived in Udukland, dying quite specifically in the settlement of Pam Bigin (near the Meban border). He was buried there, and then moved underground to come up through a particular hole in Meban country. Tente claimed to have seen the hole personally. I have already quoted from his account of the events of Leina's imprisonment and release; let me return to the same conversation, when Tente also elaborated on the 'original life' of Leina, and his resurrection:

Leina had *arum* to begin with, very much, strong. And then he died. At the time of his death, he was not *arum*. He was an Uduk, a real Uduk man [*wathim paŋ gana/*], and he died, and people buried him in a grave, dug by people there.

Then he went; he moved away and appeared in Meban country.... He had married a woman from the earth there.... They appeared together, the two of them, he with his wife, to live outside [i.e. outside the grave, above the ground]. They lived together outside; and the woman stayed, until she had had enough. Then she said to him, 'Ay! *Thah!* I'm going back to our place. Our country, which is pleasant. This country outside is unpleasant. I'm going back to our own good home.'

And Leina said to her, "Heh! Good, you go first; I will stay and come later.' Leina stayed, on and on; and he married a human girl outside, a Meban.... He settled down; he ... had children, five altogether. The woman lived for a while, and then she died.... She left him outside; but he also said to her, 'I will remain outside and look after my children. These little children, they are very young and I will not leave them. Let them grow up, and I will come later, I will follow you too later.'

And he remained, and the children grew up ... and then he went. He went to follow his wives to the ground there.

He remained for a time; and then he moved away again. There is a big pool called Ba'cba'c in the Yabus valley, and he went and appeared again there. He lived in the Yabus valley, in the water there ... and people saw him there and said: 'It is Leina! Leina is there at Ba'cba'c!'

At the time Leina was in the water in Yabus, he prevented the 'Fellata' (that is, Fulani or Hausa, groups of whom migrate annually with herds and flocks through Uduk country) from taking the crocodiles. 'He spoke awful words, and was about to kill the Fellata.... The Fellata became afraid of the water and stopped killing crocodiles.' I asked where Leina was now, and Tente replied: 'He is living in the earth there. He hasn't come out, he is remaining there. Yes, he is there in the earth. He will not appear again. He may stay, stay the whole year round. If he wishes, though, he will appear again, at another time in the future. He will appear outside.'

Tente spoke quietly but with utter assurance. On another occasion, he told me of the hole he had himself seen in a swampy place near Leina's Meban home, where as *arum* he had emerged with his wife from below. He said Leina's body, on emerging, had been fully grown but eaten by white ants. I also heard Tente's account of how his father Naka saw Leina, in the form of a Rainbow. Naka had been given a spear by Leina, kept it in his hut, and 'did a little Arum work' of healing and sacrifice. It was his brother Nyere, already an Ebony diviner, who successfully treated Naka after the approach of the Rainbow. Some months later Leina claimed that this Rainbow had been himself. When Nyere subsequently fell ill, Naka interpreted this as Leina's punishment for their having abandoned special cultivation of the site where the Rainbow had appeared. It is characteristic that a diviner and an Arum man who are *brothers* join in a common resistance to this external threat.

It was the rainy season. And Leina appeared in the form of the Rainbow: beer was brewed in the hut of Naka. A great rainshower poured down. The Rainbow appeared while people were drinking beer. And they came out and they fought the Rainbow ... as the Rainbow was about to go inside the hut.

People said, '*Çaah!* A great Rainbow! A great bad thing. It's going to go inside the hut and kill people!' They didn't know it was Leina ... and they struck him.

And then he remained in their country [i.e. Meban] ... and came back in the dry season, like this, when the grass is burnt. He came, and said to the people, 'Naka, why did you attack me?' Naka said, 'Ay! I didn't recognize you; I didn't know it was you!'

He laughed ... and later sought out Naka, and asked for a settlement of the debt, saying, 'Naka, you must give me a goat.' Naka took a goat for him, took a goat for him and cut its throat. And then he took another, a female goat, which Leina led away, to Meban country.

Later, it came on to rain, after he had gone home. People grew a lot of *kala* [a special type of red sorghum] in the village, in the place where [Leina] had been struck.

Then people moved site, to the other bank. But [Leina] became angry, and came to strike Nyere as he was sleeping on the ground at night, and he nearly died. In the morning, Naka immediately came outside, and said to his brother, 'Ay! Nyere, you, you were struck by Leina. What are we to do?' And his brother said to him, 'Ay! I am dying; what are we to do indeed? You should take that big goat, that big female goat, and cut its throat.' So Naka took the goat, and cut it. He cut it for Nyere, and made blood, and treated him [*nyoŋ*] with the blood.

Among the tales told of Leina are that he could seize an animal and transform it into a person (reminiscent of the Shilluk traditions about their hero Nyikang). For example, I have heard that Dali, whom I understand to be Leina's sister's son, and a leader of the cult today, was originally a crocodile. Leina seized him and now he is a human being (*wathim pa*).

These tales reinforce the idea of Leina as a living presence. If Leina had already 'risen from the grave' in the 1930s when he came to visit Udukland, he is no more dead now than he was then, and could obviously reappear at any time. As an *arum* beyond death, he is a permanent presence. Further, there is the interesting implication that the children of Leina, including his son Yaḵka, who was leading the cult in the 1960s, are themselves (for the Uduk) part-human, part-*arum*, because their father was already a risen spirit. Although I have not heard this aspect of things discussed, it does imply that the hold of the present Meban leaders over the Uduk depends on more than merely temporal succession to their father's position.

The belief that Leina was formerly an Uduk was prevalent even in the Yabus valley to the south. Puna assured me that not only was Leina an Uduk: he was a Lake, a member of the largest birth-group with the longest history, and specifically belonged to a section of the Lake resident both in the Yabus valley and in Pam Bigin.

The real Lake of course, according to Puna, have an *arum* of their own from the earliest times (see Chapter 2 (i) (*f*) above).

In addition to the reformulation by the Uduk of the image of Leina and his relationship to them, there has been a developing ambivalence in the way Leina's spirit is thought to affect the people. Although from the 'inside', the teachings of Leina (and other Nilotic religious figures) offer an understanding of divinity and the human condition in a general and benevolent sense, and, as we have seen, were interpreted in this way by Jang, from 'outside', the spirit of Leina could be intepreted very differently. Instead of being welcomed as bringing peace and health in the name of a universal Divinity, a manifestation of the power of Leina could be resisted as a specific appearance of *arum* ultimately from the land of the dead, and likely to cause danger and sickness to the community if not kept within bounds. The very enhancement of the normal powers of the cult's practitioners by the *arum* of Leina was, from this latter point of view, a danger to those around them; and indeed the way in which the cult was spreading in the 1960s indicated that the Uduk had in this way modelled the *arum* of Leina on the older dangerous presences of their known world. A sudden sickness, especially if it involved fainting, delirium or loss of consciousness, aimless wandering or loss of memory, would probably be diagnosed as seizure by *arum*: 'the person is seized by *arum*', *wathi bu'th ma rum*. It would then be an appropriate question to ask, 'By the *arum* of whom?' And a common reply would indicate the *arum* of a particular man of the Leina cult, his own inherent power enhanced by this presence within him. Full recovery from the sickness might follow rites to rid the person of the presence; or, alternatively, this might not be possible, and the person would have to be accommodated to the permanent enhancement of the *arum* in his or her body. In effect this would mean becoming a member of the community of those who 'had Arum' or 'had the Arum of Leina' in them, and thus able subsequently to treat others. Here it becomes extremely difficult for us to decide whether to use the form Arum, or *arum*, as this is indeed a crucially ambivalent area. It seemed to me that as time went on, having the 'Arum of Leina' meant less and less an ability to treat sicknesses from a variety of sources, but increasingly, rather, a capacity to treat others affected by the presence of the *arum* of Leina itself. Although in principle the men of Arum were supposed to know, from inner guidance or from dreams, what were the causes of disease, the key acts of effective diagnosis still lay with the Ebony Men who practised, as it were, in terms of *arum* rather than Arum, and who saw the spiritual power of Leina as a threat like any other.

These processes, which I understand as a part of the way the Uduk have made the cult of Leina their own, were already under way in the 1940s. The Chali notes suggest that even at the height of Jibirdhalla's influence as the leading man of Arum, it was the Ebony diviners—here 'witch-doctors'—who were making the crucial diagnosis, defining Leina primarily as a source of invasive sickness, rather than of healing enlightenment; they themselves appear to be the ones who reported to the missionaries Leina's claim to cause sickness (something I feel they may have, at the least, exaggerated), and they appear to have regularly passed instructions for sacrifice to Jibirdhalla, as 'Leina's deputy'.

To the 'Kwanim pa' there are very few if any natural causes. Especially is this true of sickness. For this reason, the divining witchdoctors flourish. They are called in event of sickness and while holding a lighted ebony wand over a gourd of water, claim to see the image of the one who caused the sickness. Sometimes it may be one who has an evil eye, or maybe a known enemy of the stricken one, but most often the 'arum' or spirit of one of several known to possess such, is accused. Just now, the popular one is the arum of Leena—the Meban rainmaker, whose deputy is Jibir-dhalla (Co-Gwasi). On a recent visit, Leena declared that when people sickened, they might know that he was the cause, and the witchdoctors fell in with it. In such a case, his spirit is said to have separated the 'shadow' (soul) of the sick man from his body. The treatment is for the witchdoctors to recover the departed soul, and then for the patient to have offered a sacrifice to the spirit, so that it may not occur again. As deputy, Jibirdhalla is responsible for the sacrificing.[21]

These notes give details of a particular case. The Ebony Men Restore the patient's Genius, or as here 'shadow', and the patient goes the next day to Jibirdhalla; sometimes he receives the payment, sometimes the Ebony Men do. Although Jibirdhalla, as 'Leina's deputy', would no doubt have given a different account of these matters, it seems evident that the Ebony Men were in control. Through their 'kindling of the ebony', their diagnoses were already defining as an 'object', circumscribing, and attempting to contain the *arum* of Leina.

[21] 'Customs', Chali, p. 2.

1(*a*). Following birth: Jilge's baby is 'brought out' to be greeted by Ha'da, maternal uncle and Arum man. He Brushes the baby with a chicken (see Chapter 2 (iii)).

1(*b*). Following death: some months after burial the grave is opened and repacked with earth 'to settle the *arum* of the deceased' (see Chapter 2 (iv)).

2(*a*). On the same occasion of Beer for the Grave the deceased's hunting and fighting weapons, and his musical instrument (here a lyre), are treated with red ochre and returned to his father's people (see Chapter 2 (iv)).

2(*b*). *Athele/* dancing, with beaten logs and simple flutes, takes place on the settled grave (see Chapter 2 (iv)).

3(*a*). Fatma, who came to control the cult of the Meban prophet Leina, conducting the pre-planting sacrificial rite at the Uduk home of Sheikh Puna Marinyje (1967)
(see Chapter 3 (iii)).

3(*b*). Jang, the priestly figure who became influential among the southern Uduk in the 1960s, with his Nilotic shrine (see Chapter 3 (iii)).

4(*a*). Ha'da, who became a devotee and practitioner of the cult of Leina following his own illness
(see Chapter 3 (iv)).

4(*b*). A healing rite of the men of the Arum of Leina (see Chapter 3 (iv)).

5(*a*) (*top left*). William Danga (centre) and Pastor Paul Rasha (behind him) conducting a mass baptism near Chali (December 1967) (see Chapter 4).

5(*b*) (*top right*). A young convert (see Chapter 4).

5(*c*) (*middle*). Christmas crowds at Chali, 1967 (see Chapter 4).

5(*d*) (*left*). Disguised as a frightening *arum*, William Danga plays in a Christmas charade (see Chapter 4).

6(*a*). Pastor Paul Rasha Angwo, the first Uduk pastor, with his first family, including twin boys (from a 1957 pamphlet of the Sudan Interior Mission, with acknowledgements) (see Chapter 4).

6(*b*). The new church at Chali constructed in metal in the late 1970s after two previous buildings were destroyed by fire. Photographed 1983 (see Chapter 4).

7(*a*). Omda (Chief) Talib el Fil of Chali, with an armed *ghaffir* in 1966 (see Postscript to Part II).

7(*b*). The new mosque opened in Chali's market centre in 1983 (see Postscript to Part II).

8. Tente, in his diviner's attire, 1967 (see Chapter 5).

9. Early initiation into the Ebony Order: the boy Cile is 'caught' by the diviners' medicine and made one of them (1966) (see Chapter 5 (v)).

9(a) (top). The boy's personal Genius is diagnosed as lost, and two diviners search at the root of a tree where he plays.

9(b) (above left). A chicken is cut over the gourd of water containing the retrieved Genius.

9(c) (above right). The gourd is poured over the child.

9(d) (left). Cile is anointed with oil and rubbed with the diviners' stones; the medicine Spice is hung around his neck with cowries.

10(*a*). Sebko undergoes graduation to seniority as a diviner (see Chapter 5).

10(*b*). The people gather for three days of dancing and singing to celebrate this occasion (see Chapter 5).

11(*a*). The diviners' set drama. They fight with Rainbow Medicine, some are 'killed' and then revive (see Chapter 5).

11(*b*). The Ebony diviners greet each other by clasping with the left hand and Spraying medicine on each other's foreheads (see Chapter 5).

12. A sequence from Nyane's treatment, 1983 (see Chapter 6).

12(a) (*top left*). The diviner Brushes Nyane's body with a chicken and presses it to her.

12(b) (*top right*). He draws out 'foreign things' from her body, using hands and mouth.

12(c) (*bottom left*). A colleague Straightens her limbs.

12(d) (*bottom right*). Nyane can relax after she is anointed with oil.

The Arum men

How does a person—almost always a male among the Uduk—become a man of Arum? We have noted already that Jibirdhalla was sponsored 'without being sick' and also that in the case of the 'real Lake', *arum* is present within them in a special manner from birth. But today, cults like that of the Arum of Leina spread through seizure.

I have not witnessed the rites which follow seizure, and make a man a person of Arum. But in accounts given me, animal sacrifice is the main feature of the rites. In the account which follows, it is interesting that the key diagnosis of the condition is made by the Ebony Men. Ha'da, who had been made a man of Arum in the late 1930s following a period of illness which apparently included smallpox, told me something of his own story (see Plate 4a). I have already quoted the earlier part of his account, of the smallpox outbreak in the Chali area at that time, and the fact that he and his sisters were accused of causing it by witchcraft. His father's people were the main accusers, which meant that Ha'da had to flee; he had no protectors; and it was at this time that he came to Pam'Be ('KP: 188–9). The account continues:

It was the *arum* which seized me, seized me at the time of the smallpox, and I went berserk [*gus adu*, literally 'the Liver running about']. . . . I lived, but a few little spots spoiled my body, here and there, at the time of the *arum*. And I knew the people of Arum who lived there in Chali, I knew them. First the *arum* dealt with me, and then the people of Arum. I had been given a different Liver inside here; it was my father's people. My fathers put a different Liver inside here. And then the Arum people treated me. Yes, the people of Arum treated me.

Ha'da goes on to describe a dream, in which he realized that he would be killed by his own father's people. The implication of his father's people 'changing his Liver' is that they were cursing and damaging him. But he was saved, and the positive healing and redemptive potential of Arum is lucidly conveyed in Ha'da's description of the dream:

I climbed up the roof-frame and I was pierced with a spear up there, just as I told you I was going to be killed like that. I was pierced by a spear up there. And my father-in-law seized me strongly and pulled me to the ground to steady me. But I overcame my father-in-law and went up again. My Liver was disturbing me, and people pierced me with a spear up there.

And the blood flowed down from above. And I came down to find my blood on the ground. . . .

It was Arum at last which ran to help me perhaps. Arum is the one who helped me. For the smallpox would have killed me to death perhaps. . . .

I didn't understand at all. I was very wretched. I appeared from a hole. I was not alive. Yes. I appeared ill. My Stomach is not as it used to be [i.e. he is no longer 'himself', having been shattered by the behaviour of his father's people]. My Stomach is bad [he is not content]. The smallpox struck me here and there, and I was about to die.

I went to a man of Arum, Ḵalpuna . . . I went at night, went to sleep at his place. His hut. And then he treated me, treated me, treated me. I stayed there not understanding anything. I came and sat silent at my own hut door. He was my brother-in-law. My brother-in-law has Arum.

Ha'da was then led away from Chali, to live in Pam'Be. He was supposed to return to Chali for further treatment, but has not done so, and still suffers. 'And the Ebony Men divined by kindling the ebony and said I was struck by *arum* from Chali there. I didn't understand. I didn't understand.' This divination was fairly recent; it seems that whereas Ha'da himself had found salvation through the power of Arum, the Ebony Men were offering a different view, that his continuing intermittent illness was the result of his original seizure by *arum* in Chali and his incomplete treatment.

I will try to give examples of the healing activities of the men of Arum (see Plate 4b). It is difficult to do so with any clarity because in practice, especially in the northern valleys, they work closely with the Ebony Men and are taking over some of the latter's techniques. Cases are frequently passed from Ebony Men to men of Arum, or shared from the start, and the distinctive contribution of the Arum men cannot always be seen these days. I return to further discussion of this situation in Part III of the book. There is, however, one affliction which in my experience is dealt with exclusively by the Arum men once it has been diagnosed, and that is when a person is 'struck by the ground *arum*', *'kosh ma ruma 'cesh*, or just *'kosh ma rum*, with the implication that one of the recently dead is involved. This is thought to happen when there has been quarrelling or bad gossip within a matrilineal birth-group, and it is the dead of this group that are thought to be expressing their anger. I have given an account of one such case in my earlier book (*'KP*: 190), and now give a brief description of another.

Shwamge, one of Tente's wives, has been ill. Tente kindles the ebony and finds she is struck by arum. *Gossip suggests this was not 'for no reason', but perhaps because she has been angry with another woman for beating her own daughter, who has been looking after the other woman's child. Tente calls in two men of Arum, Ha'da and Ruthko. Each in turn Brushes the patient, with the same chicken, passing it through her legs, and the chicken is cut. Ha'da Blows gently on the knife, towards the nose and ears of the patient; Ruthko touches his fingers in the blood and Blows it similarly. He Straightens her joints. Ha'da touches a little blood on his Arum spear, and Blows this to her nose and ears, while gently spitting on it. He then Touches the spear to her shoulders, chest, sides, legs, arms, and draws it down the length of her body. A pig is cut without ceremony; Ha'da Blows its blood to the patient as before. She is given some 'medicine of arum' to drink. Then, in conclusion, a small bunch of Wild Mint, wopo (a special plant, emblematic of the Arum men and their practice), is dipped in oil, and then Blown to the patient and rubbed on her body. Her joints are finally Straightened.*

As a minimal rite, this case has some interest: the main elements being Straightening of the patient, the offering of an animal and Blowing to her of the blood, the drinking of medicine, and the anointing with oil and Wild Mint.

In treating their patients, the men of Arum deal primarily with the central vital organ of a person, the Liver, where the blood is concentrated and which is a focus of *arum*. Things Blown to the patient, and breathed in, go down to the Liver. The sweet-smelling Wild Mint in particular should calm the *arum* within. Where a patient has been struck by *arum*, and is still disturbed, then the blood of an animal, when Blown to the nostrils, should make the *arum* leave, content.

Halid had been ill for some time, with what was thought to be *ayin*. This is an illness that makes a person very thin; and for this reason he had not been drinking milk—a food thought to aggravate (or even help to cause) the condition. He was himself a man of Arum, and though many years had passed since his initiation, he had not yet practised. In a recent consultation the EbonyMen had pronounced him struck by *arum*, and they therefore called in three Arum men (Ha'da, Dhirmath, and Ruthko). The Genius had also been seen in the previous divination; in fact it had been seen in two parts. One was in the river and one in the new sorghum fields. Koro, an Ebony diviner, had already Restored that part of the Genius in the river, and on the day of Halid's treatment by the Arum men, a second ebony consultation was held which revealed only one sign of the lost Genius in the fields. But *arum* was also seen in the water. The Ebony diviners gave me what was possibly their own opinion—that Halid was struck by the *arum* of Ture, the Arum man who had originally initiated him. That is, as I understand it, he was struck by the *arum* of Leina indirectly through its presence in the body of Ture. The only possible salvation was through a blood offering by other men of Arum.

First of all, however, the Restoral of the Genius has to be completed, and one diviner and the three Arum men carry this out. They go to the new sorghum fields and bring the remaining part of it back. On their return, the diviner does the Extraction: that is, sucking out the foreign bits and pieces from Halid's body. Then the Arum men Brush him and cut the chicken, which dies well on its side. They dip their fingers in the blood, Touch it to the patient's body and then Blow the blood to his nose. A goat is then taken, and led into the hut. When it is brought out it is walked about in a figure-of-eight circuit in front of the hut; the idea is that it should be taken to face all the places the patient is in the habit of going. The goat is made to drink water. Then it is picked up and held towards the patient's body: this is also to Brush the patient, to acquaint the goat with the arum that is disturbing him. Ha'da Touches his Arum spear to the neck of the goat, and then to the body of Halid. The goat however has its throat cut by a knife, and is dragged around the hut anticlockwise. (The arum making the patient ill will follow the trail of blood and leave him alone.) Some of the blood spurts into a gourd of water containing the Genius brought with a little earth from the fields, together with some Wild Mint. This gourd is now poured over the patient (this is known as up ka bas—to bathe in the blood). The Arum men Straighten Halid's limbs and oil is rubbed on him. In addition, some fat from the goat is heated on some dry grass placed between his legs, so that the smoke envelops him; and the fat is pressed to his body and smoothed in. A strip of the goat's skin (from the neck) is finally placed on him, over the right shoulder, and he will wear this for some time.

Although the power of healing in these rites is unquestioned, it paradoxically coexists with the ever-present danger of the same power. I have already mentioned the Ebony Men's opinion that the patient was made sick in the first place by the *arum* of his own former sponsor. There was another detail at Halid's rite that again pointed the danger of the close presence of *arum*. A young woman, Noske, in the same hamlet, was pregnant. Koro, as an Ebony Man who knew these things, told me that another pregnant woman had had a miscarriage, following a previous *arum* healing rite where she had accidentally stepped on the blood of the goat. So to prevent any such misfortune occurring with Noske, she was treated by a local Arum man—one not involved in Halid's case. He dipped some Wild Mint in sesame oil and Blew it to her nose and ears. Some oil was rubbed on her body. Then a little meat of the goat was Offered to her; she spat out the first mouthful, and swallowed the second. Her limbs were then Straightened.

Besides illustrating the methods of the men of Arum, especially in animal offerings (*mii abas*: to make blood), this case shows how their work is interlinked with that of the Ebony Men, and at the same time suggests how the Ebony Men may reinterpret as dangerous the power of the Arum of Leina. At the same time, the men of Arum are shown participating in techniques which are beyond any doubt primarily those of the Ebony Order. They are taking part in the Order's key act of diagnosis by kindling the ebony fire, and in the Restoral of the patient's personal Genius. This pattern of co-operation was common in the 1960s, and indicated a convergence in patterns of disease interpretation and treatment among the northern Uduk. The Arum of Leina was increasingly treated as a variant on an older notion of *arum*; as one more dangerous variety of spirit power which could disturb a patient's Liver. For such a condition, the remedy in Uduk eyes must lie with those who have already appropriated for themselves this form of *arum*, and can therefore treat its effects.

This takes us a long way from the universal claims of Jang's theology, from a Divinity in the sky whose blessing could be sought on the fields and to whom prayers and sacrifice for general peace and individual health could be made. But these theocentric claims derived from the Nilotic religious tradition had not penetrated and changed the northern Uduk world from within, as they were in the process of doing in the Yabus valley. Not only was there widespread reluctance among the northern Uduk to go along with the demands made by the Meban leadership of the Leina cult, but they were transforming the image of Leina from a prophet of general salvation into one more threatening spirit. Ha'da once told me (after a trip to the Yabus) that the real Arum of the 'kwanim pa was in the sky. He commented in explanation that the *arum* of the ground (from those who have died) does not strike people, as the Arum Above certainly can, and does. Others rejected what Ha'da had said, as 'maybe mission talk'. Tente's mother Dwarke simply snorted at the idea of Arum Above and said it was nonsense.

Lyife's death

The expansion of the Leina cult in northern Uduk country from 1930 onwards had increased tension on many levels. Eventually there was a major crisis in 1965. In the early rains of that year, Lyife, by far the most influential man of Arum in the northern Uduk settlements, initiated by Leina himself, and successor to the dominant figure of Jibirdhalla, was murdered.

Lyife was speared in the back as he went to the fields in his home area of northern Pam'Be. A man was lying in wait for him, a man who had recently lost a child, and who held Lyife responsible. A trial followed and the man received a ten-year prison sentence. There was no attempt to evade or cover up the fact of the murder; it had been a calculated matter and it was known that a trial would follow.

The killing of Lyife did not happen on impulse. It was the culmination of a long period of mounting anxiety in the hamlets, especially of Pam Bigin and Pam'Be, and even among the kinsfolk of Lyife himself. He was the outstanding Arum man of his time, but increasingly (and characteristically) people had come to think that from curing illness, he had turned to causing it. Various deaths, including those of children in his own matrilineal birth-group, were rumoured to be his responsibility.

I first arrived in the field at the end of 1965, and chose to settle in northern Pam'Be, without knowing anything of this killing that had happened less than a year before. I came to realize only much later that much of what I had witnessed over several years was directly or indirectly linked to the death of Lyife. It was obviously difficult to talk freely with people about this matter; but I was eventually able to gather enough to begin to reconstruct what had happened. Initial explanations offered one main theme: that the *arum* of Lyife (enhanced of course by that derived from Leina) had grown so big and powerful that it was in itself a contagious danger to others, particularly to those close at hand, and more especially to matrilineal kin (a typical problem for holders of special power).

But beyond this were suggestions that went further. It was mostly women who began to tell me, or to hint, that Lyife was causing deaths because he himself was born from a 'bad womb'. He was evil from his own birth. There were rumours that he had been born with teeth; and for at least a couple of generations the only way to deal with known *dhathu/* who were actively harming others had been by killing them. The enhancement of this man's power by that of Leina can only have made the potential danger greater, but the real question was not of the danger of the *arum* of Leina as such. It was that of an innate capacity for evil from a contaminated birth. Let me quote from some accounts of the death of Lyife.

These events are still felt to be recent. Although most of my information was obtained in the late 1960s, it was in confidence and I therefore quote informants anonymously. The first account is from a middle-aged man and the second a young married woman.

Yes. [Lyife] was a very great man of Arum indeed.

Was he bigger than others in our area?

Yes. Long ago, he stood alone. Alone. All these Arum which are so many, these ones that came later, are not really Arum. He was Arum alone.

And who sponsored him?

Lyife? He was *arum* on his own [from the *bwa*, the inside, the Stomach, the will], from his mother perhaps.

From his mother?

Yes, from the belly from which his mother bore him. You were borne by your mother; now weren't you borne by your mother yourself singly?

Yes.

You were borne by yourself, singly. But he was borne by his mother, it is said, with teeth already growing in the belly. Teeth. Teeth indeed. Heh! They say teeth had grown in the belly. He became a witch [*a'di di 'bo/u*] in the belly there. . . . Yes, be became a witch. And he grew up, and people said he was *arum*, was *arum*, from being able to excel in *arum* practice. And he grew, and when he was grown up, he went to Leina's place.

Who took him there?

He went by himself.... He practised *arum dhathu*/ ['evil ritual practices';
I have not heard the phrase elsewhere] before he went; this thing is not
understood ... and then he went to Leina. Leina treated him, saying, 'Ha!
Since you are doing these things, let me give you the proper thing.... You
can practise the real Arum rites.'

So he had Arum at last and he came home. He stayed at home. He
carried out a lot of Arum activity, and his *arum* became very big, and he
grew strong with this great *arum*.

He grew with all his Arum activity....

And then he left the Arum business of Leina ... and he began to do
some bad things, some little things which were wrong.

What were these things?

He would come in a dream at night. He dropped the practice of Arum.
He would come in a dream at night ... and people would see him as they
were sleeping, lying down. That is why he was killed, for it was said he
killed people.... Lyife [also] prevented the rain from falling for people.
He went up there, rode the rain in a dream, and the rain disappeared.
There was no rain, and the place dried up completely.

The same account claims that Lyife was anticipating his forthcoming end, and that this was confirmed by Leina. When Lyife was
visiting Leina, to introduce one of his own new protégés, according
to my informant the following conversation took place:

Lyife says, 'For myself, my feet are rather hot from travelling. I go to
villages far away ... I collect a lot of things too, in my hut here and in my
shoulder-bag, lots of my things I carry on my back. I carrry them to
people's villages there as though I were moving house.'

Leina said, 'But what for? As for me now, where is the skin bag I carry
on my back?" ... He, Lyife, said to him: 'Ay, but for me, I know myself.
Mine is mixed up [i.e. with different *arum*].... Something may happen to
me somewhere on my way; and this thing will shelter me; my things
collected here will be buried with me in my grave in the place where people
will kill me somewhere.'

Lyife said this to Leina.... Lyife said, 'Yes, what I have said is the
truth.' And Leina said, 'Yes, it is the truth. Good.'

It is scarcely surprising that among Lyife's protégés, one goes about
a good deal and is already the subject of gossip (for example, that
Lyife gave him 'his eyes'), and another one I know, though quite
senior, behaves very circumspectly.

The young woman's account follows. She was of the same birth-
group as Lyife, who was therefore, a 'mother's brother' to her. She
uses here an alternative name of his, Gur.

I was ill. People led me to the fields, the fields of Gur's place.... I went to carry grain. I then got sick permanently. People led Nyethko [a senior Ebony Man] to Restore my Genius.... My throat was hurting me here.... A certain Ebony Man, a Bunyan from the mountains, came ... they kindled the ebony for me ... while I was about to sicken and die....

I was struck by my senior mother's brother, called Gur. He died, he was speared as a witch [*dhathu/*] and he died. I saw him in a dream at night; he came right up to me, and I was about to fall quite dead.

For he didn't kill strangers. He always killed just his own kind [*bungwar*, body]; and then he eventually died, for people said he was now killing outsiders [his attacker was not of the same birth-group]. They killed him stealthily as he was weeding maize in the woods at Dhudhuru, in that flood-plain at Pany Ca'ba there. And we ran there to see him.... The Meban dug a shallow hole and he was buried in the forest.

If he had lived we would not be alive. He always killed us, those of us borne by [my mother]. We were not surviving well, we were dying. We used to die when we were still very young. She bore us like this, and when we were about to crawl, he killed us, many of us. [My mother] now lives without many children, just three of us remain....

Tente [a senior Ebony Man] came and led me to stay here, and he treated me by Extracting foreign matter, and he gave me some very bitter medicine. I improved. And Nasaran came [an Ebony Man from Lele, with mixed Uduk and Bertha background]. They said I should let them lead me to [his village]. They treated me. We stayed for a long time, three days ... they took my money and kindled ebony.

My informant's treatment was still continuing. She gave a graphic description of the scene where the body was found, with blood flowing all over the place 'like a great antelope'. The man who attacked Lyife had been very upset by the death of his child, and became aggressive. According to her, Lyife was not known to kill persons outside his birth-group until this time; he had just damaged his own folk with grain (bits of sorghum were always found in their bodies); he didn't kill a lot of outsiders because he was afraid of the spear which would kill him. The young woman also suggested that he knew that he was called *dhathu/*, and that one day someone would kill him. The Meban who helped to dig the grave in the bush were very junior persons, and soon ran away—they were blood-friends, *abas*, but it was mainly the women who were left to lift the body into the grave. I asked how this man had become bad; was it from his birth?

Yes, it was very bad, from the giving of two in birth, and he became bad. Together with his sister, who is still alive, though blind. Born from their mother, together with the first-born they are witches [uni 'boʔ] the two of them. He with his real sister. And we don't know this *arum*, it comes to make one give birth to two like that, we don't know why.

Meban reactions

The Meban leaders of the Arum of Leina cult were furious at the killing of Lyife, their chief acolyte among the Uduk. They responded by issuing instructions for special rites and collections of money in the years following 1965. In the early rains of 1966, I witnessed on three occasions a ceremony which was being held in every hamlet of Pam'Be. It appeared at first to be a normal rite to ensure the success of the new crop season, a 'traditional' point in the agricultural calendar. But in fact it was carried out on recent instructions from the Meban Arum men. The previous year it had rained very heavily (at first people said the rain was 'weeping for Lyife'). But the rain was poor for the rest of the season, and there was a meagre harvest. The Meban ritual leaders informed the Uduk that Arum was angry with the Uduk people as a whole because of the killing of Lyife. Yakka in particular was very upset, as he had been a personal friend. The ceremonies of 1966, prescribed for each hamlet cluster in the northern Uduk valleys, were to atone for the killing of Lyife, and to comfort Yakka. If he were not comforted, principally by the collection of money and other tributes from the Uduk communities, there could be a danger that the rain would fail again.

A second round of ceremonies, with collections of money and goods, was held in 1967 for the same reason. I saw only one performance in Pam'Be, but by chance saw three while in the Yabus valley: these I have referred to above, and shown how Jang was drawing such rites into an encompassing whole. In 1968, everyone in Pam'Be was waiting for further instructions from the Meban, and a visit from Yakka himself was anticipated. He was expected to announce that in every little hamlet the Arum men should again make beer, as before, and hold a collection for him. There was a long delay. The rain was very scanty during April and May. By late June Yakka had still not appeared. But in any case the rain was performing well by this time, largely due to the unconnected visit of Dhabara, a famous rain master from Jebel Jerok, and the efforts of 'the people in general'—that is, everybody else's rainstones. By 1969, the Meban no longer made demands in connection with Lyife's killing; they had found another ground for their requests, in the form of Yakka's marriage. Substantial gifts were in the event taken, 'to greet' him [*salam*, Arabic] 'because his *arum* is very great'.[22]

The versions of the pre-planting rite, the Arum Beer to Repair the Earth, that I saw in Pam'Be in 1966 and 1967 were rather sketchy affairs. I saw no effort to integrate the prescribed Meban rite with existing Uduk practice such as the use of rainstones or the Birdrites. No one took overall authority. Miscellaneous Arum men conducted the rite in each little hamlet cluster, and often seemed to have 'forgotten their lines'. The act of 'sacrifice' did not have the same central place in the day's rites. Even more telling was the dearth of comment and exegesis from the participants. There was no talk of Allah or Arum i Mis, and, as far as I was aware, no act of 'greeting Arum Above' with rising smoke or upturned palms. The collection of money and goods in kind for the Meban leaders was often delayed, and sometimes this tribute never reached them at all.

At Ruthko's at Waka'cesh in April 1966, things are being handled mainly by himself and Ha'da. As people arrive they bring digging sticks for both sorghum and for maize, large and small bladed hoes, an axe, and seeds to lay in front of Ruthko's hut. There are maize cobs; seeds of sesame, gourd, pumpkin; beans, nine types of sorghum, four types of maize kernel. Some chickens are tied up

---

[22] In the dry season there had been a visit by three Meban who informed the Uduk Arum men that they should all bring things for Yakka's marriage (the second or third). Already in early April three Uduk Arum men had brought blankets, and from Waka'cesh Ruthko (who had once been visited by Yakka) was supposed to take money, sesame, and sorghum. By late April, it was said by some that it was too late to go. The homeland was in a bad condition, unsettled and 'hot' as there had been a series of sudden deaths in southern Pam'Be. They would not be expected to go now, and would 'probably go next year instead'. However, suddenly at the beginning of June, I heard that a party of Arum men (not including Ruthko) had recently gone to Yakka, in his home in 'Len' [Liang], well beyond Boing (and therefore at least forty-five miles distant). There were between seven and ten in the group, and they took blankets, money, sesame, and so forth as gifts for Yakka. Some had taken £4 (Sudanese) and some had taken £5 (Sudanese); ŋule, who seemed to be the leader, had taken £10 (Sudanese), but Yakka declined to accept more than half that amount. The cash was raised by each Arum man selling crops from his own household, and the goods were their personal possessions. When the visitors reached Yakka's home, a large goat was cut for them, and Yakka gave instructions that all the Uduk rainstones should be brought out.

ready and a young male goat is tethered. Three Arum spears are leaning against the hut.

Ha'da calls all the men of the hamlet to stand in line, facing the fields; Ruthko Brushes the hoe and seeds and the men with a chicken, and then other Arum men and he cut it; a second is cut by a couple of Ebony Men called to the task, and then a third by the Arum men again. All die well, and the Arum men touch their fingers in the blood and blow it lightly off in various directions. The planting sticks are also touched with the blood. Water is poured on the chickens' bodies. The Arum men then take small gourds in which the seeds have been mixed, chew a little of the mixture, and spit a little on the men's feet and hands. The goat is laid on the ground and its throat cut with an Arum spear. The blood gushes out, and a large gourd of water is poured over. The men are called forward and press the blood and water mixture well into the ground, 'to greet arum'. Later the women of the hamlet (with a couple of male late-comers) are lined up, and the grain mixture is spat on their hands (they use their hands to make beer, but they do not use their feet in the fields as men do). In the afternoon all proceed to the feast and the beer. Money, beads, and metal bracelets are collected.

Since the early 1940s, the pressures exerted by the Meban upon the Uduk through the hierarchy of the cult of Leina have been maintained. There were the annual treks of Jibirdhalla with tribute to Leina; there was the grain-collecting tour of Akki in the Yabus mentioned above; on top of what must have been a regular pattern of payments for treatments and recovery and consultation, came the special atonements of 1966 and 1967, and the marriage gift demands of 1969. But the Uduk have failed to respond whole-heartedly to the repeated demands for tribute and respect made by the Meban leadership, and, as we have seen, reacted with deliberate violence in 1965 against the leading Arum man of the northern valleys.

But neither the murder of Lyife, nor its subsequent atonement, managed to rid the northern Uduk of the Meban Arum. Strangely enough, the very group of influential Arum men in northern Pam'Be who had been closely associated with Lyife were actively intro-ducing further spiritual activity from Meban country by the late 1960s. The inner tension between the authority claimed by Nilotic sources of divine inspiration, and Uduk resistance both to their theology and to their secular power, was not resolved.

(v) New appearances

I first heard in late 1967 of a new 'speaking *arum*' from Meban, and some months later was confided its name: *jis yap*, 'porcupine hole'. I assumed this was a brand-new spirit, until there was a visitation in the early rains of 1968 by Jidha, its leading Uduk practitioner from Bellila, in the Ahmar valley to the north. During this visit I learned more of the new *arum*, though despite some guile did not hear it speak. I did discover that it was also known as 'Bilan', the name of a man who had lived and died, and then reappeared from the earth through a porcupine hole—hence the name *jis yap*. The hole was in a great swamp in Meban country, called Tinku.

I have learned since I met Jidha that Leina had an assistant called Bilal Tonga (compare the official report of Leina's arrest, quoted above in section (i)). I am not at all sure that the connection was known to my Uduk friends, apart from the most senior Arum men. The flurry of activity which I had thought was some new affair of the 'porcupine hole spirit' was in fact connected with the mainstream Leina cult. The new spirit was his erstwhile assistant in risen form.

The new *arum* came to Jidha spontaneously (though he was already connected with the Leina cult). At the Head-Shaving after his recovery from seizure by the *arum* of the porcupine hole, a 'cow' (I assume an ox) was cut, and since this major Blood-rite the *arum* now speaks through him. It is said that wherever Jidha goes, Bilan goes with him, under his armpit. This *arum* had already become known in the hamlets of Pam'Be before Jidha's visit. Montaha, who was a 'brother' of Jidha from the same birth-group of Murinye and living in Bellila, had recently married Nyane, of Waka'cesh. When he was visiting in 1967 we heard that he had two little *arum*, like white chickens, which lived up in the roof of Nyane's hut when he was staying there. These *arum* were rumoured to speak, and to 'know your name as soon as you appeared'. When Montaha left again for Bellila, taking Nyane with him, he told people not to sleep in the hut for five days. One evening, as neighbours were eating outside at dusk, they saw these *arum* 'coming out of the hut'—but it was too dark to see them very clearly.

During Montaha's stay in 1967, two young women (Zeinab and Tamaŋwa) fell ill and were diagnosed by the local Ebony Men (of Pany Caran) as being 'seized by the *arum* of the porcupine hole', due to the presence of Montaha. Zeinab acted like a mad person (*mi'd me'd wathi/ ki gusu'd adu*, literally 'behaved like a person whose Liver was out of control'). Both patients were said to have been very ill and were making the sounds *waah, waah, waah*, an indication of their seizure. Montaha treated them, they recovered, and their Head-Shaving was held in 1968. This rite was the occasion for Jidha's visit; Montaha came from Bellila to shave the heads of his patients, and brought his own sponsor Jidha, the medium of the new *arum* of Bilan, to be present at the rite. This was the occasion I witnessed; and along with many others, I tried to take advantage of Jidha's presence to find out more about the new *arum*, and if possible to hear it speak.

It was a big occasion, hosted by Mathir of Pany Caran, of the Woshale̲t̲hdhe birth-group. Two or three other Arum men had come from Bellila, and with those of our own locality, there were eight or ten altogether.[23] Mathir was already participating in the new cult, and it was said he 'already had the porcupine hole spirit'. Crucial to the apparent spread of an invasive spirit is of course a trend in the diagnoses made by the Ebony Men; and in this case it was Nyethko, a leading Ebony diviner and 'brother' of Mathir from the same birth-group, who had made the diagnosis. At the Head-Shaving it was Nyethko who was organizing hospitality for all the guests.

The ceremony itself followed the standard pattern for a Head-Shaving.

The patients' hair is shaved off; a couple of chickens are cut outside the hut of Mathir, and their death throes carefully watched;

---

[23] I should point out here that there was a network of connections between the main participants in this activity surrounding the new *arum* of Bilan. Mathir for example had been fathered by the Murinye, the birth-group of Jidha and Montaha. Lyife and also Jibirdhalla, former leading Arum men, had been 'brothers' of Mathir, of the same birth-group. Lyife used to live in Pam Bigin (a settlement near the Meban border already of course associated with Leina) with his father's people, and Jidha lived there with him for some time. When Lyife was killed, Jidha came to live with Mathir in Pany Caran, later moving to Bellila. His 1968 visit to preside over a rite in Pany Caran was therefore a return to old friends.

a pig is cut near the bush; another chicken is cut by Nyethko alone near the hut, and then two goats are cut near the bush. When the food is ready, the patients hold a cooking paddle and, guided by several Arum men, stir the porridge and then scoop a little out with their hands on to a skin. The rest is served out normally by the women doing all the work in the background. A little food is offered by Mathir to the patients. Another Arum man mixes the red ochre powder, pours oil in the middle, and guides Zeinab's right forefinger to push a little red powder into the pool of oil. This speck disappears, and the Arum men snap their fingers. The ochre and oil are blended; the mixture is Blown to the noses of the patients, Touched to their bodies, and then applied carefully to forehead, shoulders, breasts, forearms, centre of the torso, and either side of the lower chest. The Arum men then use their left hands to smear the ochre evenly all over the patients' bodies. The patients go in another hut to eat. Meanwhile, in the beer hut, Mathir's home, a gourd of porridge and a pan of stew are placed at the foot of the centre pole, and a gourd of beer set aside, all for the arum. *The food is removed just before the patients come in to drink beer. Beer for* arum *is always made at a Head-Shaving; it is prepared separately from the early stage of toasting the flour. The patients come in with the Arum men; Montaha is clearly in charge here. All hold on to one gourd with their right hands, pass it around the pot (anticlockwise), scoop out some beer mixture, pour it into another pot; and all hold on to a gourd of water, circle it round the main beer pot in the same way and pour it on to the mixture in the small pot. All take a straw; these straws are touched to the patients, and then Arum men and patients drink a little beer. Then the general beer drinking, and feasting, starts.*

Jidha himself took no part in all this; he sat or reclined on a wooden bed in the shade, or in a hut, drinking coffee or beer. Later he joined in the general beer drinking. But whereas at a normal Head-Shaving the goods collected from the patients, as a fee for their successful treatment, are given to the man who actually treated them, in this case the goods were not given to Montaha but directly to Jidha. By the following morning about £3 (Sudanese) had been collected from various relatives; but Jidha made it known that he wanted £6 (Sudanese) in cash, plus various other items. This produced silence and anxious whispers, but in the end Jidha departed with his £6 (Sudanese), three spears (two others had been given back), two adult female goats and one young goat. This was quite a substantial fee by Uduk standards, although it was explained to me that it was not for Jidha himself, but for 'Bilan'.

During Jidha's stay, a number of people tried to arrange for consultations with Bilan, who was supposed to deliver explicit diagnoses and give specific advice, in the Meban tongue. This appealed to many, for the Ebony Men have become frustratingly vague in recent years, no longer naming names and frequently fudging the issue. These days, people said, the Ebony Men are afraid of the government: that is, they are afraid of being implicated as accessory to any action which may follow a named accusation. The prospect of a lucid oracle was therefore very attractive, and people flocked along to spend the evening at Mathir's hamlet in the hope that Bilan would speak. Most stayed up all night, and though I went home for a few hours' sleep, I was back before sunrise. But Bilan did not awake; he went on sleeping and I eventually gave up. However, I got an account later in the day from Boho, who had managed to get advice on a dispute over rainstones. Some of the Waka'cesh stones were with a son, Rumko, of the Woshalethdhe in Chali; and Tente in particular had long been grumbling and agitating to have them back, as well as grumbling about other outstanding debts still owed by this birth-group (hosts of the present occasion). But the verdict of Bilan went against Tente and Boho, and in favour of Rumko keeping the stones.

The *arum* of the porcupine hole continued to spread in the Tombak valley. In the following year, 1969, there were at least two Head-Shavings for this *arum*. In one case, the wife of a man who 'had the porcupine hole spirit' became sick because it 'covered up her Genius'. In both cases the fees for treatment carried out locally were handed over to Jidha himself.

Jidha's personal style was in vivid contrast to the quiet, even apologetic manner of most of the Uduk Arum men. On the occasion described he was wearing a magenta pink *jellabiyya*, sweeping down to the ground, with a matching turban. He was visually a striking figure, tall and slender, with a pronounced limp. He stayed aloof and rationed his words, gazing into the distance while others chattered and milled around him. He resembled more the professional Meban practitioners I had seen at work, rather than his Uduk fellows. Of course his new *arum* had come from Meban country, spoke Meban, and, as he knew, was guaranteed by the original inspiration and authority of Leina.

And yet these connections with the continuing line of Meban authority were not remarked in the Uduk hamlets. The new *arum* was soon known simply by the tag 'porcupine hole', far more resonant to Uduk ears than the (originally Arabic) name 'Bilan'. To the women whose illnesses were attributed to the new *arum* (the patients I heard of were all female), and to the rest of the women working away to make beer and food for the ceremonies, this was one more foreign *arum*. Like the other dangers of the wild, the dead, and the unknown which disturbed the person by entering the Liver, this had its own specialist who then had to be paid off, at a Head-Shaving like other Head-Shavings. The theological niceties, from their point of view, were neither here nor there.

The porcupine hole spirit's arrival followed earlier precedents. Leina himself had originally been welcomed into the northern Uduk country by two men of the Woshalathde birth-group who were later to become leaders of the cult: Jibirdhalla in Chali and Lyife in Pam Bigin. Although the killing of Lyife was, as I have suggested, partly at least an act of protest at the spreading dominance of the cult of Leina in Uduk country, the new *arum* practice was being welcomed by the same group of influential men who had been closely associated with Lyife. This new *arum* was making itself apparent through the diagnoses of Ebony men linked by kinship with the Arum men. The oracular wisdom offered by the new *arum* was accessible only to a few; but increasing numbers of people, especially women, were apparently getting sick from its presence. In time, the danger of this new spiritual source might well overcome its appeal; people will deal with it and domesticate it as well as they can. It might in the end leave only a name as a residue, like the *arum ma Miti*, or the *arum ma Badhiya* (Chapter 1 (ii) (*d*)). Although it promised new truths and oracular revelation, on the Nilotic model of divine possession, it was received by the Uduk as another dangerous earth spirit which had to be kept at bay. There were at the same time rumours of yet another new manifestation of a speaking *arum* in northern Pam'Be; I had heard gossip of a hostile kind about this, and suggestions that someone else might be getting a spear in the back if he wasn't careful. I later had a talk with ŋule, one of those associated with this new *arum,* which 'speaks from the ground'. The *arum* 'came from Meban, from

Leina directly'; and I understood in this context that Leina's wife was 'still alive'.

The severe demands made by the Meban upon their stubborn Uduk flock in the late 1960s have since eased. By 1983, the headquarters of the Leina cult among the Meban lay much farther away from the Uduk border. Fatma was the most important healer in the whole of Meban country, and operated from her newly-established centre known as Hilla Kujuriya (Village of the Lady Witch-doctor, to translate from the Arabic), at Jefije, some thirty miles to the north-west of Boing, on the main road to Renk. I did not hear of any Uduk travelling as far as this to consult her, and I had the general impression that although friendly relations were maintained between the Uduk Arum men and their nearer Meban colleagues, there were no longer the pressures there had been. Left largely to their own devices, the Uduk Arum men were settling down to a more comfortable *modus vivendi* with the still-increasing numbers of Ebony Men.

By the early 1980s, these practitioners together faced, with unruffled equanimity, a new wave of Christian-inspired activities throughout the hamlets of Uduk country: an autumn child if ever there were one, for the Chali missionaries had departed under government order nearly twenty years before.

4

The Sudan Interior Mission and 'Arumgimis': Expecting Christ

'The fear of the Lord is the beginning of wisdom.'
Quoted by Malcolm Forsberg in his account of missionary endeavours among the Uduk, *Land Beyond the Nile*.

(i) Constructing a Christian community at Chali, 1938–1964

In 1938 the Sudan Interior Mission secured a foothold at Chali to work among the Uduk. At the time the area had just been transferred from the jurisdiction of Kurmuk (then Fung Province) to that of Renk in the Upper Nile Province. This opened the way for the extension of mission education to the Uduk and some of their neighbours like the Komo, as a part of 'Southern' policy. The Sudan Government from the early years of the century had favoured missions in the South which placed emphasis upon practical education, upon agricultural and industrial teaching and sound basic skills of literacy, rather than missions which concentrated almost exclusive efforts upon religious enlightenment and conversion. For this reason, the fundamentalist evangelical approach of the S.I.M. (many of whose personnel were Presbyterians from the United States) had precluded their establishing stations in the more central and important parts of the southern Sudan. They were, nevertheless, allowed to operate in what were regarded as particularly 'primitive' and difficult areas, out of the way of mainstream development, where almost any type of mission activity could be regarded as a general civilizing influence and where there would be minimal friction with government.[1]

The early days of the mission's efforts at Chali were very largely concerned with the missionaries' own survival. Their attempts to become established were frustrated by the hostilities which

---

[1] L. M. P. and N. Sanderson, *Education, Religion and Politics in Southern Sudan 1899–1964* (London: Ithaca Press), 1981, esp. pp. 240–1.

developed on the Ethiopian border during 1940, when one Chali missionary was injured in the bombing of Kurmuk by Italian forces, and two other missionaries were killed by Italian bombing at Doro in Meban country, in July of that year. The S.I.M. had to evacuate the area, but were able to take up the work at Chali again in mid-1941. It was Malcolm and Enid Forsberg who laid the main foundations of the language work, the pattern of educational and religious instruction, and the physical fabric of the station. They were joined in 1943 by Mary Beam and Betty Cridland, missionaries of outstanding ability and personal dedication who carried overall responsibility for the station through its expansion during the 1950s and early 1960s.

Although the mission had been set up at a time when Chali was a part of 'the South', it became an anomaly when in 1953, for reasons of practical convenience, the Uduk and 'Koma' *omodiyas* (local administrative units) were 'returned to the North', that is to the Blue Nile Province (successor to the old Fung Province), to be run from Kurmuk, now a bigger town than it had been before the war. Education in the northern Sudan did not (except for certain areas of the Nuba Hills) operate through a network of missions, as it still did in the south. Furthermore, it was oriented primarily to Islam and the Arabic language, rather than to Christianity, vernaculars, and the English language. Nevertheless, the mission at Chali was working well and had gained a degree of government tolerance, and so was permitted to continue its work, although within the boundaries of a northern Province. Under 'Miss Beam and Miss Betty', as they came to be known affectionately to all, a substantial church community had been built up by 1953, and continued at the peak of its activities through the 1950s.

In his book of 1958, *Land Beyond the Nile*,[2] Malcolm Forsberg has given us a vivid picture of the early encounters between the missionaries and the Uduk people, and the gradual way in which they were able to build up the core of a teachable and willing flock. Malcolm and Enid Forsberg themselves played a very important

---

[2] Malcolm Forsberg, *Land Beyond the Nile*. The President of Wheaton College describes the book on the dust-jacket thus: it 'tells graphically of privations and perils among the primitive Uduks in the mysterious and mystifying semiarid Sudan, with its famine, polygamy, and baffling taboos. There is fear of wild beasts and wild men, and flight from the invading forces whose bombings bring martyrdom to some missionaries. It is an instructive, incisive, very human account of the trials of pioneer missionaries that ends in triumph.'

part in the early years, and retained contact with Chali for many years afterwards.

The book opens with a scene of Doatgay bringing her twins for protection and help at the mission; this was in 1952, three years after the District Commissioner had threatened to bury a mother and two women helpers alive for having done the same to twins— and started to carry out the threat by having a grave dug. He relented of course, awarding prison sentences instead. Because there was no place to keep women prisoners, they were 'paroled' into the care of the missionaries, to work on the station. Doatgay claimed she had kept the twins because she was afraid of the government, but could not stay in the village. Forsberg tells us that Mona, the first Christian convert, said to her: 'You don't have to be afraid of the old talk any more, Doatgay. The paper tells us that twins, too, are people. We who believe the paper are not afraid of twins. God will help you and we will help you.'[3]

The missionaries often despaired of reaching the Uduk, with their 'polygamy problem', their evil witch-doctors, and their lewd and sensuous dancing. There sometimes seemed to be an unbridgeable gap between the 'superstitious Uduks' and the missionaries; and those points at which Forsberg himself records what seemed at the time to have been a real exchange of understanding, seem rather less so in retrospect. On one occasion he was addressing a fairly large audience of Uduk men. 'They were almost indescribable. They wore no clothing and there were gray spots on their knees where they had crawled through their grain fields, weeding. The red oil formed dirty little balls on their heads. I realized that they needed God more than any other people I had seen.' He and Mona talked of the 'way to heaven'.

When Mona had finished, an old man who sat just in front of us lifted his hands and smiled with full comprehension.

'That is just like Birapinya,' he said. 'Our people used to go to heaven. It was much nearer in those days. Birapinya was an enormous tree and it reached all the way to heaven.'[4]

In spite of Mona's trying to stop the old man, Forsberg allowed him to continue the story of the Birapinya, which he reproduces in full, even entitling his chapter 'The Road to Heaven'. The story of

[3] Ibid., pp. 17–19.   [4] Ibid., pp. 194–5.

the tree's destruction and the cutting off of dancers in the sky concluded, Forsberg questioned the old man:

'So you don't have any way to heaven now?' 'No,' the old man said wistfully. 'Heaven's a long way off.'
   'That is just why we have come—to tell you about the true way to heaven.' I made no attempt to discredit his story. 'Jesus is the way. Just as the sin of the girls in refusing to grind for the old woman brought separation from heaven, so our sin separates us from God. Jesus came to open the way for us to return to Him.'[5]

For Forsberg, the Uduk story 'showed the intense longing of the people for a way to heaven'. If one considered the Birapinya story from another angle, it might look more like a longing for those left in the sky, a morally empty place, to be rejoined with human beings on earth (see 'KP: 68–74, and Chapter 1(i) above).
   However, such points of apparent agreement, though ambivalent, made it possible to proceed. On a return to Chali in 1951, to take charge while Mary Beam and Betty Cridland were on furlough, the Forsbergs were gratified to find how much had been achieved. It was that year that a separate Christian village had become established for the first time.

Each Saturday morning I met with the elders to discuss church affairs. . . . Matters of discipline were also dealt with in the elders' meetings. Occasionally young people, and older ones, too, fell into sin. Ordinary village life did not encourage Christian living. It was like trying to keep dry while sitting in water. . . .
   'You should all move together and build a Christian village,' I said, 'as Miss Beam and Miss Betty have so often told you.'
   The idea had been suggested many times before but it had not seemed attractive. The clan had always been the basic unit in the tribe and there was an intense loyalty between brothers and sisters, more intense, we had early discovered, than that in the marital relationship. Wives frequently went back to their own villages to cook for their deserted brothers, their deserted husbands being left to shift for themselves.
   Eventually the idea took hold. . . . It was not until two young couples settled in a place apart that they made the break. Then the Christian village began to grow.[6]

   [5] Malcolm Forsberg, *Land Beyond the Nile*, p. 195.
   [6] Ibid., p. 223.

Even though the mission did not set up their school as 'a place for gaining followers' and did not want their pupils to be just 'school-boy Christians' but 'born again', the school was very successful by this time, and could scarcely meet the demand. Forsberg's book ends with the description of a communion service at which he is served by Mona, who pronounces the benediction 'Now the God of peace, that brought again from the dead our Lord Jesus, that great shepherd of the sheep ...'.[7] Forsberg left the church moved, and thankful for the distance that had been covered in Chali since the start of the mission. This was evidence of 'The Power that Worketh', the title of his concluding chapter.

An illustrated leaflet sent out by Mary Beam and Betty Cridland at Christmas 1957 (when they were again on furlough) gives a picture of their achievements up to that year. The boys' school, founded in 1948, had sixty pupils, and the girls' school, founded two years later, had fifty. The Chali church itself had been organized in 1949, with two elders, one for the Uduk-speaking members and one for the non-Uduk. The 'Koma', Bertha, and Arabic languages were sometimes used in the church, as well as Uduk. The church now had seven elders, eighty-eight baptized believers, representing 'five tribes', and a normal Sunday congregation of two to three hundred. It acted as a conference centre for a network of smaller outlying Christian centres, including the Yabus where work with the 'Koma' was soon to proceed, and maintained links with the Doro station among the Meban. There were ninety-nine adults in reading classes, the Uduk Dictionary had been produced, and several sections of the new Testament had been translated. In 1955, it had been realized that the ten orphan children being cared for in missionary homes, including three sets of twins, justified a scheme for an orphanage; special funds were donated, and the orphanage dedicated in 1956. There were six lady missionary staff based at Chali that year, including two language specialists and a medical nurse. Mr and Mrs Peter Ackley (by 1983 in charge of the S.I.M. headquarters in Khartoum) also spent a part of the year there, with their three children.[8]

The pamphlet notes that 'Already as a result of the Co-Ed Chali

[7] Ibid., p. 232.
[8] Sudan Interior Mission printed pamphlet, in the form of a newsletter from Chali-el-Fil, illustrated with photographs, dated Dec. 1957 and signed by Mary S. Beam and A. Elizabeth Cridland.

School nine couples have established Christian homes;' William Danga and his first wife were among these. A moving account is given of 'The Miracle Uduk Family'; that is, the first family to raise twins as a result of faith. 'Rusha [*sic*], a graduate of the Chali Uduk School, helped to save two sets of Uduk twins from being buried alive. Later the first-born of Rusha (he had become a Christian) and his wife Susgay, then not a Christian, were twins. Rusha, with the assistance of the missionaries, helped in the care of the babies through the long months of helping Susgay to trust the Lord Jesus to deliver her from her terrible fear as an Uduk mother of twins. She was baptized in June, 1956.' In later years, the whole responsibility for the Christian enterprise fell upon 'Rusha', or as he is now addressed, Pastor Paul Rasha Angwo (Plate 6a).

The rosy tale of progress was, however, marred by the fact that in early December 1957, the church with its 'lovely new thatched roof' completed only the previous July under Mr Ackley's supervision, was burned down. Although this turned out to be the responsibility of a non-Uduk among the congregation, it did signify a note of unease. But the church was rebuilt and the community continued to grow and to develop a network of smaller chapels and centres. Language work progressed on various neighbouring tongues, especially Komo ('Koma') and Bertha. The translation work in Uduk resulted in a complete edition of the New Testament and also the *Rules of the Church and Hymn Book* (both published in the USA in 1963).

Unfortunately, the happy achievements at Chali as reflected in Forsberg's first book and the 1957 pamphlet were soon to seem something of the past. The Sudan's 'Southern problem' was already threatening to overwhelm the fragile peace of the whole region. Violence had broken out in the far south before the coming of Independence in 1956. Restrictions placed on the work of missions and missionaries, who were blamed in part for the unrest, increased from 1958 onward with the intensification of the civil war. These restrictions came to affect Doro, and Chali also. Malcolm Forsberg published an account of the mounting pressures upon the mission in this area, particularly at Doro, in his 1966 book *Last Days on the Nile*.[9] By the end of 1963 the majority of missionaries in the southern Sudan had been prevented from continuing their work,

---

[9] Malcolm Forsberg, *Last Days on the Nile* (Chicago: Moody Press), 1966.

or had actually been deported. The following year it was the turn of the Blue Nile Province missionaries, and Mary Beam and Betty Cridland, with other resident colleagues, were deported at a few days' notice in April 1964. The consignment of printed Uduk New Testaments, the final fruit of their work, arrived just a few days before they had to go.

Paul Rasha Angwo was left behind as Pastor of the church. Although the educational and medical work of the station collapsed, Pastor Paul, with a number of staunch elders, managed to keep the church functioning, and the Christian community more or less together, through the period of the civil war. The S.I.M. office in Khartoum remained open, and regular though modest financial help was channelled through it to Chali. Uduk living in Khartoum, of whom there were maybe half a dozen, maintained links with the S.I.M. there. Norman Nunn, the Khartoum representative, was not permitted personally to visit Chali but he was able to give general moral support and specific advice when needed.

There were many ups and downs before the end of the first civil war in 1972. The church building itself was destroyed by fire for a second time in 1970. In the period from 1964 to 1972, during which I carried out my original fieldwork in the area, Chali was isolated in a way it had not been in previous decades. After the end of the first civil war, it was once more accessible. Mary Beam and Betty Cridland went back for a brief revisit as early as December 1972, and since then several missionaries, including the Forsbergs, have spent limited periods back in Chali; they have supervised again the rebuilding of the church (see Plate 6b). However, because Chali remained part of the Blue Nile Province, foreign personnel were forbidden to settle there again; while, at the same time, Chali was beyond the reach of the various new schemes for the post-war economic and social development of the southern Sudan sanctioned from Juba and Malakal. Indeed Chali remains today a remote and anomalous corner of the 'northern' Sudan (and since early 1986 completely cut off by the new civil war). The church and Christian community have largely had to fend for themselves since 1972, building on the self-reliance they had to develop from the time of the 1964 expulsion of the missionaries.

I am not attempting here to give a full history of the mission. This would be problematic for me, in any case, because of the circumstances of my own fieldwork. When I first arrived in Chali at the very end of 1965, the deportation of the missionaries was still uncomfortably close and fears engendered by the civil war, felt to be only a few miles distant, were mounting. The authorities in Kurmuk were very uneasy about contact between any foreigner and the church at Chali. In spite of a friendly welcome and invaluable help from the Chali community at the start of my work, I thereafter settled some miles away at Waka'cesh and remained something of an outsider as far as the church community was concerned. Although I have tried to evaluate the impact of Christianity upon the Uduk, I am not in a position to give an insider's account of the Chali Christian community itself.

The focus of this chapter is rather upon the wider social and cultural context within which, and perhaps in spite of which, this community grew, and upon the relations between it and the wider society. The outstanding point about this relationship is the contrast between the mission period, before the deportations of 1964, and the period since. Up to 1964 there was a carefully supervised, slow but steady expansion of the community to over two hundred baptized believers, in spite of a regular trickle of former Christians back to the villages. Many others came to spend a year or two in Chali, perhaps attending pre-baptismal classes before returning to the villages, and thus a large number of individuals did gain direct experience of the Christian community. However, the distinction between the full membership of baptized believers and the rest was very sharp, and was maintained by formal disciplinary practices. Since 1964, the boundaries have not been so clear; there have been many laxities within the fold, but more surprisingly perhaps there have been successive waves of Christian revival in the outlying villages. The church leadership in Chali was largely responsible for initiating these, but was not always able to control them. The focus of attention, both within and without the fold, had shifted away from personal discipline, formal qualifications, and rigid verbal doctrine. The new points of attention were those aspects of the Christian message which touched the moral world of the wider society; with the collapse of disciplinary authority in Chali, younger spokesmen were free to carry the inspiration effectively to 'the bush'.

The pre-1964 regime in the church community is perhaps best characterized by a summary of its official Rules, which were read out regularly and were well known to all adherents. They are listed (in Uduk only) in the printed booklet, *Rules of the Church and Hymn Book*, and I paraphrase from this source.[10]

All Rules concern those who are baptized, and those called to be believers. The first Rule prohibited the drinking of beer, the making of beer, or the giving of money or grain to make beer for work. The system of taking turns to make beer for collective work on the fields is of course the mainstay of the normal Uduk hamlet economy, and by refusing to have anything to do with the making or drinking of beer, a person is severing normal co-operative relations with kin and neighbours. Christians within the church community, settled around the mission, held collective work parties among themselves for meals, and sugared tea. Occasionally Christians would help their relatives or vice versa with the harvest or some other pressing task. But regular or reciprocal co-operation could not take place between the church village and the outlying hamlets.

The second Rule prohibited dancing, especially the *athele/* flute dancing. Christians were not even supposed to play the flutes, or watch the dancing, although this type of dancing is quite secular and has virtually no 'ritual' associations. The beating of the logs carries even further than the flutes in the night air, and must have sorely tempted many an otherwise sincere Christian. Of course people did, and do, go to these dances for flirtation as much as for the pure love of music.

The next Rule concerned tobacco, which was forbidden. Then came three more familiar prohibitions, on adultery, stealing, and lying, followed by a ban on observing false gods—that is, 'other Arum'. Specifically, believers were prohibited from consulting Ebony Men, from speaking of witchcraft (*gwon dhathu/*), from observing food prohibitions in order to avoid the sickness thought to affect an infant through its mother's milk, from going secretly to 'kindle the ebony', or to shave the head for 'Arum' or to give things for a Head-Shaving being held by their relatives. They were forbidden to discard the commands given by God [Arumgimis] and to follow the practices of other *arum* (*mii ma ruma tiya*).

There were also restrictions on ordinary social life. Believers were not to take sides and fight alongside their relatives. The phrase used here is *'kwani gun tana bas buni mo*, which means 'people

---

[10] *Mii ma Kaniisa dhala Awarkan Gway: Mmotaka Arumgimis Mo* [*Rules of the Church and Hymn Book: For praising God*], Chali Church, 1963.

who are their blood-friends' and indicates their allies, though here the intended meaning appears to be their blood relatives in the physical sense, matrilineal kin of the same birth-group (compare 'KP: 170–8). Even more destructive of what Uduk see as proper social relations is the rule, 'Women must not lead their children away from their fathers to live in the homes of their mother's brothers, because God [Arumgimis] absolutely refuses this, saying that the father of the child is the one responsible for the children.[11] This would be a particularly acute problem for a settlement of Christian families, set apart from the non-believers' hamlets, since the church community would become dispersed and uncontrolled if the children of Christian parents went off to their maternal uncles' homes as is the normal Uduk custom; most of these uncles would be some distance away. The church in Chali strove to create a new and unaccustomed pattern of family and household, based upon paternal authority. Some of those who have worked in the mission have insisted to me that an Uduk child in the villages has absolutely no regard whatever for his father, and that it was Christianity that first instilled any such regard. This view equates authority with affection. My view is that the Uduk 'family' system is more complex than this, that whereas authority resides with the mother's brothers, respect and affection are normally expected and found between child and father, and indeed that in previous historical periods it was far more common than today for children to remain with their father's household until adulthood ('KP: 145– 57). The church Rules, nevertheless, were designed in effect to enforce, in respect of family and kinship, a break with non-believers, and to create families of Christians which would remain distinct through the domestic control by a father of his own children. The remaining ban in the church Rules concerned games played with various nuts, fruits, and stones, a category newly extended to card games and thus 'gambling'.

Only in the concluding injunctions are believers exhorted to set Sunday apart as a day for rest, and for the worship of God. They should also obey the laws, both of God and of the government. However, 'If the orders of the government conflict with the Word of God, Christians must stand firm and say "No." '[12]

The aim of creating a society set apart, with strict rules of

---

[11] *Rules of the Church*, pp. 5–6.
[12] Ibid., p. 6.

membership, reached even beyond death. Christians were of course to be buried separately, and they were asked to instruct their relatives that in the event of their death, people should not gather and wail in the accustomed manner. It goes without saying that Christians did not have the normal Beer for the Grave, *asuŋ'kupaje*, that is the concluding ceremony to settle the *arum* of the deceased in the next world. All this was naturally very worrying for a Christian's relatives back in the village, who after all, in their terms, are the ones likely to suffer when these rites are not properly carried out.

By the 1950s the mission had some degree of success in creating a separate community. The houses of Christians were built in a fan around the mission complex. They obtained water from the mission well, cultivated their fields in a separate zone near Jebel Chali, and operated a system of neighbourly work-parties among themselves for tea and food. Children remained more or less with their parents and attended school. All the family participated in the Bible study classes for men, for women, and for youngsters respectively, on different days. For entertainment on Tuesday evenings there were slides, partly to illustrate the Bible but also the world in general. This occasion was known as *Montul is ma Klab*, a 'gathering to clap', and is described in the programme of activities laid out in the *Rules of the Church*. Such gatherings, with their own new jargon, replaced the forbidden worldly amusements, and their rubric evokes the way in which the mission was trying to create a separate linguistic and moral community. Personal moral discipline, and visible good behaviour, were strongly emphasized, and those who erred were called in and talked to. They might be given a period of punishment, or even expelled from the church.

It is not surprising that in view of these strict disciplines, there were many who fell by the wayside over the years, or simply opted for village life again. By 1964 there were already many former members of the church back in the outlying hamlets. A pattern was already evident of people dropping out of the church, later to repent and be readmitted, only to drop out again. The mission had theoretically created a community apart, bounded by rules designed to be as clear as daylight. In principle, there was no ambiguity about who belonged to this community and who was excluded. But in practice, individuals kept crossing and recrossing the boundary, as they kept open their social, economic, moral and religious options. The life of the villages was still the foundation of personal experience, and constituted the touchstone of 'moral community' for all the adults in the Chali church; the mission had not existed long enough for individuals to have been brought up in it to adulthood, and was neither large nor secure enough for anyone to be sheltered from the wider environment. Demands made by relatives for help with a whole range of activities and problems in the villages frequently took precedence over mission rules.

The Christian way of life certainly seemed alien to those outside. Outsiders could not, in my experience, at all appreciate the *total* nature of the demands made upon a person's life by the church. Most conspicuous of course were the bans on beer, tobacco, and dancing, bans which had come almost to define Christianity in the eyes of the village people. When on my first day in a Pam'Be hamlet, I accepted a little beer, the girls gathered around, demanded to know if I was not a 'person of Jesus', and ran off gleefully advertising my lack of faith.

On another level, the self-definitions of the S.I.M. as an evangelical enterprise basing its claims upon 'the Word', upon the written text of the Bible, offered the Uduk only an impoverished view of the *total* character of the Christian religion they wished to proclaim. Because access to Christian belief was through a written text, and the authority of this text was preached even to the non- or barely literate, the Christian message perhaps did not have the same broad appeal that it might have had with a different style of mission. There was great emphasis on 'work with the paper' in Chali, new recruits being urged towards literacy in order to read the Bible. Verbal statements of belief, of confession, of repentance, were prominent in the Christian duties of believers; there was a great deal of language work of all kinds at Chali, from Bible study classes and sermons to translation work. There were many occasions on which believers would be questioned, and would avow that they did indeed accept Jesus into their lives; the state of a repented sinner's soul would be a matter for open discussion among the church elders and even congregation. A special style of language was purposefully cultivated.

But this extreme emphasis upon the *verbal* encapsulation and transmission of *faith*, that is the accomplishment of spiritual change through *verbal* means, was alien to Uduk expectation. There are certainly many other vernacular traditions of the Sudan, which though not literate, are rich in explicitly religious language, hymns, prayers, priestly formulae, and prophetic songs from the past—for example those of the Nuer and the Dinka.[13] But apart from a few hunting songs, Uduk ceremonies and rituals do not encompass a verbal tradition, a corpus of formal texts. There were no hymns, no prayers, no priestly blessings, nor even any spells or formulae for curses. Few myths were explicitly linked to ritual practices. Even the standard modern technique of divination, kindling the ebony to diagnose the condition of a patient, is carried on in virtual silence.

A good deal of Uduk ritual and healing practice, as I have already indicated, is shared with neighbouring cultures; the very multiplicity of languages in this region might be thought to hinder the easy passage of cult and symbol from one group to another, were it not for the fact that most of these cults are celebrated through symbolic action, movement, and music, rather than defining themselves in the explicit instructions and formulae of the word. The insistence of the S.I.M. upon 'the Word', and their heroic perseverance in translating the Word into Uduk (together with their extreme Protestant suspicion of ritual and symbol) produced a new, lively, and fluent discourse as the vehicle of the Christian message while scarcely disturbing vernacular apperceptions of person, experience, or truth. The notions that the speaking of words can 'do things', or that certain texts can be authoritatively given by God and must be held sacred, were not previously familiar to the northern Uduk. Nor was there obligation to hold to verbally prescribed articles of faith, even in rituals relating to the powers of *arum*. There was, however, a rich and varied repertoire of *ritual practice* relating mainly to the person (see Chapter 2), which could flexibly accommodate elements from neighbouring traditions without the differences of cosmic doctrine they might cloak being spelled out in the open. 'Spelling out' in the open was precisely the key method of teaching and preaching at Chali.

Even the way in which faith is spoken of in the Uduk language, as the new discourse developed in the context of the mission's work, hinges upon acceptance, or rejection, of 'the Word'. In the

---

[13] Compare for example Evans-Pritchard, *Nuer Religion*, pp. 45–7; Lienhardt, *Divinity and Experience, passim*; Francis M. Deng, *The Dinka and their Songs* (Oxford: Clarendon Press), 1973.

villages of course there is never any question of stating that one believes or denies either a whole body of doctrine, or any one manifestation of *arum*, as against its other forms. It was not easy for the Bible translators to find a suitable expression for 'believing in God'. In the case of Christ, this was easier, for one could speak of Jesus entering or even piercing the 'heart', that is the Liver, and dwelling there. This is a powerful image and draws upon deeply rooted understandings of the way in which a spiritual force might seize or enter a person, and change his or her nature. But the abstract notion of *choosing* faith in God, perhaps more an active intellectual reaching out than a passive acceptance of the spirit of Jesus, has to be rendered by a phrase which seems rather to scale down God's being to the text itself of which he is Author. The expression *gam gwo is* is used for 'to believe' in the usage of the Chali mission. In the village this means 'to believe what is said', literally 'to join the words to one's body'. It implies the voluntary acceptance or even guarantee by one person of the truth of what another has said, or of what has been reported from afar. It can also, certainly, be used in normal village speech to mean 'belief' in quite a casual sense: 'Do you believe it?'—'No, I can't believe that!' This expression, idiomatically based on a bodily image, and also upon a reference to the spoken word, has been taken up by the translators and made to bear a great deal of weight, to refer in fact to the acceptance of 'the Word', that is, the Word of God, the Bible, and all it has to teach. The focus is admirably suited to the textual approach of the S.I.M. to Christian faith: 'Do you believe the Word?' (/E gam Gwo is mo?) is from their point of view appropriately equated with 'Do you believe in the Bible ('Word of God')?' (/E gam Gwo ma Arumgimis is mo?) and thus 'Do you believe in God?' Whether this might have been the formulation chosen by a different Christian approach I do not know. But with respect to the villages this was one more of the self-imposed handicaps which limited the claims of the Chali mission's teaching. The question, in ordinary Uduk usage, has a remote and academic air; does one consider this physical writing on paper true or not? The question did not demand or provoke the direct apprehension of *arum* in any form.

The Bible, potentially the whole of the Bible in the Revised Standard Version, was the text to be made available to the Uduk in their own language. Of course the S.I.M. had its own doctrinal emphases, and it is important to bear in mind what these were. It was the particular 'world-view' of the S.I.M. which guided the way in which the translation project was undertaken, and of course beyond this, the daily and secular impact that their work had both within and outside the church community. A summary of the emphases is relevant. Here is the first section of the Constitution of the Church in the East Central Sudan, an umbrella organization set up to co-ordinate the various churches in the S.I.M. area of which Chali and Doro were the largest and oldest. The constitution was adopted in 1963, at a time when the missionaries already anticipated what was to come, and were endeavouring to leave things behind them in an ordered state, should they be required to go. This organization developed after 1972 into the current Sudan Interior Church. The first section, strongly 'Pauline', is on doctrine.

We, the members of the C.E.C.S. sincerely believe and solemnly affirm the following doctrinal statement.

1. The holy Bible was written by holy men of God, moved by the Holy Spirit, under His direction. It is without error, the unchangeable, eternal, true and complete Word of God. 2 Tim. 3:16, 17; 2 Pet. 1:21.

2. There is only one God, eternal, manifested in three persons, The Father, the Son and the Holy Spirit, the triune God. 2 Cor. 13:14; Matt. 28:19.

3. Our Lord Jesus Christ is God revealed in the flesh. Being born of the Virgin Mary He became man, yet without sin: John 1:14; Matt. 1:20, 21.

   (a) His divine power was attested to by his godly miracles. Matt. 9.

   (b) His divine love was attested to by His sacrificial and substitutionary death. Gal. 2:20; Eph. 5:2.

   (c) His acceptance as our true mediator was attested to by His resurrection in bodily form and His ascension to the right hand of God the Father. Rom. 1:4; Rom. 8:34.

4. All men are lost sinners totally unable to do anything towards their salvation. They can be saved only by repentance from sin, personal faith in the shed blood of Jesus Christ, and by regeneration of the Holy Spirit. They cannot be saved by good works. Rom. 3:10; Rom. 5:12.

5. The evidence of regeneration is the progressive operation of the Holy Spirit indwelling the believer producing in the believer a holy life and witness. 1 Thess. 1:5–7; Titus 3:5; Rom. 8:1–7.

6. All who are born are made one in Christ, being members of His body, the Church, of which He is the head. Rom. 12:3–5; 1 Cor. 10:16, 17; 1 Cor. 12:12–27; Eph. 4:11–16; Co. 2:17–19.

7. At the bodily return of the Lord Jesus Christ with His angels, the dead in Christ will be raised in bodily form. All mankind must stand

before the righteous judgement of God. The saved will enter eternal blessedness with the Lord; the unsaved will be cast into eternal torment with the Devil and his angels. 1 Thess. 4: 16; Acts 24: 15; Matt. 25: 46.

8. Christians ought not to love the world nor the things of the world. 1 John 2: 15–17; Jude 23; Rom. 12: 1, 2.[14]

The booklet in Uduk (*Rules of the Church*) gives a clear doctrinal statement on these lines, with reference to the scriptures. The following paraphrase translation is a partial summary:

1. The Word of God is called the Bible [etc.].

2. The general population are lost, away from God, separated for ever from God at death, they will be cursed for ever by being thrown in a lake of fire together with Satan and his angels [those who spread his word].

3. There is just one road to salvation, belief in the Lord Jesus, who died for our sin [bad deeds]. Those who believe will be forgiven their sin and their Livers will be cleansed. They will be reborn in the Holy Spirit and become children of God, created anew in Christ.

4. God is one, but has three sides, Father, Son, and Holy Spirit. Jesus Christ was the son of God and the son of People, he was born from a real girl with a girl's womb as her mother bore her, and he in himself is God.

5. Our Lord Jesus arose from death, from where he was buried. All those who believe and who die will rise from death and resume their bodies, which will not be decayed and which will be in their adult form. All the others will also rise at the time of their judgement, which will be a punishment for ever and ever in the place of fire.

6. Believers are born in the Holy Spirit and they will live a new life of strength in the Holy Spirit. A believer will not do as he wishes [according to his own Stomach] but will believe that God will guide him.

7. Believers will live properly and well and bear witness, they will touch the Livers of those close to them and spread the good Word.

8. Jesus Christ who has shown the way to Heaven and who sits at God's right hand will come again to earth twice, his own real

---

[14] Pamphlet, 'Church in the East Central Sudan: Constitution (as adopted February, 1963)', 10 pp. mimeographed, at pp. 1–2.

body visible, and will be seen clearly. At his first appearance, there will be another age of peace and righteousness over the whole earth. It is foretold in the written Word of God [the crucial reference here is to Rev. 20: 1–6].[15]

As doctrine, this of course represents specific principles of the fundamentalist Sudan Interior Mission, and is only a particular interpretation of the meaning of the Bible. The translations produced by the missionaries reflect their doctrinal position as much as they reflect what might have been embedded in the moral theology of biblical times or those cultural sources from which the texts of the Bible itself were originally drawn. In particular, we might note that the clearly structured dichotomies of body and soul, flesh and spirit, God and humankind, around which fundamentalist doctrine is built, are not necessarily inherent in the biblical sources but to some extent have been imposed upon them. In the discussion which follows, it should be noted that I am not comparing, for example, ancient Greek or Hebrew notions of soul or spirit with modern Uduk concepts (an exercise which might in fact reveal some interesting analogies), but rather those modern fundamentalist doctrines which inform the translators' intention.[16]

The mission teachers and those who collaborated in the translation work at Chali based their evangelism and their texts as far as they could upon the existing resources of the Uduk language, coining as few new words as possible. However, the assumptions about human nature, spirit, and cosmological order, as seen in the Old and New Testaments by fundamentalist Christians, are very different from those of the older Uduk culture as I have outlined them in the first part of this book, and the translators' task was not so easy. The actual lexicon of the Uduk scriptural texts, even in unfamiliar use, is perfectly recognizable, and each item can be given

[15] *Rules of the Church*, pp. 2–4.
[16] For a sustained examination of the concept of 'spirit' and its relation to notions of the human person in the biblical context see Marie E. Isaacs, *The Concept of Spirit: A Study of Pneuma in Hellenistic Judaism and its Bearing on the New Testament*, Heythrop Monographs 1 (London: Heythrop College, University of London), 1976. See esp. pp. 35–42, and 70–82. Compare, for a discussion of modern fundamentalist attitudes and interpretations, James Barr, *Fundamentalism* (London: SCM Press), 2nd edn., 1981, esp. ch. 5 and 6. Barr remarks, 'Fundamentalism with its limited but strongly held series of doctrines thus stands as a solid and clearly marked entity against the wild, vague and speculative theologies of the main stream of Christianity' (p. 162); how much more evident this character of fundamentalism is when placed in the open texture of a world like that of the Uduk.

a more or less satisfactory 'dictionary' gloss upon which all would agree. Thus it is perfectly clear that *arum jin nyo/o'd* means an *arum* which is dirty. But before the introduction of S.I.M. teaching, the Uduk had not thought of *arum* as being dirty or clean, let alone impure or pure. A body might be impure, either in the everyday sense of rather muddy or the stronger sense of rotting, but not, I think, a spirit. Although the Bible translators were using the same language, in one sense, in another sense they were rewriting the world, and inevitably reconstructing what could be known through the Uduk language. They were using bits of an old jigsaw to build a new picture. Here and there the new combinations rang true; the New Testament in particular is rich in passages which must have a very powerful appeal even to Uduk who have little formal acquaintance with Christian theology. These are frequently passages describing details of the life and activities of Christ. But the more formal lineaments of cosmology, of the dualism of heaven versus earth, God and the angels versus the human soul, of Cosmic good versus evil, axiomatic to protestant fundamentalism and illustrated in the doctrinal statements quoted above, constituted a new world for the students at Chali.

The primary problem of Bible translators faced with a diffuse and ambivalent vernacular notion of 'spirit' is, presumably, what to call God; there is no problem with Jesus, as a special human figure, but Jesus is the son of what or whom? Forsberg has written of the early decision at Chali to use the neologism 'Arum-gimis'. It was taken up at the suggestion of the early converts themselves.

Malcolm and Enid Forsberg were working together with Nick Simponis in the first year or so at Chali, and in *Land Beyond the Nile* we read this interesting account:

Every tribe on earth had a name for God, we thought, yet we had found no such name in the Uduk language.

'In your notes you have *arum* as meaning "god"', I said to Nick one day. 'The way the Uduks use it, it seems to mean "spirit", especially the spirits of the dead.'

'God is a spirit, isn't He?' Nick rejoined.

'Yes, but His name isn't *spirit*. According to Uduk ideas when we call God *arum* we are saying that He is the spirit of a person who once died, a ghost. I don't think they believe in any one spirit who has only had spirit existence from the beginning.'

Many breakfast, dinner, and supper conversations later, we decided that it was misleading to call God *arum*.

'I studied phonetics in Bible school,' Nick said one day, 'and we were told that if there is no adequate name for God in a language, we should just use the English name. After all, no matter what word we use, we'll have to describe Him to the people and tell them who He is.'

We did not feel qualified to argue, so we started to tell the people about God. Our first attempt at a hymn, set to music of 'We Praise Thee, O God, for the Son of Thy Love' (but not a translation of the hymn), looked like this:

> God diid imis
> God diid imis
> Akim bidi yuka Yesus[17]

We taught the people to sing it but it did not sound quite right.

'That English word "God" sounds terribly out of place in the Uduk hymn,' Enid observed one day.

'I don't like it either,' I admitted.

'Nick is right in saying that we'll have to tell the people what God is like regardless of the name we use for Him,' she continued, 'and since that is so, I'd rather adapt a word of theirs that fits into the language and then tell them who He is.' Nick, too, had begun to feel that the word 'God' fitted rather awkwardly into the Uduk vocabulary. So we began new discussions. 'Perhaps we could doctor up their word for spirit,' Nick suggested.

'Why don't we just call him "*wadhi gi mis*, the one above"?' Enid added.

Nick and I agreed. We had not dreamed that one day we would be giving God a name. But that was not the end.

Later, when our first Christians began to think for themselves, they said, '*Wadhi* means a person with a human body. You say God is a spirit. We should call Him "the Spirit above".'

So God's name was revised for the last time. He became '*Arum gi mis*'.[18]

The phrase was later represented as one word, Arumgimis. It is subtly different from the phrase I have heard in the villages and referred to in the previous chapter, Arum i Mis. The latter suggests a diffuse, intangible presence of 'Arum Above'; the former, by incorporating the demonstrative pronoun gi 'which', specifies much more precisely 'that Arum which is in the Sky', an exclusive being,

---

[17] In translation this would read: 'God is Above/God is Above/His child is called Jesus.'

[18] Forsberg, *Land Beyond the Nile*, pp. 156–7.

distinct by implication from other *arum*. The more general *Arum i Mis* again comes easily to those familiar with Nilotic concepts of a diffuse divinity on high, perhaps translating from the Meban language, whereas the firmer image of Arumgimis is indeed much more appropriate to the commanding, loving God of fundamentalist teaching.

The work of translation and gospel propagation in the Uduk tongue has been taken up again in the last decade, through the efforts of former missionaries in co-operation with Pastor Paul, who has worked a good deal on his own in Chali. It was arranged for him to visit Florida in 1981. He assisted with final drafts, and read aloud the whole New Testament in Uduk, for sets of mass-produced gospel cassettes. The fruits of this work appeared in early 1983, with a new, large-print edition of the New Testament with the Psalms and the Book of Genesis (Mr Peter Ackley of the S.I.M. in Khartoum kindly made a copy available for me). The cassettes, in sets of 24 covering the New Testament, arrived later in the year at Chali. These were to be used in a new style of mass evangelism in the villages.

(ii) Rewriting the world: the Bible as authoritative text

With Arumgimis thus clearly located 'on high', the translator into Uduk is free to bracket all other *arum* together as spirits 'of the earth', and describe them as *aruma 'cesh* in the Christian context. This expression is then made interchangeable with *arum thus*, bad *arum*, and *arum jin nyo/o'd*, unclean *arum*; the former does occur in older usage, though the latter, as I have suggested, does not. Thus (and there are many other examples) we read in Mark 7: 25–6 of a woman whose daughter was *bu'thkin ma rum thus jin nyo/o'd*, seized by a bad *arum* which was dirty; she asked Jesus *mmo/ura ruma 'cesh ka pije/*, to drive out the earth *arum*. Now it is true that in older usage, *aruma 'cesh* are powerful and dangerous, and can strike people. They are associated particularly with the graves of persons recently buried, as already explained (Chapter 2(iv) above). They are dangerous to the living, but not because of any inherent impurity or moral evil; indeed it is when their living relatives are at fault, quarrelling among themselves, that the danger of their presence is greatest. They are sometimes said to be fond of the living and the life they have left. A manifestation of *aruma 'cesh* cannot be the 'unclean spirit' or 'demon' of the Revised Standard Version (let alone the 'devil' of the King James Bible).

But particularly surprising for the novice reader of the Uduk Bible is the indiscriminate use of the *aruma 'cesh* category to include every single manifestation of *arum*, other than Arumgimis, the spirit on high. The various manifestations of known *arum*, though associated with the ground and with holes, caves, springs, and so on, are fairly benign by comparison with the dangerous *aruma 'cesh* which can strike people. The *arum* of those who have died long ago and are permanently settled in the villages of the dead under their respective hills are not actively harmful to the living; they do not pounce upon or seize the living without provocation. In so far as *arum* actively enter human affairs through possessing living persons, it is misleading to label them all *aruma 'cesh*, and a real distortion to treat them as unclean devils or evil spirits. This is not merely a point of academic theology, for it denies the positive aspects of the power of *arum*. Through their special embodiment of *arum*, the masters of hunting and fishing, of Birdrites or Elephant Medicine, bring much good to human existence. Christian doctrine as taught in Chali reserved exclusive power of healing and salvation to Arumgimis and his representatives, denying even a shadow of such power to the spiritual leaders in the villages and their inspiration. Even the men of the Arum of Leina were dubbed 'rainmakers' with the rest. All healing and ritual practices of the villages were lumped together in English as 'witchcraft' by the missionaries, and one who had strayed from Christian discipline and perhaps attended the healing rites for a sick relative in the village, would be reported as having 'gone back to witchcraft'.

The existing intricate and subtle perceived interconnection between spiritual powers and the *earth* provided a ready-made spatial metaphor upon which translators could build, by contrast, an opposing sky divinity of infinite goodness, and at the same time consign all previous beliefs and practices to the dump. Following from the sharp spatial contrast of above and below, a moral polarity was set up which lent itself to the stark symbolic dichotomies of light and darkness, of day and night, of holiness and impurity, even of right and left. The broad, clean sweep of this new teaching, deceptively straightforward as a framework for moral exhortations and sermons, allowed very little room for the complexities of previous knowledge, or for the authenticity of previous experience.

Cosmic beings were another innovation. It is true that the *arum* the Uduk were familiar with frequently took human form. But these were apparitions on a normal human scale, while *arum* as an abstraction never had an overall human shape or character. The anthropomorphic metaphors of the scriptures, however, lent Arumgimis the qualities of a living person on an awesome scale: not only the physical attributes of the body, breath, a right hand, a throne to sit on, and so forth, but also the capacity for a father's anger, love, judgement, and the like. *Arum* was already conceived both within a person, and as an extension of that person after death, but as an ultimate source of life and creation it did not take the form of a human, masculine personality. Nor was Arumgimis, the Arum-on-High, the Lord or 'chief' (*Tapa*), the only anthropomorphic being populating the new universe. In addition to the problem of the Trinity, and angels, and so forth, there were the beings of the underworld, and their chief too. Satan is introduced by name, but also is rendered interestingly as the 'chief of the earth spirits' in the sense of one in charge of many (*tapa ma ruma 'cesh*). The temptation of Jesus by Satan, when paraphrased back into English from the Uduk version, reads in part like this: 'And then Jesus was led by the Spirit [*Shi/in*, breath] out into the bush and he was tried by the chief of the earth *arum* ... and the tempter appeared and said to him: If you are the Son of Arum-on-High you can command this stone to become food.... Jesus said to him, Again it is written, You will tempt your Chief Arum-on-High [*Tapa Arumgimis*]. Again the chief of the earth *arum* led him to a high mountain ... (Matt. 4: 1–5).

Although the image of Arumgimis is metaphorically human, a wide gulf strangely separates this being, as God, from humankind. I have described in earlier chapters the intimate linkage between human experience and human history, the interpenetration of the realms of *arum* and of the life and history of the *'kwanim pa*, as human beings. There was no cosmic opposition between God and Man of the kind emphasized by fundamentalist readings of the Bible, either at the mythical beginnings of the *'kwanim pa* or in the present. *Arum* had been a power known to the Uduk primarily through their own history, and intimately linked with developing humankind from the start. But the project of Bible translation imposed a division in the world, and an ontological distinction between divinity and human beings, from the beginning and permanently. The human world was itself divided on lines it had never been before, into those set apart, who would eventually go with Christ to Heaven (*Bampa/ gi Momis*: the Land-in-the-Sky), and those left in darkness. In the next world, the people were to be divided for ever between the land of bliss on high, and that of torment below. But for the ordinary Uduk, so divided and tormented in their own past, the next world had previously, in their imagination, been an earthly place close to home where all would be joined together again.

The known world had not previously been ordered by dominant, all-pervading polarities. Cosmic distinctions as between light and dark, or between right and left, as in the frequent Biblical references to the right hand of God, for example, touched few chords. In the matter of the purity of heart and life, as against the unclean state of sin from which the believer is saved, and the purity of the Holy Spirit (*Shi/in Dheleladhelel*: literally clean breath) as against the dirty *arum* of the ground, the translators are making cosmic metaphors from mundane words (perhaps against the normal grain of image-making). The opposed categories have a pragmatic, every-day meaning, certainly; but as they are not invested with the ritual sense of purity or impurity, I am not sure that these metaphors really work. The Uduk are a people whose pragmatic sense of *what is possible* has enabled them to survive a hazardous past and to scratch together a newly settled way of life. They have, perhaps, not been able to afford the luxury of contemplating degrees of purity. They have very few food taboos; they have few 'sacred' or set-apart places, persons, or times; they have few rites of the 'cleansing' or purifying type. They have few rules restricting the range of sexual or marriage partners, and are perfectly content to marry persons even outside their ethnic community. The marriage bond, once established, is by no means quasi-sacred or hedged around with sanctions on its purity. The Uduk are a people with few holy secrets. To take their everyday words for clean and dirty, and carry them through to create a world of cosmic holiness and impurity, is temptingly easy. But does that new world exist beyond the paper on which it is written?

Translation and biblical exegesis also required a reordering of the human person as previously understood by the Uduk. Unquestionably, the very best efforts were made to utilize the language in which the physical and psychical attributes and capacities of the person were already represented. Translation was throughout a joint effort between missionaries and Uduk-speakers. The importance of the Liver, for example, was appreciated early. This vital organ, *adu*, was used consistently to replace 'heart' in English. But the use of 'heart' in modern English is acknowledged to be a figure of speech, and is capable therefore of a wide variety of different (even incompatible) but often superficial applications; the heart can love, it can fear, it can be purified, swayed, gripped, frozen, Jesus can enter it, it can sink, rise, jump, sing, and so on. In the case of the Uduk Liver, there are fewer metaphors; but they are stronger. The concept is of an experiencing organ with tangible functions, not only of emotional response, but of harbouring the blood and *arum*, and thus maintaining life. The person is sometimes led by the Liver, for example into sleep, as I have described in the first part of this book (see Chapter 2(i)(b)). The Liver would appear to include, for the Uduk, some of those aspects of the personality we might popularly label 'the unconscious'. *Adu* inevitably appears in various senses in the New Testament, some of which extend its indigenous meaning considerably, as in its adoption for expressions such as spirit and conscience; for example in 2 Cor. 2:13, *adum pem* for 'my spirit', and 1:2, *'twa/ ma dum bam*, literally 'the speech of our Livers', for 'the testimony of our conscience'. But the Liver is not an aspect of the person which the Uduk would wish to operate so independently; to allow it freedom is to lose that 'self-control' stemming from the Stomach which makes us moral agents.

At the same time, the Liver is a *stronger* centre of vitality than the metaphorical English 'heart', however suitable their equation as 'seats of emotion'; and its psychical aspects cannot be separated from the anatomical, as can our metaphor of the heart. We now have many persons with transplanted hearts, but we do not regard them as being different people. We might have a different attitude to the notion of a 'mind transplant' or substitution of the brain. For the Uduk, I would guess that the idea of a liver transplant would seem more like the latter than the former, in so far as we cannot accept the existence of an experiencing mind without a physical brain, as we do conceive of, say, 'kind-heartedness' in a person who has had a heart transplant. The Liver is an organic component in the working of a person, helping to sustain the experiencing self, and not merely a bodily metaphor for an abstract capacity.

In translation, some of what modern English-speakers see as metaphors of the heart produce striking effects when transferred to the Uduk Liver, and can even take on a stronger meaning. For example, the notion of a 'change of heart' becomes a most radical and literal renewal in Uduk Christian discourse. But many other metaphors do not work, and here I would include the idea of cleansing the heart, or 'cleaning up the Liver', which although used a great deal in the Chali church and no doubt in that context acquiring a currency of its own, is just odd-sounding outside the Christian language community.

The word *kashira/* (which I have glossed as the personal Genius: see Chapter 2(i)(d)) is understandably used for 'soul', though it is sometimes avoided. At some crucial points it is unambiguously chosen. We find that he who brings back a sinner will save his soul (*kashira/*) from death (James 5: 20). More substantial is the form of words in the burial service (see *Rules of the Church*), 'For it may please God, who has all strength and righteousness, to take from this earth the *kashira/* of this person who has died; we place his/her body in the grave and wait for that day to come when all the people will appear again.'

It is in the Psalms that the soul, with its translation as *kashira/*, is most fully elaborated. The Lord is begged to 'deliver my *kashira/* in safety ... for many are arrayed against me' (54: 18), not to 'deliver the *kashira/* of thy dove to the wild beasts' (74: 19), while 'my *kashira/* is feasted as with marrow and fat ... and in the shadow of thy wings I sing for joy. My *kashira/* clings to thee ...' (74: 5–8). A recurring motif is of pleading with the Lord for protection from the snares of evil-doers (for example, Psalm 141: 9), which recalls the way Uduk represent the dangers threatening to entrap the person, in particular the personal Genius. The soul and body are sometimes explicitly paired as complementary aspects of the person, where the translation *kashira/* seems less appropriate.

At the same time, the use of *shi/in* (breath) for 'spirit' may evoke, very persuasively for the Uduk reader, associations of *arum* as the living force within the person, conveyed as it is by the breath. Consider for example some lines from Psalm 31: 'Take me out of the net which is hidden for me, for thou art my refuge. Into thy hand I commit my spirit [*shi/in*].... Be gracious to me, O Lord, for I am in distress; my eye is wasted from grief; my soul [*kashira/*]

and my body also' (31: 4–9). In places there is an appeal to the Lord
to save the _kashira/_ because the psalmist's own strength has gone;
in Psalm 22 there is a specific reference to the weakness of the
heart, here quite appropriately translated as Liver (_adu_). The underlying logic here corresponds well with older Uduk ideas: if the Liver
is weakened or attacked in some way, the personal Genius will be
threatened too; and by saving the Genius, the restorative power of
arum will also help to correct and strengthen the Liver. 'I am
poured out like water, and all my bones are out of joint; my heart
[_adu_] is like wax, it is melted within my breast; my strength is dried
up ... O thou my help, hasten to my aid! Deliver my soul [_kashira/_]
from the sword, my life from the power of the dog! Save me from
the mouth of the lion, my afflicted soul [_kashira/_] from the horns
of the wild oxen!' [22: 14–21] Here is encapsulated that elemental
struggle over the _kashira/_, in which Uduk see themselves placed
between one powerful form of _arum_ and another. As I present the
struggle in this book, it is an epic in which the relatively weak
human being endeavours to defend and reassert a moral individuality, of which an essential sign is the personal Genius, in the
face of those powerful and threatening forces of _arum_ which may
invade the Liver, attack the person, and dislodge or entrap the
Genius. The world of the Psalms, of course a pre-Christian world,
has some deep points of contact with those archival representations
of the human dilemma on which the Uduk build.

Let us take another case where the bold appropriation of _kashira/_
for the 'soul', though odd in some ways, strikes home unexpectedly
in others. In Psalm 42 we read, 'As a hart longs for flowing streams,
so longs my soul for thee, O God. My soul thirsts for God....'
This is a vibrant image in Uduk, as far as the thirsting antelope
goes. There are problems, however, with the _kashira/_, used in both
instances in these lines, for it is an integral, experiencing faculty of
persons rather than an independent _alter ego_ which can feel hunger
and thirst. 'These things I remember, as I pour out my soul ...'
Something seems odd about the translation here too, for it appears
literally as 'These things I remember, as I pour my _kashira/_ outside ...' However, when we reach 'My soul is cast down within
me,' the literal 'My _kashira/_ is thrown down inside me' is evocative
of the way the Genius _can_ be trapped, extracted, and thrown down,
often to be hidden in the ground. Thus the concluding lines
'Why are you cast down, O my soul? and why are you disquieted

within me?' which is rendered as 'Why are you thrown down on the ground, and why do you refuse my hand?' has deep resonance.

There is an even more robust image in Psalm 7, where we have in the fifth verse, 'Let the enemy pursue me and overtake me; and let him trample my life to the ground, and lay my soul (*kashira/*) in the dust.' The transposition into Uduk is striking. The idea of my enemy chasing me, trampling my life in the ground, and laying my Genius in the dust is precisely what I might be afraid of. The correspondence here with older Uduk notions is almost inappropriately good. It is perhaps because of this kind of embarrassing difficulty that *kashira/* is often avoided in the translation, particularly in the New Testament. Other available terms for 'thyself', 'myself', and 'I' frequently stand in themselves for the soul.

The way in which the various elements of the person and the psyche are represented in older Uduk thought is described in Chapter 2 above. It is true that the sense of 'I' asserted in the Stomach (*bwa*) can speak as it were for the whole, and even exert modest control over the impulses of the central organ of direct experience and spiritual response, the Liver. But this sense of 'I' is not paramount over all the other elements; the relation of all elements of the person, including the 'I' of the Stomach, is as parts to an interactive, working whole. That whole is the experiencing 'moral person' which *encompasses* the assertive element of 'my will'.

On the side of the intellect, many expressions are used in the Uduk scriptures which refer relevantly, and vividly, to the stomach, *bwa*, as the place where acquired knowledge is stored, and 'thought' over. But in this case as with the others, a reading of the texts, as well as the orders of service and hymns in Uduk, leaves the impression that although the literal references of the Uduk idiom are carefully observed, the person as a whole has changed. Over and above the several parts, the *adu* and *kashira/* and *bwa* in particular, there exists a new 'I', an assertive consciousness whose centre of being is displaced, perhaps outside the body altogether, a detached will which can actually control the response and function of the Liver, the Stomach, and so on. The idea that 'I' can change my own Liver, cleanse it, and keep it apart, is really quite novel; 'I' had formerly been led my *adu*, rather than being able to dominate it. Complementary functions are separated from their

organic context in translation, and are thus sometimes mean-
inglessly transferred to other organs. The integrity of the person is
thus dismembered. When Jesus was asked for the greatest of God's
commandments, he replied, 'Hear O Israel ... you shall love the
Lord your God with all your heart [*adu*, Liver] and with all your
soul [*ḵashira/*, Genius] and with all your mind [*bwa*, Stomach] and
with all your strength' (Mark 12: 30). Even as metaphor, the effect
in Uduk is to magnify the abstract will of 'myself', while diluting
the experiences of my felt being. It is an unfamiliar twist to my
knowing of myself, to add the moral discipline of a puritan 'I'. On
becoming a believer, you are supposed to give up various food
avoidances that you might have practised in the village; thus for
example, you might have learned to avoid goat meat, because the
sharp smell of it went right down to your Liver and made you
vomit. This kind of reaction, learned by experience, comes directly
from your Liver, and you do not expect to control it, except by
diet and medicines. But voluntary control of the Liver, far beyond
what was previously thought possible, is exactly the kind of behavioural discipline that the new Christian is expected to exercise over
his or her former being. The new doctrine, by implication, is
diminishing some aspects of personal experience of oneself by
reducing them to 'mere body', at the same time separating the
psychic functions, grouping them together on the side of the 'soul'
rather than the 'body', and giving them in the charge of a stronger
overall will. Bodily references have become weak metaphor. The
modern Protestant dichotomy of material body and ethereal soul
has been superimposed (through textual translation and the in-
vention of a new discourse) upon the existing Uduk knowledge of
being a person, in which tangible and intangible functions are more
closely integrated, and representations of the body are images so
strong as to generate what are understood as the varieties of true
experience.

There is one vital omission from the representation of the person
in the new religious discourse of Chali: that is, the *arum* within. I
have already suggested how the sharp spatial dichotomies of the
new cosmology sunder the more intricate understandings of the
old. The great divide between the heavenly realm and the mundane
world of humankind is one of these, and because of the need to
make it clear, the older Uduk notion of a presence of *arum* within
human beings is completely ignored. And yet *arum* plays a part in

the very conception of a child; it is the vital being of living creatures, indissolubly connected with life-blood and the Liver. It is the spiritual force within a person, and it is known as that aspect of the person which survives bodily death.

Conceivably, a translator could have considered the use of *arum* for that very 'soul' which is to be saved from subterranean consignment. There are passages of the translated scriptures where a clear body/soul dichotomy has been transposed to a hypothetical duality of body and *kashira/*, whereas the duality of body and *arum* might have evoked more powerfully in the vernacular something of that flesh/spirit mystery by no means unique to Christianity. Consider this passage for example: 'And do not fear those who kill the body but cannot kill the soul [*kashira/*]; rather fear him who can destroy both the soul [*kashira/*] and body in hell ...' (Matt. 10: 28). In the logic of the vernacular, if the body of a man were severely attacked, he would lose his personal Genius anyway, along with his other senses and capacities. The substitution of *arum* for *kashira/* in this rendering would considerably reinforce the notion of immortal 'soul' and would yield a sense closer to the original.

It is true that other problems would have followed from such a translator's decision. There would have been endless confusion between the nature of human souls on the one hand, and God on the other. But this very continuity, between the 'human soul' and the forces of life and creation, had to be severed in the translation project, in order to construct a disembodied Spirit. The new world as represented in the Uduk Bible, and in Christian fundamentalism at Chali, may well form a system on its own terms; but there remains this most serious of all moral revisions, leaving the person as an empty organism without vital inner life. I do not know how far the notion of *arum* existing within the person was informally recognized within the teaching at Chali, though I guess it was simply not spoken about. It was certainly left out of the written texts. Nevertheless, the idea surely must persist, at some level, in the thinking and emotional response even of wholehearted believers.

One of the ironies in the construction of a new world from the vocabulary of the old is that if the words and phrases of the old language are used in ways that are too foreign and uncomfortable, they do not make much sense; the greater the break with the old world, the less the chance of making a deep impression upon the potential believer. And yet the more intimately the translator follows the older idioms, the fewer questions are raised about the reality of that old world. The more gifted the translator, the less the linguistic shock, and perhaps intellectual challenge, for new believers. They will be able to draw comfortably upon past knowledge and experience. But even the most gifted linguists among missionaries of a fundamentalist persuasion are committed to a clean break with the past experience of a people like the Uduk.

Let me illustrate this dilemma, by reference to the two versions of Psalm 23 which have appeared among the published materials in the Uduk language. The first translation appears in the booklet *Rules of the Church*, as a part of the service of burial for a small child. The second version of Psalm 23 was published two years later in 1965 as a part of the booklet of Psalms, *Gway gi lDawuu'd*, and it is not only more comfortable in its style and rhythm but more idiomatic in its phraseology and metaphor. Inevitably this means that it recalls the (banned) ritual and imagery of village life. For example, compare the rather heavy-handed first version of 'He restores my soul,' which reads *A'di ki woth aha/ akashiram pem ka nyan'ko'd*, literally 'He helps me get my Genius back', which is no less awkward in one language than the other. The later version however reads *A'di warki aha/ akashiram pem is mo*, literally 'He returns me my Genius to the body', a style which rings true in the vernacular. It recalls the way the Ebony Men commonly diagnose 'loss of Genius', set out for the place where it has been lost, retrieve it, and Restore it to the patient (in the rite termed *lat*). But in finding such an apt translation for 'He restores my soul', the translator is drawing powerfully on those 'pagan' notions of healing that the Church was otherwise banning as non-Christian 'witchcraft'.

In a later phrase, 'Thou anointest my head with oil', the first translation gives /*E woli aha/ ayini 'kup*, 'You pour oil on my head', which has I think the same clumsiness in Uduk as it has in English. However, the second version reads /*E 'koshi aha/ 'kup pem ka yin mo*, which in literal English does not seem to make much more sense, that is 'You cover me on my head with oil', but the phrase *'kosh is ka yin*, to cover the body with oil, is the idiom used in the villages for the act which completes rites of passage and most healing treatment. The oil may be plain, it may be black, or it may be red, according to the circumstances; it may be for the whole body, or just indeed for the head. The use of this phrase for 'anointing' in the scriptural sense is very appropriate; but again it might be thought to compromise the evangelical aim of severing links with former belief and practice.

Even in the New Testament language is sometimes used in a way which would ring strikingly true in the non-Christian context. The disciples (*imancik gwo*, those who have heard the Word), when they saw Him walking on the water, were afraid and said *A'di ta'da arum mo be*, 'He has *arum*' (Matt. 14: 26). This usage seems perfectly natural to me; it seems to have come through spontaneously here despite the enormous efforts made to distinguish always between Arum-on-High and the evil *arum* of the earth. Another instance of the use of *arum*, which in its naturalness seems to me to flow from older primary assumptions, occurs in the context of Jesus' appearance in risen form, as represented in Luke. Jesus appeared among the disciples *ki is piti*, 'in His body', and wished peace among them. They were afraid and *toshki uni parkina arum e mo be*, 'thought they were seeing an *arum*'. He reproached them, and commanded them to look at His hands and feet. *Aha/ ki is pem tana a'di mo be. Budhi aha/ is ki me'd mo dhali par e mo, haala rum diki ta gi buŋgwar is mo dhala sima/mo me'd jin parkina um e mo kun taka/ mo be.* In retranslation this would read, 'This is myself in the body. Take hold of me with your hand and have a look, because *arum* does not have a body and bones as you see that I have'. He then asks for, and is given, something to eat (Luke 24: 36–43).

Beyond the written texts of scripture, which do embrace all sorts of fertile ambiguity, there developed a simpler religious language of the spoken word: the new 'mission' language as used both formally and informally in the services and general discourse of the Christian community at Chali. Here was less room for ambivalence or opaque metaphor. The world of spoken language leaves its traces; I have discussed above some written evidence for extra-scriptural usage in the formal statements of doctrine to be found in the rule booklet. In the vernacular Hymns, some of which are close translations, some loosely patterned on available models, others fresh compositions, distinctive idioms from the spoken mission language are dominant. I discuss these in detail in a separate account, but here might just note that making up joyful lyrics to praise God is far more straightforward than endeavouring to translate, and hence interpret, God's actual words.[19]

Let us turn to some more specific aspects of the S.I.M. teaching. First of all, one should appreciate the tangible immediacy of the Gospel for Uduk listeners or readers. Even those with some formal education in geography and history have very little idea of the place, or the period, of the events narrated in the New Testament, let alone their social context. Moreover, what every child in Britain or America soon recognizes as Biblical style, somewhat removed from the English language of everyday life, is lost through translation into a language which lacks a comparable tradition. And of course, immediacy is exactly what the mission teachers of the S.I.M. were aiming at in their renderings. I have the impression that the life of Jesus was assumed by most novice pupils at Chali, and even by many confirmed believers, to have been little more than a couple of generations ago. The personal and place names of the New Testament are brought closer to home by being plausibly adapted to the Uduk ear; for example, Nazareth becomes Pa Naasira, Galilee becomes Pany Jaliil. Given this foreshortening of time and social distance, it is not surprising that the Uduk New Testament conveys a sense of urgency in its prophecies and expectations for the future. Whereas, in a Church of England Sunday School, the expectation of Christ's return might well be played down and put in the far distant future, analogous to that distant past about which pupils are carefully taught, in the mission teaching at Chali the expected Coming seemed imminent. In the 1983 volume, the New Testament is printed first, followed by the Psalms and the Book of Genesis.

In many ways the events narrated in the Gospel are appealing and even convincing to the Uduk. Above all it is the person of Jesus as an active healer and his power against dangerous manifestations of *arum* which catch their imagination. He is able to stop a whirlwind over the water (Mark: 4: 35–41); and, equally vivid in Uduk idiom, he sends demons among the Gadarene swine (especially the version in Mark 5: 1–20). Moreover, Christ's concern for the poor and the suffering comes through clearly and strongly. The text of the New Testament in translation is subtitled every dozen verses

---

[19] See my essay 'Uduk Faith in a Five-note Scale: Mission Music and the spread of the Gospel', in *Vernacular Christianity: Essays in the Social Anthropology of Religion, Presented to Godfrey Lienhardt*, ed. W. James and D. H. Johnson (Oxford: JASO), 1988.

or so, signposting the stories, and illustrations help to focus the reader's attention. For example, passages about healing, exorcism, and the prophecies of Jesus are thus thrown into relief.

One of the main themes highlighted in this way is the coming death of Jesus, and its surrounding events. The three times when Jesus foretells his own death and Resurrection are each given subtitled headings where they occur in the Gospel, and there are in each case descriptively headed paragraphs for the Crucifixion, the death of Jesus, the burial, and the subsequent appearances. A particularly strong emphasis was placed upon the Resurrection in the Christian teachings at Chali, and several hymns celebrate it.

This focus on the Resurrection and expected Return is characteristic of much evangelical enterprise.[20] But it has found a particularly sensitive audience among the Uduk; in spite of the difficulties over the theology and cosmology of God on High, the Trinity, and the cosmic struggle of good and evil, all of which seem to belong to a world apart, the story of Christ's death and what follows makes live contact. In respect of this event, the Christian message did reach out beyond the church community, and since the mid-1960s this has been a prime element in the wider appeal of Christianity. But again we are faced with an irony: although this was the key message taught by the mission, the response it has since received outside Chali can be read in many ways. The events of the Resurrection are supposedly unique in past history, for the Christian believer. But the theme of resurrection is an old one in Uduk thought, and the case of Christ is not necessarily understood as unique. Indeed it has touched an existing chord. The image of Christ as a man who had the power of *arum* strongly within him from his own birth, who then died, rose from the grave, appeared in bodily form, and may return at any time, is very arresting. So is the promise, emphasized, as we have seen, by the Chali missionaries, that the people themselves may expect a bodily resurrection one day. The continued existence of the *arum* after death is nothing special. But the notion of the *arum* after death retaining or regaining a *bodily* existence, overcoming fleshly decay and even returning in bodily form to the living community, is very special indeed.

It is sometimes suggested that the appeal of Christian missions has owed something to the secular and general education which

---

[20] See for example the discussion of millennarianism in Barr, *Fundamentalism*, pp. 190–207.

they have offered, and the opportunities that they have therefore opened up to rural populations for the first time.[21] There was an element of this with the mission at Chali, though the education it offered never gave priority to practical or academic success. Nor were those educated at Chali strongly encouraged to go on elsewhere, either to secondary education or into careers in the cities. The aim of education in Chali was to provide a degree of literacy so that the Word of God could be made known to as many as possible, and general knowledge introduced so that the people could live happily as a Christian community on the land. One should not therefore overstate the benefits of education as such offered at Chali in the mission days. Even the material benefits of medical services and so on were fairly limited. In the years since 1964 when the missionaries had to leave, the material advantages and opportunities offered by conversion to Christianity have been virtually negligible. Whatever incentives may have led village people to take a greater interest in Christianity since 1964 than they did before that date, they have scarcely been material ones. The remarkable revival of Christian religious activity and associated social life that has been seen among the Uduk in the last generation has to be understood in other terms. There is perhaps a general prestige in joining the church, at a time when the presence of Islam is increasingly conspicuous. But this circumstance aside, it is the figure of the dead and risen Christ which touches the thought and feeling of the Uduk in a way for which Islam, for example, can offer no parallel.

Even the early missionaries at Chali were aware that in their teaching on the Risen Saviour they had found a touchstone in existing belief. Malcolm Forsberg writes of one of their encounters in the early 1940s as follows:

One day Enid was telling a group of men about the power of Jesus to raise the dead and heal the blind, and they countered with their own hero.

'That sounds just like Leina,' they said.

'And who is Leina?' Enid asked.

'He's the biggest Maban [sic] witch doctor,' Gari replied.

Enid was disturbed at the comparison but Gari went on to tell her about Leina.

[21] Compare for example R. G. Lienhardt, 'The Dinka and Catholicism', in *Religious Organization and Religious Experience*, A.S.A. Monograph 21 (London/New York: Academic Press), ed. John Davis, 1982, 81–95.

'The District Commissioner didn't like what Leina was doing, so he took him to Kurmuk and chained him. That night Leina slipped the chains off by his own power and escaped. When the District Commissioner tried to catch him, Leina sat under the water in a stream for three days and they couldn't find him. After they went away, Leina got out of the water and went home.'

Gari saw the look of disbelief on Enid's face. 'You don't join my word to your body,' he said.[22]

It was thus in the context of belief *in Leina* that the Forsbergs came to learn the idiomatic phrase *gam gwo is* (join word to body) for 'believing' in general. It is not unlikely that the sustained emphasis on the Resurrection in Christian teaching at Chali has ironically served over the years since the early 1940s to sharpen Uduk opinion about Leina's also having risen; and thus to have prepared the ground thoroughly for the subsequent widespread acceptance of the Christian message.

(iii) Christianity spreads to the periphery, 1964—1983

On arriving in the field in early December 1967, I found that astonishing changes had taken place since I was there previously in May of the same year. There had been a sudden, and to me quite unexpected expansion of Christian activity, not only in Chali but in the surrounding countryside. I heard from Pastor Paul himself that 523 people had been baptized in a single day the previous month, and that many more were being prepared. I do not believe any baptisms took place from early 1964 up to mid-1967, and in the old days baptisms were held for individuals or very small groups after intensive classes.

But now, throughout the Tombak valley, younger people were all wearing bright new clothes and had given up red ochre, beads, and charms. They had abandoned the usual log-and-flute dancing, and taken up hymn-singing, Bible classes, and team games. The church in Chali and also the smaller outlying churches of Beni Mayu and Belatoma (in the Yabus valley) were overflowing each Sunday and quite a number of hut-sized chapels were being built in hamlets where no such activity had been seen before. In Waka'cesh bush had been cleared and trees felled over a large area to make a football field. William Danga was holding regular baptismal

[22] Forsberg, *Land Beyond the Nile*, pp. 154–5.

classes, and youths and girls were practising tug of war by day and hymns like 'Onward, Christian Soldiers' late into the night. They were in the process of building a chapel. Danga told me that this had all begun in Chali and Pijaulu shortly after I had left the previous May, then it spread to the south side of Pam'Be, and a couple of months previously had come to northern Pam'Be. The movement was taken up in village after village by ex-members of the Chali church now resettled with their relatives; they were mostly young men with a number of years of schooling, who had sufficient knowledge of Christian doctrine and practice and the way of life of the old mission community to become themselves teachers and preachers in the new revival. I know of at least ten who started holding Christian classes in the villages. Some of these had formerly had hopes of continuing their schooling, which would have meant leaving Chali, but civil war was closing down the schools in the southern Sudan and going to school in Khartoum was expensive, so very few managed this, and many were frustrated. The new movement gave them an outlet for their talents and knowledge.

On 17 December a second mass baptism was held, which I attended. In the church Pastor Paul's rhetoric became expansive as he called upon all the *'kwanim pa* to become believers; and then, he promised, he would bring the Bunyan (Arabs and clothes-wearing people in general) to Jesus as well. From the church we went in a very long procession to the river, and in groups of seven, Paul baptized the new believers (see Plates 5a and 5b). I counted 186, though the crowds milling around made it difficult to be sure. Those baptized were nearly all youngsters, though two or three older people—including an old man known and enjoyed for his eccentricities—were later baptized in the church. According to William Danga, who kept careful records of his own flock, 42 of the new Christians were from his class, and had received their Christian education almost entirely in Waka'cesh; but 14 more from the Waka'cesh area had also been baptized even though they had not been in William's class. They had stood up in the service at Chali to affirm their belief, and on this basis were accepted for baptism. Two boys from another village who had not been to their local class actually entered the water to be baptized, but their local teacher pulled them back and there were angry words.

There was tension between Chali itself, where the movement

had started and where church leaders desired to keep control and retain the initiative, and the outlying villages where the movement was in the hands of the new teachers. It was felt both in Chali and outside that things were being rushed, but no one was prepared to slow down. Certainly some of those I saw being baptized were not dressed properly by mission standards; not all the girls had covered their breasts, and some were still wearing (forbidden) beads under their new clothes. Those already baptized included a man with two wives, and two women who were co-wives. Not only were these two cases highly irregular, it was explained privately to me, but in the old days a course of classes for baptism had lasted three months, and now it had been shortened to 36 days (much less, in some cases, according to William.)

How had this revival started, and why? Chali church had certainly faced a predicament following the departure of the missionaries in 1964. Pastor Paul was responsible for keeping up the fabric of the church and other buildings and their contents, and for maintaining the Christian community, as well as he could. Foreign teachers, medical personnel, general missionary helpers and administrators, together with services such as the regular flights of the Missionary Aviation Fellowship to Chali, had all disappeared. A small allowance continued to reach Paul from the S.I.M., through a sympathetic Greek merchant in Kurmuk, but it was clearly impossible for him to keep up the material standards of the place, let alone the medical, educational, and other services it had provided, or his own standard of living and that of his closer colleagues. In the circumstances he was doing a very brave and difficult job. It is surprising that the church survived as well as it did. But the membership declined, as the rules of Christian discipline were in theory kept up, and those who erred were encouraged to return to the villages. There were few incentives, and no material advantages, such as education, employment, or medicine, to encourage people to return to the church, or to draw new recruits. Revenues began to dry up. After three years, Paul and the remaining church elders had reached a point where something had to be done. A new evangelical campaign was an obvious option.

Pastor Paul himself has told me that the new belief began when he started to tell the people that they should wear clothes, because the Bunyan were abusing them for going about naked. Paul himself somehow managed to buy and to distribute some lengths of cloth, and this seems to have had a persuasive effect. However, the real spark I believe to have been less prosaic.

It was on 6–7 June 1967 that the sudden attack by Israel on Egypt led to the third Arab–Israeli war. This caused great nervousness and excitement in the Sudan, freshly alerted to its Middle Eastern role; diplomatic relations were broken with the USA, and American aid was withdrawn in consequence. There was a new, and mounting, sensitivity to the presence of Westerners in the Sudan (the new Sudanese Staff Association of the University of Khartoum, gratified at the departure of all American colleagues on US-supported salaries, was even debating how to get rid of British colleagues). The general apprehension might well have exacerbated the latent hostility of Muslim, Arab-speaking circles in Kurmuk towards the Chali church, known still to maintain links with the S.I.M. overseas. This might explain the 'Bunyan abuse' mentioned to me. Paul himself was very anxious to have news from me about the state of Arab–Israeli relations when I arrived in December, and I thought it odd at the time that he was so interested in discussing the war of the previous summer.

Later, I realized why. From several sources I heard that people were afraid, because Jesus was soon to return. People had heard in the Church that there was fighting against Israel, fighting in Jerusalem, and that the temple was being rebuilt. When it was finished, Jesus would come to judge people, so they should all be ready. There were rumours that if one did not join the church, since 'Paul had been given a certificate to do this work', one might be put in prison. Supposed instructions were being passed on, saying that Christian boys, if they found a rite of the Ebony Men in the villages, should tip over the gourds of oil, burn the Ebony Men's skin bags, and if they saw women smoking the *kos* pipe (only old women do this) they should throw the pipe away in the bush. Paul himself was reported to have prompted Christians to break the logs used to beat the dance rhythms.

Christmas Day at Chali church, 1967, saw an enormous gathering (Plate 5c). There were hymns inside, and sports and games outside. I saw William Danga dressed in sacking and an old hat, his face whitened, running around scaring children; this was described to me as '*arum* games' and something which always used to happen at Christmas, though this seemed a little odd (Plate 5d). There were far more guests than the dwindled resources of the Christian village could cope with. Food was prepared in the households near the station, but this was far short of what was needed for all the guests from outside. A few chickens were killed, but no big animals. Meanwhile, however, at Beni Mayu Christmas was being celebrated separately, for the first time ever, and a wonderful time was had by all, with meat for three days, plenty of grain-porridge, and sweet tea. Here they had planned and saved money. The Beni Mayu church, which had about two hundred in the congregation on the Sunday after Christmas, was operating almost independently of Chali by this time, and had already celebrated four marriages since the people had begun 'to believe anew' the previous rainy season. These couples had already eloped in the normal Uduk way, but the marriages were then confirmed in the church. Constitutionally, according to the *Rules of the Church*, it is not within the powers of people other than a Pastor to conduct marriages; but Beni Mayu at this time was a law unto itself.

I had to leave Uduk country in early January, but returned again as soon as I could, in mid-April 1968, to discover how the Christian revolution was faring. As far as Waka'cesh was concerned, it might as well never have happened. The football field was overgrown, the nice clean clothes reduced to rags or set aside, young people were once again wearing beads and red ochre, and evening hymns had given way to dancing. The half-built chapel at Waka'cesh remained with no roof. The older people were relieved, as the money they had gained from sesame the previous year had all gone on clothes and soap for the youngsters. The adult women had had no help from the younger girls in fetching water, grinding, cooking, and so on for various village ceremonies (including a big Gurunya Head-Shaving) which took place during early 1968. Young people of both sexes had on occasion even abstained from helping their elders with secular work-parties held for beer. But now, William Danga had given up his local Bible classes and had been disciplined by the Chali elders. Pastor Paul himself was in difficulties with the S.I.M., as might be imagined, partly because of financial embarrassments resulting from his various outlays, and it took some months of correspondence for matters to settle down.

The extraordinary euphoria of 1967–8 did not recur on such a scale. But since then there have been repeated waves of evangelical activity. The pattern was stabilized somewhat after 1972, with the establishment of civil peace in the Sudan and the forming of the new local Sudan Interior Church, of which Chali is today a major component. This development, based at Melut in the Upper Nile Province, was supported to some extent by the re-establishment of medical assistance and some other services, for example at Doro, and at Gufa, also in Meban country. None of this was possible at Chali however, for, as I have explained above, it remained a part of the Blue Nile Province and was not open to major development and overseas aid in the 1970s and early 1980s as were some areas of the southern provinces. There is still no obvious material advantage to be gained from joining the Christian movement in Udukland; what educational and medical facilities are available in Chali are not under the Church.

But the movement has gained a great deal of ground, and through the renewed efforts of mission bodies overseas, as well as the S.I.M. headquarters in Khartoum, this has been consolidated. A second, and in 1983 a third, Uduk Pastor were ordained. The latter was ordained at Gindi, where 116 had recently been baptized. Pastor Paul told me in 1983 of some sixteen churches throughout Uduk country and many other smaller Christian groups, though the number of firmly founded churches seems rather to have been eight.[23] Paul mentioned that there had been 224 Christians in 1964, when the missionaries had left, and he now claimed a total of 1,119. Several young men were being trained as evangelists, some at the S.I.C. theological college in Melut, and a few others abroad, particularly at a S.I.M. college in Nigeria. He himself and the other Pastors visited the smaller Uduk churches including those in the Ahmar and Yabus valleys as often as they could. But these were largely in the hands of local evangelists, and dependent in the main on revenue they could raise themselves. However, the general support from overseas was on a visible level, and efforts of the S.I.M. and former personnel of the Chali church living abroad, or in a few cases working with the S.I.C. in the Upper Nile, together with funds and equipment they could find, helped to keep up morale.

Given this background, it is not surprising that Waka'cesh in 1983 had its own little church, and a Christian community of up to a dozen families living around it. Large numbers of others swelled the congregation from time to time, though they dropped

---

[23] *Kalaam as Sudan* (SIM mimeographed newsletter, distributed from Khartoum), No. 50, June 1983.

away as easily as they appeared. But nearly everyone in Waka'cesh and surrounding hamlets now had some outfit of clothes that was suitable to go to church in if they chose to go, and all, especially the younger people, were familiar with the church hymns. In 1983 I held sessions of songs and stories for the tape recorder, as I had often done in the 1960s. But now people were volunteering hymns as often as not. There seemed no longer to be a dilemma about being or not being a Christian. One could in fact participate in Christian life without bringing normal productive life to a halt, or even without relinquishing, completely, one's reliance on the rituals of the village.

Indeed it is difficult to see how people could be expected to give up their consultations, for example, with the Ebony diviners, when belief in Jesus no longer opened an avenue to medical treatment. Modern medicine was sought in Chali, though not often with success, and people were very discouraged. The previous year, Ha'da had been very ill, and people carried him to Chali on a bed to seek treatment. But the government dispensary had no suitable medicine, and so they carried him back. Fortunately he recovered, and was in good shape when I saw him.

In the little rectangular church, built three years previously in the traditional materials of woven wattle walls and thatched roof and sited just a hundred yards or so from the other hamlets of Waka'cesh, I heard a sermon preached by a young evangelist doing the rounds in May 1983 on a text taken from Mark, Chapter 13 (verses 24–37). In the Uduk New Testament this passage is given the subtitle 'On the way in which the Son of the People will appear', and it includes the prophecy 'But in those days ... the sun will be darkened ... and the stars will be falling from heaven.... And then they will see the Son of Man coming in clouds with great power and glory.... This generation will not pass away before all these things take place.... But of that day or that hour no one knows.... Take heed, watch; for you do not know when the time will come.' The message was made even more pointedly urgent by the preacher. Christ could come, and rescue the saved, either by day or by night; in the rainy season, or in the dry.

I had an interesting conversation shortly after with Rusko. He was now a leading member of the local Christian group though he had been a reluctant apprentice of the Ebony Order in his youth. He had not been present at Sunday's sermon, but in telling me

about the spread of Christian teaching, he also emphasized that
the idea of Jesus' Return is as strong as ever. He said that people
expect this to happen in the rainy season, and they fill up the church
at this time. In the dry season the message has less appeal, and they
disperse! I think this has more to do with the normal cycle of
expectation in the villages, of anxiety at planting time, hard work,
and then relief at harvest time, when all enjoy some relaxation.
The dry season is a time for travel, and also for many visitors,
including nomad Arabs who may rudely interrupt Christian
worship by shouting outside the church (as happened during the
service I attended). The rainy season is a more 'private' time for
Uduk communities.

Rusko himself pointed out (as had the young preacher) that the
Return may happen at *any time at all*, and that people should
therefore remain alert. He claimed there were 250 baptized believers
registered at Waka'cesh, and, although the congregation had been
two or three dozen that week, they would all return when it started
to rain. There would also be others, who had attended last year
but had not yet reached the point of baptism. Let me quote a part
of my conversation with Rusko.

I have come here today and will tell you about the growth of Arumgimis
in this area. The church which is among Uduk today started with No. 1,
the Chali Church. Then the second was the church of Marko, at Pa
Yanwosh. Those were the churches for the Uduk here. Then there were
their little ones, No. 3 was in Pan Gindi, that is Pam Pija/ulu. Then another
was at Mushwawosh, in Bonya. It serves the Uduk. And another in Pan
'Koshe, in Pan Kamil, in Bonya, serves the Uduk. Then it come to Pam
'Be, on the other side, doing work for the Uduk. And then, it came and
became established here in Pa Waka'cesh. It came here so that the people
of Waka'cesh would know Arumgimis here. And they were happy to
know all about Arumgimis. Formerly, when you came here, they were
sitting pointlessly still, and Arumgimis had not spoken to them, the Holy
Spirit [*shi/in*] had not entered their Livers, and they had not believed in
Jesus. Later, they gave up many practices, various *arum* matters and
Ebony Men's practices. And then we were very glad, and we came and
built a church in Waka'cesh ...

Last rainy season, the young people filled up the class for new believers.
They wanted Jesus very much. But then the heat grew, and in the dry
season they went away! They dispersed, and left only three or so. Later,
they all returned; in the rains they came back, to gather and believe.
Thinking they were seized by Jesus [*butha* Jesus] they came to the

baptismal class, but again in the dry season they left. Of all these, just a few remain now.

Why?

Well, something is affecting their Livers. It is as though they were told by Jesus that He would be coming in the rains. Then when they see that Jesus has not come, they go away again. When it rains, they are afraid in their Livers, there is fear in their Livers. . . . In the rains they are afraid . . . but this is not right. If you believe, you should believe permanently, because [the time of] Jesus is not known. He will appear, either in the rainy season or the dry season. . . . Jesus could appear any time, any place . . .

We discussed what had happened in 1967, and Rusko confirmed that the expected Return had prompted the first large-scale conversions of that year.

Yes. They thought Jesus would come soon. . . .

Everyone accepted this word?

They accepted it! But they didn't understand properly. When they heard that Jesus was coming in the future, they thought it would be very soon. They thought maybe they would wait for a year, and He would appear. That's why they all came and took the word of Jesus. Then when the year had gone and Jesus had not come, they went back home, to sit back again.
     The Uduk are silly.

But Christianity did mean more to the villagers than just going to church. According to Rusko and to others, there was much less talk of *dhathu/* than formerly. Twins were no longer killed. The presence of small churches scattered through the Uduk villages meant that a woman, even one who was not necessarily, I understand, a baptized Christian, could bring her babies, if she bore two, to the church for blessing. The community would then be perfectly happy for her to bring them up. I should mention here, and will develop below, the point that in the new Waka'cesh, it is not *only* through the church that twins can be saved; but it was certainly the church that offered the most easily available solution to this dilemma, and others have remarked that the earlier example of the Chali mission in saving twins has now convinced many that they can grow up to be perfectly acceptable people.

The context of the new attitude to twins is no doubt the protection from *dhathu/* and associated dangers that people feel is offered them by the church. I would go as far as to guess that affiliation to the church, in villages which are still not overtly

Christian, is seen as a way of acquiring immunity from witchcraft. I realized this from pondering my transcription and translation of the 1983 conversation with Rusko. We had been discussing the killing of Lyife, which seemed an easier topic now that it was nearly twenty years back, and Rusko explained for me:

Because for Uduk, the man was *dhathu/*. If a man is ill, they say he is made thus by another [*miin ma kamu/*]; and from not knowing about Arumgimis. If a person knew about Arumgimis, he wouldn't do this. From not understanding, that's why one person will kill another. A man is ill and people will say, that is the man who caused it to the other; he dealt with the other in the night. It was done like that always, from long ago, people were always being killed, and this has ceased recently now. Because Jesus is very big. People get to know Jesus and leave this behind. Because it is bad to kill a person with a spear.

Rusko then affirmed that the killing of twins had been left behind.

Yes, this has been left. A woman will give birth to two children, she will keep them in the house, a lot of people will be happy, they will come and carry the babies outside and greet them with money. Yes. People will take it with those children and give it to Jesus. At the church there. Put the two children there. The person in charge, for Jesus there, they take the children to him. People praise Arumgimis *very* much, saying it is very good to prepare you, to give a woman many children. He is very happy to counsel her. And you, you must care for their souls [*kashiram puni*] very well.... It is good to watch over them.... Yes, people bring those children outside.... Some give birth to three. People then bring all three children out, to carry and give to Jesus; people praise Arumgimis, saying look after these children, these children are yours for ever. They grow, and come to believe.... Many things are done like this now. And then people come out, go off, and eat things at the father's home. The father takes a goat, cuts it, and buys sugar, ten *rotls* [1 rotl] = 1 pound weight], buys coffee, five *rotls*, lots of people gather, we sit and then eat food. Then we sing songs, all are very happy, and greet the children with money. You put a cup on the ground, and greet with money. You give a pound, you give five reals [100 piastres or 10 reals = 1 Sudanese pound]. Twenty-five piastres.

Like the Gurunya practice?

Yes, like the Gurunya practice! You give the children money, and it grows, it becomes ten pounds. It is divided, and with five pounds, the mother will buy clothes for one child. Then the other five pounds is for buying the other child clothes. If any is left, a chicken is bought, and is looked after by the father of the children.... Everyone sitting outside there knows this word. They are not believers ... but they take the child to Arumgimis.

Danga also told me of this new acceptance of twins: you bring out the children, greet them with gifts—such as two chickens, or two eggs, or two coins of the same value. This rite, however, came from the Jum Jum (the immediate source of the Gurunya rites, and the new Ebony diviners).

Rusko mentioned various households in which twins were now living, and several were brought to see me. The baby Gurunya in the coloured frontispiece to 'Kwanim Pa, on her mother's back and covered in red ochre, is now a young married woman and a Christian; and a sister of hers has borne and brought up twins.

The idea of the church as a protective institution seems to have played a part in its growth among the Uduk in the last few years. It can protect one from the dangers of the old kind, against the dangers of aruma 'cesh quite explicitly, and against the evils of invasion by dhathu/, as the village people see it. If these dhathu/ come and give one twins, there is now a way out of the dilemma; for Jesus is very great, and can offer some security.

Now again from the older village point of view, the Ebony Men and indeed the men of Arum are also aiming to protect the people, especially from dhathu/. In the old days of the mission church, before 1964, the activities of the Ebony Order and men of Arum in the villages were all classed together as evil witchcraft; but of course the Ebony Men's main task is actually keeping the dhathu/ at bay, and providing treatment for those who have been caught by them. From a village point of view, it is perfectly natural for Ebony Men themselves to attend services, now that the churches are rooted in the countryside, and accessible to all. Shokko is one of the leading diviners in Pam'Be, and with an enormous if slightly teasing grin claimed that all the Ebony Men go to church these days! The diviners certainly do not discourage people from going, as I believe they sometimes used to, and they do not oppose or challenge the church in any way, now that it is visibly in Uduk hands, open to all, and in receipt of (modest) help from outside. Whether or not people are specifically recommended to take up Christianity by the Ebony Men or not, I do not know.

I do know however that women, at least, from among the village church communities still go along to the Ebony Men for consultations. The new Christianity may not hold with the activities of dhathu/; but what effective means does it offer of combating disease, infertility, and so forth? Apart from a few facilities available from the late 1970s to 1983 in Doro and Gufa (no longer so because of the new outbreak of civil war), and a very sad apology for a medical dressing station at Chali, the Uduk do not have access to modern medical help. The new Christianity must rely on faith alone.

I was giving out a few aspirins and sticking plasters during my brief revisit, when a woman came late, as the sun was going down, and asked quietly if I had medicine for the Liver. I was a little impatient and tried to get rid of her. A neighbour explained that she tended to pass out, and have fits, and this was why she needed 'liver' medicine. She had already been for help to Gufa, but her problem had not gone away. I asked her if she had not been to the Arum men. She asked 'You mean the church people? [Arum *ma cassis*, using the Arabic term for mission.] They don't have medicine.' I explained that I had meant the men of Arum Leina. The answer was 'No,' she hadn't. She departed.

I realized only later that she was a Christian. This young woman, a new convert, still needed practical help of a kind she could not obtain from effective medical sources, and yet was inhibited from consulting non-Christian practitioners. Her faith would thereby be compromised; but while this faith did seem to endorse the 'spiritual' importance of the Liver, it could not itself at this time provide access to medical help for 'fits' thought to stem from it. The distressed lady in search of medicine for the Liver faced a dilemma indeed.

Postscript to Part II

Living with Islam

The southern Funj region has been a part of the Sudan's Islamic frontier for a long time. There is some evidence that mosques were first established in what is now Bela Shangul in the seventeenth century.[1] Jay Spaulding's masterly study of the 'Heroic Age' in the Kingdom of Sennar gives full recognition to the vitality of the southern hilly marchlands in the growth of that polity. With the development of trade and with increased immigration from the northern Sudan in the course of the mid-nineteenth-century Turco-Egyptian period, Islam and the Arabic language became the dominant cultural features of the ruling groups of these border mountains. Later, as international complications produced economic, political, and military activity on this frontier, which was increasingly exploited as a slave reservoir, Arabic and Islam came to represent for many of the surrounding peoples the language and religion of an oppressing class.[2]

It is this context which makes the Sudan–Ethiopian border region rather different from otherwise comparable regions, such as the Nuba Hills of the central Sudan, when one comes to consider the place of Islamic ways in the life of the local peoples, or the broader relations between Christianity, Islam, and local belief systems. Recent history in this region has been a much harsher school for the shaping of attitudes to Islam than in the Nuba Hills, largely because of international pressures, in particular the extending spirals of violence which have characterized the modern history of the Ethiopian state.[3] These spirals have extended as far as territories like Bela Shangul, annexed to the Ethiopian Empire as late as 1898. Because the established rulers of Bela Shangul were already adherents of Islam, the violent depradations which they carried in

---

[1] Alessandro Triulzi, *Salt, Gold and Legitimacy*, esp. ch. 3.
[2] Jay Spaulding, *The Heroic Age in the Kingdom of Sinnār* (Michigan: African Studies Center), 1985.
[3] Donald Donham and Wendy James, eds., *The Southern Marches of Imperial Ethiopia*, esp. ch. 1, 5, and 8.

turn to the western lowlands have left their mark on the local people's view of Islamic religion and society. Unfortunately it is impossible to set aside the pervasive stereotype of the 'Bunyan'—that is in general any clothes-wearing person but usually a northern Sudanese—a negative image drawn from their experience of the Arabic-speaking, Islamized Bertha slave-raider of the last century.

This book does not examine in detail the place of Islam or Sudanese Muslim society in relation to the Uduk; no field study can go in equal depth into every question. But this is beyond doubt one of the most important matters that face the Uduk, or anyone who wishes to understand them. With the imposition of Islamic law throughout the Sudan in September 1983, the problems of those communities adjacent to the old Islamic frontier have become particularly acute.

From the edge of the *dar al-islam*, the world of Islam, the peoples outside, and particularly those in the Nile valley beyond its southern frontier, have little standing. The Islamic religion, like the political community of Islam, is viewed on a frontier like this not as a universal world, but as a bounded system, defining law, faith, citizenship, and even the moral status of persons, with reference to that system. Outside it, there is no law, no faith, and little dignity of the person. The crude use of the Arabic term *'abid*, slaves, is still commonly heard among the Muslim communities of the Ethiopian border to refer to the adjacent lowland populations. I once had to explain my research to a group of very charming, hospitable ladies, in the women's quarters of a Muslim merchant household in Geissan, in Bertha country. I pointed out that no book had been written about how the 'Burun' live, and carry out their farming; I could not explain that I was studying their 'history' (often a very useful ploy for anthropologists) because we all knew only too well that the 'Burun' had no history, except for their being enslaved by families like the very one with whom I was staying. One of the ladies became quite interested, and said quite sincerely, 'Ah, yes. That would be *most* interesting. The slave peoples [*awlad al-'abid*] are indeed *very clever*. I have seen that myself.'

Clever, whether helpful or cunning; loyal or treacherous; hard-working or lazy; but always, *slaves*, even in what is seen in these regions as their state of natural freedom. A view of natural right-lessness of course complements the old Islamic right to enslave infidels, but it has long outlasted the technical abolition of enslavement, slave-trading, and the holding of slaves in the Sudan. These reforms, nevertheless, came much later in Ethiopia and there is evidence that the old trading families of the border were sending slaves over to Ethiopia at least as late as the 1920s.[4]

Given that within the Islamic world, faith and society are ideally one, and given the particular history of contacts between the bearers of Islam and the indigenous peoples of this frontier zone, it is not surprising that few among the latter can conceive of 'Islam', the religion, as such, apart from the power and secular morality of those who are its bearers. I emphasize again that I am not speaking of all Islam, everywhere, a notion the complexity of which Michael Gilsenan's work has illuminated,[5] but specifically of the local frontier Islamic society of this borderland. The ordinary Uduk, for example, do not use the abstract noun 'Islam' at all. They occasionally use 'Muslim', but much more often they will speak of 'Bunyan' custom, or activities, including in this description those practices of 'Islamic' society they may have encountered. They are widely familiar with the word 'Allah'; but the colloquial usages which employ the term are so common throughout the Sudan that it is not easy to be sure what 'religious' significance a given expression has for those who know, as most Uduk commonly do, only a modest amount of Arabic.

It was during the disturbances of the late nineteenth century that the Uduk first had intimate experience of Muslims. Many Uduk, together with Bertha (and others) were captured or otherwise absorbed into the domains of the powerful rulers of the Bela Shangul mountains, and saw at first hand the processes of political and social power which carried the Islamic religion into these mountains. After the pacification of the border region by the Anglo-Egyptian government of the Sudan in 1904, many of the Uduk held as slaves or serfs by the border rulers were allowed to return to their villages, where they were rejoined by others who had fled to the protection of Sudan government outposts such as Jebel Gule. These people too would have seen something of the harsher and intolerant side of local Islamic society.

[4] A. J. Arkell, 'A note on the history of the country of the Berta lying East of Kurmuk within the Abyssinian frontier—with special reference to the recent discovery of a considerable import of Berta slaves into the Sudan', 12 pp. mimeographed. NRO.

[5] Michael Gilsenan, *Recognizing Islam: An Anthropologist's Introduction* (London: Croom Helm), 1983.

Following pacification, the excesses of slave-raiding and trading decreased, and were to some extent replaced by what the new government regarded as legitimate trading in the region, though on a small scale. The figure of the itinerant, or even settler, merchant from the Bertha hills became a familiar one among the Uduk, and in recent times many have felt they know the 'Bunyan' or Muslim trading way of life very well, through knowing merchants of this kind (and often getting on well with them personally). Personal relations with the nomadic Rufa'a el Hoi are also normally good (at least up to the new outbreak of civil war in 1983).

But since the beginning of the century very few Uduk have become Muslims; the conceptual distinction between Muslim and unbeliever has indeed sharpened, while everyday interaction between them has probably increased. Uduk are well aware of the presence of 'Islam', they know it is a permanent part of the situation with which they have to live, and to some extent they are seeking a *modus vivendi*. But it is still virtually invisible in the Uduk villages. The Omda (see Plate 7a) and most of the sheikhs of the Uduk in the 1960s were at least nominally Muslim, and a few of them had married Muslim Bertha women. A handful of other Uduk had become Muslim, some through settling and marrying in Kurmuk, one or two others through the patronage of local merchants. But the vast majority of the Uduk population appeared to hold themselves apart from Muslim ways.

Islam has not, on the whole, been understood as a *religion* by the Uduk. They have seen Islamic observances as part of a way of life, a social and political identity embraced by those who in the past have exploited the Uduk and in some ways continue to do so. Why should they emulate the manners, dress, and social *persona* of those they have good reason to mistrust? The public aspects of Islamic life are very visible to the Uduk, whether among the local merchant or official families, or among the nomad Arabs of the Rufa'a el Hoi.[6] These include the wearing of the northern Sudanese long robe, *jellabiyya*, or the shorter tunic, *jibba*, for men, and swathing with the all-covering *tob* for women. Uduk observers can see all too clearly the restrictions which are placed upon the freedom of both men and women, but especially women, in the Islamic marriage relationship and indeed all family relationships. They

[6] Abd-al Ghaffar Muhammad Ahmad, *Shaykhs and Followers: Political Struggle in the Rufa'a al-Hoi Nazirate in the Sudan* (Khartoum: Khartoum University Press), 1974.

find male circumcision, a diacritical marker of the Muslim in the southern Funj region, distasteful; and the idea of female pharaonic circumcision (which in the Kurmuk District, as in many other parts of the Sudan, is expected of Muslim families) they find abhorrent. Dietary restrictions, with regard to pig meat for example, they see little point in, and find amusing. They are always glad to receive from the Rufa'a meat of animals which have died of their own accord and are 'unclean' to the Arabs. Disapproval of beer-drinking does not make sense to them, and there are indeed very few compensations they can see in the Muslim way of life. Until very recently it has not even been associated with any real opportunities in the educational or employment fields.

The village of Chali itself has for a long time been the main focus for a Muslim presence in Udukland. The name Chali is almost certainly derived from an early merchant settler claiming 'Ja'ali' descent, from the riverain northern Sudan. Since at least the 1920s there have been Muslim merchants in Chali, but the contact they have had with the Uduk, even when they can actually speak the vernacular, has been very limited. The men appointed as government chiefs of the Uduk have also frequently been Muslims.

There was, however, from the early period of Condominium government a clear understanding that this region should be regarded as a part of the southern sphere of the Sudan from the religious and educational points of view. In 1926 the Governor of Fung Province wrote to the District Commissioner of Southern Fung at Roseires (his use of 'Barun' includes Uduk, Meban and others):

The following are laid down as the main lines of administrative policy to be followed by you and your A.D.C.:

The Barun and the Ingessana are to be regarded as belonging to the Southern Sudan. It is definitely the policy of the Government that they should not be Arabicized.

Other Arabicized populations north of the Baruns and surrounding the Ingessana will of course remain Arabicized.

Care must be taken that zealous local Inspectors of Education do not start the local Arabic Khalwa system among Barun and Ingessana. Educational policy in respect to them will eventually be assimilated to that of the Southern Sudan.[7]

---

[7] Governor Fung Province, to DC Southern Fung, 1926. NRO Civsec 36/4/13.

As we have seen, this policy culminated in the establishment of the S.I.M. in 1938 at Chali, in the same year as the Uduk were transferred to the Upper Nile Province. The 'Hill Burun' and Ingessana, however, remained in the Blue Nile Province, and in fact became officially regarded as potential Islamic converts.

The spread of Islam was seen therefore in political and social terms by the government, as it was, though in a different way, by the local people, and it is scarcely surprising that very few individuals among the Uduk, apart from the Omdas and Sheikhs and their immediate families, should have been attracted in the early days by the Muslim faith. However, in 1953 Chali was handed back to the Blue Nile Province, with the mission already established. This was a year of great change in the Sudan, for political decisions had been made to proceed quickly towards independence of the country, and political parties were campaigning for support among the population in the preparations for the Sudan's first elections. A delegation from the Khatmiyya order of 'Abd al-Rahman al-Mirghani, upon which was based the National Unionist Party, came to Kurmuk and Chali to rally support. This party was already strong in the Blue Nile Province.[8]

The speeches and receptions were accompanied by the drumming and marching of the order, and proclamations of the Islamic faith. All this colourful activity seems to have made a big impression upon the people. The Chali rally was the first public challenge to the Uduk to accept Islam, or rather as they saw it, to join the practices of the Muslims. There was by 1953 a certain amount of tension, connected with the general rise of nationalistic feeling, between the small Muslim merchant community and the Chali Christians. This also was a time of maximum tension between the mission station, approaching the height of its influence, and the outlying villages. These were among the background factors which help to explain why the Khatmiyya had a surprising impact, not only on existing Muslims in the Chali market area, but on fringe members of the church community—and on uncommitted persons in the villages. A large number of village men, in particular, showed interest and rallied round. It seemed as though Islam had arrived, all of a sudden. A majority of the Uduk men of the Tombak valley

---

[8] Peter Woodward, *Condominium and Sudanese Nationalism* (London: Rex Collings), 1979, gives a detailed account of the run-up to the 1953 elections (pp. 126–35).

apparently 'became Muslims', to use their own words, though they did not go as far as taking Muslim names, or accepting circumcision. Tente, even then an experienced Ebony diviner, was among them; he became, I was astonished to hear, an 'Islamic teacher', *mu'allim*.

But the new fashion, as it turned out to be, soon passed. The next year, 'Islam' was given up, and the people returned to cultivation. They had spent so much time praying, washing hands and feet, and killing goats and chickens for meat, that they were very hungry; they had neglected the fields, and so the next year gave up the demanding new faith. I am not at all sure how far it was understood that their votes rather than their souls were being courted in 1953. At all events, their suitors did not persevere after that election year.

Danga caused much mirth as he told me (in 1967) the story of the Khatmiyya's visit. Understandably, one of the things that really appealed to the people was the order's drumming parade (known in local Arabic as *shabab*). Danga, then a mission schoolboy, argued several points of theology, insisting to his new Islamic instructor that God was Three, and not One.

In the year those people came, I was sitting studying in school. But I became angry and left for home in May.... One Bunyan came, to teach us a song. This was while I was still in school, and I had learned to read and write as a child, and I was a child of God [Arumgimis]. And I had understood the teachings about the God of Jesus Christ, being in three parts.

And the man who taught us said, 'Repeat: God [Allah] is One.' He asked us, 'How many is God?' [*Allah kam?*—Arabic.] All the boys said, 'God is One.' And then he asked me, 'You, boy! How many is God?' [*Allah kam ya walad?*] And I said, 'God is Three.' [*Allah talata.*] That is what I said, that God [Arumgimis] is in three parts. And that was how he came to teach us the way of the Muslims in Udukland. He taught us one song. *Haya bina. Haya bina. Haya bina.*

Danga was one of four boys among the first to be given instruction. What he now remembers best seems to have been instruction on performing the parade of the Khatmiyya. He remained with his group for a month before being taken back to school on orders from the mission. Whatever the hopes and fears of the missionaries

(and there were plenty, as Forsberg has made clear[9]), the Uduk
Christians began to suspect the Muslims of planning violence.

They came in the dry season, and they played drums energetically ...
they had in mind to destroy the Church and were intending to kill the
missionaries there. We all gathered in the Church there, the missionaries
and the young Christians; they were not very many.... And just a few of
us went off to wait and watch them. They did their dance and sang a
lot.... And later, a Bunyan came from Nyille there [a Bertha village] to
teach people, and show them the way in which the *shabab* is done [the
parade].... And he taught us another song, *La ila illa Allah Muhammad
arasul Allah*....

Later that year this practice expanded fast.... It spread and spread,
and people took it up and worked very hard at it, for one year. And then
the Governor came, from Wad Medani. The Governor came, in 1954, to
Chali there. The people collected for a big *shabab*, and he brought police
too, and they marched with drums.... And the people brought things,
athele/ [flutes and logs for dancing] included; but the *athele*/ people were
not many and were crowded out by the *shabab*.

Danga went on to describe how the people spent all their time at
meetings and gatherings for spreading the new ideas, and how the
grain and animals were used up in hospitality. 'Then hunger struck,
and they left this work saying "Ah! We shall give up this thing and
cultivate again." '

At this point in the conversation, Tente joined us, and Danga
laughingly reminded him that he had been a *mu'allim*, a religious
teacher, along with Shokko, another leading diviner. He agreed,
and then began to explain how things had soon gone sour. He used
the phrase 'Ansar', the sect politically opposed in recent times to
the Khatmiyya; but this term is used very widely in the southern
Sudan to refer to any Islamic propagandists since the time of the
Ansar activity in the nineteenth century. It does not mean that the
modern Ansar visited Chali.

Tente, that year you were a mu'allim?

Yes.... They wore *jellabiyyas* in the special way, in the style of the Ansar.
They wore them just like real Ansar. It was worn by many Uduk that
year. Everybody became Ansar that year. But they didn't know the
meaning [*'pemen*, literally 'roots'] of it. It was just done by them as a
thing in itself, but they didn't know its meaning.

[9] Malcolm Forsberg, *Last Days on the Nile, passim*. Ch. 22, for example, describes
the enforced change from Sunday to Friday as the weekly day of rest throughout the
schools in the southern Sudan.

Tente elaborated on the events of that year, referring to the followers of the Khatmiyya as 'people of the *shabab*'. He himself had
become disenchanted when large numbers of curious Meban visitors
came to his village on a day when beer had been prepared for a
work-party in the fields. Alajabu (alias Samuel, a brother of Pastor
Paul) was a leader of the new activities, and had tried to make him
stay to entertain the guests. He even threatened Tente that the new
Arum would attack him with a big curved stick. Tente, nevertheless,
went off to cultivate, and found the beer nearly finished when he
got back. Then visitors turned up from Chali and finished off the
goats brought by the Meban guests as a kind of homage to Tente,
their host.

Yes, that business became distasteful to me [*shina bwa*, bad in the
Stomach] when lots of people came from Meban. There was a big work-
party of mine, and the beer was fermenting. People slept at my place, it
was full up, *mu'b*. I thought *thah*! I would go and cultivate. That Alajabu
said, '*Caah!* You are not going to cultivate. If you go off to cultivate,
caah—you will not come back again; you will go and die out there under
the grass.' I said, 'What! What is this, that I shall die under the grass?'
Alajabu said, '*Caah*. This great Arum, we don't understand it. This Arum
which has come now, we don't understand its actions. But it carries a
great curved stick. If you go it will kill you out in the tall grass. You will
die in the grass and lie there until you are shrivelled dry. Just lying there
under the grass.'

And the whole thing became bad in my eyes. I said, '*Caah*. You say
this, and so how can I stay? [i.e. people will think I am afraid]. I am going
to break away from this business and cultivate.'

But I didn't go to cultivate. Just three went; Gure, and the brother of
Jethen ... and Ha'da. They went to cultivate, came home, and found no
beer. A little was left for them, but very little indeed. All those people of
the *shabab* just sat in the village and dealt with the beer completely. There
was very little left for me. That is what upset me. I didn't want this, and
I broke away from the *shabab* business. I just stayed without it. But lots
of people continued doing it. I looked at it, cursed it, and gave it up.

Because people had nothing. They had no sorghum [the staple grain].
They were living without anything. They were busy with just the *shabab*,
always, always, always. At dawn, people did *shabab*. The moon was rising
late, but in spite of this, people would light a fire with flames so that they
could do the *shabab* [rather wasteful of firewood], and in the morning at
dawn again they would do the *shabab*.

Then the Chali people came in crowds, and massacred the goats the
Meban had brought, cutting their throats just like that and eating them.

Some time later, Tente told us, there was a big expedition to Kurmuk, for a political rally. A large number of Uduk men went along, but there was nothing to eat on the journey, and nothing to eat when they got there, and 'even Alajabu was neglected and hungry'. Few of those newly attracted to Islam by the exciting events, the parading, and exhortations of 1953 remained as permanent converts.

Little more happened locally on the Islamic front until the mid-1970s, when the immigrant Muslim population of Chali began to increase with expanding commerce (see Introductory Essay). A mosque was opened in 1983 (Plate 7b). A small place for prayer was under preparation in Beni Mayu. The people had again been given encouragement to take up Islam, and it was well known in the villages that by going to pray in Chali one would easily find gifts of cloth and clothing. A number of the older men had gone along with this. But the younger men and youths were said to be firmly rejecting these offers. The new *mahad* (Islamic Institute) in Chali provided some local employment but as yet had no Uduk students. It goes without saying that these developments scarcely affected the women at all.

But in 1983, any talk that touched on the new mosque in Chali moved quickly on to the fresh phenomenon that had appeared in the Yabus valley. A certain Sheikh Ahmad, an itinerant holy man of a kind well known in the Sudan as *feki*, was attracting attention and had visitors from far away—Kurmuk, Damazin, and beyond. He claimed to have healing powers, and the Uduk in Chali and Pam'Be were very curious about him. People were saying that he 'had *arum*'. When I asked what *arum*, the answer was 'the Arum of Muhammad'! The institutional Islam of the Chali mosque was never spoken about in this way.

Sheikh Ahmad was said to have come from Roro, an outlier of Jebel Gule (where interestingly a Koman language, now virtually disappeared, used to be spoken). I have no confirmatory evidence. Some people said he had spent six years (and some said twelve) in the bush and forest, on Jebel Bisho, eating just leaves. (Jebel Bisho is a mountain from which the great majority of the Uduk claim to have come.) Sheikh Ahmad was reported to me as having a large following among the Uduk of the Yabus valley, but I rather doubt this. He certainly recommended to patients certain medicines and made suggestions about planting crops, and also prescribed conversion to Islam. Men were said to be regularly packed off in lorries to Kurmuk for circumcision at the hospital. However, I understand from Joachim Theis that the 'Koma' are very wary of Sheikh Ahmad, and I believe the reports of his success that circulate in Chali may be exaggerated. Rusko was one of those who told me about Sheikh Ahmad, who was also described to me by Joachim Theis as a striking figure with dreadlocks. Rusko said,

You know something, there is another *arum* now. In Yabus.... People are about to take their children there. The Uduk, all of them want to go over there. Yes. To see this *arum*, they say.

What arum?

The *arum* there ... called Feki Ahmad. They want to see, if they take a child who is sick, if he will treat him. The child will get better, they say....

And what does he tell a sick person?

He tells a sick person, he has only one instruction, you should take the person to Kurmuk for circumcision. He should pray to *arum* [*luŋ arum*], pray to the Arum of Muhammad, and he will get better.

And do some people get circumcised?

Yabus, yes, and this area. Some of our older people have been circumcised, in Chali there. People give them prayer beads. They wear them, and sit and count them. Because those people at first, they brought a lot of cloth, a lot, and Uduk went from here, to pray there, and the people would give them clothes.... They gave the *jellabiyya* to wear, and to pray.

Are they different from Sheikh Ahmad?

Yes, different. They don't know the way of Ahmad. People wonder at what they have heard, and go and see him. Because they don't know his name.... The Yabus people are all circumcised now. People fill up the lorries, again and again, and go to Kurmuk to get circumcised.

Even allowing for a little dramatic exaggeration, the appeal of new spiritual claims seemed to have caught the attention of the Uduk once again, at least in the south. It is interesting to note that the new *feki* was seen by the Uduk in some respects as a kind of diviner, with knowledge not only of sickness but also of the welfare of the crops, and the rain. A rival (of whose identity I am not sure) had apparently locked up the rain in a trunk the previous year, and in 1983 Ahmad was reportedly saying that this man would open the trunk and let out the rain.

Whatever may be the long-term results of Sheikh Ahmad's influence (and he seemed to have kept a low profile for a long period in

1985), it is quite clear that the particular appeal he had for a number of Uduk in 1983 derived from his personal interest in their everyday problems, and his personal spiritual claims. Two poles of the Islamic world, the constituted doctrine of official Sunni Islam, and the charismatic and mystical claims of the Sufi tradition in the person of the itinerant Sudanese *feki* or holy man, have now both touched the Uduk. The mystique of the holy man has long played a part in the spread of the Faith in the peripheral regions of the Nile valley,[10] and Sheikh Ahmad's arrival in the Yabus valley may signal a permanent southward shift in the 'Islamic frontier'. But even if the Uduk come to demonstrate a new allegiance to the Islamic faith on any scale, and in the very long term this must be a very serious possibility, it can exist only in an equivocal manner with older traditions, as is still the case with the Bertha. With or without the spiritual inspiration of a charismatic person, and with or without subscription to theological doctrine, it may be that the Uduk will increasingly participate in a Sudanese framework of 'civil society', to adopt a concept which Gerhard Baumann has suggested on the basis of his work in the Nuba Hills, which although not requiring *faith* does define that structure of civility in terms of behaviour, manners, dress, and a social code which stems from the Islamic tradition of the Sudan. The political factor of living on the north–south boundary in the Sudan is likely, however, to remain more sharply divisive here than anywhere in the Nuba hills, and this boundary itself may inhibit the growth of a 'civil society', locally or indeed nationally.

---

[10] Triulzi, *Salt, Gold and Legitimacy*, ch. 3 on the coming of the 'Wise Men'.

PART III

The Ebony Speaks

5

Becoming Ebony Men

Observers and informants alike agree that there has been an enormous upsurge in the activity of the Order of Ebony Diviners (ŋari/) in the last two generations or so. Mary Beam and Betty Cridland put it to me when I met them in 1971 that there had been a great increase in 'witchcraft' during their time in Chali.

Throughout my fieldwork the rituals and general activities of the Ebony diviners had commanded my attention, even more insistently than the Gurunya rites and practices (described in 'Kwanim Pa). It was evident from the start, and made explicit by informants, that while the Gurunya cult for the saving of infant life was the special concern of women, the ŋari/ practices were not simply a 'men's version' of the women's rite. Though run by men, the ŋari/ practices encompassed the women's specialism; the Gurunya people were sometimes described as a kind of ŋari/ themselves. The Ebony Order worked for the saving of the life of the people as a whole, and was the concern of everyone.

I had been taken aback in the 1960s by the conspicuous numbers of Ebony Men in the villages. I would estimate, generalizing from my own survey of Waka'cesh (see Appendix 3), that among the northern Uduk well over a third of adult men, together with a small proportion of women and children, were apprentices or full graduates of the Ebony Order. There was almost no overlap with the membership of the cult of the Arum Leina, and thus, when the whole range of ritual specialisms is taken into account, nearly two-thirds of the male population appeared to be practitioners of one kind or another. There is a special term, indeed, for 'lay people' without any specialism—'kwani e 'te/, 'just people'. These are in a small minority among men, though might be a majority of women, especially of younger women. For everybody, therefore, sources of oracular advice and healing treatment were close at hand. The Ebony Men offered initial consultation and diagnosis, through their technique of 'kindling the ebony', and were more accessible than the Arum men, whose role remained more that of specialized consultants to whom patients were referred. Among the Ebony Men, perhaps only a quarter had graduated to senior status, and the rest were still apprenticed to the Order, though fully active practitioners. This structure in itself reflects the growing success of the Order in attracting recruits; or rather, in sponsoring diagnoses of patients which included a requirement that they should be brought into the Order.

The Ebony Order, like so many institutional practices of Uduk social life today, has an immediate 'external' origin. However it was well established long before the time of Leina. It has played a role partly counter, and partly complementary, to the cult of the Arum Leina since the 1930s, and in the last decade seems to have reached an accommodation (and a sharing of responsibilities) with the Arum men. During the mission period, the Ebony Order was identified by the missionaries as their chief adversary; and this no doubt helped in some ways to sharpen its image within the villages peripheral to Chali. From the 1940s onward the numbers of adherents increased, many being recruited to new branches of the Order which had become active among the Jum Jum near Wadega. Since the departure of the missionaries in 1964, and the gradual increase of Christian activities in the villages, the Order has ceased to be a focus of opposition to the Church in the way it had been; and today, the Ebony Men seem actually to be smiling on the new advances of 'Arumgimis' (see Chapter 4).

The relationship between the diviners' Order and Islam has to be interpreted in a regional and historical context, and not simply within the horizons of present-day 'Uduk society'. We recall in particular the Islamization of the Bertha, immediate eastern neighbours of the Uduk, and the spread of Islam in regions like the Nuba Hills. Whereas Christianity at Chali arrived relatively late, was always small-scale by comparison with the main missions in the southern Sudan, and, though extended, remains institutionally fragile even today, the presence of the Islamic frontier is a substantial and, as far as we can foresee, a permanent social and political fact. To speculate, in the very long term, the Order of Ebony Diviners may come to represent a focused antithesis to Islam among the Uduk, as it has proved already in other parts of the region which never had their own mission Christianity: in particular, in Bela Shangul, the homeland of the Bertha.

This mountainous region still looks towards the Sudan although it was largely incorporated into Ethiopia at the end of the last century. It received large numbers of Arabic-speaking Muslims from the central Nile valley during the nineteenth century, settlers who through intermarriage produced a stratified society in which the Arabic language and Islam had privileged status over the indigenous Bertha language and culture. Our knowledge of the history of Bela Shangul, of the making of this stratified society and the subjugation of Bertha institutions, comes from the work of Alessandro Triulzi. Triulzi has described the way in which certain motifs of ancient belief and ritual are treasured by the Bertha as bearing something of their distinctive past and present identity, in the face of the successive waves of immigrant rulers whose way of life and religion have given their homeland its modern character. There is more than a hint that the old Bertha rites have served, at least symbolically, to limit the power of immigrant rulers. The main ancient cult of the Bertha centred on a sacred rock, from which the expression 'Bela Shangul' itself is directly derived; and the formidable priest of this cult was the *ŋeri*.[1]

There is no doubt that in one or two senses the Uduk have 'taken over' the Bertha institution of the diviner, transcribed by Triulzi as *ŋeri*. The term *ŋari/*, so thoroughly at home in its Uduk context that the people say 'The Bertha also know the name *ŋari/*', is one of very few words in common between these quite unrelated languages.[2] The other shared terms, as far as I can discover, are all obvious loans, referring for example to certain musical instruments or to throwing-sticks which the Uduk have adopted from the Bertha. These cultural adoptions almost certainly post-date the arrival of the Uduk in their present homeland from further south (probably in the first half of the nineteenth century, possibly a little earlier). The term *ŋari/* (with slight variations in pronunciation) is now used over the larger part of the Kurmuk District north of the Yabus River. It may also be found north of the District. Its local

---

[1] Triulzi, *Salt, Gold and Legitimacy*, ch. 1.

[2] The term *ŋari/* or a cognate is found in several other parts of the Sudan–Ethiopian region. The most detailed account is of the various kinds of *ngarrec* of the Murle, in B. A. Lewis, *The Murle: Red Chiefs and Black Commoners* (Oxford: Clarendon Press), 1972. There are four main types of these 'witch-doctors', who possess special insects in their heads, which are linked with rain serpents: sandal throwers, pebble diviners, fire doctors (mostly women), and augurs or seers who read sacrificial intestines (pp. 137–42). Jon Arensen has confirmed the basic account of Lewis, and is conducting new research upon the Murle.

use is coextensive with the loose organization I have called the Order of Ebony Diviners, which has its centre at Jebel Silak, a peripheral Bertha-speaking community.

In this border region of tiny language communities and intricate local patterns of coming and going (quite apart from the imposition of state structures and national frameworks of language, religion, and culture), it is probably quite false to think in terms of cultural 'traits' having a single centre of origin, and a subsequent pattern of diffusion. Alessandro Triulzi has suggested (in discussion) a most helpful image. A border region of this kind is like a pattern of sand-dunes partially obscured beneath a shifting sea; what has been lost at one time, may be found by someone else in another place, when the sea later retreats. What is underneath, may be obscured completely for a time, but may surface again unexpectedly. The fundamental substance is always there, beneath the surface waves; but its elements are continually shifting and rearranging themselves. This image, which reminds us of the very long time perspectives of cultural continuity in the Sudan–Ethiopian borderlands, may help us to accept the significance of correspondences even where we cannot specify sources, routes of contact, or context of diffusion.

It is important to find a way of picturing the assorted local cultures of this border region not as a patchwork quilt, the pattern of each arbitrary scrap unrelated to the others, juxtaposed in space but lacking organic connection. A tapestry would be a better image: for the same main threads run through while creating areas of distinctive pattern and image scattered over the whole; even in the field of ritual repertoire, discussed for the Uduk in Part I, many elements recur among the Bertha, Koman peoples, Hill Burun, and Meban, though in different combinations and with different emphases in each community, and no doubt in the same community at different times.

The main achievement of the modern ŋari/ among the Uduk, I believe, has been the regathering and rearrangement of older elements of knowledge and ritual into a freshly intelligible series of authoritative interpretations, a newly explicit discourse. Some of these elements are no doubt 'imported', even along with the 'institution' or role of the ŋari/ himself: where this is the case, the older resonances of common understanding across this 'pre-Nilotic' region may facilitate their acceptance. But it remains true that the larger proportion of elements drawn into the new discourse stems from within the older traditions of the Uduk themselves, which we have already described as their 'cultural archive' in Part I of this book.

I have adopted the expression 'Ebony Man' for the *ŋari/* among the Uduk, and the term Order for the admittedly sprawling organization which links him to his sponsors (now to be found mainly at Wadega) and his sponsors' sponsors (theoretically at Jebel Silak). It seemed to me that 'diviner', a translation I have used in previous writings, suggests a too exclusive function for the way the Uduk have developed the role of *ŋari/*, and limits its significance (though I use the phrase 'Ebony diviner' in contexts such as professional divination and diagnosis). But the modern *ŋari/*, besides divining the causes of illnesses and other problems, is an interpreter in a broader, stylistic and representational sense; he acts out an image of and for the people, through his songs, his dances, his costume, and his attitudes. For this reason I frequently use the term 'Ebony Men', and occasionally its singular, which better evokes the representational *persona* of the *ŋari/* than does the functionally specific 'diviner'.

With so many people, especially young men, becoming *ŋari/* these days—each hamlet or household supplying apprentices—the institution has become more open, more democratic, than it once was among the Bertha. Moreover, the knowledge which the apprentice acquires, although it has its specialized aspect which comes with the authority of the Order, is not *secret* or arcane. It is rather that the authority of the Order has its sources in the existing moral knowledge of the people.

The term *ŋari/* has taken on a wider, as well as a specific application. Outside the context of the Ebony Order, it can be used quite generally of ritual specialists, even including the men of the Arum Leina cult; and as I have mentioned, it can specifically be used of the specialists of the women's Gurunya cult. In the very widest sense, I think the term *ŋari/* could be extended to all the older Uduk ritual specialist roles, such as the Elephant master. The word is used, moreover, in a range of general ways even in the mission context. It comes in very handy for the Egyptian magicians called to interpret Pharaoh's dreams in the translation of Genesis 41: 8; and a wall barometer at Chali, by which 'you could tell when to sow seeds', was known as 'little *ŋari/*'!

(i) The *ŋeri* diviner in Bertha history

There were a number of independent chiefdoms among the pre-nineteenth-century Bertha. The ruler (*agur*) of each had a *ŋeri* to advise, in priestly fashion, to divine, and to sacrifice for him. The *ŋeri*'s prayers were said to have been addressed to the 'rivers, trees, stones, and the rain' and Triulzi suggests that he combined the traditional powers of a rain-maker, diviner, and medicine-man. Triulzi also describes some rites for the protection of crops from animals, birds, rain, and wind; and he has emphasized in discussion that not only the chief, but all could have access to the *ŋeri*. The role of *ŋeri* was hereditary, passing from father to son; however, if a ruler of one group lacked a *ŋeri* (and no Bertha group was complete without one), he could request a *ŋeri* from another group to come and train a young man for him. '*ŋeri* teachers were borrowed from one group to the other in exchange of crops, grain, or honey to the *agur*,' Triulzi was told; and he concludes that it is not surprising that the *ŋeri* was later to 'play an important part in resisting foreign intrusion in Bertha society'.[3]

It was a prime responsibility of this Bertha *ŋeri* of old to divine the future by burning ebony wood, a technique known to them as *shangur*.

The *shangur* was the reading of the future through the flame of a particular kind of ebony wood called *tari* or, lacking this, of any high-burning wood (*bibi*) or, at times, of a special grass named *abandu*. The reading was performed traditionally by the medicine man or diviner among the Bertha (*ŋeri*) or sometimes by the elders of the community. Today, when Islam has pervaded several aspects of Bertha society, both the *ŋeri* and the practice of *shangur* are waning, being restricted to isolated communities; but in the past both had an important function in Bertha society.

The *shangur* is said to have been performed or consulted 'before any major event, hunting, harvesting, gold extracting, a long journey for trade, moving from one area to another'. *Shangur* is equalled by Bertha informants to the Arabs' Qur'an, it is 'the book' of the Bertha: '*Shangur* is good. We cannot live without it. The Arabs say they cannot live without God. So also we cannot live without *shangur*. The *shangur* sends messages and receives messages from God. What God wants us to do and what we want him to do for us is done only through our fathers' *shangur*.[4]

---

[3] Triulzi, *Salt, Gold and Legitimacy*, pp. 27–8.
[4] Ibid., p. 26.

Triulzi quotes further accounts of how the *shangur* of the earliest known ancestors of all the Bertha led them in their migration from Gerri to their present home in the Ethiopian foothills, from which they displaced Mao and Koma populations. The *shangur* reportedly warned them that if they moved even further, the leopards would destroy their goats. He quotes one informant from among the (Muslim) elders of Khomosha who equates the *ŋeri* with the very highest conceivable authority: he claimed that the *ŋeri* of the Bertha were spiritual fathers like the *'ulama* or *wali* of the Arabs, and feared (in 1972) more than Haile Selassie. Since a *ŋeri* 'can bring disaster and wrath upon the land', the Bertha respect him.[5]

It is quite clear from the evidence of these modern informants that they counterpose the *ŋeri* of the past to the Islamic teachers and holy men of the Arabs. Moreover they see the burning ebony oracle as the counterpart of the written wisdom of Islam. Alessandro Triulzi has kindly shown me unpublished material from his notes, including a text in which a *ŋeri* and a *feki* (Islamic holy man) engage in dialogue. Triulzi's informant, himself a Muslim, states 'The *fekis* reject the truth in the *ŋari* [*sic*] practice. The *ŋari* work with the power of Satan, while the *fekis* believe in the power of God ... although there are villages where both *ŋari* and *feki* live as neighbours.' It was claimed that the Bertha *ŋeri* were very active until the time of Shaikh Khogali al-Hassan (that is, until the late nineteenth century). The informant described a visit by Khogali to the greatest *ŋeri* of his time, Gaussa; Khogali asked him to cease the practice of magic in his domains, but at the same time asked the magician to keep off the rains until he had completed his journey! Gaussa then forecast Khogali's own death, and in fact survived him. Triulzi notes that during the Mahdiyya, the *ŋeri* did not contribute to any direct uprising among the Bertha, but did complain about the prohibition upon their beer and tobacco; and moreover 'the *ŋari* may have been helping the people by telling them what the *shangur* [ebony oracle] was saying against the Mahdists'.[6]

Even though this evidence is based on present-day oral tradition, we can be fairly certain that during the last century, the old Bertha institution of the *ŋeri* came to represent in some ways the antithesis, even the rival, to Islam. This has no doubt given it a political edge,

[5] Ibid., pp. 26–7.
[6] Alessandro Triulzi, fieldnotes.

which helps explain its spread in this Islamic frontier area among peripheral and formerly subjugated populations. It is almost certain that the earliest introduction of the role of *ŋeri* 'diviner' to the Uduk came directly from the Bertha, during the period of the late nineteenth century when many Uduk were enserfed, along with Bertha, in the domains of Khogali, Ibrahim Mahmud, and Hamid Hassan. The later influence of the *ŋari/* institution has spread directly from outlying modern Bertha communities in the Sudan, especially from Jebel Silak.

(ii) The spread of the Ebony Men

To set the scene I would like to quote one account of how a man was saved by the Ebony Men from a potentially fatal encounter with Allah. Lothdha told me the story of Allah appearing to him in the form of a whirlwind. He was knocked over, became ill, and could have died. But Karis, an Ebony diviner from the Tombak valley, came to the Yabus and saved him, with his medicine of Spice (*jiṯ*). This is a wild aromatic root, the emblematic medicine of the Ebony Order.[7] But it was not the medicine in itself, alone, which saved him. In conjunction, Allah necessarily permitted, and aided, the recovery. It is clear from the account that the Ebony Man and his Spice medicine facilitated an accommodation with the external power which otherwise might have killed the unprepared, and unprotected, victim. Since first wearing the Spice, Lothdha has himself graduated as an Ebony diviner. This story can be read as a parable of the wider protective salvation that the Order has offered, and still offers the people.

Allah was about to cut my throat [i.e. I was about to die—this is a common Uduk idiom, and can be used of *arum*]. People would not have been seeing me now. It was the Spice of the Ebony Men which helped me. That is why I am alive and speaking now. I would not otherwise have been seeing people.

I was very young; and Allah was about to cut my throat. I didn't know people [I was not my normal self]. Karis was the one who helped me with his Spice. I lived, and I can speak to you now. I was struck by—Allah was about to kill me. And he helped me with Spice. Now I can speak and see everybody. A great whirlwind struck me under the fig-tree, while I was digging out yams [previously stored there]. I was about to die....

[7] I have not been able to establish a botanical identification for this plant.

And Ḵaris made you an Ebony Man?

Yes, it was Ḵaris who made me an Ebony Man, with his Spice. Allah enabled him to do this [*Allah ki ci a'di me'd*, literally, 'Allah gave him a hand'], to help me like that, and now I can speak and see people.

There are various kinds of 'diviner' and 'medicine-man' among the peoples of the Kurmuk District, all known in colloquial Arabic as *kujur*. Among the Komo for example, to the south of the Uduk, are some who divine by throwing cowrie shells; and Joachim Theis reports divination by burning fat and feathers among the Kwama. But these diviners are not as assertively conspicuous as the modern Ebony Men among the Uduk, arrayed in animal skins, feathers, and charms on professional duty, unpredictable, moody, and sometimes aggressive. Joachim Theis tells me that the Uduk diviner, slung with skins, whip, and medicines, can easily be spotted downstream from Yabus Bridge, in the linguistically mixed communities of the south bank of the river.

Uduk speak as though there had always been some *ŋari/*, though everyone emphasizes that in the past they were very few in number. There were also fewer diseases; one of the frequently cited causes of the diseases so common today is the unprecedented number of practitioners—including Ebony Men—in the community.

All my informants agreed that the earliest modern Ebony diviners were the *ŋariny je Arum Allah*, literally, 'elephant diviners of Arum Allah'. One of the first who could be remembered was Co Punya, said to have lived before 'Kujul' (Khogali Hassan) and the 1904 battle of Jerok ('*KP*: 39–40). Another was Rawa, who lived in 'Cogo', between Bertha country and the Uduk. Rawa sponsored Nyere, who himself sponsored many others including William Danga's father Ledko. Nyere must have been active during the 1930s. He was a paternal uncle of Tente's, and his protégé Ledko originally sponsored Tente himself (see Plate 8). There are quite a number of the 'Arum Allah' diviners still practising, such as Ḵaris who treated Loṯhdha. They are I think still the main type of diviner found south of the Yabus. The 'Arum Allah' diviners, sometimes just known as the old-style *ŋariny je*, that is, old-style 'elephant diviners', are still associated with the 'Cogo', a category of people who today speak both Uduk and Bertha, and seem to be descended from slaves escaped or freed from Bela Shangul. The link back to the Bertha, and the explicit 'Islamic' connection in the reference to

'Allah', remind us that when the Uduk took over the ŋari/ institution it was already defined, through antithetical opposition, as counter to Islam.

(iii) The five branches of the Order

The earlier organization of diviners of the 'Arum Allah' persuasion among the northern Uduk has now been supplanted, by the popular acceptance of sponsorship into newly-fashionable branches of the Order. These have become known to the Uduk from the Jum Jum people around Wadega, but they have their centre at Jebel Silak, to the north, where a dialect of the Bertha language is spoken. From Silak, I understand, the new Order spread to Melkan, and the Jum Jum took it from Melkan. They have now passed it on not only to the Uduk but also the Meban, and to the Hill Burun of Jebels Abuldugu, Mufwa, Maiak, and Surkum.

I visited Silak briefly, at an early stage of my travels in the region. With some companions I climbed the hill for the view. I did notice that near the top of the hill there was a *kujur* living in ostentatious isolation; he and various others that day happened to be in their professional garb of goatskins and charms; and I was shown quite an impressive cave and waterfall where a rainbow was said to live. At the time I had no idea how significant this would later seem. Much later, from Uduk and Jum Jum informants, I heard of the big Rainbow in Silak (the context demands a capital letter): it was a hungry meat-eating Rainbow, living in a cave with water.

At Silak new Ebony Men are initiated in the cave, by immersion. But before they enter the water, the meat of a sheep or a goat is lowered into it; if the meat is consumed in the water, the Rainbow creature is well pleased, its hunger is satisfied, and the novices can safely enter, and acquire knowledge; they 'learn everything'. However, the water which splashes out from the hole of the Rainbow creature 'kills' the novices. They are then revived with Spice.

Silak is the historical, and symbolic, centre of the modern Ebony Order and the rites of the Rainbow Cave are now acted out in many communities far from Silak. The Jum Jum around Wadega to the south were keen apprentices, and through an expanding network of sponsorship, have passed their practices on to the Uduk.

Most senior Uduk Ebony Men have themselves had Jum Jum sponsors.

As the Uduk have received the Order from Wadega, it embraces five branches. There is some regional variation in the way these branches are named and grouped over the Kurmuk district, but as they are perceived among the Uduk at present they are as follows:

1. *Je* (Elephants). This branch has 'long' been associated with Jebel Wadega. Distinct from the 'old-style' Elephant diviners qualified as 'Arum Allah', these new *ŋariny je* are in the majority in Uduk country today. They wear their roots of Spice carved into long points like elephant tusks, with white scars down their length. The Elephants use red ochre in their rites and 'fear the Rainbow'. 'Fear' (*ko*) has the ritual sense of 'avoid, respect' as well as the ordinary sense of fearing a danger (compare the Dinka or Nuer *thek*).[8]

2. *Cirtaŋge* (Dik-dik). Also an old branch from Wadega, and known in Uduk country for some time—at least a generation. There are few representatives; I believe their Spice is shaped like the horns of the dik-dik. The name is a mispronunciation of the Jum Jum *ter dhuŋke*, 'diviner of the dik-dik'. In various ways the *cirtaŋge* diviners are special. They are shy and delicate, and 'fear' the others, they do not fight the others in the set dramas which form a part of the Order's rites of passage, but sit and eat apart and 'fight among themselves inside the hut'. This is all 'from their *arum* of long ago'. When the other Ebony Men drink milk and break wind, as is their practice, the *cirtaŋge* don't like it and weep. They are given eggs to eat, 'like the Gurunya'—the child who Sits Black to avoid the threat of death (*'KP*: Chapter 7). The right foreleg of any animal killed at an Ebony rite is given to the *cirtaŋge* present, and they eat it apart from the others. In the details of the rites of passage through which apprentices pass, *cirtaŋge* are treated in the same way as *je*.

3. *Thuk* (Guinea-Fowl). Also 'long' associated with Wadega, though in a minority in Uduk country today. They too resemble the Elephants in the details of their rites of passage. The Spice they wear is rounded, with white spots, like the flecks of the guinea-fowl.

---

[8] Evans-Pritchard, *Nuer Religion*, esp. pp. 177–83; Lienhardt, *Divinity and Experience*, esp. pp. 123–5, 127–32.

4. *Japa* (Throwing-Stick). This branch is the main one associated today with Jebel Silak. It only recently came to Wadega, and then to the Uduk, where it is a very fashionable development. There are a large number of newly-initiated Throwing-Sticks, and they have replaced the older branches to some extent. While Tente, for example, used to be an Elephant of the old 'Arum Allah' type, he later became a Throwing-Stick. His new sponsor (*com*, which can also mean 'owner' or 'father') was Mabruk, a Jum Jum. The Throwing-Sticks do not 'fear' the Rainbow in the hole; but because the Rainbow does not like red ochre, they do 'fear' red ochre. They use black oil (*jiso*), and the white ash of river snail shells (*homod*), in their rites. Their Spice is shaped in a plain J-shape to resemble the throwing-stick. Sometimes they are associated with the weasel, *leheny*, which is an animal found around the hamlets rather than far out in the wild bush.

5. *'Bu'th* (Monkey). This branch is said to have originated in Jebels Keili and Kukuli, Bertha-speaking hills close to the Ethiopian border, but it reached the Uduk via Wadega. The Monkeys carry a whip, like the monkey's tail, and their Spice is thus shaped. At their graduation rites, the apprentices are spotted in various colours (to be described below). The number of Monkey diviners also seems to be increasing among the Uduk.

There are minor variations between the branches, each of which has specific relationships with the wild animals and is permitted to use skin bags of specific types, whilst 'fearing' a range of specific animals. But all these variations are mere decorative details of the Ebony Men's paraphernalia, the way their rites differ, or the role they take in set dramas. They do not, as far as I am aware, affect the methods of oracular consultation, diagnosis, and the treatment of sickness, which are common to the various branches. From the patient's point of view, an Ebony Man is an Ebony Man, regardless of whether he (or occasionally she) is an Elephant or a Throwing-Stick. This becomes crucial only if the patients are diagnosed as *bu'th ma jit̲*, 'seized by Spice', for this means that they are seized by the Spice of a particular Ebony Man, and necessarily therefore of a particular branch. The patients should then go through the succession of complicated rites leading them to graduation as new members of the Order.

(iv) Accepting the Ebony Men

There are many stories on the lines of 'how I became a ŋari/', but apart from unusual accounts like that of Lothdha (given above), they tend to resemble one another and repeat a few well-worn motifs.

1. Manjal

You see at first I refused to become an Ebony Man. Then my feet became painful. It was at the time Miss Beam's people [the missionaries] were here. Later I moved up here, and people made me an Ebony Man and I became very happy because I recovered. I recovered with the Ebony Men's treatment, while I had at first refused to be one, because I didn't want to eat people's chickens for nothing.... Yes, I used to despise this kind of thing.... Then the Ebony Men treated me, after I had been going to the [mission] dispensary. They healed my foot. ... After they made me a ŋari/, I really got better.

2. Kutha

It was when people were dancing athele/.... We went to dance at night, and a man called Tanga, brother of Joc'ko, took off his shorts and hung them up. Then we took the pair of shorts, which contained some Spice. We wore the shorts and scattered the Spice on the ground. Then the Spice seized me. I went on my way; but when I was seized by the Spice I became very ill indeed. People kindled the ebony and said I was seized by Spice and was about to die.

But I disagreed with this and I went to Bellila. He [Tanga] came and brought me from there; I stayed here and they made me an Ebony Man. I was about to refuse, and then I thought to myself, let them make you a ŋari/. Then I went to the dispensary and drank some medicine and returned home. Still my body was sick.'

3. Shokko

Why were you made a ŋari/?

Why? It is always through sickness that people are made Ebony Men.

What was your sickness?

Just sickness. I was made a ŋari/ when I was ill, very ill. I got sick for no special reason: I got sick from God [Allah], from Arum.

Were you seized by Spice?

No, I just got sick without any special cause, a real illness. I was not seized by Spice.

Were you a child?

Why? I was big, I was grown-up ... I got sick from Arum. I was sick; and then the Ebony Men came and took charge, they made me one of them. They took me over there, and kept me in Nyethko's hut. I stayed and stayed, and they treated me there in Nyethko's village.

And a certain Jum Jum called Jidic was there to teach us. As the sun was low like this, we were beaten with whips [the practice of the Monkeys]. I was beaten until my fingernails were almost off! ... We were beaten with the whip like this, *cuw*, *cuw*, *cuw*. Every day; one day, beaten! Next day, beaten! We were bathed with water very early in the morning, we ran about and stayed without warming ourselves. We were once chased in the morning, and we ran and struggled over the door of the hut.... Then people brought us out, and we were beaten and we jumped on their backs ... I was very thin from my illness.

4. Sebko

The Ebony Men came from Wadega there, when people of this area didn't have this business.... It came, and they started putting Spice on people here. That is why the Uduk have Ebony Men now....

Sometimes with sickness, a sick man will confound the Ebony Men. Because your *arum* is sick, you will in addition be seized by Spice, and die. And there is no means of treating you successfully. You are treated until they get tired. You will remain without recovering.

What is the work of Spice?

It is worn because of sickness.... It heals people. You who are very sick, if you are seized by Spice, and they treat you, you will get strong. You will go and eat with people. If you are seized by Spice, and if people treat you without putting Spice on your neck, you will never get better from the illness. You will die. If you are treated, you will recover, by washing with water every morning very early. You will bathe always, always, with the stones in it. Stones in the water ... Ebony Men's stones! They are taken out of the bag, and put in the water. You will take a bath while the air is very cold.

The very familiarity of such stories within the community suggests that becoming an Ebony Man is not the strange and special event that being seized by *arum* can be. At least for a young man, it is now almost a standard expectation, as if being sick through vulnerability to a strange power or through contamination from Spice itself, and recovering so as to be in control of what made you sick, is a 'rite of passage' which might form a part of anyone's life. All lay people are closely related to an Ebony Man. The Order is not at all an exclusive society 'set apart', but has become an integral part of every person's world.

However, it is not surprising, given the characteristic occasional obstinacy of Uduk and the presence of so many competing ideologies and faiths, that some people not only 'refuse' the attentions of the Ebony Men at first, but go on doing so. Rusko, initially having been given the Spice to wear as a baby, hated the rites he was obliged to go through as a boy. These rites are parallel to those of the Gurunya cult, and like them include, for example, the use of dirty things. The diviners are even supposed to consume dirty substances at the rite for Showing the Banks or 'learning the boundaries', the first major step in apprenticeship. Rusko's account, from 1968 when he was already attracted by the Christian revival, follows on from a passage I have already quoted in explanation of the Gurunya rites ('KP: 218).

When I was made an Ebony Man at first ... people did the rite for Showing the Banks. We went, and people took a lot of dog-dirt which they had collected while we were sitting on the ground, not noticing. People took it secretly from the ground there to mix with our food. They poured sauce on it, and poured oil mixed with sesame paste. They took it and put it in an open place. People gathered us together, saying, 'Come and swallow down this food.' We flocked around the pot; 'Don't use the right hand!' they called. 'Just scoop it up with the left!' [Among the Uduk, the right hand is normally used for eating.] We went on eating, and later I saw a lump of hair. I didn't go on eating. I dipped in with the back of my hand, and I went _thuup_! [spitting out instead of eating]. Again I dipped in, and went _thuup_! People saw me, and said, 'That one's not eating!' ...

I said, 'I don't want this! To eat filth; I may become ill from eating these things.' ...

People said 'You are living now; but you will soon die.' I asked why, and people said, 'Because you refused the Ebony rite. Don't refuse the Ebony rite. It is something attached to you from when you were small.' I told them I was not sick. I was taken when I was very small, just from drinking milk as a baby.

Rusko even returned his special skin bag to his sponsor, an insulting act which risked his sponsor's wrath. Since then, he said, the Ebony Men had continued to badger him. Whenever he had a complaint, they would remind him that he needed them.

Then there was the time my foot swelled up, and people told me I should kindle the ebony to _lat_ my foot in the playing field [to Restore my lost Genius]. I said there was nothing wrong with me. I had broken my little toe, it was perhaps from being tired; then it came to the sinew here, it hurt here and then moved to the other side. That is why it hurts like that.

They said I was bewitched [*ceshu*]. I was buried in a hole in the football field there [i.e. my Genius was there]. They said I should make a little beer for people to Restore me and pick me out from the hole in the football field. Pick me out from the place where I was buried in a hole. I said, 'I am not going to make beer. I am going to stay like this and I am going to recover with just my own *arum*. *Arum* is the one which will help me.'

There had been an earlier snake-bite, which might have accounted for the infected swelling on his foot. Rusko went to the modest government dispensary at Chali, and I also administered an anti-biotic. By this time people were suggesting that the Ebony Men were themselves preventing his recovery, and if he didn't accept them, he would eventually die.

I continued to refuse the Ebony Men. People told me that the Ebony Men were the ones doing this. 'The Ebony Men ordered you to wear Spice again, that is why your foot is hurting you like that.... If you go on behaving like this, you will die one day.'

He did eventually recover from the swollen foot, but later there were more sicknesses, and he attended the dispensary in Chali several times. People were saying that *dhathu/* ('witches') had shot him with an arrow. Eventually he did rejoin the Order, though with great unease. He described to me his distaste at their various techniques, and his worrying inability to suck out foreign objects from patients' bodies, as they seemed to do. He summed it all up as being due to his own inner nature, his Liver. He said of the Ebony business, 'It is from my *adu* that I don't want it.'

Rusko's experience of several years as a 'reluctant diviner' was followed, after a period of mission schooling, by his becoming, understandably, a leader of the new Christian movement in the 1970s. In his account of this, which I have quoted in the previous Chapter, it is again from the Liver, the centre of being, that the word of God is accepted or resisted. The way individual people experience and tell the tale of their encounter with the Ebony diviners, as with the representatives of the Nilotic divinities, Christianity, or Islam, thus illuminates the history of these '-isms'. We now turn to the formal structure of the Ebony rites.

(v) Apprenticeship and graduation

The rites of passage of the Order of Ebony Diviners form two separate series, corresponding at many points in name, structure, and symbolism to the sequence of Gurunya rites I have already described ('KP: Chapter 7). There is a preliminary rite, known as *deha jit* (Wearing the Spice) at which the new recruit is given a necklace of the Spice root medicine to wear. This is followed fairly soon by the basic entry rite, *tora gap* (Showing the Banks), focused on the crossing of the river. At the conclusion of the rite the novice is covered with red ochre, after which we may call him an 'apprentice' Ebony Man. I number these rites 1 (a) and (b). The new diviner will go through other specific rites at which advice and instruction is given, as for example the *montor kanycir* or Lesson in Kindling Ebony. After this, he may practise professionally, and even sponsor others, but in a fairly junior capacity.

Final graduation as a senior Ebony diviner comes only with the second series of rites, connected with the large colourful and dramatic occasion of the Diviners' Horn Dance, *ce ŋari/*. Shortly after this dance comes the concluding *thes 'kup*, the trimming or Styling of the Hair in specific patterns. I number these rites 2(a) and (b). I describe here examples of these rites as I have seen them. At all the main gatherings, and indeed on any occasion when they meet in large numbers, the Ebony Men may enact set dramas, which are described separately below.

1(a) *Wearing the Spice* (Deha jit)

I saw this for Cile, the three-year-old son of Dhirmath and Badke (for illustrations, see Plate 9). Dhirmath himself was a Throwing-Stick, but his little son was to be made an Elephant. Cile was suffering from *peŋgwar*, a hard lump in the upper abdomen. (This may have a number of causes of course, including chronic malaria.) I heard various expressions—that he was 'sick from the Ebony Men' ('*ba'tha'd ma ŋari/*), 'seized by Spice' (*bu'th ma jit*), and even 'struck by the *arum* [Arum?] of the Ebony Men' ('*kosh ma rum ŋari/*). This was deduced because he was sleeping in a crouching position, that is *ki luŋgu'b*. The phrase can mean both 'low down' and in a westerly direction, but in this context the suggestion was that he was crouching low like an animal. Koro, an Elephant who was taking charge of Cile's case, demonstrated the position for me; I recognized it from the set dramas I had seen. After he had been given Spice to wear, Koro told the boy he would sleep normally. He and two other Elephant colleagues had made the diagnosis by kindling ebony, and saw among other things some Spice in the water, as well as the Genius of Cile.

The Ebony Men, including Dhirmath, go off to Restore the Genius, which is found in two different places. The first is a tree a few yards from the village where children are in the habit of playing. They all tap, poke, and stroke the tree with their spears, and one Sprays out a little finely masticated Spice from his mouth. The others dig around in the soil at the foot of the tree, and with something of a flourish, scoop up some mud, supposedly containing a part of the Genius. They all Spray Spice on the tree. We then cross to a muddy pool on the other side of the village, another children's play area. A ball of mud is retrieved from this place, presumably with the remaining part of the Genius, Spice being Sprayed the while, and we return to Dhirmath's hut, where all the mud is put in a gourd of water.

The Elephants then do the ye for Cile: that is, vigorous sucking of his body, back and front, to Extract any foreign matter which might be partly causing his illness. Each Ebony Man spits out from time to time, and then goes to the bush to throw something away. Then each puts a rounded pebble from his bag into the gourd of water with the Genius, chews Spice from his own necklace and Sprays it into the water. Koro takes a chicken, passes it round the bowl, and uses it to Brush Cile. The others take the chicken and do the same. The chicken's throat is cut and blood pours into the gourd. The chicken spends some time on its front, but Koro spits and it turns on its back to die, which is good. The blood of the chicken is Blown to Cile's nose; and then the contents of the gourd are poured over him, to be followed by clean water. A necklace is then strung for the child, made of alternate pieces of Spice and cowrie shells, given by the Elephants. It is put in the gourd with the Ebony Men's stones, and some oil. Later the necklace is taken from the oil, swung round the child, Blown to his nose, put around the neck of the adult Ebony Men one by one, and then tied on Cile's neck, and his body rubbed with oil. A large black stone is put in his mouth for a moment, and then rubbed all over his body.

He is Sprayed with Spice, and his body Straightened (in this case crossing of arms, lifting up, and bending of the back). Everyone then settles to a modest meal which has been prepared.

Cile was to wear his Spice as a necklace right up to the time when, we assume, he would have his final graduation years later. After this he would wear it diagonally across his chest. One boy I heard of lost his Spice, and became ill. Beer was made for the Ebony Men to come to treat him and give him new Spice.

1(b) Showing the Banks or 'Learning the Boundaries' (Ṭora Gap̱)

About a month after Cile had his new Spice, preparations were made for the first big rite, Showing the Banks. A couple of days beforehand, at sundown, a number of Ebony Men gathered to put the toasted flour into the beer pot, for fermentation. All the women and girls who were to assist in making the beer came too. Tente and Koro took their special antelope horns. All crouched low around the flour, spread out on skins in the hut. Tente guided Cile's hand as he sprinkled the fermented grain on to the flour, and then Tente and Koro Sprayed the horns, screamed, and blew them. Everyone joined in, the women then escalating into their high-pitched ululation. Tente and Koro moved the horns through the flour, mixing it up well. Cile then held one of the horns, with a little flour mixture on its tip, and guided by Tente took it back to the big pot in which the beer was to be brewed. The diviners then Sprayed everyone with a little Spice.

Two days later, the beer is ready. There is an early storm, which delays the proceedings; everyone should have been down to cross the river before sunrise, rather than just after. Cile, his parents, and the women and girls who made the beer are lined up. Spice is Sprayed on the horns and they are pointed at each person. Then all go off in procession to the river. Because this is late in the rainy season, and the grass is very tall and wet, we go to the nearby Wora Bwaman stream-bed instead of the main Tombak river. One of the Ebony Men carries Cile, and as we approach the river, some scream into their horns, and others grunt, humph, humph, as the women begin to ululate. All throw grass they have taken from Dhirmaṯh's hut into the stream-bed, to 'show it the banks', cross over, move along the bank and come down. Cile, and then everyone, is doused in water taken from a hole in the stream-bed. Spice is Sprayed on each person's forehead as they regain the near bank.

Back in the village, Cile and his mother, and all the women who made the beer, have a little hair snipped off and Blown to their noses. Their heads are completely shaved and Sprayed with Spice. As Cile was made to put the flour in the beer pot, so now his hand is guided with the grinding stone as he grinds a little maize. The hand stone is Blown to his nose, and to his mother's. The child and his parents, and the women who made the beer, are Brushed with a chicken. The diviner's stones are put in a gourd of water. The chicken is cut over the gourd, and Cile and his mother have the contents poured over them. Two more chickens and a goat are cut without ceremony, and then everyone concentrates on preparing the feast. In the middle of the day Cile, his mother, and the women who made the beer are covered with red ochre, and the beer drinking follows. Towards late afternoon, the diviners' stones are dipped in oil and placed in Cile's mouth; they are knocked together over his head, Blown to his nose, and pressed to his body as it is Straightened. Spice is Sprayed again on his head. His necklace is also dipped in oil, swung to his body, and put on.

As far as Cile was concerned, the day's rites were over and he was apprenticed to the Order. But by this time twenty or so Ebony Men had come to share the beer. Whenever they gather on these occasions there is a good deal of special business: for example, greeting in pairs by Spraying each other's foreheads with Spice, then grasping each other's left hand and snapping their fingers apart in the air (normal greetings are by shaking right hands and parting with a snap of the middle finger). A special pot of beer is brought out for the Ebony Men, and placed in the centre of the village, for their set drama. I will describe these dramas below, and also deal below with the occasion when the apprentice is shown how to divine with the Ebony. After this, he is able to practise, and he may go on practising for many years before his final graduation as a senior diviner. This graduation is the big Horn Dance, followed shortly by the final Hair-Styling which completes the whole sequence. These rites are the largest social occasions seen in the Uduk villages, and require a great deal of preparation. They also demand large-scale hospitality, and for this reason have to be anticipated about a year in advance, so that extra grain can be planted. If there is a good harvest, several may be held. Visitors can be expected from all parts of Uduk country.

2(a) The Diviners' Horn Dance (Çe ŋari/)

I have seen the big Dance three times (see frontispiece and Plate 10). I shall describe only one occasion in Pany Caran when four Ebony Men were graduating, and two whole hamlets were involved in the preparations. The candidates were Dhirmath (father of Cile, whose earlier rite is described above) and Ria of Shokko's hamlet, and Sebko and Shi of the new hamlet known as Sebko's. Sebko was a Monkey, the other three Throwing-Sticks. Their graduation had been anticipated in the rains of 1966, and by early April 1967 things were really under way. The candidates and all the women and girls who were to help in the making of the beer had their beads removed to Sit Black from the day the preliminary grain was put to sprout. Women from three or four different hamlets were helping.

The Ebony Men dance only when the moon is waxing, and so these early preparations began at the end of the previous month. When the new moon appeared a week or so later, the appointed women began to grind the main bulk of grain for the beer. During the time they are Sitting Black, however, during the whole period the beer is being prepared, special precautions are observed; neither graduating Ebony Men nor the women making beer may sleep with their spouses; the candidates themselves must sleep outside, without a fire. Small beer-parties may be held during this preliminary period for specific tasks, such as bringing firewood. Tente, as one of the most senior Ebony Men in northern Pam'Be, went off to Wadega in the second week of April, to give the news of the forthcoming Horn Dance to his own sponsor, Mabruk (a Throwing-Stick), and to invite him and other senior representatives of the Order from the Jum Jum. The sponsor of the three Throwing-Sticks was Tirriya, a senior Uduk diviner from Bellila, near to Wadega, and our own Shokko was the sponsor of the Monkey, Sebko. Mabruk, in the event, did not come, but Beshir, another very senior Jum Jum Throwing-Stick, did turn up. In each of the two hamlets preparing beer, a special dancing place had been cleared on the west side of the settlement, and a rough shelter constructed at the far side of the clearing. The shelters were for the Throwing-Sticks to rest in during the three days' celebrations; no shelter was necessary however for the Monkeys, who would 'just sit under trees as usual'.

There was a lot of activity even among those who had no special connection with the Order or the forthcoming rite. One young man in Waka'cesh went off to Kurmuk especially to buy new shorts and shoes for the Dance. All the girls were making new beads and bangles. Visitors were expected from Gindi and from Bellila, and in the event there were three or four hundred, I would guess. There was plenty of expected confusion and argy-bargy at the gathering. Several senior Ebony Men wanted a hand in directing affairs, and, as activities were divided between hamlets anyway, it was not easy to follow all that was going on. Some preliminary dancing started when the main beer was put on the fire at sunset, but did not last very long. The next evening, Tente opened the proceedings proper with a few of the special diviners' songs. When all the available horns had been collected together, he Brushed them at Sebko's hut and cut the chicken. The blood poured on to the horns, and the chicken died well.

This was the formal opening of the Dance, and the women and girls began to join in as the Ebony Men sang and beat their horns. There was some argument as the senior visitors had not been summoned to Sebko's, so the whole dancing party moved slowly along the path to the other hamlet, meeting them half-way; there were angry words—almost *de rigueur* on these occasions—and the party divided up, to dance in both hamlets. Tente announced sharply that all the Ebony Men ought to wear skins on these occasions. Beshir, the important visitor from Wadega, was not doing so—in fact he was wearing the short Sudanese robe *jibba*— but Shokko defended Beshir, and demanded to know why Tente always picked quarrels at events of the Order. The two had to be separated, and Beshir ordered a fine of five goats each (later reduced to three, and then two).

During the dancing, Shokko suddenly 'killed' five young apprentices with Rainbow Medicine; we saw them laid out on the dance floor. They included the four who were about to graduate. Other senior diviners 'revived' them by Spraying Spice, Straightening their limbs and bodies, and slapping them with throwing-sticks. Each senior swung an apprentice up behind him, to crouch and ride on his own back.

The dancing continued more or less all night, though drinking water was short and had to be collected at intervals from hamlets in the vicinity. The next morning, I became involved in a complicated plan to negotiate the loan of a barrel from a fairly distant village, take it in the Land Rover to be filled at a water-hole, and deliver it to the dance place. This was the big day.

The special songs of the 'diviners' horns' are much loved, and whenever sung evoke the euphoria of the big Dance. Some are taken from the Jum Jum, and either sung in their tongue (many of the chorus not understanding the words) or adapted from it; some are in Uduk, and of these, not a few have been lifted from older contexts. There is, for example, the rainstone song, and there are the hunting and violent death songs (*gwaya kaŋis*, of which I have quoted one, the leopard song, in Chapter 1 (ii) (*b*)). Here are two very popular songs: I quote only the key lines, on which the lead singer elaborates, and to which the chorus responds.

1. The Cockerel's Song:

In this song, the novice, referred to by the Jum Jum word *akoke*, cries because he is only an apprentice who doesn't know much. Because he is so junior, he doesn't find rewards. People give him only chickens for his services, and so he cries. At the end, any personal name of an apprentice can be inserted, in this case A'daŋa. The *yee* is simply for extending euphony and rhythm. After the song, the Ebony Men strike up the dance beat on their horns, and everyone joins the great wheel of the dance until another song is started.

Leader:	*Adhoŋgolaŋwa yee*	A tough old cockerel!
	Akoke	Akoke, the novice
Chorus:	*Ko'd ja ŋwa*	He cries at the chickens
Leader:	*Adhoŋgolaŋwa yee*	A tough old cockerel!
Chorus:	*Kokaliko*	Cock-a-doodle-doo
Leader:	*Akoke yee*	Akoke, the novice
Chorus:	*Ko'd ja ŋwa*	He cries at the chickens
. . .		. . .
Leader:	*A'daŋa'dee*	Oh, A'daŋa!

2. The Rainstone Song:

This song is entirely in Uduk, and has been added to the corpus of the Ebony diviners from an older Uduk tradition. Luge is the name of a person, though I could not find out anything about him.

Leader:	*Asho'k ma tata ya'di yethee*	The rain of my mother's brother is to fall.
	Dhalki ya'di yeth waa	Let it come and rain!
Chorus:	*Aa lama sho'k*	I washed the rainstones.
Leader:	*Luge, Luge*	Luge, Luge.
Chorus:	*Aa lama sho'k*	I washed the rainstones.
Leader:	*Asho'k ma tata ya'di yethee*	The rain of my mother's brother is to fall.
Chorus:	*Aa lama sho'k*	I washed the rainstones.
Leader:	*Pa madu, pa madu*	In the deserted village, in the deserted village,
Chorus:	*Aa lama sho'k*	I washed the rainstones.

The dancing went on through the morning. Some food was prepared for the seniors, and a few preliminary gourds of beer were provided too. Some animals had been cut, without much ceremony. In the centre of the dance-space a little ring of Ebony Men gathered, each with an antelope horn and a short chunk of soft wood for beating it. Some horns were long and twisted, and others short and only slightly curved. The rhythm of each song was beaten out on these horns. The difference in pitch between the large and small horns, finely adjusted by pouring in water, was a musical fourth, and the rhythms played on this interval formed the interlude between each song, or bout of singing. As the songs were started, usually with a senior figure giving the solo lead, everyone stood still and joined in the responses; after the verses, the horn-beating began, with girls often accompanying the horns by beating pairs of sticks, and the crowd started to dance. They moved in a rhythmic shuffling step, sometimes individually, sometimes in pairs, mostly girls with cross-clasped hands, in an anticlockwise wheel around the tighter ring of Ebony Men. On the fringe of the main wheel of dancers, groups of young men, often in matching gear, or wearing broad leather body belts said to have been Jum Jum warriors' garb in the old days, swirled in formation, breaking the dance only to leap high and whoop in concert.

In the mid-afternoon there is a break in the dance. At Sebko's hut, the four candidates, together with the twenty or so women and girls who have been making the beer, have their heads shaved. Then the Monkey apprentice and half a dozen girls are carefully spotted all over their bodies in three colours: a yellowish-green colour (gwo'dgwo'd) to represent the black monkey (which is in fact rather green greyish), red to represent the red monkey, and black (to represent the black fur round the monkey's eyes). Sebko himself is also dabbed with white spots, but Tente tells me later that this was just a mistake. Meanwhile, the Throwing-Stick candidates and the rest of the women and girls have a white mixture, of the ash of homod shells (river snails), beef fat, and water, smeared on their heads. (I think they already have jiso, black oil, on their bodies, or at least plain oil.) Feather head-dresses, dhurpa *(ceremonial wear of the Ebony Men), and necklets of Spice are then Touched to the four candidates, and fitted on them. The spots of the Monkey people (including the women and girls) are then all smeared together. The Throwing-Stick people are picked up by Tirriya and other seniors, slapped with a throwing-stick, and put down in front of the hut, facing it. A little soap is scraped on to their heads, 'for the perfume'. The Monkey people, with some other Monkeys present, then go in the hut. Chilli is being burnt and they have to breathe the smoke. The men go in crouching on all fours in 'monkey' style.*

We hear a lot of coughing inside. As the men come out first, in monkey style, each is beaten with a throwing-stick. The girls then come out, but are not beaten. Sebko, however, remains for some time; he is said 'to have died' (wu'd mo), and we hear sounds of vomiting and sobbing. Eventually he comes out quietly. Food is then provided for the candidates and the girls. They all eat greedily and roughly, using their left hands 'like animals'. One spectator exclaims 'Just like a lion!' Then they enter the hut to start the beer, and there is general eating and beer drinking. The dancing resumes; in the evening the crowd moves to the other hamlet and continues dancing until dawn. The candidates are now sometimes spoken of as 'girls' and seniors may play at mock sex with them during the dancing.

The following morning, the Throwing-Stick candidates were scratched with the claws of a wild bird known as *wulu/* (the tawny black eagle according to the Uduk Dictionary); three or four parallel scratches were made on the small of the back, thighs, arms, and foreheads. I have never seen this rite, though have been told of it many times, and seen the consequences. We arrived (with another barrel of hard-won water) mid-morning, to find the dancing still under way. It would have continued all day, but around noon news came of a death in a village a few miles away, and so the dancing ended a little early. The horns were collected at Shokko's hut. They were Brushed again, but this chicken was not killed. Spice was Sprayed, and then each man was free to take his horn home.

A big wind blew up shortly after this—reminding us that the dry season was nearly over—and the Ebony Men all pointed with their fingers and Sprayed Spice. I heard the comment, in Arabic, 'Ah! The rain at last.'

Several goats, a pig, and many chickens had been provided for the feast. The Ebony Men are allowed to seize and cut chickens without permission on these occasions, and at least three extra had gone from Shokko's home. The candidates also have to give certain things as fee payments to their sponsors: in addition to the goats, probably three each, to be killed at the feast, the candidate might have to find 50 piastres in money, six spears, four loaves of tobacco, and many other things. Candidates would raise what was necessary from their brothers of the same birth-group, but might expect a male goat in addition from their own fathers, and chickens from other members of their paternal kin.

2(b) Hair-Styling (<u>Thes</u> '<u>Kup</u>)

I have seen this rite, which completes the final graduation, twice. I will describe the occasion when in April 1967 I saw it performed for two Elephants and one Guinea-Fowl, and merely note a few contrasts with the occasion when I saw it done the following year for two Monkeys and one Throwing-Stick. In the first case, which took place in a Bellila village, the Horn Dance had been held about two weeks previously, and the moon was nearing its demise. The new graduates and their sponsors were all Uduk from Bellila. We arrived to find a goat and a pig already cut; these animals, as is usual for the Hair-Styling, had been given by the graduates' fathers. The three graduates and about ten women who made the beer, all of whom had slept the previous night apart from their spouses, were lined up outside the beer hut. Their hair was trimmed. As they had been shaved clean a couple of weeks previously, there was now a neat close growth, in which patterns could be made with a razor-blade. All were given the same style, a 'skull-cap' with two indentations, each a couple of inches long and half an inch wide, over the brow. These represented the tusks of the elephant. The hair was carefully collected, I believe for disposal in the bush. There

was an argument as to whether a chicken should be cut or not, and
in the end it was not.

*The principals and women of the beer sit in a row on the 'left
hand' of the hut (as you faced it), looking towards the west, which
is required as 'they are Elephants'. Then they all line up, facing
west, in three lines in fact, each person with his or her left hand
on the back of the person in front. Water is sloshed over all of
them, and each vigorously washes the one in front, with the same
hand. They all walk forward and back, still in line, trampling the
ground 'like elephants', while the women watching ululate. Water
is poured over them continuously, so that the trampling of all the
feet makes a lot of mud, 'like elephants'. (The word for mud, as
far as I can see, is the same as that for elephant: je, which has
always puzzled me, though there might be a tonal difference I have
not heard.) The seniors Spray Spice on their new colleagues, and
on the women, and Straighten their bodies. All then retire to a line
facing the hut, while the seniors sing, in Jum Jum, the songs of
thes 'kup. The candidates and supporting women then join in the
choruses, and start to dance, first anticlockwise around the soloist
and then in a formation of two facing lines, which move as one
towards the hut, and then away. At the end of the songs, the women
ululate and point their left-hand fingers in the air. Other songs
follow, mostly in Uduk. There are no beaten horns at this time,
just voices and the stamping of feet.*

*Later in the day, a gourd of red ochre is produced, and the
seniors first Spray Spice into it, and then pour a little oil. This oil
forms a pool in the centre. The third finger of the first graduates's
left hand is placed in the ochre, and he flicks a little into the centre
of the pool of oil. It rests a while; he continues to point at it, the
seniors snap their fingers, and the people call out his name. The
ochre sinks slowly, accepting his name, and everyone shouts and
ululates. This is repeated for the other two graduates. At this point
there is an argument; the senior diviner present objects that things
have not been done properly, and rushes for his spear, but others
restrain him. The oil and ochre are thoroughly mixed; the seniors
Blow it to the noses of the principals, and Touch it on their bodies
(forehead, a stripe down the chest, and across each side). Meat and
porridge food are given to the graduates; they eat politely, by
contrast with the occasion of the big Dance, though I hear the*

remark, 'Let him bite like a lion.' Then the red ochre is spread liberally over the heads and upper bodies of the graduates and their supporting cast of women, some even being rubbed over a few other Elephants within reach.

Finally, a bir *(the beaded nick-ring worn by women) is taken for each graduate. It is dipped in oil and Touched to each of the three men, and then put around his neck. The girls and women who made the beer are given the same. If there had been more beads, bangles, and anklets available, the graduates would have been more elaborately decorated as women (recalling other rites of passage: see for example Chapter 2 (iii) (b)). The general feasting and beer drinking then proceeds. Later there is an elaborate charade, followed by some more singing and dancing. The* bir *neck-rings will be worn by the men until they retire at night, and returned to their owners in the morning. When all the beer is finished (and there is more for the morrow) the new hair-styles will be completely shaved off.*

The rite I saw on a later occasion for Throwing-Stick and Monkey graduates differed in one or two details: for example, the hair-style, which this time was a 'skull-cap' with two horizontal parallel stripes over each ear. These marks were to resemble the curved head of the throwing-stick. Another difference was in the final anointing, which consisted of plain oil for the body. This time I saw the graduates being adorned with their new strings of Spice, diagonally over the right shoulder and chest. They were also given feather head-dresses, but I did not see them being dressed as women—this may have been special to the Elephants.

Before concluding this account of the richly elaborate passage rites of the Ebony Men, I should mention that they also have special funerals. I have not seen an actual burial, but I have seen the final Beer for the Settling of an Ebony Man's grave. This is an occasion for great celebration, and the horns are brought out. There may of course be *athele/* dancing for lay persons, at this time. But for an Ebony Man there is beating of the horns and singing of the diviners' songs. On the other hand, people do not go hunting at the final Beer for an Ebony Man (cf. Chapter 2 (iv) above). They would not dare: for instead of finding gazelles and other hoofed animals worth hunting, they would find only the dangerous clawed animals, the lions, leopards, and wild cats.

(vi) Set dramas

On big occasions of the Order, the Ebony Men may put on special set dramas: people say 'the Ebony Men are playing' or 'acting' (*ŋari/ lo'bon*) (see Plate 11). The form these dramas take depends on which branches of the Order are present, how many seniors as against apprentices, and how many individuals willing to put on a good show. It is usually when the beer is brought out in the afternoon, when the main rite is over, that things start to happen. At one rite for Showing the Banks, when thirty or forty diviners were present, I suddenly became aware that the Monkeys and the Elephants had lined up in two queues.

Leaping or plodding like their namesakes, on all fours, the diviners approach the beer pot. Suddenly the Monkeys nudge the Elephants right out of the way; they are 'fighting over the beer'. Seniors, meanwhile, waving throwing-sticks or whips (according to whether they are Throwing-Sticks or Monkeys) try to supervise re-forming the line, with Monkeys and Elephants in alternation. Suddenly they start to fight again, Spraying out medicine, I believe here the Spice, at each other. Many are apparently struck down helpless. The seniors approach carefully, leaning over the prone bodies, placing saliva carefully in their nostrils one by one, hauling them up, and whipping each one (Monkeys) or slapping them with a throwing-stick (others) so that they jump up on the back of the senior. The whipping and jumping up is repeated once or twice, and then the two shake hands, with the left hand. After one final light whip the apprentices all appear normal again, and are lined up.

A senior Monkey (Shoḵko in fact on this occasion) circles watch-fully round the lines in monkey fashion, pauses, gathers speed by revving up his 'back' legs and dashes suddenly down the line, spitting Rainbow Medicine in all the boys' faces. The women ululate and the apprentices fall back like ninepins.

I am prevented from moving closer, for my own protection, because of the danger of the Rainbow Medicine. A crowd rushes off after the senior Monkey, catches him just before he is able to get up a tree, and brings him back to loud ululation. Meanwhile, most of the younger Ebony Men lying 'dead' have been revived in the same manner as before, though one remains in a trance-like state, apparently lifeless, even though water is poured over him.

Many of the people present join in a procession anticlockwise round the hut of beer, singing; the boy in a trance-like condition is carried round with them as they sing and dance. More water is poured on him, Blown in his face, and various seniors Spray Spice on him, until eventually he recovers. A little later in the afternoon, the Ebony Men take partners, each senior with an apprentice, whipping him lightly and then jumping him on to his back, to 'ride' about with him, grunting as he goes, and then jumping him down again. The pair then greet each other with the left hand, parting with the usual 'flick' of the middle finger as they raise their hands on high. They then Straighten each other's shoulders back and Spray Spice on each other's foreheads.

This set drama explicitly enacts the confrontation with the Rainbow in Silak. Here, however, the apprentices are 'killed' by the Rainbow Medicine rather than by the Creature itself, but as in Silak, are revived in the name of the Order by the medicine Spice. It is, I believe, only the most senior diviners who have charge of Rainbow Medicine.

The Rainbow epitomizes, for the Uduk today, the dangers of the wild, the *arum* power which is endemic there, the unknown and unknowable aspects of the world beyond the home (see Chapter 1 (ii) (*d*)). This power can be faced and tamed to some extent by those whose own being is fortified by previous contact with it, and who participate in the realm of that same power themselves. The Ebony Men embody in themselves something of that power of *arum* derived ultimately from the wild, and through their medicines, particularly Rainbow Medicine and Spice, assist in protecting the community from that power and thus help it to survive. If you ask what the Ebony Men's work really is, you may sometimes be answered in these terms. People may say that the work of the diviners is really 'to fight the Rainbow', or 'to ride on the Rainbow'.

It is appropriate to recall here the awe with which the Uduk talk of the rainbow, the exciting tales they tell of meeting one in the bush. Leina is of course said to have appeared as a Rainbow (see Chapter 3 (iv)). Such encounters continue to take place, and the younger people are regaled with tales of them (while tales of encounters with big game are rare these days). As far as I can tell, there was no older cult among the Uduk connected with the rainbow. But associations are now frequently made between the

Ebony Men and the Rainbow, as the following account by Danga clearly illustrates.

I haven't seen a Rainbow. I would have seen one, but I wasn't there on that day, recently, in November ... but some stories which people tell are not true. They speak, but the meaning of what they say is not true; they said that the Rainbow was about to go into a house.... I don't know: what was it going to do in the house? What was it going to do by entering Tente's house there? Was it a diviner's Rainbow? What was it looking for? Do Ebony Men have Rainbows?

This is what people say: in times long ago, the Rainbow would come looking for a diviner's house. It would come and put its mouth right in the doorway of a diviner's hut. The one that came that day was perhaps about to do the same. And I wanted to come and see it but it wasn't there. It was just a little distance away, and then it disappeared.

And once before, at the end of the rainy season like this, while people were killing fish, they hooked a Rainbow with a very large hook, gog! If you hook a Rainbow in a soft place, and you want to pull it out, you won't succeed.... And the one which was at Yinkutha E there, it was just touched by the hook, and some scales were pulled away [the same word as is used for fish scales].... When the people saw this, they fled out of the river. They came out of the water, refused to fish and left the river.

And the body of the Rainbow, according to what people say, has ears like a camel, and a mouth like a camel, but I haven't seen it. I don't know what its body is really like. Whether it has a body or whether it is just a thing like the wind, it is the rains which it carries with it, because it is red. And you will see another part which is green, there is a very green part. But I don't know much about its body. Because from there, if a Rainbow is very near you, you will only see a great redness. It transforms the place and people's bodies; everyone's bodies, and you too become coloured like the Rainbow....

Nuur went with his wife, when they were newly-weds, only just married, to bring firewood from a place called 'Rainbow Hole' towards Pany Ca'ba there. They were about to drink water; and according to people ... he said, 'Why is the place smelling like a pipe?' From that ... he got sick. *Arum* had seized his Genius there. And the Rainbow kept his Genius.

So people then made beer for the Ebony Men who came to *lat* [to Restore the Genius]. Liyasi came with ŋule, and Monkey diviners came too, and Ria came. Ria was very junior and Liyasi forbade him to go in the water. 'Stay outside, for you will run from the Rainbow and get sick and die. You must wait outside.' And ŋule went into the water, following Liyasi. And then, Liyasi dived down there and found the Rainbow which was holding the Genius of Nuur.

Then the Rainbow became very angry ... but Liyasi also became strong. It coiled round him. With the Rainbow folding around him he still went on in spite of it. He attacked the Rainbow with his Medicine. He pushed on past it and found the Genius of Nuur right in the place where the Rainbow was curled up, and he scooped it out. ŋule went into the water there, and says he was struck by the Rainbow right here. Scratched right here with a great *gaw*! He was cut and bleeding. And ŋule ran off, because of the Rainbow scratching him here and making it bleed. He ran out. Then they came home, bringing back Nuur's Genius.

Besides adopting a certain sceptical tone, Danga's account describes what purports to be a real experience shared by several people, an experience confirming not only the power of *arum* within the Rainbow, but also the power of (senior) Ebony Men to counter it. This supposedly true story closely follows the emblematic struggle, the cosmic work, of the Ebony Men.

But another answer to 'what the Ebony Men do' may be more down to earth. A more pragmatic answer would point out the everyday tasks of the Ebony Man in arranging consultations and treatment for a very wide range of problems brought to them by the people. These include minor and major illnesses, as well as queries over the source of damage by wind and storm, the significance of dreams, the suitability of marriage partners, the problem of infertility, the timing of planting and harvesting, and so on. Their power is not unambiguously benign. In the matter of assisting women troubled by infertility, for example, if the diviner becomes irritated with a woman's persistence he may give her medicine which will go too far, and produce twins. Of all their responsibilities, dealing with illness takes by far the greatest part of the Ebony Men's attention. Crucial to this work in particular is the initial act of divination by the 'kindling of the ebony', followed more often than not by diagnosis of a displaced or lost personal Genius. Restoral of the individual Genius, in the face of so many threatening irruptions of *arum*, is the prime healing act of the diviners.

6

Kindling the Ebony:
Divination, Diagnosis, and Treatment

The Uduk have many uses for the wood they call *cir*, and which is commonly known in the Sudan as *babanus*, translated normally as ebony, though strictly an ebony substitute.[1] It grows straight and slender when young, and hard and gnarled when old. The young wood is white, but the older branches and trunks develop a black core. The straight young growths may be used for fire drills, and the iron-hard black wood for arrow tips. A popular style of throwing-stick is cunningly fashioned with a pointed dark head of the core wood, and a curving handle of black and white, from the natural shape and colour of the ebony branch. The wood burns bright and sharp, and is a first-class fuel, increasingly marketable in Chali. The older trees may still be found in thickets well away from settlements, and near the hills. Trees near the hamlets have usually been culled, but younger whippy growths are often spotted around old stumps. It is this new growth which is used for oracular consultation.

A person with a problem, usually of illness, goes off into the bush (or sends a relative) to search for straight young growths of ebony wood, about a metre long. When several have been collected, the enquirer strips off the outer bark and thorns, and takes the peeled, ivory-coloured wands to an Ebony Man. The problem is explained, and the diviner normally agrees to seek the source of the illness, or other difficulty, through 'kindling the ebony', *kany cir*, sometimes briefly termed 'kindling fire', *kany o'd*.

It will be recalled that the priest-like *ŋeri* of the Bertha consulted the *shangur* oracle by making fire, typically by burning ebony wood. According to its revelations he gave advice to the chiefs and guided the people in their migrations (see Chapter 5 (i)). The

---

[1] '*Babanus*, a small tree, *Dalbergia melanoxylon* G. and P., with black heartwood. Ebony.' This definition is given in J. D. Tothill, ed., *Agriculture in the Sudan* (London: Oxford University Press), 1948, p. 942.

Bertha compared the importance of this oracle, to them, with that of the Holy Qur'an to the Muslims. Ordinary people could also consult the oracle, through the *ŋeri*, about hunting, marriage, and so forth. The modern Uduk have come to place just as much reliance upon the oracle as did the Bertha of old—but there are important differences in the way the ebony is consulted in practice. There is no chiefly authority corresponding to that of the Bertha ruler to control oracular consultation, nor is there a priestly role for the diviner. The oracle is accessible to all, in the sense that anybody may take ebony wands to an appropriate diviner—that is any member, even an apprentice, of the Ebony Order. Each local community, instead of having one or two particular diviners, has dozens; each Uduk Ebony Man operates independently of any sanctioned authority; instead of the institution being primarily hereditary, it spreads freely, senior Ebony Man energetically recruiting others, through the verdicts of the ebony oracle itself. The way in which those verdicts are read offers another point of contrast: although the physical signs, if photographed, might well look similar, the interpretation given, and thus the oracular advice revealed by the burning ebony to the Uduk today, is surely rather different from what was standard for the Bertha of the last century. Unlike a 'religion', an oracular technique carries no cultural message in itself. Rather like someone else's computer, it will process and offer you back largely what you feed in. The modern Uduk have made the ebony oracle respond to the world as they know it, to the problems they themselves define. Kindling the ebony is a way of asking questions on your own terms. Even though you may have learned the technique from a different cultural tradition, the answers you will wish to pursue through it are framed from within your own.

The ebony oracle has been appropriated on a very democratic basis by the Uduk. It is true that the kindling of the fire is a particular prerogative of the Ebony Order, and cannot be performed by lay people. But in spite of this jealous guarding of their privilege, the Ebony Men have begun to share it with their colleagues in the cult of the Arum of Leina, with whom they now co-operate closely. It is also true that few women are members of the Ebony Order, and this does mean in practice that many consultations consist of women approaching men on behalf of themselves or their children. Certainly the majority of patients in the cases I have observed are women, which is partly, however, because children are often ill and their mothers are treated together with them. But I do not think one can properly speak of a privileged class who have access to the oracle, and a deprived class who do not. There is no suggestion of anyone 'owning' an oracle or of having a monopoly over its verdicts. The ebony itself, in so far as it has an owner, belongs to the clients, or the patients; and it is at their initiative that the consultation takes place. Diviners do not investigate the state of patients on their own initiative; the ebony has to be brought to them. Furthermore, the range of possible diagnosis is widely known and even canvassed in advance of a consultation, and the choice of diviner or diviners very open. A patient's own dreams may be given much weight in the making of a diagnosis. Whether between men who are members of the Ebony Order and men who are not, or between the collectivity of diviners (who are nearly all men) and the collectivity of women (few of whom are diviners) I do not think we can speak of a divide between those who control the sources of 'true knowledge' and those who are dependent on them. Access to the oracle is not as political a matter as in the case of the Azande, for example.[2] There is very wide participation in the search for the revelations of the ebony oracle, and what was an institution linked, though loosely, with the authority of the old Bertha chiefship has not only been taken over by the Uduk, but its former exclusive authority has been dispersed.

I have heard it claimed, by Puna Marinyje in the Yabus valley, that divination with ebony wood was long known to the Lake, the historically central birth-group of the Uduk. He traced the Lake back to the mythical beginnings of humanity, and claimed for them a particular *arum* power of their own, derived from their (matrilineal) descent. I have already referred to his account (Chapter 2 (i) (*f*)). Puna's father, Marinyje, had been a Lake, and according to his son, had powers directly from the 'Arum Lake'. He was not initiated by any other person. In a dream, *arum* (?Arum) showed him the divination with burning ebony, and also medicines. At one time, he sacrificed a black 'cow' (probably an ox) because the locusts were eating all the crops. It was only later that Leina initiated him into the cult of 'Arum Gwara' (Arum of the Meban).

---

[2] Compare particularly Evans-Pritchard's account of the poison oracle, and its control by male household heads and rulers, in *Witchcraft, Oracles, and Magic among the Azande*, Part II.

In general, Puna said, the Lake used to become ŋari/ diviners and men of Arum by themselves, and needed no sponsors.

It may or may not be the case historically that the divinatory use of ebony wood was known to the Uduk long before nineteenth-century contact with the Bertha. It is possible that Puna was exaggerating the antiquity of the burning ebony oracle among his people, in emphasizing the autochthonous origin of the special and all-encompassing powers which he attributes to the Lake. Even so, ebony in itself has long been known as a potent substance. The wood grows quite freely in the savannah regions of the Sudan, and is of vital importance to hunting peoples, being the hardest wood and therefore good for arrows and other sharp weapons. It may be that the particular use the Bertha made of the *babanus* in their major oracle made good sense to the Uduk on the basis of an older set of ideas about this wood. As far as my own information and that of Joachim Theis goes, the present-day divinatory practices of neighbouring Koman peoples do not include kindling the ebony. North of the Yabus, however, the ebony oracle seems to have been widely diffused by the first decades of this century (J. D. P. Chataway refers to this oracle as 'common throughout the Kurmuk district', in 1927[3]). Let me sketch the technique as it takes place today.

(i) Reading the ebony

The diviner who has been presented with the ebony wands will probably ask two or three colleagues to assist in the consultation, as they prefer to act in small groups. They gather and sit quietly around the fire in the client's hut. A gourd or pot of water is supplied. Each diviner takes an ebony wand and lights the tapering end in the fire. He holds it in his right hand as it flames, downward, over the gourd of water. It burns erratically, in fits and starts of flame, sometimes a firework-spurt shooting out sideways, sometimes a curl of grey smoke floating down, sometimes a black smudge dropping off. Patterns of blotchy grey, black, red, and white form on the surface of the water, and flecks of ash and oily patches join in a slow dance. It is quite fascinating to watch, especially when three or four wands—I have seen six—are burning

---

[3] J. D. P. Chataway, 'Preliminary Notes on Uduk Tribe', typescript of 5 pp. (plus 3 pp. on the language), at p. 4. NRO Dakhlia I 106:112:L:7.

together. After some minutes the Ebony Men sigh and seem satisfied, extinguish their wands by dipping them in the gourd, and put
them aside. The whole process takes place, normally, in complete
silence, everybody intent on the flames and water, but saying
nothing.

As the diviners leave the hut, they seem to know exactly what is
required, and set about the necessary preparations. There may be
a later, discreet, consultation with the patient or close relatives, in
which something is revealed of what has been seen. I have seen the
burning ebony a couple of dozen times, have been told the results
of another couple of dozen consultations, and pestered many people
with my questions. I still have only a partial understanding of
how to 'read' this style of divination, though sufficient perhaps to
indicate its range and explanatory power.

We are already familiar with the way in which the Azande put
appropriate questions to their poison oracle. By contrast, the Uduk
do not seek anything specific of their ebony, but passively attend its
revelations. The ebony provides spontaneous information, which is
then interpreted by the diviner. He himself remains silent, allowing
the ebony to respond, of its own accord, to the wider circumstances
of the patient's condition. This response is possible, Uduk consider,
by virtue of the innate sensitivity of the ebony wood. This sensitivity
is a part of its wild nature, from the forest where it grows. It is a
property of the species itself, the growing tree, to absorb sounds
and other signals, perhaps especially those of 'psychic' phenomena,
from its surroundings, and reveal, in the consultation, what it has
picked up.

One has to be careful in selecting ebony wands to take to a
diviner. Ebony growing very near to a settlement will have become
confused by too much noise. This ebony nearby can 'hear' the
everyday shouts and conversations of the people, the crowing of
the roosters and clucking of the chickens, and will not be able
to distinguish between the general chatter and goings-on of the
community and the really important signals which carry further.
However, ebony growing far out in the woodland between the
hamlets will know of grumbling over debts (which can activate
rainstones and cause storm damage); it will know of the actions of
arum, and of *dhathu/* (witches) and other sources of psychic
activity. It will know how, where, and why a Genius has become
detached from a person. The ebony of the woodland can reveal

such hidden aspects of events to the human community, through the diviner's reading of the signs.

I realized these properties of the ebony wood only when Tente told me of new instructions he had been given by a visiting Ebony Man, Dhabara, from Jerok in the border hills. Dhabara was the first to tell Tente not to use ebony from close by a village, for this would be confused, and circle round and round, without going straight, '*ber*! (like the sound of a moving arrow) to the source of the trouble (such as a person in another village). He was to use ebony from far out in the forest. (It was also a new idea to Tente that an accused person could be approached and asked to assist in helping the sick man recover.)

You said that the ebony can hear people talk?

Yes, it hears talk, as it hears the cries of the chickens, he said. The chickens cry near the village, and because we are speaking there too, the ebony hears our words at the same time.

And so when people kindle it, it remains confused, meandering around in the village area, and doesn't show the way properly. But that which is far away, if it is sought out, broken off, and brought back, it will tell us clearly: 'Ay! It is *that* person, right over *there* [pointing], who is dealing with this [sick] man.' It will tell a man like that.

Yes, and people—the ebony tells people these things, and people will go and lead that man from there. And many of us in these villages here should scoop a little ash from the hearth, and touch the man on the body there, the man who is sick like that. And he (the man brought from far) will also do it, and the sick man will recover.

How does the ebony hear people's words?

The ebony itself knows that. . . .

You heard this from Dhabara?

Yes, I heard this from him recently. For he said the chickens are heard by the ebony growing around the village . . . and when the ebony is kindled, this ebony remains circling within the village here, because of that crying of the chickens and also because of the talking that we do. It doesn't show the way very well, he said. . . . If you bring ebony from far away, it will not remain meandering about in one place . . . it will immediately go from the place where it is kindled here, '*ber*!—to show you the way over there.

In the actual consultation of the ebony, as I have already described, silence prevails. When one can later reconstruct, in part, what was 'seen' in the water, or in the fire of the burning wand, signs and symptoms are explained in the intimate language of those notions of the person, the body, psyche, and spirit, which I have set out in the first Part of this book and which constitute the archival foundations of Uduk self-knowledge. No doubt, when the Bertha, the Jum Jum, the Hill Burun of Maiak, or the Meban gaze into the fire and the water, they see emerging their own conceptions of the human condition. The practice of preserving silence at the actual consultation may very well have helped this technique to spread throughout the region. It is true there may be occasional exclamations of 'Bismillah!', 'Allah!', 'Shallah!' (abbreviated from 'Mashallah'), but these are Arabic expressions approximating in the lingua franca of the region to a casual 'Goodness gracious!'

Rusko (the former reluctant Ebony apprentice, now Christian leader) described how he learned to interpret the signs offered by the ebony oracle:

The matter of kindling ebony: they showed me. We did it.

How was it?

They kindled it for us, and they said, there, that was the Genius. If the ebony-fire goes in that direction there, *por, por, por,* people will say 'We should go along that way, to go and *lat* the person there [i.e. retrieve and Restore the Genius]. Don't go *that* way [the opposite]. The fire doesn't want that way. We will go on that path there, indicated by it. We will go and *lat* there.' And from there in the water, from that smoke acting in the water, people say, 'Yes: that's the Genius, it's very black there. We will go and retrieve it. The person has a very marked Genius(-sign) indeed. . . . His Genius has been there from long ago, that is why he is always sickening and is about to die. We will go and deal with him!' The ebony-fire shows people and so we go along that path. . . . You will arrive and scoop it up there and carry it away. You come back, finish the job . . . that is what is done at an Ebony rite.

One of the commonest indications of the ebony wood is that a person's Genius has been displaced, and is separated from his or her body. If this is the case, the Genius appears clearly in the gourd of water below the burning ebony. It is a dense black smudge. If the smudge moves, this may indicate where the Genius is, in the corresponding direction. If it moves close to the rim of the gourd (the boundary of the sign-area), it is likely to be found in a river (thought of here as a boundary). If the smudge is particularly dark and glutinous, 'mud' is indicated. People will then speak of a *kashiran je*, a 'mud Genius' and seek to retrieve it from a muddy place, whether from the river bank, the fields, or an old village site.

The smudge may be quite circular in shape, in which case a grave may be indicated. This means that the Genius became detached when the patient was attending a burial; funerals are very dangerous occasions, both because of the burial itself and because many *dhathu/* are likely to be in the crowd. Sometimes two or more black smudges may appear in the water, which could indicate that the Genius had been left behind partly in one place and partly in another. On one occasion I witnessed, the smudge was 'very small', and though the Ebony Men watched carefully, they decided to repeat the divination with fresh ebony and water. The same sign appeared, a little more definitely. Sometimes the Genius seems to be the only sign read in the consultation, and is often the only one mentioned afterwards. Frequently on asking what had been seen in the *kany cir* for such-and-such a person, I would be told 'Just the Genius.' Everyone knows, however, that the Ebony Men may see many things that they keep to themselves.

Specific illnesses which appear to be part of an old stratum of Uduk medical theory quite frequently appear in the water. For example, *ayin* is a complaint suffered by men. Its cause is sometimes said to be drinking too much milk, and its symptoms are a general loss of weight and abdominal pain. The corresponding condition in women is called *jelbuta*, and both these are indicated in the divination by a whitish film over the water, particularly over the Genius smudge. (When *jelbuta* was pointed out to me, it looked more a reddish scum.) A reddish film may, however, indicate urine, *dhara'c*, which reveals that a patient is suffering from contact (direct or indirect) with the urine of a particular person, to whom the diviner will then send the patient for treatment. *Gu'th*, the illness which follows careless contact with senior in-laws, that is not observing the avoidance rules, is said sometimes to be seen in the water ('*KP*: 143–4). There is also a sign for *peŋgwar*, a hard abdominal swelling. The very common attribution of infant sickness to *ako* (milk or breast), on the theory that something passed on through the mother's milk has caused it, appears as 'smoke' in the water.

There is a set of signs which indicate the presence of *arum*. I have been shown it as white flecks more than once, and I have also been told that a certain white patch indicated the white cloth of the Sudanese Arab robes which the Arum men wear. A squiggly line was once described to me as the 'rope of *arum*', *nyok ma rum*, and also as the 'rope of the Wild Mint', *nyoka wopo*—this plant being the emblematic medicine of the Arum men. The patient's husband was a man of the Arum Leina cult, and this was the rope that had taken hold of her; the same word is used of tying goats or cattle to a peg, and could be translated 'halter'.[4] *Wopo* has also been pointed out to me as a series of curly black wave-patterns.

Blood (*abas*) is frequently seen in association with *arum*, often qualified as *abas ma rum*, though it can occur on its own. It appears, not surprisingly, as a red blotch, and can simply indicate how ill a person is; there can be *abas she*, blood of a tooth, in the context of a toothache; or a very sick person's body may be perceived as 'all bloody'. In one consultation over a woman already known to have been struck by *arum*, it was pointed out to me that you could see 'the blood of her body' in the calabash. In another case where the water itself became all red, *dhir dhir* (very deep red), as well as exhibiting 'blood', I was told this came from 'the *arum* of our village', because of quarrelling within the birth-group. However, spots of 'blood' in the water have also been interpreted as the blood required by *arum* through the offering of an animal. It was said the sign meant that the patient should be 'bathed in blood', that is doused with water from a gourd in which a little blood from the animal has been spilt.

The appearance of 'blood' in the divination seems rarely to be an exclusive sign either of the patient's bodily condition or of a required blood offering. It may be read both ways at the same time, as it evokes the representation of blood as a connection between the inside and the outside of a person, a pathway for the being and movement of *arum* itself. If there is something badly wrong with the blood, this is likely to have been caused by *arum*; and blood offerings will then make *arum* content to leave the body in peace. Blood as a pathway seems to be the underlying notion in another case where the diagnosis was that a woman was struck by *arum*. She had suffered a miscarriage at two or three months (known as 'the blood coming down'), and this was attributed to her having accidentally stepped on blood at a previous *mii arum* (a rite con-

---

[4] Nuer also use the image of a 'halter' linking God to persons. Their cattle are frequently tethered with a rope around the neck, and this rope is often left trailing from the animal's neck as it wanders to pasture, sometimes even with the tethering peg attached. Nuer sometimes say that when God releases you from your halter, you die (Douglas Johnson).

ducted by the Arum men). The patient at this previous rite happened
to be her own daughter, almost a young women (with whom there
was of course the primary blood-link of substance); the girl was
struck by *arum*, and an offering (which is known as *mii abas*, to
make blood) was therefore made for her. Her mother, pregnant
again, stepped on this blood and was then struck by *arum*, which
appears to have passed from her daughter to herself via the literal
pathway of the animal blood intended to lead the *arum* away
from her daughter, as well as via the pathway of mother–child
connection. At another *arum* rite a woman neighbour who happened to be pregnant was given attention by the Arum men, with
Wild Mint and oil, the Offering of meat, and Straightening of
the body, so that she would have some protection from the danger
of accidental contact with the blood of an offering. The appearance
of a red blotch, the sign for 'blood' in the water of divination, can
therefore be read in a number of ways; and in almost every case I
am familiar with signifies that *arum* is involved one way or another.
Whatever the Ebony Men are able to do, the patient in such a case
should have attention from the men of Arum as well.

I was shown on one occasion a number of reddish smudges
which were described as the Liver (*adu*). I asked whether this was
also blood, and the answer confirmed it—*abas adu* (blood of the
Liver). The patient was already assumed to be crazy, *gusu'd adu*,
literally, 'the Liver running about'. In this particular case the
responsibility was already said to be that of her co-wife, who was
known as *dhathu/*.

Spice, *jiṯ*, the emblematic medicine of the Ebony Order, is often
seen in the water. When pointed out to me, it looked like reddish
patches. One Ebony Man told me of a person (actually William
Danga) who had been caught by Spice (*bu'th ma jiṯ*) as a child but
had not joined the diviners. When he was unwell on one occasion,
his wife took ebony to a diviner in a nearby village. The diagnosis
reportedly was that he was *bu'th ma jiṯ*; the water was all white,
shiny (*bany bany*), and had 'swallowed him up'. As Danga had
been caught by Spice originally as a small child, but nothing had
been done about it, the suggestion that the Spice was still bothering
him was scarcely suprising.

A further sign in the water which is interesting because it seems
to be a new importation from the Jum Jum, is the *maŋal* grub. It
appears as a number of white spots—the grubs themselves are

whitish. Only a few of the Uduk Ebony Men can deal with the *maŋgal* grub, which is said to get inside a person's stomach and bite it, causing pain. (Although worms of various sorts are a certain cause of illness among the Uduk, the *maŋgal* is not a real human parasite but a grub from the bush.) Tente has recently become a specialist in Extracting the *maŋgal* (a technique he learned from his Jum Jum sponsor in the Ebony Order), and any Ebony Man finding the appropriate sign in the water may send a patient to him.

It is sometimes said that the Ebony Men can see the actual face of a person who, as *dhathu/*, is causing an illness. This is a sensitive matter, as they no longer dare to name or confirm the name of a suspected witch, and I could not discover what such a 'face' (*jis e*, literally 'hole' or 'setting' for eyes) might look like in the water.

'Rain' (*asho'k*) and wind can also be seen in the water, though I am not certain how they are distinguished. From the pattern of movement the Ebony Man can judge the source of storm damage.

The signs I have mentioned are only a few from among the full range which the Ebony Men can see in the water. There are certainly many more. It is apparent that those which appear most commonly are not recent importations or innovations: they are based on well-established notions of the body, its life-giving blood, the proper place of the 'psychic' Genius within the whole and healthy personality; and the intimate presence of *arum* in human affairs.

I cannot say whether the signs read in the ebony divination by the Bertha, the Jum Jum, the Meban, or the Hill Burun are directly analogous, or how far 'translation' has taken place in the spread of this mode of divination from one group to another. But even if there were a correspondence between individual signs in isolation— for example, if the Bertha and Meban diviners also saw a sign for 'blood'—it would not necessarily evoke the same range of associated meanings that it does for the Uduk. Moreover, signs are normally perceived in groups, in association with each other, and sometimes one may stand for another, as 'blood' may stand for '*arum*'. The way in which this happens can be seen in the cases below.

Whatever the individual meaning of the signs, the way in which they are combined, and read as a whole diagnosis of the patient's condition, has a peculiarly Uduk style. In the blank surface of the

water, illuminated with the fire of the fresh-peeled ebony, the Ebony
Men draw upon the world they know from the past, and in using
this code of visible signs they make it more tangible. This would
be less evident if there were only a few practitioners who kept the
knowledge of divination and other matters to themselves. But the
Ebony Order has spread so fast, and now includes so many people
among the northern Uduk, that everyone is familiar with the main
outlines of the technique of divination, and with what it can reveal.
It has become almost diagnosis by the people, for the people: a
whole society looking into its inner self for confirmation and
redefinition of what can be known, in the face of dogmatic and
conflicting political and spiritual demands from elsewhere.

I attended one rite at which beer had been made for the occasion
of Teaching of the Ebony-Kindling, *mmotor monkanycir*. It was
for a young apprentice called Dilgo, who had been through the
initial rites some years previously but was still very far from the
culmination of the Horn Dance. He was an Elephant of the old
branch of 'Arum Allah' diviners. His own sponsor, oddly, was
not present, but Koro, of the same branch, took charge of the
demonstration, along with Tente who was by far the most senior
Ebony Man present.

*About ten Ebony Men gather in the hut of beer. Tente holds the
bundle of fresh-peeled ebony wands provided by Dilgo in the fire,
chews his Spice and Sprays it on the bundle, Touches it to the
shoulders of Dilgo, and hands a lighted wand round to each
colleague. All gather round the gourd of water, gazing intently at
their burning sticks, while Dilgo watches. As signs begin to show
themselves in the water, and in the way the wands burn, the diviners
bark out a few phrases. This is most unusual but of course the idea
is to instruct Dilgo on how to divine. Koro exclaims first, rab! (I
believe this is the Arabic Rabba, used of God by both Muslims and
Christians; the older connections of the 'Arum Allah' diviners with
the Islamized Bertha may be relevant here.) He then calls out,
'Genius! Small child!' The latter means that the Genius-sign in the
water, presumably that of the apprentice Dilgo, is still immature
as he is young and inexperienced. Another diviner identifies blood,
and then Tente exclaims arum! ter is! He then remarks in a more
level voice to Dilgo, 'Your ebony is very powerful.' At this, some
of the Ebony Men Spray Spice on their own shoulders. Tente takes*

another ebony wand, lights it, and holds it over the water, saying arum. *The wand suddenly shoots forth a dramatic spurt of flame, and a number of exclamations follow. Someone remarks that the Genius is very far away, and that there is some redness. Tente announces that the Genius is in the middle of the sorghum fields. All then extinguish their wands in the water, dip their left hands in it, and wipe their faces. Koro wipes Dilgo's face, and I am told to wipe my own, with the left hand, presumably because of what we have all seen. The rest of the water is poured away outside. Tente asks various of the Ebony Men if they are going to give their new colleague something.*

Outside, a chicken is cut over a gourd which contains some water and the Ebony men's stones. Tente and some others throw handfuls of the mixture over Dilgo while yet others Spray Spice. The whole gourd is then poured over Dilgo's back, and he is finally washed in clean water. Two further chickens are cut, and one cockerel, which expires only reluctantly. Tente comments—'It's a male; its Liver doesn't want to go into the ground.' A goat is also cut, but without ceremony. The logic of this case seems to require that the Genius be retrieved from the fields, and this is to take place later.

Following an Ebony consultation, treatment is arranged, and specialists such as the men of the Arum Leina are brought in to assist the Ebony Men where appropriate. In a few cases a patient may be tansferred to their exclusive care, but on the whole there is a co-operative division of labour, and a typical case will involve the participation of several specialists in the treatment of a patient. The techniques and methods of treatment are drawn from a wide repertoire of practices known to the Uduk, and not only from the particular esoteric knowledge of the Ebony Men or other specialists deriving from their professional training. A few cases drawn from the many I have observed will illustrate the way in which treatment following an Ebony consultation aims at the restoration of the whole person. Plate 12 illustrates some of the typical elements in a diviners' healing rite.

(ii) Restoring the Person: some selected cases

1. Emed's body pains: a simple rite

Emed, an old lady of the Wuga birth-group who used to live with
the Lake of Waka'cesh and was now in a nearby Wuga hamlet,
was generally 'ill all over', especially with headaches. Beer was
made and an Ebony rite arranged, with Tente and three others,
including Dhirmath who was (most unusually) also a man of the
Arum Leina cult. In the divination we saw red matter, interpreted
as the patient's blood, showing that she was very ill; and a black
cloudy splotch, the Genius entrapped in mud. (There had already
been one earlier divination in which more may have been seen.)
The Ebony Men then went off to retrieve the Genius. They split
into two pairs. One went to the river, because Emed had once been
'hurt by a fish' when living with Tente's people, and her Genius
found in the river, so it might well be found there again. As Emed
had subsequently married into Pam Bwawash, a part of the Beni
Mayu area, the second pair of Ebony Men went to search in the
site of her old hut there. They dug around among the three cooking
stones still in the place of the hearth, extracted a lump of muddy
soil, and brought it back.

The first pair of diviners soon came back with their part of the
Genius in mud from the river. The Ebony Men chewed and Sprayed
Spice on Emed and another lady who had requested treatment, and
Straightened the patients' shoulders back a little, turning their heads
and massaging their necks. They then performed the Extraction for
the two ladies. This involved the elaborate 'picking out of objects'
from the patients' bodies and heads. All the while they were
clicking with their tongues and exclaiming as they did so 'Allah to
pa, cha cha, Allah yi pa'—nonsense syllables as far as I know,
though the use of 'Allah' may mean they could come from Bertha
usage. They seemed to place the 'objects' they Extracted in a gourd
of water, and this was then thrown away in the bush. Tente made
as if to 'slap' the patients with his throwing-stick and they got up.
He prepared a quantity of 'medicine for body pain', *cwa isa nyor*,
a pounding a type of soft bark.

When the second pair of Ebony Men arrived, all took a preliminary drink of strained beer. Some sizeable stones were then
heated up on the fire. The two patients sat down, and were covered

over with blankets. In front of them, a potsherd was filled with the hot stones, the beaten medicine, and water. They leaned forward, under the blankets, and inhaled the fumes. More water and hot stones were added; and after three or four minutes, and considerable coughing, they emerged, sweating. The medicine mixture was then diluted, and rubbed on their bodies. The two lots of mud with the Genius were put together, applied with gentle Blowing to Emed's nose and ears by one of the diviners, and then smeared on her body in certain places (described by Tente on another occasion as 'forehead, both sides of the body, the shoulders, and the Liver'). Dhirma<u>th</u> then Straightened her body, pulling her fingers and arms, and bending her shoulders.

A small pig was provided—someone remarked, 'That's just a chicken of a pig!'—and cut in the throat with a spear by Dhirma<u>th</u>; he touched a little of the blood to Emed's nose, ears, and the same places on her body as before, and then wiped the spear—an 'arum spear'—on the roof of the hut.

This rite was unusual, in that a pig was used to make a blood sacrifice, mii abas. I have seen this only rarely; pigs are frequently used for feasts, and I have even heard that the blood of a pig is not pleasing to arum, but only the blood of chickens, goats, and cows. However, this may have been a latter-day view: Muslims have been actively trying to rid the southern Blue Nile region of pig-keeping for generations.

Some snacks were served round, and the patients were anointed with sesame oil by Dhirma<u>th</u>, before he dabbed a little oil on everyone else. The pig meat was roasted and shared, and the beer-drinking proper followed. This had been a small rite, almost a family affair, and would not lead on to a prolonged period of convalescence, nor to a debt and a Head-Shaving.

2. Tabke: one rite in the life of a sick child

Tabke, a girl of four or so, was in a chronically ill state. She was a daughter of Tente and Pure. She had little strength in her arms, a listless manner, a swollen belly, and a hard lump inside. From time to time she had fever, and an eye-infection. Her mother had taken her several times to the government dispensary in Chali, but without appreciable change. Tente and another performed the divination; there appeared in the water a dark splodge, the Genius.

It was rounded, 'like a grave', and so the diviners were prompted to seek it in the grave of the child's maternal grandmother, as she had recently been taken to the final death rite for this person, the 'fixing of the grave'. Also in the water we saw reddish scum, interpreted as *jelbuta*, and small white flecks, said to be *maŋgal*, the type of grub which consumes a person inside.

The two Ebony men went off to retrieve the Genius from the now-abandoned village where the grandmother was buried, discouraging me from joining them, and came back with a leaf wrapped around the earth they had removed from the top of the grave. Tabke was then held on her mother's lap while the Ebony Men performed Extraction; dramatically, Tente appeared to snatch out of the child's belly a large whitish grub—the *maŋgal* itself (no doubt discreetly collected on the expedition to the old village). Together with other 'things' less visible, the grub was deposited in the gourd of water and thrown away in the bush.

A very tiny chick was taken by Tente, while his colleagues produced the Genius bundle. Between them, they Blew the bundle to the child's nose, ears, and pressed it to her belly; they drew the chick over her body, Brushing it to her front, back, and sides. One held out the chick and the other carefully cut just the tip of its toe, over the Genius bundle. Tente put the toe to the child's forehead, Blew it to her eyes, and rubbed it on her arms, belly, and legs. He placed the chick on her head where it stood for a suprised moment and then fluttered down. The Genius mud was now smeared on the girl's body; her limbs were gently Straightened, and the rest of the mud poured around her feet, a little being reserved with the leaf for the roof of the hut. Medicine was chewed and Sprayed on the child, and later she was obliged to drink more. A final medicine, known as *penkel*, was rubbed on her body, with oil. This substance is most uncomfortable—it stings the skin and itches terribly. Its purpose was to kill the 'things in the body', *tom buŋgwar*, that might be doing harm, and to heal the place where the *maŋgal* grub was Extracted.

A small meal followed, prepared by the girl's mother and a couple of other women in the hamlet. This rite was again a small affair, incurring no debt, though it is likely that for major treatment a father would probably bring in a team of other Ebony Men to see to his own child.

Tabke did not survive many months after the rite I have just described, although many more efforts were made to save her.

3. Lamana: a co-wife's witchcraft

Lamana was the daughter of Yukke (Ha'da's wife, who had been married before). Lamana married into Chali, but her husband had taken a second wife. She had been ill for some time, and from a previous divination it was known that she was 'mad'—*gusu'd adu*: her Liver was 'running about' and her behaviour was sometimes out of control. This was already blamed on her co-wife, said to be *dhathu/*. Nyethko was going to do the Restoral, but he was not feeling well and so Tente and others did it. There was no public reference to the 'witchcraft' in the background of this case; this had been explained to me in confidence beforehand by a person unconnected with the rite.

Before the divination I had asked Tente what had made Lamana ill, and he said, 'Maybe the Liver', but he would be able to tell me definitely after the divination. In the water, Tente and a colleague divining, we saw the following—or rather these are the signs that were pointed out to me: Genius, mud, Liver as two or three red blotches which were also described as *abas adu*, blood of the Liver, and a grave. The diviners called Yukke, in whose hut we were, and asked if anyone had recently died, as a grave was indicated. She said that a younger sister of Lamana had died, and mentioned the (now-abandoned) village where the grave was. (At the funeral, many people who were *dhathu/* would have been present.)

Tente, his colleague Yuha, and Ha'da as an Arum man, all went to retrieve the Genius at the grave of the child, at the foot of Beni Mayu. On their return, they were joined by some more colleagues, and several performed the Extraction, first spraying water on Lamana from their mouths. On this occasion they sucked with their mouths as well as grasping with their hands to Extract things. In a most convincing manner Tente sucked hard and spat out blood, supposedly from the patient's Liver. She was then given some medicine crushed in beer, which also contained Spice. Then the Arum men Brushed her with a chicken (because of 'mud', said Tente; 'this is always done by them'—he may have meant the *mud of the grave*). The retrieved mud was Blown to the patient and

Touched on her body. The chicken was cut, and the blood Blown to her. The Arum men then Straightened her body, and she was anointed with oil. This concluded the rite, and all proceeded to drink the beer waiting for them.

As this rite was part of a series, and the young woman was suffering from a long-term complaint, I assume it very likely that after a period of time, perhaps a year or more, the diviners and Arum men who treated her would expect beer to be made for a Head-Shaving, if recovery were completed.

4. Musha's eyes

In another case, there was direct evidence of the activities of *dhathu/*. One of Musha's eyes had been giving him trouble for some months, and he was finding it increasingly difficult to see properly. Beer was made for an Ebony rite. I did not see the divination, but following the signs they had apparently read, the Ebony Men, led by Nyethko with the help of three Arum men, went to the sorghum fields to dig for the Genius. I was later told that one dug here, one dug there, and one somewhere else. Eventually Nyethko called one of the Arum men over to dig in a particular spot, where it was found that grains of sorghum were buried, together with chicken feathers, bones, and the husky remains of beer sediment. The beer sediment was from a party formerly held to cultivate Musha's field. The chicken remains were from the same occasion, when a chicken had been cut in the field to feed the workers. The action of burying a man's grain is a recognized method by which *dhathu/* may hurt his eyesight so that he cannot cultivate well. The grain—it can in some cases be maize rather than sorghum—is likened to eyes.

The hard earth brought back from the fields in this rite for Restoral certainly contained sorghum grains, which we saw as the earth was crumbled in a gourd of water. We did not however see the chicken remains; nor the beer sediment (which could not have been preserved in a recognizable state for very long). I do not know if the evidence had been set up: there are many flattened areas in the fields used for threshing, and it would be very easy for sorghum grains to become embedded in the earth in the vicinity of a threshing-floor.

Danga told me that *dhathu/* could indeed carry out actions of the kind described, even just with their own eyes. I knew already that such actions could be seen in a dream, and here was a case of the ebony apparently also revealing details of the actions of *dhathu/*. In the rite which followed, the bowl with the earth and grains was taken to the edge of the village near the bush, Brushed with a chicken, and the chicken was cut over it there, rather than in front of the hut as would be usual. Perhaps the *dhathu/* responsible were being kept at bay. After the Genius was Restored to Musha, the Arum men washed their hands in the mixture and it was, I believe, thrown away. The Ebony Men performed the Extraction, and squeezed a little medicine from some cotton on to Musha's eyes and ears. He was finally anointed with oil.

5. *Dutke: struck by the* 'arum *of the Ebony Men*'

A person need not have become very ill for an Ebony rite to be appropriate. In the case of Dutke, Nyethko's wife, it was sufficient for her to report a dream that she was bitten on the back of her head by a monkey. Her husband was of course an important diviner of the Monkey branch of the Ebony Order. Everyone immediately took this dream to mean that she was struck by the Ebony Men's *arum* of Nyethko, *'kosh ma rum ŋari/ ma Nyethko*. Dutke had already begun to feel a little ill but she was up and about, helping to prepare the food for the consultation.

Nyethko, Tente, and three other diviners came along, and first kindled the ebony. In this particular case it appeared that the ebony divination was being used to confirm a patient's dream, and at the same time perhaps to go beyond the dream, and discover other circumstances. In the water there were seen signs of the Genius, of Spice (the Ebony Men's medicine), and of blood. The Genius of Dutke was then sought outside the hut of Nyethko's other wife, after that hut had been Brushed with a chicken. All the diviners Sprayed Spice as they dug with the tips of their spears for the Genius outside the hut.

Danga suggested to me that this was perhaps the spot where the two wives of Nyethko sometimes fought: with the implication that it was because Nyethko was annoyed with his two wives for fighting each other that his 'Ebony Men's *arum*', in the form of the Monkey, attacked Dutke. The situation could certainly be read from one point of view as a way in which a man who has access to the techniques of the Ebony divination can attempt to control his womenfolk; but at the same time it was Dutke who revealed her own vulnerability through her dream, anticipating treatment, in the first place. Moreover, Nyethko knew well that too many dreams of this kind can make a man appear a threat to the community, and this could be very dangerous to himself.

In the gourd with the Genius, the Ebony Men put their special stones. A couple then Brushed inside Dutke's hut with a chicken, Brushed her, and cut the chicken over the gourd. The mixture in it was partly thrown at the patient, partly poured over her; and the stones were rubbed on her body. She was washed with clean water, and a stone put briefly in her mouth. She was Straightened. One of the diviners' stones, in fact a red pebble, was anointed with oil, popped in her mouth, then Sprayed with Spice before being used to rub oil on her body. She also drank a little medicine.

A pig was cut without ceremony for the feast, and everyone then got down to the meal. There was an easy-going and intimate air to the whole morning's proceedings, the Ebony Men ragging each other and at one point staging a mini-drama, changing partners in pairs, Straightening shoulders and Spraying each other with Spice.

6. A sick Ebony Man

The diviners themselves sometimes get sick, and there are some special features of their treatment. The occasion of a rite to treat an Ebony diviner is an excuse for plenty of high spirits and stagey business. On the day when I saw Bosha, an apprentice sponsored by Tente, being treated, the rite was followed by the diviners' set drama. On this occasion, a woman Ebony diviner was among the half-dozen or more who participated in the treatment. These were joined by a good number of others later, for the beer and the fun. I did not see the divination, for we arrived in southern Pam'Be when the Genius had already been retrieved, and put in a gourd of water with the diviners' stones and Spice.

Some chicken feathers were cut and thrown over the patient, who with his 'father' (sponsor) was then Brushed and the chicken was cut over the gourd. The contents were poured over the 'father' and boy. Then he and another young apprentice were suddenly 'thrown'—actually heaved and pushed—up on to the roof of the hut; they clawed at the roof 'like lions' as they scrambled up to the top (compare the discussion of 'Lion Eyes' in Chapter 1 (ii) (d)). The adults went up after them to bring them down; they were slapped with the throwing-stick, jumped on the backs of their rescuers, jumped down, and Sprayed with Spice. This was a signal for all the Ebony Men to take partners and Spray, slap, and jump each other up and down—that is to 'greet' each other. More chickens were cut, and Spice was Sprayed on the women and girls who made the beer. This does not happen when the patient is an ordinary mortal. Tente put a fresh Spice necklet on Bosha, who then drank his medicine mixed with beer, and was anointed with plain oil.

During the beer drinking later in the afternoon, the set drama took place. Finally, the patient, the girls and women who made the beer, and a number of Ebony Men also present, were all anointed with the oil, rubbed with the stones, and then Straightened. This day's treatment would certainly incur a debt, which in due course would have to be settled with the senior Ebony Men, at a Head-Shaving ceremony.

7. The offering of blood by the Arum men for an ailing child

Very often, as some of these cases show, the men of the cult of Arum Leina are co-opted by the Ebony Men to assist in the treatment of a patient. Sometimes the patient is referred straight to the Arum men: but I have the impression that this is becoming less common, and increasingly, the Arum men participate in the healing rites together with the Ebony Men. Indeed, it is not uncommon for them to take part in the crucial act of divination, the kindling of the ebony, as the following case illustrates.

Aa was a little girl who had been sick for some time. She was thin, weak, cried a lot, and coughed; she had a swollen, hard belly. Her father, Yuha, was an Ebony diviner, and together with Yasin, a colleague, and Ha'da and Ruthko (two men of Arum) they held a consultation. Ha'da called me, and I saw the final stages of the divination. In the gourd, they saw the Wild Mint medicine of the Arum men, in the form of an expanding series of black scalloped curves; three reddish patches were *abas ma rum*, the blood of or for *arum*, and some white specks signalling *arum*. The white specks looked to me like *maŋgal*, but when I asked, Ha'da said no, no *maŋgal*. The Genius was declared to be in an old hamlet site where the family used to live, and Yuha and Ruthko (one Ebony diviner, one Arum man) went off to get it. It was found under a big tree where the children used to play. Ruthko also brought back some sprigs of the Wild Mint plant and put it on the roof. The child was examined by the Arum men, and there was some discussion of *peŋgwar*, the hard swollen part in her side. When I asked Yuha about this discussion afterwards, he explained to me very earnestly that Ebony Men by themselves could not heal people. It was *arum* only which could heal people.

The child was taken to the edge of the hamlet for the Extraction, conducted by the two Ebony Men. The Extraction seems to be the one technique of the Ebony Men which is left entirely to them. They sucked hard at the child's abdomen, and with retching sounds, spat out in the bush. Yasin spat out blood convincingly and repeatedly. Yuha appeared to be squashing or killing something he had Extracted, beating it on the ground.

Aa was then brought back to the hut, to stand outside the entrance with her mother and baby sister. Mother and young children are often treated together, as they are considered so close. Here, the Ebony Men retired and the Arum men took over. The mother and two children were Brushed with a chicken, each Arum man not only Brushing them but also passing the chicken between their legs. Some of the Wild Mint was put with the Genius bundle, and some was laid on the ground. As Ha'da held the body of the chicken, Ruthko cut it with his Arum spear. Ha'da swang it so that the blood dripped on the threshold of the hut and on the Wild Mint, before he laid it on the ground. The chicken took quite a long time to die (this is preferred by the Arum men); there were several tense moments as it struggled on to its front, which is a bad sign, while Ha'da slowly waved his whip—a special Arum whip of hippopotamus hide—as if to influence it. It appeared to die on its front; Ha'da moved nearer still waving the whip, and with a final couple of heaves the chicken turned over and expired. Earth was rubbed on its neck and thrown into the bush. Then came the Restoral of the Genius: the Wild Mint and the mixture in the gourd were Blown to the nose and ears of each patient and pressed to their bodies, as the Arum men Sprayed them.

This rite should have sufficed, had the illness been seen as a temporary condition. But the child was known to be gravely ill, and possibly near death. So in addition, a goat was brought out, a

young male, and the Arum men performed another blood offering
on the same, though more elaborate lines. A fresh gourd of water
was set in front of the patients. Ha'da then walked the goat round
to the side of the hut (the side nearest to the hamlet centre, which
happened to be the right), then inside the hut and out again to face
the bush, to the south, and then to the north, and then back to the
entrance, in front of the patients. It was then walked around the
patients, anticlockwise, and made to drink some of the water. Then
the goat was Touched to the patients: that is, it is held up to the
nose, breasts, drawn down the chest and touched to the sides of
the mother's body, and then held to the two children's bodies in
the same way. The goat, with its head to the west, was carried
bodily by the two Arum men with a woman bystander helping,
right up over the three patients, down to the ground behind them,
and back up and over again.

Ruthko held the goat on the ground, while Ha'da touched his
Arum spear to its throat, and to the body of Aa, belly, sides, back,
and then the same for the other child. He cut the animal's throat
with his spear, and then the two Arum men lifted it so that the
blood poured liberally into the gourd; they dragged the goat around
the hut, anticlockwise, and off to the edge of the village where it
was left to die. A trail of blood was left around the hut.

Ha'da and Ruthko took a little of the mixture in the gourd into
their mouths and Sprayed it on the patients, flung some more with
their fingers, and finally poured it over them. The wet bodies were
then rubbed with Wild Mint, and doused with clean water.

The children—of whom there were now three as another infant
had been brought along to benefit—were naturally screaming by
this time, and Aa vomited. But she still had to drink some medicine
in water, prepared by Ha'da, and have the remains smeared over
her body, along her limbs, down and across her torso. This was
followed up with sesame oil, and the very uncomfortable itching
medicine *penkel*. Ha'da also took a little of the fat of the goat, and
burned it over a few straws, to windward of Aa, so that she could
breathe the smoke. The burnt fat was also rubbed on her, with the
ashes of the straw. Finally, the Straightening of limbs took place;
Ha'da did this for Aa while Ruthko dealt with the others, pulling
and turning all their joints, crossing their limbs over and back,
accompanying this with gentle spitting.

The girl's father, Yuha, had now done what he could as an

Ebony diviner, and so had the Arum men he co-opted. Had there been sufficient grain, there would certainly have been beer for this occasion, but it was July—that is before the harvest, and the previous year had not been a good one. There was however a substantial meal, prepared with contributions from several households and by several women. Chirga, the mother of Aa, confirmed to me that maybe next year, another ceremony would be held, to Shave the child's head, drink beer, and anoint her with red ochre; that is, if Aa should recover. Like so many other young children, she had little chance, and died a year or so later.

8. A typical Head-Shaving

Finally I should describe briefly a Head-Shaving to conclude a debt to the diviners and Arum men after a successful recovery. In this case, the patient was Alagathe, an adult man who had been treated during the previous rainy season for the wasting disease *ayin*, and also for the hard internal swelling *pengwar*. This was now the very end of December, the sorghum harvest had been a good one, and plenty of beer was being made for various rites and ceremonies. The rite took place at Kuseje, near Beni Mayu. *Ayin*, a wasting disease with abdominal pain, can be treated mainly by Extraction. The Ebony Men could sometimes extract a piece of red wood some inches long from the Stomach, I was told. However the present case was caused not by *dhathu/*, in which case Extraction would have been a sufficient cure, but came from *arum*.

While a person is undergoing treatment, for most complaints, but especially for *ayin*, he or she should be very careful about foods, even fasting. The safest thing is to eat plain grain porridge with watery stew. A patient should avoid sesame, and if possible meat and milk. After the Head-Shaving, restrictions are lifted. The original divination for Alagathe was done by Amee, an Ebony Man in a hamlet on the far side of Beni Mayu. Alagathe had stayed with him for several days for the Extraction. He was then referred to a man of Arum, Yiskale of Kuseje, who 'rubbed oil on him from his gourd and gave him *ayin* medicine'. Fortunately, he recovered.

Some women of Kuseje first shaved the patient's head, completely. Four Ebony Men then performed a token Extraction on him, as they thought there might still be something in his Stomach. Then a goat was brought. Invited to participate as an

Arum man, Ha'da touched a knife to its throat, then to the patient's body. He cut the animal's throat, some distance from the hut.

Tente then took the red ochre which had been ground, and Blew it on two arrows to the patient—these arrows were part of the debt settlement. Oil was poured into the gourd of red ochre powder, and a little of the powder sprinkled on top; it lingered, and then sank in to joyful cries of 'Aiwa!' (Arabic, 'Yes!') Yiskale and Ha'da then Blew the oily red ochre on to the bangles which were to be given as part of the fee, and applied it to the patient's body in spots, before smearing it all over him. A diviner chewed Spice, Sprayed it on to the mixture of meat and beans which had been cooked for the feast, Blew a little to the patient, and Offered it to him to eat, before taking some himself. Other Ebony Men came forward and did the same with a variety of other foods that had been prohibited during convalescence. As the Arum men did the same, Alagathe took care to spit out a little of the first bite he took, on to the ground, only then accepting the Offering of a real mouthful. This is a common motif in those rites which mark recovery from illness, restoration of normal social relations, or successful conclusion of a rite of passage. A Head-Shaving is a time for relief, a kind of thanksgiving.

Male guests who come to a beer ceremony for Head-Shaving of a patient are supposed to bring one arrow to contribute to the fee payments, which are divided among the diviners and Arum men. Some may bring spears. The patient will also have to find a number of goats, chickens, perhaps sesame, tobacco, and bangles for the diviners and Arum men who healed him, though the amount varies according to who is treating whom, as well as for what.

These case studies draw together a number of the threads in my presentation. In particular, they reveal the way in which the techniques and activities of the Ebony diviners are drawing together various current ritual practices among the Uduk, including those of the men of the Arum of Leina. At a deeper level they are assembling into a coherent corpus a large proportion of the elements of what I have termed 'lay ritual practice' from the archival cultural stock. The main elements, which appear from available evidence to pre-date the Ebony Order, are set out in Chapter 2 (iii) (d) above. It seems safe to guess that the Ebony diviners have developed two particular specialisms of their own:

one is the Extraction of foreign objects from the body (though this is a technique found among practitioners throughout the region), and the other is the Restoral of the personal Genius, *kashira/*. This rather special technique has become the hallmark of the Ebony diviners' practice, at least among the Uduk. It seems to me that in the face of mounting dangers, in particular those conveyed by new and strange powers of Arum, the individual Genius is experienced to be under threat in a way it might not have been before. The historical endeavour of the Ebony Order, in this suggested per-spective, is to assist in the reconstruction of indigenous discourse about the maintenance of individual identity, consciousness, integ-rity, and autonomy among the people in the face of the forces which threaten to overwhelm them.

(iii) Interpreting the success of the Ebony Men

The image that local Arabic-speaking Muslims have of the Uduk is of a people Godless and naked, uncircumcised and uncivil, who eat polluting meat and themselves behave like animals in not restraining their sexual or other passions. Unfortunately we have to accept that this image is not very different from that held by at least some of those involved in the mission enterprise at Chali. The Nilotic peoples who border them perhaps do not distance themselves to this degree, but also relegate all the 'Cai' ('pre-Nilotes' or Burun) to a lesser status, as cattleless and therefore inconsequential groups, who may know a good deal of magical wizardry but do not recognize the divinities.

These attitudes do not bother most Uduk. Indeed, the activities, dress, behaviour, and general style of the Ebony Men seem to take up, act out, and even celebrate this apparently negative image. Even as short a time ago as the 1920s, however, there would have been only a few diviners, and these might or might not have indulged in the extravagances of latter-day Ebony Men. Diviners from neigh-bouring communities, such as those of Jerok, various Bertha villages, and even the Jum Jum, look rather ordinary today, and though they may be members of the Ebony Order, do not 'look' in an Uduk setting like real Ebony Men. I vaguely wondered why until I realized they were wearing the plain Sudanese robe, *jibba* or *jellabiyya*, with a single skin bag or string of Spice, at the most, slung over it. By contrast, even on minor professional duties, the modern Uduk Ebony Man tries to look as stylish as possible, with goatskin wraps around the hips and all manner of bits and bobs. On major occasions the scene was worthy of several film crews, as some dozens of Ebony Men beat their horns, danced, mimed, acted out their animal roles, cracking their whips, leaping, biting, grunting, and Spraying out their Spice with loud hissing sounds. Since well over a third of the male adults in the Tombak valley were Ebony Men by the 1960s, and a large number of other people were involved in ancillary and supporting roles, these occasions involved whole communities. I do not believe the Uduk have always 'looked' like this. Not surprisingly, the performances of the Ebony Men confirm the existing prejudices of passing Arabs and other visitors. Some are understandably a little shy to look on for very long (though just occasionally the odd Arab may come discreetly for a consultation with an Ebony diviner). There is more than a veiled hint of hostility in the Ebony Men's rites. These rites after all celebrate the powers of the wild.

Tente once told me of an occasion when the diviners had been sorely tried by the behaviour of a 'Bunyan', I think a nomad Arab, who spent the whole day hanging around and making comments while they were holding rites. The Ebony Men were about to perform their set drama in the late afternoon, and had already finished most of the beer, when suddenly tempers broke. Tente came out of the hut, growling like a wild animal, and attacked the visitor, jumped on him, and bit him. Others joined in, until they were restrained.

You want me to speak until the sun goes down?

Yes!

People were having a beer for Showing the Banks at the home of Dholo'th. There were a lot of Ebony Men. There was a Bunyan, called Hisnein. He stayed around annoying people from the early morning. He was moving about among the Ebony Men, and people told him, 'Go away! You will be bitten by the Ebony Men!' Still he refused to stay quiet, and continued moving around, all the time [and making offensive remarks]. Then when the sun was about so, in the late afternoon [when the diviners would be preparing for their set drama], Boji said to me, 'Come outside please. Take a look at this Bunyan. He's not behaving himself. Why should this Bunyan disturb us all day?'
I remained in the hut for a long time, and finally I came out. He was

sitting like this, with his back near the firewood. This firewood was kept by Mina.

I came out from the hut, going *kwah*, *kwah*, *kwah*. He was gazing at me in silence. Then I jumped behind him there, and he was moving about from side to side; then I jumped on his back, *ka'bat!* I seized him with my hands and scratched his back with my fingernails, all over, down to his feet. Then I bent his head over like this, and bit him with my teeth, *ruth!*

He was red all over with blood, his teeth were red. All the Ebony Men then gathered, and seized him, *kwan*, *kwan*, *kwan*. He was moving about, but couldn't get away.

Then people came up and stopped the Ebony Men. I ran off, leaving all the others; I who had bitten him first, ran off and left them. He was about to cry. He was quite helpless in front of the Ebony Men. Quite powerless.

Tente was acting out the latent political symbolism of the Ebony Order. This brief scene reminds us of the historical context in which the organization has been able to spread; and in which it has had such a deep appeal for those communities of the southern Funj (like the outlying Uduk) who lie just beyond the direct control of local centres of power, money, police, public order, and official religion. Centres, that is, like Chali.

(iv) Historical recapitulation: the local power structure counterpointed by the Ebony Men

Through the various periods of Chali's history, outlined in the Introductory Essay, the Ebony diviners have been able to hold their own in the peripheral settlements. Far from being in retreat as one form of religious authority or another has waxed in Chali, they would appear to have risen to meet the new situation; for example, the peak in the post-war expansion of the Ebony Order coincided with the heyday of the Chali mission. The diviners have been able to integrate a range of miscellaneous older ritual practices into their corpus, and also to reach at different times specific accommodation with other religious and ritual systems. They have done this most conspicuously with the Meban cult of Leina, while periodically offering resistance, and a similar counterpoint may be seen in their developing relations with Islam, Christianity, and again Islam in Chali. They appear to have moved towards whatever religion has been identified from time to time as chief rival by the dominant orthodoxy of Chali. (I have also suggested, though only on the basis of slender indications in the oral evidence, that there

may have been a time, before the present century, when the position
of the Lake birth-group was politically more central as a patron of
others than it is today, when the ritual powers of the Lake were
respected and even feared, and the dreams and oracular diagnoses
of the people were directed against them.)

Let me sketch the evidence for this interpretation, period by
period. Apart from oral tradition which suggests that there have
always been diviners among the Uduk, and that the earliest diviners
of the modern Ebony Order spread from the Bertha, our first
recorded evidence for the presence of ŋari/ in the Chali area appears
in the notes that J. D. P. Chataway, Assistant District Commissioner for the Southern Fung (Roseires), made after interviewing
Sheikh el Fil in Chali in 1927. This was a couple of years before
the disturbances connected with Leina and other Meban prophets,
and a decade before the arrival of the Mission. Under the heading
'Religion' Chataway notes, 'I was told by one man that there
were three Gods. One of the people, one of the rain, and one of
cultivation. When I protested that three seemed a lot he replied
"yet the Arabs pretend that they have a fourth to look after them."
The God of people is responsible for all deaths. Another said
Lingari their God came and talked to them in their sleep and gave
them advice. In all probability the Sun is their chief God. But I did
not get on sufficiently intimate turns [sic] for them to discuss their
religion freely.'[5] We can leave aside the Sun God. Otherwise the
passage makes sense; in his word list, Chataway gives 'Arrum',
distinguished with an initial capital, for 'God'.[6] From what we
know today, it is perfectly understandable that his informants
should have spoken of the *arum* of the *'kwanim pa* as causing
deaths, the distinct *arum* practice of the rainstones, and that of the
fields (almost certainly the Birdrites). The Arab deity is seen as a
separate, fourth type of *arum*, and no concern of theirs.

The reference to 'Lingari', I am quite sure, is to the Ebony
diviner. Chataway's interview, with the Arabic-speaking Sheikh
and a few others, would have been in Arabic, and in that language
the definite article would surely have been used when speaking of
the ŋari/, that is '*el-ŋari*'. It is understandable that in this context,
as indeed in others where minimal Arabic is known, the 'el' may
become 'le-', and in this case could account for 'Lingari'. The

[5] Chataway, 'Notes', p. 3.
[6] Ibid., p. 2 of vocabulary list.

description might mean that he is able to make contact with all these various *arum* in his sleep; or it might conceivably mean that persons can apprehend advice from the diviner in their own dreams. Chataway tells us under 'Rainmaking' of a 'Ngeri', different from the doctor, also 'Ngeri', 'who performs in the manner common throughout the Kurmuk district i.e. with a bowl of water and a lighted piece of "babanous".[7] It is welcome to have firm evidence of the use of this oracle by the Uduk half a century ago.

Chataway's account, though not very full, does give an elaborate account of the use of rainstones; these rites are less complicated today, and might well have been a little reduced as the rites of the Ebony Men have partly replaced and partly absorbed them. This could also well have happened to the Birdrites. However, these various activities seem to have been carried on quite well in concert in 1927, and the term ŋari/ seemed already to have become, in some contexts, a generic category, as it is today.

The Uduk were only beginning to feel the established presence of government in the late 1920s. Previously it had been a liberator and saviour, and according to oral tradition some Uduk had adopted the practices and role of ŋari/ from the time before liberation, during the period when a number of them had suffered side by side with the Bertha under the Bela Shangul sheikhs. Bertha ŋeri diviners were known for their counter-position to Islam. This background could have explained their willingness to elaborate a little to Chataway on the practices of the ŋari/ diviners. But the government was now wielding its own arbitrary powers. In 1929 the police shot dead some of the followers of the Meban healer, Leina Muali. This news must have caused some consternation amongst the Uduk, and it is not surprising that after Leina's arrest, and period of imprisonment for nothing other than being a 'kujur', the Uduk apparently were willing to accept his authority. Since the 1930s, the functions of the Ebony diviners and the men of the cult of Leina have come increasingly to complement each other.

Leina's influence with the Uduk was firmly established by 1938, when the area was transferred from the Fung to the Upper Nile Province and the Sudan Interior Mission arrived in Chali. As we have seen, the Uduk countered missionary stories of Jesus with their own accounts of Leina's deeds, as well as with their own

---

[7] Chataway, 'Notes', p. 4.

myths accounting for '*arum* in the sky' and so on (the people stranded up the Birapinya Tree were of course *arum*, and they are presumably still there). The typescript notes from Chali (mid-1940s) record the way the Ebony diviners were even at that date beginning to control the presence of the Arum of Leina. According to this evidence, the crucial diagnoses by ebony oracle were being made by these diviners alone, and we can detect a trace of hostility on their part towards the growing dominant influence of Leina's men.

The notes describe the 'divining witchdoctors' as flourishing. Using the lighted ebony, they claim to see the one who has caused an illness; it may be one with the 'evil eye', or an enemy, or the 'arum' or spirit of someone. The popular one of that time was 'Leena—the Meban rainmaker', whose deputy was Jibirdhalla.[8] The *ŋari/* diviners perform the *laṯ* and *ye* (these vernacular terms are used) and then hand the patient over to Jibirdhalla for further treatment and sacrifice. A clear division of labour is described, between the several *ŋari/* diviners, on the one hand, and Jibirdhalla, alone, on the other.

However, whatever rivalry there might have been between the Ebony diviners and the Leina cult at that time, it was irrelevant when set against the active disapproval by the mission of both kinds of practice. This is clear throughout Forsberg's writings, and from other sources. As early as 1940, a government report acknowledges the collaboration of the mission in curbing the Ebony Order: 'A jum jum Kujur who escaped the police last year and has since been extorting much wealth from the Uduk was reported by Mr. Forsberg of the S.I.M. to be at Chali. He was not at home when A. D. C. Renk went there, but has since been arrested and sent to Kurmuk.'[9] As I have described above, it was explicitly forbidden for Christians to have anything at all to do with what was all lumped together as 'witchcraft' by the Christians, and in the booklet of Church Rules later published there is a specific prohibition on consulting the ebony oracle. Meanwhile, there would seem to have been an increase both in the activities of the diviners, and in accusations of what the village Uduk would have translated as witchcraft (*dhathu/* actions). Mission and government authorities collaborated in the prosecution not only of those who

---

[8] 'Customs', Chali, p. 2.
[9] Monthly Diary, Northern District, Renk, April/May 1940. SRO UNP 66.E.2.

had taken part in the killing of persons for witchcraft, but also of those diviners who had been accomplices to the act in the sense that they had helped in some cases to identify witches. A number of diviners were sentenced and imprisoned in the 1950s, and this served to moderate their overt activity. But it did not, I am sure, diminish their significance. It seemed to lay people that disease and witchcraft were multiplying, and that they were increasingly in need of the diviners' services.

In particular, because the missionaries talked so much about twins, drove around the countryside collecting them up for the orphanage, and notified the authorities in cases where they had been disposed of, it seemed to some of the Uduk that women were now giving birth to twins all over the place, in far greater numbers than before. Bukko implied in a conversation with me and Danga that it was the very presence of the mission which had led to so many cases of twin birth. Missionaries and administrators used at times the crudest forms of threat to impress upon the Uduk that they should not kill twins. Forsberg has published an account of how a visiting DC threatened to bury two women alive as a punishment, and had the graves actually dug in front of their eyes to terrify them out of such wrongdoing. He did of course relent, before sending the women off to work at the mission in lieu of imprisonment.[10]

It was at the very height of the mission's influence, when it was quite the most prominent centre of power within Chali, backed by government policy and keeping the local merchants happy through its patronage, that the Uduk and Koma areas were transferred back from the Upper Nile Province (that is, 'the South'), to the Blue Nile. This was in 1953, when Sudanese independence was suddenly an imminent reality and nationalist feelings were running high. The Chali merchants now had influential friends in Kurmuk, and the local political scene began to change. The visit of the Khatmiyya, which I have described, took place the same year. Tente, who had always kept the mission at a distance, was already a prominent Ebony diviner. His being a 'kujur', however, did not hinder his embracing the new Islamic activities, indeed taking a leading part. A turning-point had been reached. The diviners were moving towards a *rapprochement* with their former Islamic adver-

[10] Forsberg, *Land Beyond the Nile*, pp. 18–19.

sary, becoming followers of Islam and demonstrating openly their distance from the regime of the mission in Chali. It was, as it turned out, a fleeting episode; but the pattern, in retrospect, is unmistakable.

In seems to have been during the same period of the early to mid-1950s that the new activities of Ebony diviners began to influence the Uduk from Jebel Silak, via the Jum Jum. It was not long after the collapse of the Islamic episode that Tente became freshly apprenticed to the new Throwing-Stick branch of the Order, with a Jum Jum sponsor. He has since played a leading part in the spread of the five new branches of the Order among the northern Uduk. There would seem to have been a large number of new adherents of the Order from the mid-1950s onwards. If I am not mistaken, the new aggressiveness of the Order posed something of a challenge to the Leina cult. Diagnoses directed against the spreading dangers of the *arum* (?Arum) of Leina appear to have increased. We might recall here that Tente and other Ebony Men were among those who spoke most explicitly on the real identity of Leina as a risen Uduk *arum*, and who related tales of his coming to threaten the Ebony diviners in the form of a Rainbow.

The tension between the Uduk Ebony Men and the cult of Leina broke out into hostility in 1965, with the killing of the influential Arum man Lyife. This was only a year after the enforced departure of the missionaries: it is not insignificant that the incident happened at a time when authority of all kinds in Chali had waned. Not only had the foreign personnel departed and church-backed authority collapsed, but also, because of the intensifying war in the southern Sudan, there was very little business or regular administration going on in Chali. The peripheral Uduk areas were left more to themselves than they had been since the 1930s. The killing of Lyife, however, was followed by increasing pressure upon the Uduk from the Meban leaders of the Leina cult; for a time Meban country seemed to be the main source from which 'outsiders' were trying to control the Uduk. It was during this period, of the mid- to late 1960s, that in the southern valley of the Yabus the religious leader Jang was able to construct something of an integrated religious system; but his death in 1968 was predictably attributed, at least among the northern Uduk, to his having succumbed to the power of the Nuer Arum.

By 1969, the time of my last long visit to the field, 'foreign' influence and powers seemed generally to have waned. Meban pressure had fallen off; there was no more threat from Nuer divinity; there were no heavy demands either from the church in Chali or from the police or civil authorities, who still maintained only a token guard over this region so close to the war-torn Upper Nile. That part of the Blue Nile Province to the south of the Yabus was not administered at all. The people of Chali's peripheral settlements now began to take up Christian activities: but, as I have explained above, this was on their own terms, and not on orders from above.

The conclusion of the civil war in 1972 led to an increase in the activity of business, police, and army in Chali, while the church community remained relatively weak, not being able to benefit from the new dispensation for foreign mission organizations available in the South. Chali was still part of the 'North', though political ferment occasionally arose over its eventual status. As the size and character of Chali grew, and national policies of encouraging the spread of Islamic institutions took effect, with an Islamic Institute in Chali in the mid-1970s and later a brand-new Mosque, the new Christianity in the peripheral settlements (and including the Yabus valley) began to take a firmer hold. In these circumstances, who could be surprised to find the Ebony diviners looking benevolently upon the new Christianity, even going to church, and helping out the odd Christian patient who came for consultation? The pendulum had swung back again; the diviners had again come to an accommodation with a former rival, this time Christianity as against Islam, now the dominant religion of Chali. Because of the renewed outbreak of civil war in the southern Sudan—as of 1983— external support for the Christian revival has once again withered. The Ebony Order may eventually find themselves facing, without the ally of Christianity, their historic confrontation with the power that is represented by the Islamic frontier.

As for Sheikh Ahmad, the holy man of the Yabus; he had charismatic promise, for a time. And he was quite different from the Muslims of the Mosque in Chali, mainly the business and government community. Danga told me that Feki Ahmad never came to Chali. 'Chali was not a good place for him at all.' A good part of his appeal could have lain in the fact that he placed himself physically in the 'bush', and politically outside the power of Islamic 'civil society'. Of course he also preached the healing of persons.

(v) The Ebony Men and the cultural archive

In interpreting the 'success' of the Ebony Order, it is useful to remind ourselves of the obvious ways in which the organization and practices of the Order, especially as they have learned it from the Jum Jum in the last generation or two, appeal to the Uduk. For example, there are the many feasts and festivals, with music and song, dancing and play-acting. There is a rich array of costuming and personal decoration to catch the eye. By contrast, the Arum Leina cult has no music, dance, or poetry, and prescribes the solemn dress of the Arabs. Mission Christianity had of course many songs and the poetry of the Bible to offer, but otherwise, mainly puritan restrictions. Uduk exposure to the Islamic religion has been very limited; but to talk of the brief flirtation with Islam in 1953, is to recall the singing and drumming (see Tente's account in the Postscript to Part II).

Moreover, the activities of the Ebony Men, and their rituals, draw in a very broad majority in the community. Even though there are only a few female diviners, women participate far more in Ebony rites than in those of the Arum Leina cult. By contrast, women have played only a subdued role in the mission community and in the recent Christian revivals; and no role at all in relation to Islam. But in the Ebony Men's rites, the women who make the beer are given a prominent place in the ceremonies, passing through a black period and so forth as do the principals themselves. The diviners address themselves very directly to the problems of women and children, as part of their concern with the everyday difficulties faced by ordinary people, to a much greater degree than the practitioners of religious faiths. A woman might well feel she can discuss problems with a diviner, far more than with the more formal men of Arum, let alone the mission or Islamic authorities. Moreover, since such large numbers of people have become Ebony Men, there is little shyness about consultations with them. Virtually everyone, men and women alike, has access to an Ebony Man 'within the family' as it were, and they are likely to understand immediately the problems that are put to them.

A feature of the Order which makes it immediately acceptable to the lay Uduk is the focus upon medicinal practice. The Ebony Men's activities do not concern themselves with any particular spirit or divine power, but they do concentrate upon the healing of the personal body, through the use of Spice and other medicines. Affliction by Spice is a condition which itself may require incorporation into the Order. The conception of a healing power in the control of specialists and embodied in particular medicines from the bush is well known to the Uduk, having an older model for example in the practice of Elephant Medicine. By contrast, the cult of Leina, Christianity, and Islam are all predicated upon an immaterial conception of divine spirit, and a view of the human world as contingent upon, and subordinate to, that Divinity. The power of such Divinity is seen by the Uduk as a potential threat to the balance of the human system; it may invade the Liver, and dislodge the *kashira/*, turning a person into a patient who requires treatment to restore the working balance. The diviners treat mainly the Stomach and the Genius, referring patients with seriously disturbed Livers to the Arum specialists. The diviners are engaged on the side of individual humanity in the face of powers that they admit are beyond their own control. They have made the Restoral of the personal Genius their particular technique, a rite which continually reasserts the personhood of the humblest and weakest who is thus helped to withstand the overwhelming forces of 'pure spirit'.

Beyond what the Ebony diviners explicitly do, are the inner correspondences between the nexus of the Order's symbol and rite and the older experiential and imaginative world of the Uduk, which I have referred to as a hunters' archive. The Order is firmly oriented to the wild. Four of its branches are named after wild animals; the fifth is linked by antithesis to them as an order of the homestead, with its emblem of the hunting weapon, the throwing-stick. The diviners sometimes combat the wild, as in their perennial cosmic struggle with the Rainbow creature; but are in themselves partially wild, and in dreams or after death can appear as dangerous animals. They play-act their wild-animals namesakes in the dramas, and their body-decoration and paraphernalia recall the wild in many ways. Their medicines are mostly barks and roots from the forest, and with their main emblematic medicine, Spice, they strive with their privileged knowledge to protect the community from invasion by the powers of the wild, or the dead. The ebony wood from the forest gives them the detailed insight they need to do this.

In all these ways, the preoccupation of the Uduk with the wild, the animals and the forest, and their own struggle against it, finds plenty of scope in the symbolism of the Ebony rites. There are, moreover, direct analogies between the techniques of the Ebony Men, and some of the older Uduk cults; for example, their use of stones, which matches the Birdrite stones and rainstones with which the Uduk have long been familiar. The way in which people are 'caught' by Spice has earlier analogues in the way people are 'caught' for example by *dhara'c*, urine. It is the owner of the 'urine' who can cure the patient. Again, with Elephant Medicine, the parallels are very clear; the Ebony Men are fighting the Rainbow as the master of this Medicine fights the Elephant.

The structure of the Ebony Men's rites is familiar in outline to the Uduk, from their domestic rites of passage, and from their older rites of sickness, convalescence, and healing, such as in the case of Elephant Medicine. The diviners draw heavily upon the existing repertoire of lay ritual actions in their healing rites. Moreover, the symbolism of the diviners' rites of passage is easily understood by the Uduk, from the 'seizing' of a person by a medicine from the bush, through the rite where he or she crosses a river, Sits Black, and eventually is anointed with red oil. The 'wild animal' elements in the rites have deep reverberations. Unfamiliar details of rite, word, and symbol are fascinating rather than baffling to the Uduk because they have a framework in which variants can be interpreted. (Details of the Nilotic-derived cults, on the other hand, do not always find an appropriate place.) There is also the explicit close connection between the Gurunya cult and the Ebony Order. The women who handle the Gurunya rituals are sometimes spoken of as *ŋari/* themselves; I have discussed in my earlier book the tremendous appeal of the Gurunya cult, and it is for very similar, more general, reasons that the Ebony Men's activities have become established among the northern Uduk. The Gurunya practice and the diviners' practice are close analogues of each other. Salvation in grand style from outside, offered through theological discourse and by the hand of a foreign authority, may be attractive in many ways; but salvation on one's own terms, practically dealing with one case at a time, seems surer and safer. The broad appeal of the Ebony Order, largely in the hands of men, and the more specifically focused Gurunya cult, in the hands of women, have together quite thoroughly permeated the world of the modern Uduk, often defining its essentials to themselves and to outsiders.

But beyond the visible externals, the Ebony Order has re-evoked and reconstituted that implicit moral world so often passed over by the advocates of theistic faith. This has been possible because of the ebony oracle. Although this oracle was associated with particular centres of authority among the Bertha of old, today among the Uduk it is open to all. It does not in itself bring new dogma or judgement, but it is a technique which enables the Uduk, in a very unauthoritarian way, to investigate themselves.

In adopting the practices of the Ebony Order, the Uduk have not accepted any revised theory of the world. The diviner is there not to instruct upon a new vision of human nature, nor upon a newly-dominant divinity of the sky or anywhere else. The diviner is there to *answer* the people, rather than to instruct them, and so from the start he is dealing in known matters, assumptions as to the nature of the human world which do not even need to be stated because they are taken for granted. The everyday illnesses and problems of a client are posed to the neighbour-diviner for a solution; his solution can scarcely go against the grain of the fundamental notions he shares with his client of the way experience is known to a person, of the hazards of human encounter, and of the presence of *arum* within and beyond it all. This foundation of implicit moral knowledge is certainly worked upon by the diviner, and sometimes creatively. But he answers the questions put, and does not impose the pre-condition of a new faith before answering. The ebony wood reveals a community's own secrets to itself. The ebony belongs to the people perhaps as their dreams belong to them. They certainly see it as a source of knowledge in much the same way. It can even reveal something of the foreign 'powers' which have invaded the land, and indicate how these should be dealt with; this has been true especially of the Arum Leina and other manifestations of *arum* from the Nilotic world. To some extent the *cir* can combat the influence of these powers; my case material has shown instances of 'anti-Arum' diagnoses by the diviners. I have also put forward evidence of the diviners treating 'Allah' in the same sort of way.

These diagnoses seem in line with the people's own expectations, especially in a case like that of the death of Jang, immediately attributed by everybody, without formal diagnosis, to the consequences of his taking on the Nuer Arum. In general, there is (perhaps quite rightly!) a feeling that there are too many Arum specialists and practices about; and that the very presence of all these cults is in itself a threat to the people. William Danga elaborated on this theme, echoing the words of Bu*k*ko that I quoted in the Introductory Essay:

Long ago, they say, long ago: the true words which we have been told say that at that time there were no Arum activities. There was no Arum practice. But the diviners' practice was important. There were only a few diviners. But people didn't get ill. People stayed well. The only *arum* was the *arum* of Mi*t*i [see Chapter 1 (ii) (*d*)]. That was present in the land of the Uduk. It had a horse, and a gun in its hand, that type of rifle that the police use. They always used to race their horses in the late afternoon.

But all these Arum, the Arum which strike people dead, they did not exist. The Arum which make people sick did not exist.

There were just the *arum* which gathered to play the *athele/* [the dance with logs and flutes]. They danced the *athele/* in the old days, and the dance called *baraŋgu/* [the dance of the old days, associated with mythical times].

Were these arum *from people who died?*

Yes, from people who had died. They danced the *athele/*. You would hear them dancing the *athele/* like real people. They made the *yisaŋ* cry like people do [a high whooping call of the girls]. *Guy, guy, guy,* and W*a! Mum*! like real people [echoing the percussive beat and roar of the dancers].

There was nothing else apart from this. And you would go, and you would look around the place and think that people were dancing the *athele/* in that village over there, while the *athele/* in fact was being danced in the heart of the forest at Bathan there, for *arum*. And they often danced the *baraŋgu*. The *arum* were not feared, in the past. When the sun was there [indicating] ... in the later afternoon, they would dance *athele/*. They were not feared in those days. For there was nothing [i.e. no disease, no trouble]; people stayed well in those days without anything [to disturb them].

Didn't the ground arum *strike people?*

Ç*aah*, That didn't strike people all the time. Just occasionally. Very occasionally. They just struck people from time to time. Not continually.

Because evil talk didn't exist, long ago. There was talk, but no sitting and wagging tongues [criticizing, grumbling]. If you quarrelled with your brother, you would immediately fight, and the thing would be settled, and the *arum* would not strike anybody. Not at all. It happens from evil words which you mutter: *arum*, the ground *arum* [*aruma 'cesh*] will strike you. If you fight, you and your brother, the *arum* will not strike you, because you will soon get it over and settle down.

And in the past, they say, there were things, there were animals, in plenty. There were plenty of fish, and a lot of gazelles, right among the villages, among the villages in the places where people lived. People were not struck by hunger-for-meat ['*kosha kwa/a*]. People ate many, many things. Everything. And for sesame, they say you would cultivate a moderate patch, say from here to that little hut of mine there. And you would harvest sacks—about five sacks—from that little clearing for sesame.

But now?

Çaah! Nowadays the earth has gone bad. You will cultivate a great field of sesame, from here right as far as that [indicating the edge of the hamlet]; and will you find anything? Very little; you'll find only about ten *kelas*. [Sudanese Arabic measure: a *kela* is one petrol tin.] That's all. But formerly, *çaah!* A really small clearing, a tiny little patch, produced a great quantity of sesame, they tell us.

And now people get sick a great deal?

They sicken because there are so many diviners. There are many Arum, the place is full of them, the earth there. Arum fill the earth, that is why as soon as a little thing is done [i.e. a little mistake is made], people easily get sick, straight away. Because the place is full of Arum. Because Arum— the sickness perhaps says, 'Heh! There are plenty of people who will help with treatment!' There are Arum—there are people of Arum and Ebony Men, and that is why people get sick all the time.

Where do all these Arum come from?

They come—the Arum proper which is practised, comes from Meban there. And that Arum of the Ebony Men comes from Wadega.

In suggesting that people are getting sick from the presence of too many Arum specialists and diviners, Danga is only partly joking. The presence of powerful medicine, as in the old Uduk model of the Elephant Medicine, can make people sick who are in close contact or relationship to it. It is on this model that the Uduk have again and again patterned the incoming 'spirits', the Arum Leina and the Arum Dhamkin; the specialists in these forms of Arum are certainly supposed to protect the community from that particular power, but at the same time they are dangerous to those around them. The danger would perhaps not be seen in the same way by the Meban, and certainly not by the Nuer. But for the Uduk Jang's death was another demonstration of the power and the danger of a foreign spirit; and in the case of the killing of Lyife, the people themselves took action to rid their community of a power which had become dangerous, not necessarily in itself, but because it had fallen into dangerous hands. The older Uduk cults were not those of Arum as such; *arum* thought of individually were the relatively harmless ghosts of the dead, and those mythical part-human beings which existed before death came. *Arum* thought of as a general power, or force behind living beings, could ultimately be said to have given life to the world; but this was never framed as a purposive act. To this extent we could say that the old Uduk world was without a 'divinity': and certainly a world without a God. It was a humanistic world, in which the main story was one of the unfolding of human life itself, and the consequent differentiation of the intimately linked power of life, *arum*. The world of *arum* in their imagination was a continuation (in some respects transposed) of the known world, and drew its own 'history' from the passage of life and death in the community of the living people. In so far as *arum* could enter the living world afresh, it could do so in the form of a returned being from the land of the dead. There was no direct inspiration or possession from 'another world' of divinities and non-human existence.

But precisely such 'other' divinities have come from neighbouring cultures, and from the revealed religions, to the Uduk. Their apparently easy acceptance of these new 'Gods' and enthusiasm for new religious practices is deceptive. These foreign divinities have, in at least the case of Leina and associated manifestations, been recast as risen human spirits, their presence in the living community operating very much in the manner of the old 'medical' specialisms of the people, inevitably causing suffering from time to time but giving vital protection to the community against the world of the wild, the dead, and increasingly in recent times, against the threat of foreign invasion and domination itself. Islam exists as part of the context in which the Uduk live and have lived for generations; they have, on the whole, resisted conversion to Islam, but at the same time, one of the older-established branches of the Ebony diviners is explicitly termed 'Arum Allah'. 'Allah', consciously being introduced into the discourse of the southern Uduk in particular, ironically through the greater assimilation of Meban ritual practices and also Nilotic cult, is part of the world which the Ebony Man must interpret. Levels of comprehension and interpretation may be complex; on one occasion I asked why a sick diviner, when undergoing treatment, should be thrown up on to the roof of the hut. The reply came back, 'Well, Allah is up there. The mother who gave birth to us all is up there!' The task of interpretation, of course, is also a protective one, and we have seen how the diviner may actively put forward diagnoses of a patient's condition which represent both 'Allah' and the Meban-derived Arum Above as a danger. The scope of the diviner's work potentially extends this response to all introduced and taught religious dogma.

I have already noted that the diviners are now going to church, at least on occasion. It is possible, within the framework of old and newer Uduk thought, to accept or reject the explicit advocacy of one or another 'religion' or belief, but the work of the Ebony Men is not on the same level. You cannot so easily accept or reject the advocacy of the ebony oracle, because in itself it stands for no dogma. In silence, it is attuned to the implicit assumptions of the proper balance within a person. It reveals the workings of the vulnerable inner person, relations between people, relations between the living and the dead, relations between people and the world of the wild. These matters, elusive, 'open-textured', and adaptable, constitute a part of what I have called in this book the archive of 'moral knowledge', and these fundamental levels of silent knowledge can weather a good deal of vocal debate about the dogmas of a higher theology. Advocates of Islam, Christianity, and even the Nilotic divinities, rarely confront these basic representations of the Uduk, but succeed to some extent by finding a way through their loose texture, which remains undamaged. These dogmatic faiths have rarely touched the deeper levels, and are open to partial reinterpretation by the Uduk on their own terms.

The Ebony Order, so astonishingly successful in the last generation or so, draws its strength not from explicit new doctrine but from its quiet tapping of the older sources of experience and knowledge. In the process, perhaps a good deal of what was opaque has been given a clearer definition, a process which in itself might be seen as a rendering visible, and a reaffirmation, of the archival contents. Inevitably, a number of matters which were previously implicit and not much discussed, have been brought out in the open by frequent consultations with the ebony oracle. Until this technique was available to the Uduk, for example, I do not suppose that anybody had actually 'seen' a personal Genius, except as a shadow on the ground; nor afflictions of the Liver, or the work of *arum* and *dhathu/*, except in a dream. To some extent the old notions may even have been redefined through the explicit diagnoses of the ebony oracle. But they are not completely new. The revelations of the ebony are always comprehensible to the people. What they have heard of Islam is another world. At the same time, much of the teaching of Christianity, for example, even though in the Uduk language, cuts so cleanly through what they implicitly know, that it leaves the older certainties almost undisturbed, and the older questions still open. This is why the people have confidence in their own diviners, who can in principle give them a diagnosis of themselves that they can understand, as well as of the world and its powerful advocates of strident and jealous Gods.

Epilogue

In the Prologue to 'Kwanim Pa I quoted Emed's version of the myth of Woman's discovery of Man; she told us how women at the beginning of things lived in the village and men were wild creatures, *arum*, out in the forest. The Woman of the story called on what she thought was a Gurunya bird, a glossy starling, to throw her down some fruit from the fig tree where he perched. He did so; she called him down, found him to be Man, mated with him, and took him home. The story bears some intriguing resemblances to the tale of Adam, Eve, and the apple tree.

A mimeographed translation of the Book of Genesis was available at Chali in the 1960s, but only in 1983 was the text published and widely circulated, in the form of the new Uduk Scriptures. The book of Genesis is also included on the set of Bible cassettes introduced for evangelical work the same year. Eve, Adam, and the fruit trees of the Garden of Eden have an oddly familiar sound when translated into Uduk, and it is instructive to dwell briefly on the resonances, and oddities, of the story as it appears to its new audiences.

In the Uduk myth, Woman and Man are separate beings from the start, one in the village and one in the bush; they did not have a common source in one original body, nor did they cleave as one flesh, as in the Genesis text. The beginning of things is essentially the encounter between the two. There is no primeval and timeless Creator who judges them, or indeed made them. The presence of *arum* in the Uduk story is not that of a third entity; it exists within the compass of the first beings themselves, especially the wild male creature, himself the source of the woman's fertility. Whereas in Genesis, it is the woman who gives fruit to the man, in the Uduk myth Man gives fruit to Woman. There is no suggestion that this fruit is forbidden or dangerous, any more than that nakedness or sexuality is shameful. There was no One to prescribe such rules, or such shame.

In Genesis, Adam is the one to initiate dialogue, whereas in the Uduk tale it is Woman who speaks first. She also initiates sexual relations, hiding her Man in leafy branches of the fig tree not from any God but from the other women. She takes him to her village;

whereas in Eden, no 'village', whether of men or women, is yet formed nor cultivation begun. As a result of the first Uduk mating, and the subsequent demands of the whole female community, the first Man weakens and dies: by contrast, in Genesis it is Eve who is promised sorrow and pain, especially in childbirth, and she is informed that her husband will rule over her.

In the Uduk story there is no 'evil' beguiling animal who deceives human beings (the Gurunya bird's part is quite innocent). In associated myths there are several accounts of animals helping humankind, such as the Dog who brings fire, the rat who shows women how to give birth properly, and so forth (see Appendix 2). In the story of the great Dance when the wild animals were about to kill us all, the Dog alerted us and we overcame this planned treachery. In so far as the Uduk stories give some account of the beginnings of evil, they seem to place it in fragmentary and contingent ways outside human society, in the world of the wild bush and its animal life: not on a cosmic scale within the frailties of human beings themselves, as they are defined and judged by any omnipotent God. The notion of an ancient burden upon human beings, or a state of original sin or uncleanness of any kind, is not present in the myth, nor in the general cosmology of Uduk tradition. Rather, there is a more optimistic view of human beginnings; we did not sin, we were not banished by Authority, but succeeded ourselves in establishing some authority over the rest of the creatures, and started to construct a new world. Certainly things were spoiled as the process unfolded; some animals did foolish things, like the two lizards who quarrelled and dropped the Moon Oil, thus losing the last means of revival after death. Certain human beings also took destructive action, like the woman who burned down the Birapinya Tree and cut off part of the human race in the sky. But actions like this were taken piecemeal. There is no fatalistic suggestion that yesterday's moral faults (any more than today's) are produced by, and inevitable because of, an original cosmic failing.

However closely the individual elements of the two stories can be compared as a rearrangement of motifs, it cannot be denied that there is a profound difference in the moral worlds they depict, when taken as a whole. As a result, the Genesis story can touch few deep chords for the Uduk hearer; it must seem in some ways an odd, quirky, and inconsequential tale, as so often the myths of some other peoples appear to us. The indigenous story, however, is full of moral resonance. Does it matter that there are these differences in the myths of early times, if one is considering questions of present-day religious faith? I think it does.

There are two particularly pertinent points in this case. First, the fundamentalist Christian teaching at Chali emphasized the literal reality of Genesis, as of the New Testament, giving more weight by implication to the Fall story than other missions might have done. Second, the doctrine of original sin was given great prominence, with the insistence on Jesus as the only means of purification. This emphasis makes the Genesis story quite alien to Uduk assumptions: for not only do they counter the hierarchies of God and Man, Man and Woman, with an integrated and egalitarian vision, but they regard the fruitfulness of sexual encounter and the birth of children as a source of positive good. There is very little association of sex and procreation with defilement; childbirth is normally a 'cool' and auspicious event. A new-born human being is a fresh beginning, and a promise for the future.

I believe that those moral views which colour any possible readings of the vernacular myths have scarcely been displaced by the discourse of theistic religion, which has drawn attention to the nature of Divinity rather than looking deeper into humankind; and in so far as it has touched on matters human, it has been reduced to questions of public practice and prescribed and prohibited acts (perhaps especially in the case of Islam). The plural character of religious allegiance among Uduk-speakers does not necessarily reflect deep divisions in their common moral world.

The outstanding individuals who in the last generation have promoted Nilotic faiths, Islam, and Christianity among the Uduk have not torn themselves or their followers from each other or from the main body of the population. There have been fashions and factions, and coalitions of interest around particular issues or particular leaders. But these have rarely been long lasting; the issue in question has either subsided altogether or it has become absorbed, as one more variant interpretation, even one more latent theological dilemma, in the general ferment. Public figures who have accepted outside patronage, such as the Chali Omda, Talib el Fil (who by virtue of his office, became the leading Muslim among the Uduk), Pastor Paul Rasha Angwo of the Church, or spiritual leaders like the late Jang of the Yabus who placed their faith in a Nilotic heaven, seem to have broken away from 'tradition'. But not one of these competing religious advocates severed his ties with the world of the ordinary people. Each of them in his own way, has acted as their mediator, representative, and interpreter in relation to the outside world. Let me conclude this study by turning specifically to Pastor Paul and to Tente, men who have more in common than their formal differences of status and declared faith would suggest.

I had heard of Pastor Paul some time before I ever arrived in Chali. He and the Chali Church were well known in the Blue Nile Province in the 1960s, among traders, administrators, students, nomads like the Arabs of the Rufa'a el Hoi, and also the few expatriate travellers or workers who knew the southern parts of the Province. As a Christian outpost, right on the border with the rebellious South, Chali had already acquired some notoriety. Pulling the Church through the civil war period, when outside financial aid and other help was reduced to an intermittent trickle, was a real achievement on Paul's part, and required a political tightrope act of no little skill. Members of the local merchant community had always tried, to some extent, to keep him under their wing, extending credit in difficult times and so forth, but he was able, nevertheless, to sow the seeds of the extraordinary Christian revival which began in 1967 and to keep it going, not always by the most orthodox methods, until the flow of outside assistance was re-established after 1972. Pastor Paul now presides, almost elder-statesman-like, over a much expanded network of Church groups, and his diplomatic strategies have broadened to encompass relationships not only with the strengthened Muslim presence in Chali and the return of foreign missionary workers to places nearby in the Upper Nile Province, but also the (locally startling) arrival of representatives of the Catholic Church.

He is regarded by most outsiders as a spokesman for all the Uduk. Paul has little in the way of conventional education, but his fluent English (slightly Southern-States American, and slightly Biblical) gives no hint of this; his cheerful and easy social manner makes any visitor feel welcome. I first visited Chali at the invitation of some young northern Sudanese administrators and health workers stationed in Kurmuk, who had established their own friendly relations with Paul, as many local Muslims did. It was 24 December 1965, and they suggested to me that we all go to Chali for Christmas. We did; Paul and his helpers put on what with hindsight I realize was a remarkably good meal for all of us, and when my companions returned to Kurmuk, I stayed on to make the most of Paul's hospitality and to formulate a plan of extended fieldwork among the Uduk.

Paul has visited the USA a couple of times, most recently in 1982, to assist with the preparation of cassettes to be used in evangelical teaching. References to his foreign trips again convey an impression of familiarity with the world. He is fond of joking with guests that he is a Republican.

In the heyday of the old mission station, when Paul was being prepared for ordination, he wrote a short autobiography in English. This document eloquently speaks for itself, placing the phenomenon of Christian acceptance in its historical and social context more vividly than I ever could. With his permission, I quote the whole document, as Paul showed it to me, with only minimal editorial correction.

The Sad Testimony and Good News to the Uduk Tribes:
June 30, 1961

Before, when I was not a Christian, I was a bad boy.

I hated all the boys and men and women, I did not like anybody to tell me anything, even my brother or my sister I used to fight with them all the time because I was a proud boy. I loved my mother and my Daddy because when I did wrong, they did not correct me. When I fought with some of the boys they said to me, 'This is the kind of thing we want you to do, to fight and we need you to do bad things so that you might be a good man when the time of fighting comes and you will be able to help yourself with your own hand.' When you folk heard this talk you folk would say in your heart, this is a very very wrong way my Daddy and my mother were leading me into the way of destruction.

They said that, because from the beginning the Uduk people did not have a home, they just lived in the forest like rats. When the rain is raining it fills their holes completely, then the rats begin to run to the dry land to save their little life. Well in the same way the Uduk people did not have any peace in their life, because there was fighting between them and the Ethiopian people. One among their tribes is called Khujle [Khogali Hassan], he is the highest among the Bertha people. He made all of them his slaves, and took them to sell in Ethiopia. When he went to the Ethiopians himself he reported to them about the Uduk tribes, he told them that the Uduk tribes are a poor people. You could just come and fight with them for a few minutes and you will overcome them and take them to be your slaves. So the Ethiopian people they came in two tribes, that means the Khujle who came with the Ethiopians to fight the Uduk. But the Uduk people are not many tribes, they are just a few people. When they saw the great multitude they went inside their fence, for they lived in their fences because of enemies. When the Ethiopian people and the Bertha arrived in the Uduk land, they began to fight with them for four days and the Uduk people did not run out from the fence. They fought inside the fence for four days, and the Uduks were very very very very tired from their fight, so they told their women to fix them a fire to put their spears and arrows in the fire, so that the spears and arrows would be hot so that they might shoot the Ethiopians and Berthas with hot spears to let them die real quick. Yes they did it very badly [i.e. acted severely] to the Ethiopians and Berthas. And one thing they can do is put poison on their arrows and shoot the Ethiopian people and Berthas. So when the Ethiopians and Berthas saw the hot spears and arrows on the top of the fence they ran and left part of the fence open, and the Uduk people found a way to come out from the fence and killed many of the Ethiopians and Berthas. So they ran home with nobody in their hands to be their slaves as they had wanted.

And the second time Ethiopian people and Berthas they came together like armies of locusts surrounding them. So the Uduk people made an agreement among themselves. They said, 'Let us chop solid bamboo like a spear and let it be sharp on both sides, and don't cut it short, let it be eight feet so that we will pierce them and push them down from the top of the fence.' Yes, they hurt them very badly and they put the poison on too, but the Ethiopians did not mind and kept coming in groups. The poison that the Uduk put on their arrows and spears has roots like an onion.

So they put it too on the sharp solid bamboos and pierced the Ethiopians and Berthas, but they didn't all come together, some of them sat down and watched their people when they were coming in to fight; but the Uduk killed a lot of them, and when the Ethiopian people saw their people had been killed they sent in another group. So the Uduk people were very very tired, not just in the body but in their arms too. So the Ethiopian people and the Berthas they came in and took some of them and cut their heels so that they would not run home. They just made them their slaves as they wanted it to be, they used them to wash their women's feet and cook for them and put a lot of loads on them, like a donkey, carrying on both sides. They took my [... *illegible*] grandmother. But three of them ran back to the Uduk land and gave birth to my mother. This is a Miracle from the Lord, because God knew it that I will be His own. All of this bad attitude is just coming from the devil who blinds people's eyes not to see the way of Salvation. As Paul said in the Epistle of Romans Chapter 1: 29, 30, 31–2. He said those people who are in the darkness they have a heart that has been filled with all unrighteousness, Fornication, Wicked-ness, Covetousness, Maliciousness, Full of Envy, Murder, Debate, Deceit,

Malignity, Whisperers, Backbiters, Haters of God, Despiteful. Proud, Boasters, hateful to God, Insolent, Haughty, Boastful, Inventors of evil things, Disobedient to parents. Without understanding, Covenantbreakers, Without Natural affection, Implacable, Unmerciful. *This is a Good News.*

Because the Gospel of the Lord Jesus Christ arrived in the Uduk's Land in 1938. But I was a little boy at that time, seven years old or something like that in my age. I went to another country [i.e. another locality] and the Italian war with the Ethiopian people found me there. When the war was over my mother went to that country and brought me back to my home Chali El Fil and I was very happy to be with them. The Missionary was already there in the Uduk area and they began to help the people to know the true God. But the Missionary did not know enough of their language so they spent their time learning their language. When they learned their language they began to help them a little bit with the paper. But the Uduk people were just afraid of the white sheets, they said 'If we touch these white sheets we will die, because it is a bad thing that the white people brought to us!' And one thing they said was the white people have not been born, but they just come out of the river. They aren't persons [i.e. *'kwanim pa*] they are just ghosts [i.e. *arum*] because they have soft skins and they keep the rain from raining on us any more.' So later the Missionary went in to their village to visit with them all the time to learn their language and to call them to sing a little song about God. And some of them did come, and the Missionary entreated them to let their children come to school. But it was not a real school, just a day school. So my mother told me that I cannot go to school because I was a mischievous boy. But I refused her word and ran to school in 1946 but the Missionary did not have a real school. We came to school at 8:00 to begin our class until 11:00.

Then in 1948 the Missionary had a permit from the Government to build the dormitory, so we have a real school. Then in 1949 I began to be a mischievous boy. I did not listen to the word from my teacher, I was just doing with my stomach [i.e. behaving as I wished] all the time. Then one day my teacher gave me a punishment, and I told my teacher 'If you are going to give me this punishment, I will run home, I cannot stay in the school for one minute.'

So my teacher hit me four times on the bottom, but this punishment did not do me any good, it just made me worse, so I ran home. Then word was sent to my uncle to bring me back to school, but I refused his word absolutely, so he went to call a policeman to take me by force. Yes, the policeman came, so I told the policeman 'Can't touch me because blood will be shed right now!' But in that moment Miss Mary Beam came and stopped me from fighting with the police and Chief, because the Chief was there too.

So she told the Chief and police that she would take care of me and she said she would give me another punishment to help me sit right [i.e. to stay quiet and behave well]. The punishment they decided to give me was to tie me under the tree with a chain. When I heard that talk I was very angry with Miss Mary Beam and even my friends too. I did not let anybody come close to me. I gathered all the rocks together under the tree with me to hit those who came to feed me and told everybody not to give me water and food; that I should sit without anything to eat and drink was my thought. Then afterwards I recognised that I was guilty before God because I did such things as not honour the big people. So I began to be a shame to myself because my consciousness rebuked me thoroughly. So in 1948 the Uduk people had a first Conference and every Chief brought his people to the Conference from far districts; the names of the places are here: Fu'da/om & Belatouma & Bemby [i.e. Pam'Be] & Fija/ulu & Borfa & Golnugura/ & Benawayu & Soda & Balila & Chali. And from that Conference I stood up to receive Jesus Christ as my Saviour, and from that time I began to be a good boy because Jesus was in my heart. The Leader for that Conference was Miss Mary Beam, and Miss Betty Cridland was the speaker, and they led me to the Lord Jesus Christ, and many people too they led to the Lord. And they treated me like their own child, sure I am to them in the Lord Jesus Christ. But when I finished my fourth year in Elementary school in Chali El Fil I went home again because I didn't want the P.E.O. [referring to the Province Education Officer] to take me to another school, because it is not the custom of Uduk to go to another country. They say we are not foreigners [i.e. 'Bunyan'], we are the Uduk people, that means the 'Village People' [i.e. 'kwanim pa, people of the home]. We are not wanderers like other people. So when I finished my fourth year at Elementary School in Chali El Fil I went home in 1949 and did not come back to the Church for three and a half years. I covered myself with beads and red dirt color and played with the unbeliever, I danced with them and drank beer with them and smoked with them. The first time when I tasted a Cigarette it hurt my heart and I was so dizzy from the morning to the evening I could not move my body, and the people were so shocked they couldn't do anything. So my mother came and took water and poured it on me to cool my body, but the water did not help me. But when I woke up, I said 'This is a punishment from God because I did not believe in him with a true heart.' I know it too that the power of God showed me how bad cigarettes are, because they contain 18 poisons. But when I got well from the poison of the cigarettes I did not stop drinking beer, and I still went to the witchdoctor [i.e. Ebony diviner] for no good reason. I was just playing with my life like that. But in 1952 I was called by the Government to be a scribe for the Chiefs of the Uduk people, so I did it for one year, though I did not like it for sure. But in 1953 my heart turned back to the Lord. So I resigned from being a scribe, then in 1954 I was called by my people to be the President of the Club of those who called [... *illegible*] Chali. From that time I came to be close to the Lord when I was still in the village, and Miss Mary Beam and Miss Betty Cridland they gave me the Bible to read. While I was still in the village with my people, I read the Old Testament that tells the word of how God gave Isaac twins. So I told my wife, that I wanted God to give us twins. Oh my head, she was very very angry with me and she said to me 'Why do you curse me like that?' Because the Uduk people did not like twins, they said they have an evil eye. Yes, when I said that word, God gave the twins in 1954 and I have [... *illegible*] had a hard time with my wife [... *illegible*] from that day because of the twins that were born. One boy did not have a left ear. He is [the second?] but the first one has two ears, so my wife wanted to kill him that had one ear. So Miss Mary Beam and Miss Betty Cridland they spent their time helping me with her. But not only just their time [... *illegible*] after years because my mother-in-law she came with her relatives. They came to search for my wife to kill her and the twins too because they said my wife and the twins were Wizard. It is good to kill them thoroughly without any question about them. So when I saw the people coming in groups with their long sticks towards my house I ran to Miss Mary Beam to call her to come and help me. So we locked the twins inside. So we kept the twins alive. But the names of those twins has become called *A Miracle UDUK FAMILY* because they have grown up in their parents' home. When they were still little babies a doctor told Miss Mary Beam and Miss Betty Cridland that those twins would not stay alive because they were very thin. But on top of that word, God increasing His grace helped those twins from the sickness. Yes, all the time both of them were almost about to die, but Jehovah [... *illegible*] put his hand on them and healeth them. But now they are boys, and the one that has the one ear, the doctor did an operation on him this year for his tonsils, but now [... *illegible*] well. And both of them are seven years old and they are in the school this year, but on October 30, 1961 they will be eight years old on Monday. Before they went to school they were baptized on March 19, 1961. So we thank the Lord Jesus Christ for love and His kindness towards His Saints as it has been said in the Psalm 16: 1–3 the portion that David said is Preserve me, O God, for in thee do I put my trust. But to Saints that are in the earth and to the excellent, in whom is all my delight so in Psalm 101: 6 the Lord said, Mine eyes shall be upon the Faithful of the land, that they may dwell with me, He that walketh in a perfect way, he shall serve me. Psalm 119: 1, 2 Aleph. Blessed are the undefiled in the way, who, walk in the law of the Lord. Blessed are they that keep His testimonies, and that seek him with the whole heart.

This message is from the Pastor Paul Angwo and his testimony.

Since, the Church that is in the Sudan is having difficulty because of the activity of the Muslim Religion. But my aim is that the Church in the Sudan may be yielded completely for Christ and bring the fruits of Righteousness to it. As Paul said, I am not ashamed of the Gospel of Christ, for it is God's power working unto Salvation for deliverance from eternal death to every one who believes with a personal trust and a confident surrender and firm reliance, to the Jew first and also to the Greek.

Paul may one day update his account. But it is clear even from this early writing about his own life that he was able to find in Christianity not only an appealing message for its own sake, but a way of handling some very practical problems. He and his wife and children were featured in the literature of the S.I.M. as 'The Uduk Miracle Family', as they were the first to bring up twins. Although Paul has since married again and has a second family, his commitment to Christianity has remained constant since his conversion and the early events of his first marriage. The new synthesis of the post-missionary Christianity revival is very much Paul's creation. The more recent translations and revisions of the scriptures are themselves largely Paul's work, and the key emphases of the new local evangelism, with its heightened expectation of the Second Coming, are inspired by him. His has been a creative synthesis of the old language and a new vision; and at present, it 'works' in its appeal to a large number among the younger population.

In a recent conversation with Paul, he explained to me that, since the revival of Christianity in 1967, people see Jesus as an alternative to the *ŋari/*, 'to protect them from the darkness and the death'. He also told me of a visit he made in 1983 to Sheikh Ahmad, the popular holy man in the Yabus. They had a theological discussion, in which they debated who was king; Ahmad apparently said that when Jesus came again to earth, Muhammad would be king. Paul represented his case as well as he could.

Tente flirted with Islam briefly in 1953 when the Khatmiyya was, literally, drumming up support in Chali. But otherwise, he has remained aloof from the various advocates of new religion in Uduk country, and implicitly suspicious of their motives. He has been many times married and many times bereaved; something in the order of ten of his own children have died, while he has only four still living. Because of the deaths of his mother, a brother, a sister, and another child, I found in 1983 that he had even left the village of Waka'cesh and settled across the river with other relatives. He had been throughout his adult life one of the most active members of the Ebony Order among the northern Uduk. In the dress he affected in 1983—an orange Muslim skull-cap, together with 'Western' trousers and shirt—he seemed almost to be mocking both Arab and Western styles. His main experience of the 'outside world' has been prison, for minor matters in Kurmuk and, in one case, for a more serious matter in Roseires (when most of the male population of Waka'cesh were taken off for a year, following a fight and a death in 1981). Tente had learned to be wary of 'the government' for a number of reasons, among them the cases which took place when he was younger in which diviners were implicated in naming 'witches' and thus held accessory to their subsequent killing. He had been consistently wary of the activities of the mission, and when I first had discussions with Mary Beam and Betty Cridland in 1971 they remembered what a sceptic he had been.

As a boy Tente was taken by Lyife to see Leina, to seek advice on a problem with his leg. The sore was attributed to the wild animals, for Tente had been an active and successful hunter. The leg later healed. Tente first became apprenticed to the Ebony Order when he was still quite young, I would guess in the 1930s. He joined the old-style Elephant diviners of the 'Arum Allah'. But some time later, after his brief encounter with Islam, he was drawn into a new branch of the Order, the Throwing-Stick diviners, through a Jum Jum sponsor. Thereafter, Tente sponsored many others, mainly younger men and boys, as Ebony Men. In colloquial idiom, they were his 'children'. He also had various special practices which came from older sources, in particular the practice of Elephant Medicine. As an Ebony Man, he had recently acquired a particular speciality, dealing with the *maŋgal* grub. A stomach pain might be attributed to this, and Tente had learned to Extract the grub in true wizardly style.

I am sure that Tente saw no contradiction between his work as an Elephant master and his work as an Ebony diviner. He was, however, loyal to the interests of the Ebony Order against the men of the Arum Leina cult, and resisted the revisions that this movement was introducing. He often maintained a diplomatic silence when I forced discussions in public, but just as often came round later to explain things to me in private. Tente himself could never be led into making clear doctrinal statements, but was an excellent commentator on ritual practice. He often adopted an open, agnostic position on questions of 'divinity'. He once said to me that it was *arum* which made us (*uk ana*, created us, using a word for a potter making pots) and keeps us alive. '*Arum* made people, *arum* made moths, made trees, made tomatoes, made coffee.' I said, 'So *arum* is very good. Why does *arum* hurt people and make them die?' Tente responded, 'How can we know? *Arum* gives birth to us, makes us tall and strong, and then kills us. Why? We don't know.'

Although the techniques of the Ebony Order were pragmatically satisfying for Tente, if not always effective, the ultimate grounds of health and sickness were beyond the reach of the Ebony Man. I have already quoted his account of the presence of the life-sustaining *arum* within the ordinary person. Even the Ebony Man is ultimately the creature of the *arum* within him, and when he is sick, all that the others can do is carry out a treatment aimed at the recovery of that *arum*. In the following explanation Tente refers to the treatment of Ebony diviners, and it is clear from his reference to Losko (a very old man who had no ritual specialism) that there is, nevertheless, no fundamental difference between their treatment and that of ordinary people:

See: the Ebony men treat each other. There may be one whose *arum* does not want him to recover, and he will die. If his *arum* is one which wants him to live, this Ebony Man will live. Every year, many Ebony Men are tossed up like that, and another one, and another one. And some from among the rest are prevented [from recovery] by [their] *arum*, and they die. And another *arum* which is content, will keep you outside [i.e. outside the grave], keep you outside, outside here. And again, one day you may sicken, people will again do something for you, the Ebony Men will again gather to treat you. Again they will throw you on the roof, and again take a goat and cut it.

If the goats are cut for you again, and again, and again, repeatedly, while your *arum* doesn't want them, it is about to die. It dies, and you will die as well. You will die together with your *arum* after all this. Yes! Because it is *arum* which keeps us alive. If your *arum* dies, you will also die. If yours will always remain strong, as with those old people who live until a great age, now their *arum* are still alive and that is why they remain living for so long.

Look at Losko now, his *arum* is still alive. His *arum* has not died. It is alive all the time. It goes like this, bent, bent double as he now does; it is his *arum*, it is old, as he is now, and sits in one place. If it should die, he will die too together with his *arum*.

Tente was among those who spoke most convincingly of Leina, the Meban prophet, as a risen Uduk; and of his appearance in the form of a Rainbow. He used to sing the old hunting songs and the rainstone song, all now adopted by the Ebony Men, with style and grace, and he threw himself wholeheartedly into the music and dancing, the rituals and dramas of the diviners. For him certainly, the rites of the Ebony Order were a very satisfactory way of mobilising the Uduk. No one could really be expected to save the people if they did not try to save themselves. The diviner, his Spice, and his listening Ebony promised a way of doing this.

Paul was aiming at eternal salvation. For Tente there was no need to worry about the hereafter. He was concentrating, as far as his knowledge could take him, on saving bodily life and its precious, if mortal, individual psyche for the here and now. To outward appearances, the Christian Paul, and the Muslim Omda Talib el Fil, the Nilotic spokesman Jang, and the sceptical diviner Tente were ranged as ideological opponents, and represented a people divided (at least) four ways. But as I hope to have shown in 'Kwanim Pa and the present book, all belonged in a fundamental way to one moral community. The differences between them reflected the various powerful influences exerted upon the Uduk people from the world outside, through discourses and practices which characteristically co-opted the younger menfolk. But the continuities of interpersonal connection, and the knowledge stemming from shared language and history, have remained. These evidences of moral community are partly hidden, implicit rather than spelt out, and they are given substance primarily through the network of kinship links through women. Indeed the community of the womenfolk, though drawn into Nilotic cult, Islam, or Christianity in a marginal way, has been the main source of indigenous response, the guardian and treasurer of the archive. The prime reason for the acceptance of the Ebony Order among the Uduk was its enthusiastic endorsement by the women, whose problems and sufferings it spoke to directly. Through the women, all religious innovators traced their most important personal links, including those with each other. Omda Talib el Fil and Pastor Paul were related as brothers-in-law; and Pastor Paul and Tente too were related as members of the Lake birth-group, regarding themselves as sharing common matrilineal descent. The notion of blood relationship, whether substantiated through known matrilineal links or used as metaphor to extend the rhetoric of kinship between those whom history has thrown together, remains the essence of 'moral community' for the Uduk; the womenfolk themselves remain its part-visible, part-hidden embodiment.

Appendix 1

Koman parallels, the archive and the pre-Nilotic context

My own first-hand knowledge of the various peoples of the 'pre-Nilotic' border region, in addition to the northern and southern Uduk, and some general travel through Bertha country, amounts to a couple of weeks in the Koma–Ganza settlements south of the Yabus in the Sudan in the mid-1960s; in Ethiopia in the mid-1970s, I spent two–three months among the Gumuz, six weeks among the Komo–Kwama and Shyita settlements of the upper Jokau, and a couple of weeks in the northern Mao villages of the upper Dabus. In addition to the historical researches of Alessandro Triulzi among the Bertha,[1] and other original findings which are beginning to be published such as those of Charles Jedrej and Akira Okazaki on the Ingessana (Gâmk), and Christian Delmet on the Meban,[2] it is the recent fieldwork of Joachim Theis among the 'Koma' of the Yabus valley[3] which is now beginning to make real comparative study possible. I here make a few suggestions as to some of the areas in which we may seek correspondences at the 'archival' level between the cultural practices of the four Koman peoples (speakers of Komo, Kwama, Shyita as well as Uduk) which in principle might be extendable to other communities of this 'pre-Nilotic' borderland.

[1] In addition to Alessandro Triulzi's monograph, *Salt, Gold, and Legitimacy*, see particularly his articles 'Trade, Islam and the Mahdia in Northwestern Wallagga, Ethiopia', *Journal of African History*, 16 (1975), 55–71; 'Center-Periphery Relations in Ethiopian Studies: Reflections on Ten Years of Research on Wellega History', in *Proceedings of the Seventh International Conference of Ethiopian Studies*, ed. Sven Rubenson (Arlöv, Sweden, Berlings), 1984, 359–63; and 'Central and Peripheral Rule: the Case of Neḳemte', in *The Southern Marches of Imperial Ethiopia*, ed. Donham and James.

[2] M. Charles Jedrej has published several articles on the Ingessana, including for example 'The Social Organisation of the Ingessana', *Sudan Notes and Records*, 56 (1975), 108–19; and 'The Cult of the Dead among the Ingessana (Sudan)', *Anthropos*, 74 (1979), 40–6. The same people have been studied more recently by others, and a paper which presents information on their religious ideas has been published by Akira Okazaki, 'Living together with "Bad Things": The Persistence of Gamk Notions of Mystical Agents', *Sudan Sahel Studies* I, ed. M. Tomikawa (Tokyo: Institute for the Study of Languages and Cultures of Asia and Africa), 1984. For recent data on the Meban, see Christian Delmet, 'De curieux Nilotiques: les Maban du Haut-Nil', *Production Pastorale et Société*, 15 (1984), 41–58.

[3] Joachim Theis is preparing a thesis for the Free University of Berlin on the 'Koma' of the Yabus valley. He has prepared several preliminary papers, culminating in his contribution 'Case-study: Research among the Koma' to the 'Final Report on the Sudan Research Project at the Institute of Ethnology at the Free University of Berlin' (Project leaders Fritz Kramer and Bernhard Streck), 1985.

I should establish in advance, however, that as far as we can tell, the central integrating notion of *arum* as held by the Uduk does not seem to have a cognate or a corresponding substantive correlate in the other Koman languages.[4] There would appear, perhaps significantly, to be rather more heterogeneity in the spiritual vocabularies of the Koman peoples than in their repertoire of terms for the body and its parts, the animal world, the elements of their ritual practice, and their mythical themes.

A commitment to hunting and gathering is an obvious starting-point in any comparison of the Koman peoples. Joachim Theis has vividly described a hunt in which he participated south of the Yabus, which included members of several different ethnic groups under the leadership of the 'Koma' *kitiman ba mata*, 'hunting master.'[5] Theis has also told me of the way in which a killer of a large antelope such as a roan is treated. (In the particular case he witnessed this was a man of the Ganza, a small group who speak what is probably a northern Mao tongue and live on close terms with the 'Koma'.) He is secluded from the community, shaved, dressed in beads and red ochre, and has to stay in a hut with a smoking fire (this recalls the special status and rituals of the leopard killer and other hunters among the Uduk: and while the antelope is not a 'dangerous' creature in the way the leopard is, it reminds us of the moral kinship in Uduk thought between human beings and the antelopes).

There is evidence that Komo ideas about body and personality are analogous with those of the Uduk. Let me give a few examples. The word for body, *esh* or *ish* according to Theis' preliminary work, and *is* in the extreme southern Komo communities I visited, corresponds to the Uduk *is*. The term for liver is the same, *du*, and has comparable emotional reference, being similarly translatable in suitable contexts as 'heart'. There are also 'psychological' states associated with the stomach/belly though the term for this is not cognate (*kimi*).[6] Shades of the dead (*yileli*) may wander around at night, but the 'spirit' that may reside in a person appears to be different. Through a specific rite, a child receives a spirit *bεs*,

---

[4] The Dinka, intriguingly, refer to the sacred ibis as *arumjok*, though Godfrey Lienhardt advises caution over making a connection. Among the Atuot, however, diviners may call out *arum*! as they apprehend the approach of a power. John Burton gives as a translation ' "Everyone keep still!" ' in his text, but in the glossary gives 'In the course of exorcism when the diviner becomes possessed by a power he will call out *arum*, to signal that the power is about to speak through him' (*God's Ants: A Study of Atuot Religion* (St Augustin: Anthropos Institute), 1981, pp. 110–11, and p. 146). Compare the Majangir word *yarum* for blood, which may be a loan-word from old Majoid, and may there represent an interchange with early Nilotic (H. C. Fleming, 'The Importance of Mao in Ethiopian History', in *Proceedings of the Seventh International Conference*, ed. S. Rubenson, p. 36).

[5] Joachim Theis, 'Hunting, Beer and Kinship—Sketches of Inter-ethnic Relations in the Yabus Valley (Southern Funj Region)', 'Preliminary Reports of the Sudan Project', Institute of Ethnology, Free University of Berlin, 1983, pp. 37–9.

[6] Joachim Theis, personal communication.

normally from his father; the community of common *bɛs* is normally a
patrilineage, though those who cultivate together may be brought into the
same *bɛs* community regardless of descent. *Bɛs* may become mixed up, in
which case they have to be sorted out again; and they may be lost, in
which case they have to be retrieved. There are some points of comparison
here with the Uduk Genius (*kashira/*); while the Komo *keshire* appears to
mean sorceror or witch. There are then *wal*, which appear to be protective
medicine-spirits (as in various Nilotic languages); they may harm others,
or be used in curing. There is a rather imprecise idea of a heavenly spiritual
presence, in one form *kumbamish*, 'sky-mother', but in more recent usage
walemish, 'sky-spirit', the phrase used by the former Sudan Interior
Mission translators for God.[7] The Komo use chickens in a partly oracular
way, as do the Uduk, and they also use them to Brush a patient. This
action (*wup* or *wup is* in Uduk) is *wob* in Komo. According to Theis the
purpose is to take out a *wal* or *bɛs* from the person, or to greet its presence
there. The word *lat* is used for the rite of retrieving a lost *bɛs*, for example
from the river (as is it in the corresponding Uduk rite for the Genius), but
since this is usually carried out by an Uduk specialist, we need not assume
an independent use of this word in Komo.

I have learned further from Joachim Theis that there is a ceremony for
cleansing twins of 'evil witchcraft powers'. They are carried in a special
ceremony to the bush, by the hunting master and a helper. Hunting songs
are sung and the grass is burnt, to drive the witchcraft into the bush to
kill the wild animals. After the ceremony, known as *bibi ke 'ina*, or 'eye
of the witch', the women and children go home and the men from the
whole area set out for a hunt.[8]

The general cultural style of the Komo, their dress, their social conventions, the way they marry, build their houses, organize their work and
share their beer, is very similar to that of the Uduk; and they play
much the same kinds of music for dancing. Even in the details of myth,
correspondences are found. I limit myself here to the quotation of one
myth only, from among those which I collected on the upper Jokau in
Ethiopia, which made me feel quite at home. It pictures the great primeval
dance of all the creatures, at which the music is again that of the *baraŋgu/*
flutes. A mother, embarrassed by the Fox's criticism of the smell, knocks
her daughter back into the grave whence she had reappeared. Since then,
people no longer reappear after death.

> When the young people were playing the *barku* [corresponding to the
> Uduk *baraŋgu/*], there was one who was buried in the earth, she had

[7] Samuel Burns and C. J. Guth, 'Koma Language', mimeo. grammar and vocabulary,
n.d. (Available in the library of the Institute of Ethiopian Studies, University of Addis
Ababa.) Also see SIM mimeo. materials on the scriptures in 'Koma'.
[8] Joachim Theis, personal communication.

died, and people wept for her and forgot her.... Beer was made and
... the people all came together to dance the *barku, yit, yit, yit*. They
were dancing like that, and she who was buried, she got up, and came
with her grave-goods, the things she was buried with. She was a stranger
... she appeared outside like that, and she danced. The Fox is the one
who curses people, he came to the place where people were dancing the
barku. 'Oh, what a bad smell,' he said.... 'What smells like a dead
thing here? Where is it coming from right now, like a decaying person?
It smells like death here.' The mother became angry because of what
the Fox had said.... She said, 'My child, I wish I had left you at the
place where I buried you. I should have left you there.' ... She led away
her daughter, led, led, her away with her grave-goods, led her like that.
She entered into the grave. The mother followed and picked up a stone.
'My child, don't you come out! You are cursed by people outside here.
You are decaying.' She picked up a stone like that; 'Don't come out,
my child!' *Wep*! she went, on the head of her child.... So we now die,
once, and are not to be seen any more.[9]

Puleni, the old lady who gave me this story in the upper Jokau valley in
1974, linked it with various other themes that were familiar to me from
the Uduk. In fact she returned immediately to the theme of the moon's
spittle, which had been taken by the snake; her point was that if the people
had been able to receive this, the girl would not have decayed as she did.
There was a strong suggestion in this tale, however, that once decay sets
in, it is good to keep the deceased at bay, and prevent them from returning.

It is perhaps in the area of death representations and practice that the
most striking correspondence can be demonstrated, not only between
Uduk and Komo, but Kwama as well. I will not go into the range of
cognate vocabulary here, but focus on ritual practice. For this topic we
are fortunate in having historical evidence to draw upon, as well as recent
observation. The 'Komo' to the north of the upper Daga/Sonka valley
were visited by the Dutch traveller Juan Maria Schuver in 1881, though
from his vocabulary list it appears that his informants spoke Kwama.
Schuver reported from his visit to the upper part of the Sonka (Daga)
valley that at least for important people among the 'Komo' there was no
immediate burial at all. These persons were left, dressed in beads, in
special corpse-huts, for seven to ten years, on platforms where they were
protected from termites. Gifts were brought to the corpse. Burial, of only
the dry remains, was finally carried out in or near the hut where the
deceased had lived.[10]

---

[9] James Waro assisted me with language work and translation in Komo, although his
mother tongue was Anuak.
[10] Juan Maria Schuver, *Reisen im Oberen Nilgebeit*, Supplement No. 72 to *Petermanns
Geographische Mitteilungen* (Gotha: Justus Perthes), 1883, p. 69.

Grottanelli, who half a century later (1939) attended a burial and the rite which followed five days later in a 'Koma' (probably also Kwama) village in western Ethiopia, concluded that the custom of exposing a body had been abandoned, but from an informant who spoke some Oromo he gathered that in past times funerals of elders were performed in a very different way.

> The body of an elder would be exposed on a platform (*wuss*) inside his hut, clad in all his ornaments, garments and arms, and left there for several years, until the hut showed signs of complete decay. The bones were then collected and buried in a small round grave just outside the hut. Now this form of burial is described by the Dutch explorer J. M. Schuver . . . and his words confirm my information.[11]

Mr Samuel Burns of the Sudan Interior Mission worked for a number of years in the 1950s at Yabus Bridge, and to him we owe a great deal of linguistic information about the Komo, together with some ethnography. In a set of manuscript notes prepared in about 1956 he tells us that a common phrase, 'the old people', is used of both the aged living and the dead together. He notes that nowadays the body is usually buried the same day, 'by Government order', though it is sometimes kept for four or five days, and begins to stink. 'No one ever remarks on this, even though, to an outsider, the stench is poisonous. "One day you'll stink too! Do you want people to turn their noses away from you?"' Burns tells us that a big beer-feast, *shataga* (which must be the Arabic *saddaqa*, also used sometimes by the Uduk) is held after about twelve months. The notes continue, concerning these Komo who sought refuge from Ethiopia in the Sudan during the Condominium period:

> Before coming into Sudan and under Government order, body was kept until rotten. Meat 'filleted' from bones and dried in sun like biltong. Then folded up, put in a 'mwalda' (skin bag) and hung up in roof of house. Bones taken to river, scrubbed clean with sand, and stored. After about a year a 'shataga' (feast for dead) was called. Each guest brought a ring of metal, a string of beads or other ornament. The dried body was laid out in sun, and decked out with the ornaments, as well as those possessed in life. Often resulting mass was so heavy, took several men to lift. The bones were then taken and carefully polished.[12]

[11] V. L. Grottanelli, 'Burial among the Koma of Western Abyssinia', *Primitive Man*, 20 (1947), 71–84, at p. 81.

[12] Samuel Burns, 'Notes on Koma Culture', 12 pp. mimeographed, at p. 5. I am grateful to Joachim Theis for drawing my attention to this manuscript, which along with the language work of Mr Burns and his colleague Charles Guth is a valuable source for our knowledge not only of the Komo but the Koman peoples in general.

The body and bones were then buried in a grave which consisted of a narrow shaft down to a room-like chamber below, with a bench on one side. This is like the old-style Uduk grave still made today.

I was not aware of these earlier sources of evidence when I first heard among the southern Uduk in the 1960s that the Komo disembowel a corpse, bury the entrails beneath the beer pot in the hut and place the body up in the rafters where it will dry out in the smoke from the domestic fire. I also heard that younger in-laws are obliged to accept morsels of food from the hand of the deceased at his or her funeral. Then, during my stay among the Komo of the upper Jokau valley in 1974, I learned indirectly from my Anauk assistant James Waro that what I had earlier heard and had since read in Schuver was true in principle: that the disembowelled body was dried on the roof-platform of the living hut, and buried outside only after five or six months. However, this practice (he said) was stopped by the British (the people of this area had formerly lived at Wadesa in the Sudan). The British had explained that 'when a person died, he would never live again, everything was finished'.

There is an initial appearance of linguistic, cultural, and social heterogeneity among the Koman-speaking communities and an even wider variety if one extends the survey to other peoples of the 'pre-Nilotic' belt of the Sudan–Ethiopian border. Some of these have previously been included in the Koman language grouping, such as Gumuz, 'northern Mao' and Ganza, though recent research queries this classification.[13] Others have long been known to be linguistically quite distinct, such as Kunama, Nera ('Barya'), Ingessana (for which alternative names have recently been suggested, Gâmk or Gaam), Bertha, Hill Burun, Meban, and I would add Majangir. Members of these various groups are in many cases culturally assimilated in part and socially linked to larger neighbouring populations, and many speak a second language besides their own, such as Amharic, Oromo (Galla), Arabic, Nuer, or Anuak. In the case of the Hill Burun and Meban, there is the very interesting phenomenon of peoples speaking languages which are themselves undoubtedly Nilotic, while at the same time certain themes running through their social and cultural practice strongly resemble those of their 'pre-Nilotic' neighbours. This is true of the Meban, for example, even while Christian Delmet has been able to argue the 'Nilotic' character of their sacrificial rites.[14] In their ritual repertoire, the Meban share many elements with the Uduk, Komo, and Bertha, for example the action of _wup is_, the Brushing of a patient, with a chicken, elements which are quite unknown to the main body of Nilotic-

---

[13] See particularly Lionel M. Bender, _The Ethiopian Nilo-Saharans_ (Addis Ababa: The Artistic Press), 1975; Bender, _et al._, eds., _Language in Ethiopia_ (Oxford: Oxford University Press), 1976, Part I, ch. 2; and Bender, ed., _The Non-Semitic Languages of Ethiopia_, Monograph No. 5 (Michigan: African Studies Center).

[14] Delmet, 'De curieux Nilotiques'.

speaking peoples, or as far as I know to the Oromo. Further research is required before we can begin to interpret the patterns; but for the present I think it useful to remember that in this fragmented region, there is no simple correspondence between 'language' and those enduring elements which go to make up a people's culture in the broadest sense.

At the deeper, perhaps the 'archival', level, there would seem to be in this region elements which have long circulated between the various 'pre-Nilotic' peoples. These could be regarded as belonging to a common archival stock, from which particular items are drawn and put in circulation from time to time, passing from one group to another in spite of contrasts or changes in language and explicit religious or other systematic discourse. The pattern of diffusion of one element in isolation may not yield a rational history; the set of elements should be seen together. Elements crop up here, there, and then somewhere else, in variant combination; movement has been in different directions at different times. The patterns of association between peoples, association based on common language, intermarriage, political or other ethnicity, common cult following, and so forth, have changed shape many times and are still doing so. But an archival level it might still be possible usefully to distinguish the 'pre-Nilotic' cultural region. The population base for the continuity of this cultural region is thus not a linguistic community, nor is it a racial or genetically definable group, nor is it even based on endogamous principles. It is rather a political–historical *niche*. This *niche*, as a borderland, has played an important part in giving cultural identity to a series of peoples, perhaps of different provenance, who have severally and collectively found in it a home, and defined themselves as outside the framework of the more powerful societies, and major states, lying on either side.

Appendix 2

Further Uduk tales

1. At the great dance: Hare and the elephants (by Kinna)

[There is a repertoire of stories and story-motifs associated with the primeval dance, about the animals and their encounters with each other. These can stand on their own as 'folk-tales' but are often prefaced with a phrase such as 'The animals were dancing and ...' which links the story with the mythical scenario. Elements of the stories are split and recombined in the telling, and may refer in different texts to different animals. Hare may trick Elephant, or Fox may trick Hyena; in the text below, Kinna slips unconsciously from Hare to Fox as hero. Animals may be referred to impersonally, as members of their kind, but often are treated as individual characters, even to the point of receiving a special prefix, *Mo-*, with the sense of 'Mr' or 'Sir'. Here I use capital initials or even a title. I have attributed gender though this is not necessarily implicit in the Uduk names or pronouns.]

People were dancing the *baraŋgu/*, and Hare was wearing leaves of the *gali'th* plant [with edible seeds] as shoes. He was stamping his feet, *te'b*, *te'b*, and an elephant said to him, 'Oh, Hare! What is it you're wearing that sounds like that?' He replied, 'Just the soles of my feet which I have cut off [for shoes].' He said to the elephant, 'All right, you can come tomorrow and I will see you.' And the elephants came, and more came, and more came, until they were finally gathered. And the Hare brought a knife, to cut the elephants' feet. For one without much fat, he just pared off the surface, but for one with much fat he carved right in, *gag*. The elephant cried out '*Oog!*' Hare said, 'O great one, a famous person like you, crying out like that?' Again another came, and again he just pared off the surface of this one without much fat. But he carved up another fat one, *gag*! He cried '*Oog!*' And the Hare said, 'Why do you cry like that? You whose name is famous, "Mr Elephant, Mr Elephant", why do you cry?' And when he had finished, he carried away the feet, and put them inside a granary. Then he told the elephants: 'All right. Now you must all go and brew some beer. You must make beer, and you, and you. Then you all come back to me, and I will cut shoes for you.'

And later they came back, coming from here, and from there, and there, and there, coming from all over. And he, that Hare, went right inside the granary and stayed there imitating the sounds of shoe-making, *kosho'k*, *kosho'k*, *kosho'k*, while in fact he was crunching the things all up. Until there were just a few left, to make the sound with like that. The elephants said, 'Hey, you are sitting in there busy like that, why don't you bring everything outside?' He said, 'The things are all here.' He stayed there making the sound as before, and then the great left-handed elephant rushed forward and threw down the granary, *dhus*, and grabbed him, *'ce'th*. he grabbed him, *'ce'th*. The elephant was about to beat him on the ground; but he said, 'You shouldn't beat me on the ground. Roll me along so that I will break into pieces completely.' And so the elephant just rolled him along; and he scampered off.

He ran, ran, ran, and threw himself under the roots of a tree. He went right inside the roots of the tree there. Then the elephant came up, *'tum*, *'tum*, *'tum* [in a lumbering way] and seized his tail. He said, *'pulupulum*! [a teasing taunt] Someone has taken hold of a tree-root, thinking it's my tail!' And a *juk* [a harmless reddish snake] nearby said, 'No, Mr Elephant, that is Hare's tail, there, get hold of it properly.' He abused the other: 'O Mr Juk, you have nasty sunken eyes like a snake.' And the elephant heard Hare's words and let him go.

He ran off. Ran, ran, ran, and rushed in among some girls who were fine-grinding grain for beer. He arrived among the girls, *buum*. The girls took off their beads and put them on him, *dhoro'th* [this suggests a mass of beads]. The elephant came and found him, and said, 'Hey, who is that looking like our Hare there?' He said, 'Impossible! Does your Hare look like this?' The elephant again listened to his words and went away. Hare again ran off quickly. Ran, ran, ran, ran. The girls all cried out, 'Oh, oh! Fox, give us our things back!' But he went on, without stopping, ran and ran and ran.

2. Tortoise and Elephant (by Bukko)

Tortoise was sitting being admired by Elephant. Tortoise went along, *kwash kwash kwash*, spinning a big cotton belt, to dance there among the people, going *kwash kwash*! Elephant admired her very much. She said, 'Mr Elephant, have I put on my things yet? I haven't put on my beautiful things yet.' She deceived Elephant with his nasty words like that. While the giraffes were all together there dancing, *thu'k thu'k thu'k*! The people were dancing; was anyone left out? ...

And then ... Elephant had his liver cut out by Tortoise with a metal blade. 'Please weren't you admiring me? Open your anus for me and I will enter your stomach. Because you admire me very much.' She got to work snipping Elephant in the liver there, bit by bit, *'tha'k 'tha'k*, and Elephant said, 'Ooo!' 'Why are you crying out, I'm just moving my elbow about.' Was it her elbow? While all the time he was being snipped away bit by bit in there.

Then Elephant bumped to the ground. She said, 'You're crying like that because of me. Open your anus and let me jump down.' She jumped down when she had finished off Elephant's liver. Elephant collapsed on the ground, *dush*.

3. The Birapinya (by Uḵka)

[Uḵka was herself Ganza but married to an Uduk husband, living far to the south of the Yabus. In her version the dance has been modernized from the *baraŋgu/* to the *athele/*. Here the woman burned down the tree because she was offended that her daughter, newly risen from the grave, was cursed for stinking at the dance. It follows that we no longer arise from the grave.]

Haven't you heard the story about the *pinya*? A woman died, and was buried. And she stayed for two days, and then appeared from the grave. She came back, appeared out, and the *athele/* was sounding. And her friend, with whom she danced, said, 'Let's go to the *athele/.*' But her mother refused to let her go. Her mother was toasting grain for beer, they say, and she stopped her; but [the daughter] went on. They went to dance *athele/*. And other said, 'Why is your body smelling like that? Why is your body smelling rotten?' They spoke like this and she took offence and left. Crying she left offended and ran home. And her mother said, 'I told you that you should stay at home today. Why did you go?' Then she, the mother took a handful of burning cinders and threw it at the foot of the thing there. It burnt up.

People had no path to come down, they just dropped to the ground. Some came and survived. The tall ones landed and died.

This is what they say; it was heard by us just like that. The people who would have told us properly, we don't know them. This is what people say, and we just heard this. That's all. That's why we die for good now, because of the burning of the Birapinya.

4. The little rat who taught the women (by Emed)

[Following mating and the first conceptions, women did not know how to give birth. They would slit open the belly when the labour pains came. The small rat *dhothany 'cena*, whose name literally means 'giving birth among us', which lives in association with the *'kwanim pa*, finding shelter and scraps of food around the eaves of houses, taught the women what to do.]

People did not know how to give birth. It is said that they used to just cut open the belly. They cut around the children and plucked them out, and then sewed up the hole again. Then the little rat came by, and said, 'Oh! What is that you're doing?' The people said, 'We're plucking out the children from the belly.'

'Now please, sit like this,' she said. 'Give birth *so*, give birth *so*, give birth *so*.'

'*Twa'c* [the women did it], '*twa'c*, '*twa'c*, '*twa'c*. The babies were very red, crimson. She made a fire, and said, 'Arrange the cooking stones like this. Put the cooking stones like this, and heat some water. Then you can bathe. Bathe yourselves in water like this. Bathe your vagina here with water, *kaw*, *kaw*, *kaw*. Then strip some bark like this, strip some bark of the kwaye tree, and wear it over the vagina, '*the'c*.'

People then became human beings ['*kwanim pa*]. The woman gave the child milk. Because she had bathed in warm water, and was able to get up and go about. From giving up that business of cutting out the children. And now we always give birth. We know how to give birth and to cut the navel cord. And people remain alive.

Appendix 3

Ritual practitioners in northern Pam'Be, 1966

These lists give what positive information I was able to discover, and there may be several other practices and practitioners I did not hear about. Only a minority of women have a practice, and even they are probably underrepresented in these lists. The one practice run by women is the Gurunya cult. Names are those of adult men except where indicated otherwise.

Waka'cesh (at least 13 out of 21 adult men have a special practice)

Ngau	Hunting, rainstones
Ha'da	Arum Leina, rainstones
Ruthko	Arum Leina
'Koshol	Arum Leina
Tente	(Hunting of father's people affecting him); Elephant Medicine, Elephant and Throwing-Stick diviner, *maŋgal* grub expert. Sometime Muslim leader
Koro	Elephant/Arum Allah diviner
Yuha	Elephant/Arum Allah diviner
Kutha	Throwing-Stick diviner
Hama	Diviner (branch not known)
Baden and Lishka (his wife)	'Urine'
Danga	(Diviners claim him); Christian leader
Halid	Arum Leina
Gamu	*Minkuth* (groin speciality)
Yukke (F)	Gurunya, 'urine'
Rapka (F)	Elephant/Arum Allah diviner

Kalagorko (10 out of 11 adult men have a special practice)

ŋule	Arum Leina, rainstones
Thia	*Badiga*, body swelling speciality
'Tabko	Birdrites, Elephant diviner
Rusko	Former Elephant diviner, now Christian leader
Jeden	Type of 'Urine' affecting knees, Arum Leina
Thuga	Type of 'Urine' affecting head, Arum Leina
Badko	Throwing-Stick diviner

Nyoa   Throwing-Stick diviner, Arum Leina
Lol   Hunting
Yapko   Former dik-dik diviner
Maya (F)   Gurunya, Elephant/Arum Allah diviner
Oiyga (F)   Gurunya

Pany Caran (at least 15 out of 27 adult men have a special practice)

Nyethko   Monkey diviner
Denge   Birdrites, Elephant diviner
Rabesa   'Urine'
Manyjal   Monkey diviner
Mathir   Arum Leina, *arum jis yap* (porcupine hole)
Dhoge   Special Bunyan diviner, Arum Leina
Sebko   Monkey diviner, rainstones
Tagir   Small red ants speciality
Shi   Throwing-Stick diviner
Mathe   'Urine'
Shokko   Monkey diviner
Dhirmath   Throwing-Stick diviner, Arum Leina
Ria   Throwing-Stick diviner
Ya'ka   Elephant diviner, rainstones
Kaygo   Arum Leina
Cile (boy)   Elephant/Arum Allah diviner
Ridaŋ (F)   Elephant Medicine

Pam Jodko (at least 3 out of 5 adult men have a special practice)

Jodko   Monkey diviner
Algo   Diviner (branch not known, maybe given up),
                         Arum Leina
Yila   Guineafowl diviner
Emed (F)   Arum *pi 'ce* (she blows into ears if sore)

Pa Yasin (at least 3 out of 5 adult men have a special practice)

Yasin   Throwing-Stick diviner
Bogi   Throwing-Stick diviner, Arum Leina (recent)
Shamma   Throwing-Stick diviner, Arum of the pipe

Summary

Of the adult male population of 69 in this small area (which I would guess is typical of the northern Uduk), at least 44 (or 64%) have one or more ritual practices. At least 14 have the Arum Leina (20%), and 27 are members of the Order of Ebony Diviners (39%). In all settlements except one, at least one diviner also holds the Arum Leina practice (a total overlap in this sample of 5 individuals only). All five modern branches of the Ebony Order are here represented, as they have spread via the Jum Jum, as well as the older Elephant/Arum Allah variety which came directly from the Bertha. In all settlements, there is a numerical preponderance of Ebony diviners over all other practices, including the Arum Leina. Each major practice includes a small number of women, and occasionally a child. If these are included in the statistics, the community of practitioners appears even more substantial.

Glossary

abas   Blood, 'blood-friendship', relatives thus connected.

adu   Liver; seat of passions, and translated into English idiom in this context as 'heart'.

arum   In a diffuse sense, the animating spiritual essence or power in living creatures. In a specific sense, the shade or ghost of someone who has died.

Arum i Mis   Spirit in the Above; used by Uduk to translate for example the heavenly divinities of Nilotic theology.

Arumgimis   The Biblical God. Literally, 'That Spirit which is in the Above', the Sky Spirit.

aruma 'cesh Literally 'spirit in the earth'. Used in the traditional sense of the shade of one recently dead, newly buried, and not yet settled in the after-world. Used in the Christian context in opposition to God in Heaven, as 'spirits of the underworld', to include all manner of unclean and devilish spirits, Satan, etc.

athele/   A form of secular music and dance. The music is produced by an ensemble of eleven flutes, and eleven slightly curved and concave logs. Each player blows a flute held in his left hand, and beats a log with a short stick held in his right hand. The dancers move around the players in an anticlockwise wheel.

baraŋgu/,   A dance also performed with flutes, longer and deeper
  bargum   but no beaten logs. Rarely seen today, and regarded as a dance of the old times. Frequently appears in myth, for this was the style of the great primeval dance at which all the creatures, including proto-humankind, were gathered.

Bunyan   A clothes-wearing person; frequently thought of as a non-Uduk, though many Uduk are now said to be 'becoming Bunyan'. Characteristically, an Arabic-speaking Muslim Bertha from the Ethiopian foothills, likely to be on petty commercial business these days, though his forebears were feared as slave-raiders and traders.

bwa   Stomach. Seat of conscious deliberation, rational decision, will.

c̱a'b ki 'thi To Sit Black. During an illness or at times of ritual vulnerability, such as the middle transitional phase

of rites of passage, one Sits Black by removing all
the beads and decorations, refraining from the use
of red ochre, and in some cases using plain or
blackened oil (*jiso*). This period will normally be
concluded by a rite in which beads and red ochre are
once again used, marking return to health and
normality.

çiŋkina/   Historically, lost person, foundling. A slave, servant,
kinless, bereaved person.

cir   *Dalbergia melanoxylon*, Arabic *babanus*. A tree with
black heartwood used widely in the savannah
regions of the Sudan for firewood. Commonly known
as 'ebony'. Used as oracle by Bertha, Uduk, and
other diviners. *Kany cir*, 'to kindle the ebony',
diviner's action of lighting the end of an ebony
wand, over water, to make an oracular consultation.

çi 'twa/   Literally, 'to give to the mouth'. A ritual action, to
Offer, in which a little food is given, rejected, and
then given again to be swallowed. A senior in-law
may do this for a newly-married spouse; or a diviner
for a patient, recovering from an illness. It concludes
a period of 'avoidance' and re-establishes a
relationship.

cwa   Tree, root, medicine. *Cwany je*, Elephant Medicine.
Cwam pe'do/, Rainbow Medicine. *Cwa ŋari/*,
diviners' medicine (in general).

dhathu/   Condition of being born from a matriline carrying
inherent spiritual power. Formerly restricted to
certain lines, e.g. the Lakeŋ Golga, but more recently
thought to be transferable from one line to another.
In the middle decades of this century regarded as an
evil contamination, and those thus stigmatized
thought capable of causing illness and death around
them ('witches'). Twin births were a sign of such
contamination, as were other unusual signs such as
being 'born with teeth' or what we would regard as
real deformities. Adults thought responsible for
deaths would be killed, and one or both twins
disposed of.

ga/   To avoid something; for example, foods which you
know from experience make you feel queasy. Also
used of avoiding in-laws; and among the southern
Uduk, children 'avoid' the name of their father.

gurunya/   A dark glossy starling. A cult devoted to the saving of

	children born to bereaved mothers is named after this bird, and the bird also appears in myth. See *'Kwanim Pa*, Chapter 7.
jit	Spice. A wild aromatic root, not an ordinary medicine, but used in rituals by diviners. It is an emblem of their profession. The plant grows up to a foot or more, with thin long grassy leaves, parallel veins. It is wild, but planted by diviners around their homes. The root is up to two or more inches long, very hard, dark brown with white core.
kashira/	The 'shadow' of anything. But also a non-material element of the person, Genius. The *kashira/* is active during dreaming, and is thus able to signal a forewarning of mystical or spiritual harm. Its loss can make a person vulnerable to sickness, and Restoral of the *kashira/* (*lat*) is the commonest of the services provided for patients by the diviners.
koŋgoro/	A set of ritual practices which belong to the older Uduk tradition, concerned with the protection of growing crops from insects and birds. Birdrites.
'kwanim pa	Plural of *wathim pa*, the human being, sometimes specifically used to mean an Uduk as distinct from other people. Literally, 'people of the home'.
kujur	A common term in Sudanese colloquial Arabic, which we can translate 'magician' or 'witch-doctor'. Used by Arabic speakers of the Bertha and Uduk *ŋari/*, though it would also be applied to other ritual specialists. Carries the sense of 'pagan mumbo-jumbo', though at the same time many good Muslims in the Sudan are fairly careful to give the *kujur* a wide berth, to be on the safe side.
lat	The ritual of retrieving, and Restoring, a lost Genius (*kashira/*).
mii abas	'To make blood', that is, to offer an animal by cutting its throat, or spearing it.
mii arum	Rite for *arum*, usually a healing rite at which men of the cult of Arum Leina officiate. 'Arum business' in general.
mii ŋari/	Diviners' rite.
mushu	A special medicine, to counteract the consequences of having killed a human being, or a leopard.
ŋari/	Among the Bertha, the *ŋeri* was in the last century a priest-like diviner, adviser to the chief. A modern

cult has spread from the Bertha to several other peoples of the Kurmuk District, including the Uduk. Among the Uduk today, a substantial proportion of the population have become ŋari/, or members of a diviners' order which I term the Ebony Order after their oracle. This is now a mass-movement among the Uduk and I speak of Ebony Men as well as of diviners, to suggest this.

nyoŋ   To straighten, in the geometric sense. To Straighten, or put right, in the context of healing rituals.

'thi 'kup   To Shave the Head, a phrase used for the final rite which marks recovery from an illness, or the conclusion of a major rite of passage. The head is shaved, and any debts to the healers are finally paid off.

thoson   To treat, to mend, to fix or repair things. Used in reconciliation and in healing contexts.

to'k is, todosh is   Used only in ritual contexts, as far as I know, to refer to the pulling, stretching, and Straightening of the torso and limbs, at the conclusion of a healing rite.

wathim pa   Singular of *'kwanim pa*; a human being, an Uduk. A living and complete personality.

wuk   A ritual action, of Touching a spear to an animal before offering it, for example.

wup is   The ritual action of Brushing a chicken up and down a person's body, or Brushing it over some objects, such as rainstones or dance-flutes. This is a way of 'greeting' *arum*. It is used for welcoming guests in a village; and particularly before rites of healing and the offering of animals.

ye   The ritual action of diviners in Extraction, that is sucking and pulling at a person's body, to remove supposed foreign objects.

Select Bibliography

A S A D, Talal, 'Anthropological Conceptions of Religion: Reflections on Geertz', *Man*, 18 (1983), 237–59.

B A M B O R O U G H, Renford, *Moral Scepticism and Moral Knowledge* (London: Routledge and Kegan Paul, 1979).

B A R R, James, *Fundamentalism* (London: SCM Press, 2nd edn., 1981).

B O U R D I E U, Pierre, *Outline of a Theory of Practice* [1972], trans. R. Nice (Cambridge: Cambridge University Press, 1977).

C A R R I T H E R S, M., C O L L I N S, S., and L U K E S, S., *The Category of the Person: Anthropology, Philosophy, History* (Cambridge: Cambridge University Press, 1985).

C O L L I N S, Steven, *Selfless Persons: Thought and Imagery in Theravāda Buddhism* (Cambridge: Cambridge University Press, 1982).

C O L S O N, Elizabeth, 'Heroism, Martyrdom and Courage: An Essay on Tonga Ethics', in *The Translation of Culture: Essays to E. E. Evans-Pritchard*, ed. T. O. Beidelman (London: Tavistock, 1971).

D O N H A M, Donald and J A M E S, Wendy, eds., *The Southern Marches of Imperial Ethiopia: Essays in Social Anthropology and History* (Cambridge: Cambridge University Press, 1986).

E V A N S - P R I T C H A R D, E. E., *Nuer Religion* (Oxford: Clarendon Press, 1956).

F O R S B E R G, Malcolm, *Land Beyond the Nile* (New York: Harper, 1958).
—— *Last Days on the Nile* (Chicago: Moody Press, 1966).

F O U C A U L T, Michel, *The Archaeology of Knowledge* [1969], trans. A. M. Sheridan (London: Tavistock, 1972).

H A R R I S, Grace G., *Casting Out Anger: Religion among the Taita of Kenya* (Cambridge: Cambridge University Press, 1978).

H E E L A S, Paul and L O C K, Andrew, eds., *Indigenous Psychologies: The Anthropology of the Self* (London: Academic Press, 1981).

J A M E S, Wendy, *'Kwanim Pa: The Making of the Uduk People: An Ethnographic Study of Survival in the Sudan–Ethiopian Borderlands* (Oxford: Clarendon Press, 1979).

J O H N S O N, Douglas H., 'Foretelling Peace and War: Modern Interpretations of Ngundeng's Prophecies in the Southern Sudan', in *Modernization in the Sudan: Essays in Honor of Richard Hill*, ed. M. W. Daly (New York: Lilian Barber Press, 1985).

—— 'C. A. Willis and the "Cult of Deng": a Falsification of the Ethnographic Record', *History in Africa [A Journal of Method*, published by the African Studies Association of the USA] 12 (1985), 131–50.

L I E N H A R D T, R. G., *Divinity and Experience: The Religion of the Dinka* (Oxford: Clarendon Press, 1961).

—— 'The Dinka and Catholicism', in *Religious Organization and Religious Experience*, ed. John Davis, A. S. A. Monograph 21 (London/New York: Academic Press, 1982), 81–95.

MIDGLEY, Mary, *Heart and Mind: The Varieties of Moral Experience* (London: Methuen, 1981).

MURDOCH, Iris, *The Sovereignty of Good* (London: Routledge and Kegan Paul, 1970).

PARFIT, Derek, *Reasons and Persons* (Oxford: Clarendon Press, 1984).

POCOCK, David, 'The Ethnography of Morals', *International Journal of Moral and Social Studies*, 1 (1986), 1–20.

ROSALDO, Michelle Z., *Knowledge and Passion: Ilongot Conceptions of Self and Social Life* (New York: Cambridge University Press, 1980).

SPAULDING, Jay, *The Heroic Age in the Kingdom of Sinnār* (Michigan: Michigan State University African Studies Center, 1985).

TRIULZI, Alessandro, *Salt, Gold, and Legitimacy: Prelude to the History of a No-man's Land, Belā Shangul, Wallaggā, Ethiopia (ca. 1800–1898)* (Naples: Istituto Universitario Orientale, 1981).

Index